"... Dramatically affected [   ] and planning. We have sent all our directors of marketing worldwide a copy of the book and made it required reading."
—Christina Tabora, Director of Marketing Communications, Hyatt International

The traditional methods inherited from the mass-marketing era no longer work well. Now *The Great Marketing Turnaround* offers a bold strategic vision of new marketing made possible by today's powerful computer and telecommunications technology. This book reveals how you can:

—Create direct-response advertising that identifies your most promising prospects and develops an exclusive relationship with them
—Use database-driven strategies to win over your competitor's customers
—Explore alternate channels of distribution without endangering your present channel
—Maximize sales and profits with the new individualized marketing

Filled with case histories and dollars-and-sense inspiration, this book will show business readers how to cast off outmoded marketing strategies and begin to implement the great marketing turnaround in their own organizations.

"INVALUABLE . . . A REAL KNOWLEDGEFEST ABOUT THE NEW MARKET FORCES."
—Jerry Conlon, Director of Marketing Information, NIKE, Inc.

"Key insights to the real meaning of relationship marketing."
—Peter T. Main, Vice President, Nintendo

STAN RAPP and TOM COLLINS are co-authors of the best-selling *MaxiMarketing*, which has influenced marketing thinking around the world. Co-founders of the Rapp & Collins international advertising agency network, they currently devote their full time to speaking, writing, and consulting. With Richard Cross, they are co-founders of the CCR Consulting Group, which is currently working with major corporations in the United States, South America, Europe, and Japan.

THE GREAT MARKETING TURNAROUND

The Age of the Individual
-and How to Profit from It

STAN RAPP·TOM COLLINS

A PLUME BOOK

PLUME
Published by the Penguin Group
Penguin Books USA Inc., 375 Hudson Street, New York, New York 10014, U.S.A.
Penguin Books Ltd, 27 Wrights Lane, London W8 5TZ, England
Penguin Books Australia Ltd, Ringwood, Victoria, Australia
Penguin Books Canada Ltd, 10 Alcorn Avenue, Toronto, Ontario, Canada M4V 3B2
Penguin Books (N.Z.) Ltd, 182-190 Wairau Road, Auckland 10, New Zealand

Penguin Books Ltd, Registered Offices: Harmondsworth, Middlesex, England

Published by Plume, an imprint of New American Library, a division of
Penguin Books USA Inc. This is an authorized reprint of a hardcover edition
published by Prentice-Hall, Inc.

First Plume Printing, January, 1992

10 9 8 7 6 5 4 3 2 1

Ⓟ REGISTERED TRADEMARK—MARCA REGISTRADA

LIBRARY OF CONGRESS CATALOGING-IN-PUBLICATION DATA
Rapp, Stan.
    The great marketing turnaround : the age of the individual, and
how to profit from it / Stan Rapp, Tom Collins.
        p.   cm.
    Includes bibliographical references and index.
    ISBN 0-452-26749-8
    1. Marketing.   2. Advertising.   3. Sales promotion.   I. Collins,
Tom.   II. Title.
HF5415.R3247   1992
658.8—dc20   91-36647
                                                                 CIP

Printed in the United States of America

"The trade of advertising is now so near perfection that it is not easy to propose any improvement."

— Dr. Samuel Johnson, 1759

Contents

Introduction

In the mid 1980's, we wrote a book called *MaxiMarketing* in which we sought to describe a great wave of change taking place in marketing — and to systematize the ways in which the smartest marketers were learning to ride it and not be smashed by it.

"The 80's," we said then, "will be remembered in marketing history as the decade of transition" to a dramatically new marketing territory.

"In this new land," we wrote, "you will know the name and address of the end-user of your product — regardless of where or how the purchase is made. Your advertising will be linked directly to measurable sales. You will hunt down individual users of competing brands and lure them away with a dazzling array of value-added services."

And we pointed out ways in which much of the traditional mass marketing approach was losing its efficiency and would be forced to give way to a new way of relating to the consumer.

In the short space of five years, what had seemed like a radical view of marketing at the time is now beginning to achieve widespread acceptance.

A front-page story in *The New York Times* dramatically confirmed some of the pains of transition we had warned about.

"SHIFTS IN MARKETING STRATEGY JOLTING ADVERTISING INDUSTRY," trumpeted the lengthy front-page story by Randall Rothenberg on October 3, 1989. It marked a turning point in press recognition of an historic shift in direction for marketing:

> After five years of stagnation, the American advertising industry is facing a dim and uncertain future...Advertising agencies are adapting only fitfully to a profound change: the splintering of the mass market into hundreds of smaller markets, and the development of new ways of communicating with them...The growth of mass adver-

tising has come to a virtual halt, agency profit margins have been cut in half, and advertising agencies are going through a painful consolidation that is reaching into the deepest corners of the industry.

"Things are changing and changing for the worse," the article quoted Martin F. Puris, the chief executive of Amirati & Puris.

"...It's a crisis more than a transition," said Don E. Schultz, professor of advertising at Northwestern University's Medill School of Journalism.

Rothenberg elaborated on the historic development taking place when he was interviewed for one of the programs in the public television series, "Adam Smith's Money World." During the program, which was devoted to "Madison Avenue Blues," Rothenberg was asked where the advertising business was going in the next ten years, and he replied:

> There'll be continual introductions of new media forms, which will continue to diminish the power and reach of mass media, network television, mass circulation magazines. Another thing that's going to happen is new research technologies are going to enable advertisers and their agencies to pinpoint much more exactly who their target market is, or markets are.
>
> It's going to require advertising agencies to be able to focus in a much more rifle-shot approach on these specific markets, using the specific media. Given the fact that it is an industry that was built on mass media and mass markets, that presupposes a dramatic change. [1]

"THE PARTY'S OVER," a story about food marketing on the front page of *Advertising Age* had announced earlier in the year. According to the story, food marketers were putting the brakes on big advertising budget increases.

This was soon underscored when Quaker Oats announced it was reducing marketing spending for the summer quarter by $35 million. This "was not a cutback but rather part of a planned reduction," explained a company spokesman. "What we are trying to do is improve our profitability and eliminate dollars that were relatively ineffective."

Reading between the lines, it sounded like the company had concluded that $35 million of its previous summer marketing expenditure had been at least partially wasted. A few months later, it was reported that "The Quaker Oats Co. will jump into database marketing starting in September [1990] with an initial budget in excess of $18 million." Quaker's move to develop one-to-one contact with their end-users was positioned as a means of "building relationships that Quaker hopes will translate into brand loyalty."

It was one more sign that advertisers large and small are being forced to rethink their mass marketing philosophies.

"Advertisers are saying they are not sure advertising works," the chairman of one of the largest agencies, Ogilvy & Mather, had lamented earlier. "They're not saying it in words — they are saying it in actions, by cutting media budgets, by cutting agency compensation, and by moving money into promotions."

In May of 1990, Campbell's Soup Company announced it was cutting its headquarters staff of 1,952 by 19%. Noted *The New York Times* reporter wryly, "Analysts have sometimes criticized Campbell for turning out award-winning advertising and scores of new products with little effect on profits."[2]

Another leading agency, Lintas U.S.A. "began telling their clients that the foundations of modern advertising — including mass-circulation magazines and far-reaching television networks — are eroding beyond recogition."

Tom Peters, the noted co-author of *In Search of Excellence*, added his voice to the rising chorus with a nationally syndicated column headlined, "MASS MARKETING IS OUT, DATABASES ARE IN."

"Marketing is moving into trying times," the eminent Madison Avenue veteran Alvin Achenbaum has warned. "The end of mass marketing as marketers knew it for over 30 years is now upon us. Marketers must change the way they address the marketplace, and they must change the way they communicate with it."[3]

The director of advertising for mighty General Motors added the voice of a mammoth advertiser when he redefined the company's desired relationship with consumers: "GM wants to deal with you as a buyer rather than as a collection of buyers...to learn how to communicate with you on a one-to-one basis."[4]

IS IT REALLY THE END OF MASS MARKETING?

What's going on here? Is the old mass marketing really dead? And if so, is there life after death?

Don't send flowers yet. There are still plenty of big advertisers of products that have big markets and need big media.

What is clear, however, is that the affordability and cost efficiency of traditional strategic thinking is being shaken to its foundations. Yet so far just a comparatively few marketers not only recognize the problem but also understand the complete reversal of thinking which is necessary for the solution.

The problems resulting from the changing marketplace are

not limited to the large advertisers. Many smaller advertisers who have always addressed general audiences with general statements of company image or product excellence are also being forced to reexamine their advertising and promotion strategy and consider more effective new options. And not only advertising and promotion, but every aspect of the marketing process must be reexamined in light of the disintegration of mass marketing.

Profound changes in the marketplace are forcing the development of a whole new way of thinking about the very nature of the marketing concept first developed in the 60's and 70's by Kotler, Leavitt, and Drucker.

The new realities are going to deeply affect, either favorably or unfavorably, everybody involved in the marketing process— large and small retailers, large and small branded products and service companies, large and small advertising agencies, promotion agencies, advertising media, suppliers — just about everyone involved in moving goods from producers to consumers.

Not everybody will be hurt, of course. The problems facing marketers today also represent tremendous opportunities. In this book we are going to show you how the most innovative companies, in the U.S. and throughout the developed world, are taking advantage of the changes taking place.

Since our first book was published, many other voices have joined us in questioning some of the basic shibboleths of traditional marketing. And there have been many daring probes into the future of marketing by innovative companies in the U.S. and throughout the world — companies that have scored breathtaking successes by turning away from conventional marketing practice.

After the bottom fell out of the home video game market and it was considered dead, a company called Nintendo made a roaring comeback, with sales soaring to $2 billion almost in a matter of months. They did it with a dynamic combination of new product excellence and a dramatic new kind of marketing.

In the U.K., Austin Rover cut in half its cost per incremental sale with a breakthrough one-to-one marketing program. Then they went on to build an unusual customer-rentention program that is a model of the new individualized approach to marketing.

A little tea company in Oregon vaulted into fourth place in national tea sales without spending a penny on conventional brand-building advertising, relying instead on direct customer cultivation and the synergy of a unique multi-channel distribution system.

Kraft General Foods has built a relational database of some 25 million brand-user households and is experimenting with innovative ways to communicate directly with various segments of it. According to John Kuendig, director of direct marketing, they have been running as many as 18 different database-driven marketing programs at a time and four have been rolled out nationally with remarkable results.

John Deere has found a way to get their advertising for their big-ticket home and garden equipment into the hands of 600,000 prime prospects at what conceivably involves no net advertising expenditure at all.

Canon office equipment in Belgium swept from nowhere to a strong position in that market with a program that is a classic of the new emphasis on event marketing combined with individual attention in business-to-business marketing.

THE COMMON DENOMINATOR IN THE NEW MARKETING

We saw in all of these and many other happenings an important common denominator: what we came to identify as a great turnaround in marketing thinking. The power of image-building and product-awareness advertising was still important, but the desired relationship with individual consumers was put in the forefront of strategic thinking.

In our preface to *MaxiMarketing*, we recounted a luncheon conversation we had in 1985 with Clay Timon, then the newly-appointed director of worldwide advertising for Colgate-Palmolive Company.

"Do you remember," asked Clay, "in the movie 'The Graduate,' when the family friend takes young Dustin Hoffman aside and murmurs that famous one word of advice? 'Plastics!'

"Well, when I was coming up through the ranks in the 60's, the magic word we would whisper to one another in the corridors was *marketing!*

"And do you know what they are whispering in the halls at Colgate these days? It's *direct marketing!*"

Five years later, shortly before this book was completed, Clay told us that there was a new magic word being spoken in the halls at Colgate and at other packaged goods marketers. "This time it's *database marketing*"!

Colgate-Palmolive now has database-driven marketing programs involving eight brands in over fifteen countries around the world.

Timon predicts that by 1995 at least half of their brands, which include such familiar household names as Ajax, Palmolive, Colgate, Fab, and Irish Spring, will be promoting sales by cultivating ongoing relationships based on information in their user database.

But there are many companies who don't quite know what to do with — and about — database-driven marketing targeted to the individual today, just as many didn't quite know what to think and do about direct marketing in the 80's.

Some companies seem to be squirreling away millions of consumer names in their computers without a very clear idea of how this new kind of resource can be turned to profitable use.

As Ray Schultz, the editor of *DM News*, observed wryly in an editorial commentary, "Some of these efforts are pathetic. In most cases, a big shot is hired to come in and play around with the base for a year or two. But corporate attention gets diverted. The database stagnates. The big shot is fired."

The problem is that developing a database is by itself not the solution to anything. A database is only a means to an end. The end is direct contact, dialogue, and involvement with the individual prospect or customer leading to increased sales and brand loyalty. It is really a question of applying to consumer marketing what the authors of *In Search of Excellence*, Peters and Waterman, called, in talking about industrial marketing and management, "getting close to the customer."

Since we wrote our last book, we have been tracking the experiences of dozens of companies who are finding new ways to accomplish this and who are making personal one-to-one marketing the engine that drives the company's growth strategy. But we have also seen many companies who only give lip service to this idea and resist allocating the budget dollars needed to implement it well, and other companies standing aside in perplexity with a wait-and-see attitude.

So we decided that a new book was needed which would pinpoint exactly how the marketing of the past is being forced to change. And the book would suggest the lessons to be learned from the daring companies that are gaining a commanding lead by making a turnaround in their thinking and programs, away from the old ways of mass marketing and toward a new kind of Individualized Marketing.

We will start by examining the profound social and market changes which are making this complete turnaround necessary.

Then we will define and describe how The Great Marketing Turnaround is beginning to take place. We will show how, when confronted with the complexity of the new marketing changes, you can succeed by making a single basic shift in thinking which is a reversal of what was the conventional wisdom in the 60's, 70's, and 80's.

We will identify ten significant trends which are the reverse of traditional marketing thinking and which together add up to what we see as The Great Turnaround.

We will provide striking examples of each trend, and extract from them Idea-Starters you can use to stimulate your own marketing thinking, whether you are part of a large or small company, a manufacturer, a retailer, or a service company.

We will show how, in the shift from mass marketing to the new Individualized Marketing, some of the old tried-and-true marketing practices and the new elements work together.

We will illustrate how this is happening with case histories of some of today's most impressive marketers. We will tell you what we learned in conversations with people like Bill White, ad manager for Nintendo...James Spector, director of consumer promotions of Philip Morris USA...Susan McIntyre, a marketing executive at Stash Tea...Edson de Godoy Bueno, president of Amil, Brazil's second-largest health-care plan and its fastest-growing company...John Kuendig, director of direct marketing for Kraft General Foods...Jean Sémah, who as manager of Sopad Nestlé France took them from a 20-share to a 30-share in less than four years... Ron Fusile, manager of sales promotion for the Buick Motor Divison of General Motors...Jeff Silverman, who started Toddler University to make infant and toddler shoes at the age of 23 with a loan of $3,000, and built it up to an annual volume of $30 million in less than four years...David Jones, the CEO of Grattan's in the U.K., who changed the look of catalog marketing forever with his visionary Next Directory...M. Nakagawa, assistant promotion manager for Procter & Gamble Far East, who is pioneering in Direct-Relationship Marketing in Japan... and other leaders of the new wave in marketing that is transforming the relationship among producer, distributor, and consumer.

We will point out how a number of other companies are not quite "getting" it. They are going through the motions of getting closer to the customer, but in a half-hearted way that fails to exploit the real opportunity.

We will reveal how many retailers are quietly taking the lead in creating databases that lead to profitable ongoing relationships, while brand advertisers are often still merely doing studies or accumulating names for one-shot projects.

We will explore "the reinvention of the art of advertising" – and the emergence of new media, as well as new forms and uses of existing media, which are making it possible to find true prospects and turn them into loyal customers.

We will also explore the dramatic rise in the importance of sales promotion and its merger in many areas with direct marketing. "Promotion these days has a new and expanded mission," writes Laurie Petersen, editor of the Promote section of *Adweek's*

Marketing Week. "It still must make something happen, but squeezed budgets will force marketers to pay attention to the messages their promotions are delivering."

We will look at the shift to real-time research that focuses on what consumers are saying this month, this week, this day — and does it in startlingly effective new ways.

We will observe where the new ideas and the new programs of the new marketing imperative are coming from. Those leading the way are not only coming from the maverick world of direct marketing, as you might expect. Some have backgrounds in a variety of other marketing services, and some are talented people who are "cross-overs" from mainstream advertising , sales promotion, and other forms of traditional marketing.

UNTANGLING OUR TERMS

In writing about advertising and marketing, we find ourselves frequently bumping up against the limits and vagueness of existing terminology. For instance, in writing this book, we had to face again the general confusion over such terms as "image," "awareness," "direct marketing," "direct response," "direct mail," and "mail-order," — terms that have been used with all sorts of meanings and argued about for over thirty years. In order to keep from getting tangled up in these confusing terms, we offer a glossary on page 46 showing how we use them in this book.

You will also find references in this book to MaxiMarketing. Briefly, what we outlined in our book by that name was a nine-step process for incorporating, reviewing, and maximizing all of the new marketing capabilities involved in relating directly to individuals who are your ideal prospects and best customers. The nine steps are:

1. **Maximized Targeting** — prospecting for your most desirable customers in all media
2. **Maximized Media** — new ways to reach the consumer
3. **Maximized Accountability** — proving that it works
4. **Maximized Awareness** — advertising appealing to the whole brain, both "left" (rational) and "right" (emotional)
5. **Maximized Activation** — inquiries and sales promotion
6. **Maximized Synergy** — double-duty advertising
7. **Maximized Linkage** — joining the advertising to the sale
8. **Maximized Sales** — through database and share of mind
9. **Maximized Distribution** — adding new channels

The MaxiMarketing concept applies a unified strategic approach in which people who are actually or potentially your best customers are identified, contacted, persuaded, motivated, activated, converted, and cultivated in a way that maximizes sales and prospects.

By applying the nine steps of the MaxiMarketing model, there is improved performance along the entire continuum which turns likely prospects into long-time customers. MaxiMarketing is the practical application of everything you need to do to succeed in the new era of Individualized Marketing. Put another way, Individualized Marketing is where the action is in the 90's, and Maxi-Marketing is an aid to maximizing your results.

Now, in the five years since we wrote our first book, extraordinary developments by pace-setting marketers have expanded our own thinking. The basic steps in our MaxiMarketing model of 1986 are still valid. But in using these principles, the best and the boldest new marketers have gone beyond what we imagined then. They have shown how all the separate disciplines of awareness advertising, sales promotion, direct marketing, public relations, event marketing, point-of-purchase, and customer satisfaction programs can be fused into a database-related whole which adds up to a remarkable turnaround in marketing.

In this book, we will show how you can incorporate into your own thinking the lessons that can be learned from these new marketing pioneers.

THE CHALLENGE OF FERRETING OUT INFORMATION

One of the challenges we faced in gathering information for this book is that many marketers are extremely guarded about certain key details of their breakthroughs. They are like great chefs who will proudly give you the recipe for one of their most successful dishes but deliberately omit one or more key ingredients which would permit competitors to copy their success. In the same way, marketing directors may withhold certain facts about actual results, but otherwise may be generous in sharing the broad outlines of their new programs.

By searching through what has been revealed in trade conferences and business publications, and supplementing this data with interviews, conversations, and our own experiences as advertising agency executives and marketing consultants, we have been able to piece together a surprising number of examples illustrating the reversal in marketing thinking and practice already taking place.

If here and there you find missing some details of the degree of success of the marketing program being discussed, you will understand that this is proprietary information which is being withheld by innovative marketers to prevent competitors from following too quickly and boldly. But we were able to gather enough information for you to see what the most imaginative marketers are doing and how well it seems to be working. We will also suggest how you might be able to adapt what they are doing to meet your own needs.

In writing this book, we have kept in mind not only what is happening in the U.S. marketing scene but also what we have observed in Canada, Europe, South America, Japan, and around the world. You will find case histories and references drawn from a wide spectrum of business categories in many countries. The subject matter of this book deals with fundamental marketing forces that are making themselves felt throughout the developed world.

So come along with us and see for yourself how you or your company can be one of the winners in the increasingly complex marketplace of the 90's. The great turnaround in marketing is already beginning to happen — and you can be one of the first to realize its full potential.

You have a choice. Either you can stand to one side as a fascinated spectator watching marketing leaders of the future race ahead with their new-found capabilities, and then have to scramble later on to catch up with them. Or you can be one of the pacesetters in turnaround thinking yourself, and enjoy the satisfaction of seeing your competitors struggling to catch up with *you*.

1 Trouble in the Marketplace

The disappearance of Mr. and Mrs. Average Consumer...
Personal time as the new currency...The Darwinian pressure
on products, services, stores...Network TV slippage...
Threats to brand loyalty...Clutter, clutter everywhere...
The spectre of waste and lost opportunities...The need for
a break with past practices

There is a new kind of strategic marketing thinking that is providing an important advantage to those who use it first in the 90's. It is the culmination of a gradual shift that has been taking place for several decades. It doesn't fit every situation and every product equally well. But where it does fit, understanding this shift in direction can be essential to gaining the advantage over competitors, and in some cases even to surviving.

Before we define and illustrate what we believe is the new marketing imperative, it is important to look at why it is happening and why it is necessary.

To appreciate fully how the foundations of mass marketing have been weakened, one needs only to look around at the floodwaters of social, lifestyle, distribution, and media change that continued to creep upwards throughout the 80's.

Many of these changes, viewed separately, may not come as a surprise to you if you read the advertising and business press. And yet the total effect when added up is startling, even shocking.

So here, in broad outline, are the seven root causes behind

the need for turning away from marketing practices of the past and rethinking the basics of marketing strategy in the 90's.

1. CHANGING DEMOGRAPHICS AND LIFESTYLES

Consumers are no longer neatly lined up as large, simple, visible target groups. The Norman Rockwell all-American family of breadwinner father, housewife mother, and two and a half children, swearing by their Lipton tea, Wheaties breakfast cereal, and Tide detergent, has almost become an endangered species.

As the 80's drew to a close, *Business Week* summarized the problem in a cover story, "Stalking the New Consumer":

> Life used to be much simpler. Mass marketers such as Procter & Gamble Co. would cook up innovative but fairly utilitarian products and advertise them on network TV. All the housewives between the ages of 18 and 34 watching "Search for Tomorrow" or "The Edge of Night" would see the ads and rush out to buy disposable diapers and dish detergent. The commercials were boring, but they saturated the airwaves and repeated the products' names over and over. Supermarkets stocked their shelves, and consumers came and bought.
>
> Things don't work quite that way anymore. Real product innovations are rare. And most women 18 to 34 aren't sitting at home watching the soaps. They're in college, or they're working as lawyers, cab drivers, or lathe operators. A 15-year-old boy may be doing the family shopping. Many customers are single, many are old, and many don't speak English. And some can't even read. Few of them are watching dull, name-dropping ads.[1]

America's constantly changing demographic mix means that often yesterday's targets are simply not there today. Today 53% of all U.S. households have only one or two members. Of the 10.4 million new households formed between 1980 and 1988, half were formed by singles. And most of the changes taking place in this part of the world have their parallels in Western Europe, Australia, Japan, and other developed markets.

One in four U.S. homes now consists of a person living alone, compared to about one out of ten 30 years ago. The Census Bureau estimates that this group will continue to expand, growing to 33.7 million households by 2000. Experts say these loners are more prone to impulse buying because there's no other household member around to disagree with or question the purchase.[2]

The number of unmarried couples living together has risen

in the last two decades from about half a million to 2.5 million.

The number of women in the workforce continues to rise, up near 58 million in 1990, about 10 million more than a decade earlier. Today 56% of U.S. women are working outside the home.

And this is a world-wide phenomenon. In Japan, half of the married women are working outside the home. In the U.K., the magazine *Woman's Own* reports: "Back in 1980, the year after Margaret Thatcher became Britain's first woman prime minister, there were twice as many men as women employed in the printing and publishing industry. Now women are fighting towards an equal share of the action not only in that sphere but in a whole lot of others as well. Of the 25,000 dentists in Britain, 6,000 are women, and the British Dental Association reports that half of those enrolled in their present training program are women."

This means less time and energy available for cooking at home. Of the three meals a day, it is estimated that in the U.S. one and a half are eaten away from home, and of the remainder, half are ready-prepared.

It also means that the family operates differently. It is estimated that $40 billion in family funds is now spent by teen-agers, mostly for groceries and other household items. And teen-agers are not known to be avid readers of women's service magazines.

Thanks to the two-income family, with less time to shop and (sometimes) more disposable income, direct-order marketing has continued to boom. Today American households receive over 21 billion copies of some 8,500 different mail-order catalogs a year, an average of almost 50 catalogs per household.

Because Mom's so often not home, companies like Avon and Tupperware have been forced to turn to other selling methods. After Tupperware sales declined, the company turned to holding parties at offices, day-care centers, churches, and recreation centers, and experimented with selling via a mail-order catalog. Avon estimates that 25% of its $2.67 billion in business is now done in the workplace. Electrolux vacuum cleaners now make 15% of their sales in its own 750 shops and are now expanding into shopping malls because, they say, "that's where the people are."

For years marketers have been preoccupied with the young baby boomers. But now the size and power of the youth market is shrinking. The "bulge in the python" has moved further along. The 77 million U.S. Baby Boomers are reaching middle age. "This will create a new consumer culture and dramatically alter the financial landscape of America," predicts Doris Walsh, publisher of *American Demographics* magazine. "Service will be valued above price, quality over quantity."

Did you know that about one-fourth of all U.S. population

growth in the last decade came from immigration, and that half of all of the new immigrants came from Asia? How much do you know about this new market? How are you communicating with them and selling to them?

People are staying healthier and living longer. In 1776, life expectancy was just 35 years — today it's 70. There are 30 million people in the U.S. over 65 — more than the entire population of Canada. The American Association of Retired Persons is now the second-largest organization in the country, surpassed only by the Catholic Church. Its magazine, *Modern Maturity,* is the largest-circulation publication in the U.S., with circulation of 22 million. In Europe, by the year 2,000 between one-fourth and one-third of the people there will be over 50 years old. By the year 2010, about 25% of the population of France will be 60 or older, compared to 18% a generation earlier.

In Japan, life expectancy is now 77 years for men and 83 years for women. In Brazil, in 1980, half of the population was under 20. By the year 2,000, the under-20 segment will have shrunk by 20%, and the increase in the adult population will be in the over-40 segment.

Declared *Adweek's Marketing Week,* "An era dominated by youth is ending. What we eat; what we wear; where, how and when we travel; what we buy and why we buy it — all will change as vast numbers of consumers face the opportunities and milestones of their journey beyond youth."

And marketers can stumble in seeking to adjust to this new reality in the marketplace.

Concluded an article in *Fortune* on this new-old market: "Mass marketers who don't get acquainted now with the mature consumer will regret it...The smart ones are making their mistakes before making them gets too expensive." [4]

(And even better than making mistakes and learning from them is avoiding them in the first place. Part of the secret, as we will see, lies in getting and staying in closer touch with your true prospects and best customers.)

2. THE DEMANDS ON PERSONAL TIME

Oh, for those wonderful Radio Days immortalized by the Woody Allen movie by that name. Almost every evening, the whole family sat around in the living room and listened to the radio.

They had plenty of time and willingness to hear and absorb every word of Jack Benny's artful plugs for Jell-O or Ed Wynn's zany skits for Texaco. (Nobody worried in those days whether the stars of the show were sullying themselves by pitching the sponsor's product.)

And as people listened, they might also browse slowly and carefully through the great weekly magazines that were an important fixture of their lives — *Life, Look, Collier's, The Saturday Evening Post.* Or they might be reading one of the several evening newspapers available.

A generation later, we might still find the nuclear family gathered around that fascinating new novelty, the television set, watching "Father Knows Best," "I Love Lucy," "The Honeymooners," still without an undue amount of competition from other activities.

What a difference today! We are adrift in a new world — almost a complete reversal of the old. Advertisers must almost literally run down the street to catch up with and buttonhole the hurrying consumers.

For millions of people, almost every minute of their waking hours is blocked out and booked up for working...commuting... computing...jogging...shopping...entertaining..."quality time" with the children...movie-going and movie viewing at home on cable or VCR...and each member of the family "grazing" separately at the refrigerator or microwave at different times. More and more people are giving up leisurely dining and turning to bolting their food standing up at a fast-food restaurant — or gulping a quick cup of soup zapped in the microwave — or having a pizza, Chinese food, or even a gourmet restaurant dinner delivered to the home.

Market researchers and poll takers report growing complaints everywhere about pressure and lack of time. "It's true in Portland, Maine and in Evansville, Indiana," reported researcher Judy Langer. Her findings showed that "everybody seems to feel worn out" by the demands of work, family, and personal achievement.[5]

"The whole society is becoming time-poor and money-rich," according to Professor Jagdish Sheth of the University of Southern California. "Consumers are looking for value in time, not just value in money." And woe be to the marketers who fail to take this into account, both in their advertising plans and in the development of their products and services.

"Time will be the currency of the 1990's," says Tony Adams, VP-market research at Campbell Soup. "Heating is replacing cooking, and 'You are what you heat' will be the catchwords of the 90's."[6]

Today this is a fact of life in Madrid as much as it is in New York. In Madrid you can continue doing business while stuck in a traffic jam, courtesy of a company that hands you a mobile phone for a three-minute call while you are waiting. And already one out of ten meals in Spain is eaten outside the home.

A study by the European Economic Commission asked workers

to choose between an increase in pay for more hours or the same pay but a decrease in hours. On the average, one out of three workers was prepared to choose the extra time over the extra money.

But if time is money, large companies are often slow to catch on. It is often the small, nimble, quick-footed entrepreneurs who are darting into the market with time-saving services for time-deprived consumers, while the giants come lumbering in afterwards to emulate them.

3. OVERCROWDING BY TOO MANY NEW PRODUCTS, SERVICES, AND STORES

There is a grim Darwinian law at work in the birth, survival, and spread of new products, services, and stores. Born into a favorable environment, they multiply swiftly. Inevitably the time comes when they start running out of new customers to feed on, start stealing from each other, and many die off.

As the big brands fought it out in the major mass-merchandise categories, they started running out of new customers. So to expand, they began uncovering and serving niches with increasingly specialized products and line extensions. But in today's computer-controlled production and quicker turnaround time, as soon as one company develops a hit product, the competitors can quickly and easily imitate it and improve on it.

So as soon as one marketer discovers a profitable niche, others leap in to compete for its trade. The result is a bewildering proliferation of product choices.

When Procter & Gamble came out with a new ultra-thin disposable diaper called "Ultra Pampers," Kimberly-Clark's Huggies failed to respond at first due to faulty research. Huggies' market share dropped from one-third to one-fourth. But then the company hurried to put out a thin diaper of its own and regained its one-third market share. [7]

The outpouring of new products and line extensions has led to a fierce battle for retail shelf-space. According to SAMI, a market research firm, the number of cereal brands that sell at least $1 million grew from 84 in 1979 to 150 ten years later. And the number of toothpaste brands sold in food stores rose from 10 to 31.[8] The various divisions of Revlon alone are reported to offer a total of 2500 different products!

There is simply not room for most stores to carry and display all these products. (Although a liquor store in the Little Poland section of Brooklyn boasts of carrying 118 brands of vodka!)[9]

In many product categories, marketers of famous old brands are faced with an alarming trend toward "commoditization." To compete for the low end of the market, they introduce a cheap, convenient, mass-produced product like a throwaway razor or ballpoint pen. Others follow, and the product quickly becomes a commodity sold on price, not by brand, driving down sales on the more expensive heavily advertised products. (This has also resulted in something called "consumer bimodality," in which the consumer chooses either the cheap commodity version or the expensive luxury version — and often it's the same individual consumer under different circumstances.)

In such a circumstance, mass advertising of a "commoditized" product may not be affordable, and also may simply drive people into the stores to buy a competitor's commodity. For growth, a whole new strategy, even a new product line, may be required.

In packaged goods, various figures are put forth concerning the number of new products introduced each year.

The most commonly accepted figure seems to be 10,000 new food and non-food items per year, at a cost of $15 to $20 million per full-scale introduction. Yet the typical supermarket has space for only 17,000 items on its shelves.

Peter Rogers, as executive vice president of Nabisco Brands, has called this outpouring of new products "sheer lunacy." He pointed out that *less than 1%* of the 45,000 new food products introduced in the previous 16 years by all manufacturers had achieved annual sales of $15 million or more.

"We would have done much better had we just taken our new product dollars to the bank and put them in an ordinary passbook savings account," he declared. [Italics ours]

He made the startling admission, according to the story in *Marketing News*, that "Nabisco's new products have enthused the sales force and maintained the interest of the consumer...They have failed, however, to increase tonnage or market share and have not enhanced the value and position of existing brands."[10]

In other words, it would seem that Nabisco has had to run very hard with new products in order to stay in the same place.

Overcrowding of store shelves is not a phenomenon restricted to the American marketing scene. In Japan, there are 3,500 to 4,000 new products introduced each year in food stores. And only one out of ten is believed to succeed.

SATURATION EXPERIENCED IN OTHER FIELDS TOO

With many service establishments and retailers, the story is the same.

In the $60 billion fast-food industry, growth is leveling off and the franchise chains are fighting to steal customers away from each other. By the end of the last decade, it was estimated that 20.8 % of fast-food meals were being bought at a discount through couponing or specials. According to a financial analyst, the market was experiencing a softness as a result of long-term problems such as the overbuilding of new restaurants.[11] Just as there is a limitation to the number of products you can put on supermarket shelves, there is a limit on the number of fast-food outlets the public's appetite can support.

In the budget hotel business, there is also a "fierce competition for market share." Fifty chains are battling it out for their share of the inexpensive rooms market.[12]

Banks have become almost frantic in their urgent pleas to depositors to switch. The cost of the incremental sale, of getting that one more depositor or cardholder, is soaring. Often, perhaps, it can only be tolerated by concealing this reality from themselves. It is similar to the way we as individuals sometimes deliberately conceal from ourselves the imprudent costs of our expensive hobbies and pastimes by not adding up all of our expenditures.

In retailing, the department stores are being buffeted by the saturation of discount chains on the one side and the sharper targeting by specialty stores on the other.

Shopping malls are suffering from an over-supply of malls and stores. There are now almost 35,000 shopping centers and malls. Many stand half empty. For many people, the novelty of going to the mall just to wander and browse has worn off.

The gloomy outlook for retailing was summarized by a blunt story in *The New York Times*, which said, among other things:

> Retailing has fallen on hard times as industry profits continue to slide and some of the best names in the business are now on the auction block.

> Recent headlines may tell the tale of how at least seven crown jewels of retailing, including Bloomingdale's, Saks Fifth Avenue, and Bonwit Teller, are being sold by their parent companies. But these sales — the unpleasant aftermath of a leveraged buyout wave that swept through retailing in the last few years — are only symptomatic of deeper forces reshaping the industry.

> Once a growth industry that racked up profits from a rising population tide, retailing has matured into a business where one store's gains now come only at the expense of another. The massive over-building of shopping complexes during the 1970's has left America "over-malled."

> "There's a war going on," said Howard Davidowitz, head of his own retail consulting firm. "We've overpopulated America with stores." Alan Millstein, publisher of the *Fashion Network Report*, a monthly

trade letter, said: "These are the most dire times for the industry since the Great Depression of the 1930's." [13]

While the bankruptcy of the B. Altman department store chain and the shaky state of others is certainly due more to the leveraged buyout binge of the 80's than to a failure of marketing, it certainly has put pressure on many marketers to find new and better ways to sell. The upscale beauty products market, so dependent on department store distribution, is one that is especially endangered.   Reported *Adweek* after the Campeau Corporation dragged its Federated and Allied department stores into bankruptcy court, "The potential shakeout is forcing some [beauty products] companies to look harder at alternatives to department stores." [14]

Faced with this over-malled environment, some retailers, both large and small, are finding ways of fighting back with skill, swiftness, and imagination. We will be pointing out how in some fields small retailers are banding together to underwrite powerful target marketing and customer cultivation with their own databases.

The smartest manufacturers of branded products also are finding ways to separate themselves from the crowd. They are engaging in private "conversations" with consumers, carrying on individualized direct communications out of sight of their competitors.

The overcrowding of the marketplace is a fact of life that absolutely must be taken into account in the strategic planning of all marketing today.

4. THE WEAKENING OF THE MAGIC IN NETWORK TELEVISION ADVERTISING

For a full appreciation of how the foundations of mass marketing have been weakened, one need only look at the slippage in network TV's domination of the national advertising landscape.

Because of the escape routes provided by independent stations, cable TV, the VCR, and the hand-held remote control device — as well as the demands on personal time that we have looked at — the audiences for network television commercials keep going down, down, down.

By the start of the 90's, VCRs were to be found in over 65% of U.S. homes, and more than 330 million blank tapes a year were being sold.

Meanwhile network television advertising rates (per ratings point) have continued to go up, up, up. And American households are bombarded by more, more, more commercials, which keep getting shorter and shorter.

As advertisers were squeezed by rates rising faster than the cost of inflation, some began to wedge two 15-second commercials into their 30 seconds of purchased time. Finally, in 1986, the networks bowed to demand and began to sell 15-second commercials at half the cost of a 30-second commercial. Within three years, 38% of all network commercials were 15's.

Now advertisers are having second thoughts. "The use of 15's has hit a saturation level," according to one agency media director. "Only so many advertisers can tell a story in 15 seconds, and clutter is impacting the medium." Advertisers find themselves caught between the punitive cost of 30's and the declining effectiveness of too many 15's. [15]

Over the years, the total network share of prime-time viewing audience has gone steadily down — from a peak of 92% during the golden years before 1980 down to 68% at the beginning of '89. At that time, the heads of CBS and ABC predicted the decline would bottom out at 64%, but the president of NBC said it could go as low as 55%. [16]

Marketing Professor Eugene Secunda of Baruch College in New York surveyed top advertisers and found that 53% would consider making a significant shift in ad dollars if the three networks' combined share dropped to 65%.

"It's like those folks who kidded themselves that the Roman Empire was going to go on forever," observed Professor Secunda.

And the share of audience for network TV *commercials* could be far lower than 65%— actually, nobody knows quite how much lower — since many viewers wander off to the kitchen or the bathroom or flip to another channel with the remote control during the commercial break.

(There's some disagreement over usage of the terms "flipping" and "zapping." Although some writers refer to channel flipping as "zapping," we prefer to reserve that word to describe the custom of hitting the fast-forward button during the commercial break when playing back a home-recorded television program.)

One survey found that 75% of all TV homes have remote controls.[17] Another study found that people with remotes changed channels an average of once every five minutes, while a typical heavy flipper might change channels a thousand times a day. People with remotes changed channels 5.3 times as often as those without.[18] Based on a sample of viewers in the New York area, flipping cuts a prime-time advertising audience by 10% or more. Networks are understandably nervous about progress being made toward measuring this slippage more accurately, since each rating point can be worth approximately $80 million in advertising revenue!

Another study found that the highest-income households,

those considered most desirable by many advertisers, do the most flipping. Households with incomes over $75,000 flip an average of once every 2 minutes and 42 seconds![19]

And even if we viewers do happen to see your commercial (or part of it) as we go flipping past, how much more can our poor brains absorb and retain? Just one two-hour movie on U.S. commercial TV is interrupted with some 50 spots and promos.

Dave Vedehra, president of Video StoryBoard Tests, found that the number of people who say they pay "absolutely no attention" to commercials increased from 13 percent in 1983 to 20 percent in 1984, and this trend was expected to continue.

Mona Doyle, president of Consumer Network, a market research and consulting firm, recently made a similar report. "When we asked consumers last year to tell us the best and the worst television commercials, a number told us that they simply don't see them any more. They don't have to zap them by remote. They have tuned them out mentally." [20]

This decline has very serious implications for national advertisers. "The inability to efficiently reach consumers with the benefits of a new brand is tied directly to the decline of the influence of network TV," according to the president of the nation's 11th largest advertising agency. [21]

"Gone forever is the great electronic funnel through which we could pour our products into the mainstream of American awareness," bluntly stated J. Tylee Wilson, chairman of RJR Nabisco in 1986. [22]

And not only is network television losing viewers. It is possible that *all* television has lost some of its magic. "The ratings results from the A.C. Nielsen Company over the last three months have displayed a rather startling trend: millions of viewers appear to be abandoning television," reported *The New York Times* in April of 1989. "That is, viewers are not just abandoning the networks for cable channels or Fox Broadcasting, or for rented videocassettes, but are simply shutting their sets off for the sake of other, unknown pursuits." [23]

While all this is bad news for the networks and a problem for the major advertisers, what does it mean to smaller advertisers? As the big companies begin to rechannel more of their massive ad expenditure into other media, the law of supply and demand will undoubtedly drive up these other rates. (Mail-order advertisers who have thrived on the two-minute commercial on cable are already being squeezed out of that happy hunting ground by the rising demand for cable time.)

There is also a positive side to the money flowing into alternatives to network TV.

It is causing all kinds of media forms and channels to thrive and expand, offering more opportunities to *all* advertisers.

It's absurd even to think of writing off network TV in America as a powerful and prosperous medium. As we write this, the networks show signs of bouncing back, with trimmer staffs, smaller audiences, and higher rates per thousand. Network television remains the easiest way to get maximum reach from this extraordinary advertising medium. But this does not eliminate the challenge to advertisers to find new ways to make the medium more cost-efficient by using it to identify and contact true prospects, as we will be showing you later in this book.

5. THE DECLINE IN BRAND LOYALTY

Another problem many brand advertisers face today is that the public is saying, like Rhett Butler to Scarlett O'Hara, "Frankly, my dear, I don't give a damn." The ability of manufacturers to copy one another's most successful products, and the brand-hopping encouraged by tempting discounts, may be seriously weakening the grip of brand loyalty in many categories.

There is a fierce debate raging in the advertising community about whether the intensity of brand loyalty is fading or not. But there is impressive authority for claiming that it is. And if it is true, then a significant amount of the more than $100 billion a year spent on national advertising, most of it devoted to creating and maintaining awareness of branded products and services, must be going down the drain.

"Traditional brand management is dying, a victim of decreasing consumer brand loyalty and increasing retailer clout," was the way *Advertising Age* paraphrased a top Kraft Inc. executive. In the same story, Donald Schultz, a professor of marketing at Northwestern's Medill School of Journalism specializing in advertising research, pointed out that market managers' past experience in a growing market may leave them ill-prepared for a no-growth economy in the 90's.

Supermarket scanner data are providing some startling views of U.S. consumers, according to Schultz. "The belief that once consumers buy a brand, they will stay there, is not true." [24]

In a Needham Harper Worldwide study, the percentage of consumers saying they try to stick with major brands dropped from 80% to 60% during an eight-year period.

There seems to be broad agreement among the pessimists that two factors have tended to erode brand franchise: price-cutting promotion and product parity.

A front-page story in *The Wall Street Journal* raised the issue with this challenging headline: "AS NETWORK TV FADES, MANY ADVERTISERS TRY AGE-OLD PROMOTIONS...THEY SWITCH TO DIRECT MAIL, COUPONS, AND PR PLOYS. WILL BRAND LOYALTY SUFFER?" [25]

According to William C. Johnson, an undisputed leader in sales promotion, "Every time the brand is discounted or promoted, confidence and respect is withdrawn until eventually the account is empty."

Then there is the problem of lack of product difference in the eyes of the consumer. A study by BBDO worldwide found that two-thirds of the consumers surveyed in 28 countries believed that no differences existed in the quality of brands in 13 different product categories. [26] So why not buy by deal and coupon instead of by brand?

However, brand loyalty is more important in some product categories than others. The same consumer who couldn't care less about the difference between Charmin and Cottonelle toilet tissue may be prepared to engage in a fist-fight over the difference between Toyota and Chevrolet.

Brand loyalty also varies by demographics. "Successful blue-collar" families have been found to be more brand-loyal than the average consumer.[27]

Paradoxically, consumers seem to prefer any brand than no brand. Generic products in supermarkets — plain old unbranded "peas" and "paper towels" — at one time seemed to be the wave of the future. But generics hit their peak in sales in 1982 and 1983, when they reached 2.4% of grocery sales, and have been declining ever since.

It's too soon for branded package goods to heave a sigh of relief, however. As we will see later on, retailers are building the potential to launch a powerful alternative to the major brands with their own private labels, backed with the power of their own customer database and the clout to deny shelf-space to any advertised-brand product they choose to exclude.

Brands are not about to disappear. That's not the issue. The question is how do advertising-supported brands defend and expand their profits when those profits are besieged on three sides by three enemies of profitability — declining media cost-efficiency, the increasing costliness and wastefulness of price-cutting sales promotion, and the retailer's growing power.

The retailer as enemy of brand profitability? Yes, the retailer. Not only because of retailer demands for trade deals and slotting allowances, but also because of the ever-present threat of competition from the retailer's own brands.

Borrowing the idea from an innovative supermarket in Canada, New York's D'Agostino supermarkets have introduced a new premium store brand, President's Choice. *And D'Agostino's own Decadent Chocolate Chip cookies now outsell Nabisco's Chips Ahoy, the heavily advertised leading national brand.*

Says Carol L. Colman, managing partner of the consulting firm Inferential Focus, "Today the retailer is holding the cards, earning a higher return on each product and competing on home ground with his own suppliers. Aided by computer power — scanners and warehouse link-ups that give the chains daily feedback on which products are moving off the shelves — the supermarkets have a clear competitive advantage over the manufacturer-suppliers."

In Rochester, New York, the Wegmans chain of supermarkets has been carrying a new brand of disposable diapers to compete with Pampers, Luvs, and Huggies. It's Wegmans' own Ultrasofts (actually made for them by Weyerhaeuser Co.), with many of the premium qualities of the Big Three but selling for as much as 10% less. And you better believe it, Ultrasofts has no trouble getting well stocked and displayed in Wegmans' supermarkets.

"The Loblaws and A&P chains have already announced their intentions to concentrate on fewer lines in many categories, *supplementing the leading brand with their own,*" reports *Adweek's Marketing Week.* [Italics ours.] "Other supermarket chains with dominant market positions have hinted they would follow suit." [28]

To break out of this encirclement, national advertised brands have got to find new ways to *add value* to the product without adding materially to the production cost, *cut waste* in advertising and promotion, and *improve communication* with prime prospects and wavering customers. We will be looking at how turnaround thinking opens the door to addressing all three of these challenges.

6. ADVERTISING CLUTTER, OVERKILL, AND WASTE

The department store pioneer John Wanamaker is supposed to have said, "Half of all I spend on advertising is wasted. The trouble is, I don't know which half."

Now this is changing. Not the wasting, but the knowing.

We believe that the half that is wasted includes the billions of dollars that are squandered on non-prospects in order to reach and convert prospects...the additional billions lavished on giving away cents-off coupons to loyal customers, coupon cheaters, and brand-indifferent bargain hunters...and more billions spent on unaccountable image advertising that does nothing to lead to a sale.

Professor John Philip Jones of Syracuse University, iconoclast author of *Does It Pay to Advertise?*, says bluntly, "I believe that people continue to spend enormous amounts of money on advertising because they're scared to death to stop. That's the fundamental reason."[29] Needless to say, there were plenty of indignant rebuttals from other advertising experts. We found one rebuttal that took a curious turn. Wrote Martin N. Grant, vice president and group management supervisor of Chiat/Day/Mojo New York:

"My theory is that there are so few clients that spend enough on advertising to be seen that any measurement of advertising effectiveness is ridiculous. I can count the clients on one hand who spend enough on advertising to be effective. Yet there are a sea of marketers who spend $3 million to $4 million a year on advertising and then say it doesn't work...I've told clients in the past that if you can't spend $8 million or $10 million, don't spend your money."[30]

Isn't that a rather extraordinary observation by a prominent agency executive? Can this really be true? A "sea" of marketers are spending only "$3 or $4 million a year" on advertising and then finding it doesn't work! In other words, wasting their money!

But they are getting off cheap. Remember the famous "Where's Herb?" campaign for Burger King? It cost $40 million, and while it was running Burger King's share of market actually declined.

Advertisers lavish millions on campaigns in order to achieve some penetration of public consciousness with almost no solid evidence that such awareness will lead to an increased share of market.

And advertising and trade publications seldom mention the actual sales results of most campaigns. They limit themselves for the most part to subjective critiques of the creativity displayed, or to surveys of public awareness of the campaign message or admiration for its cleverness.

In a rare exception, here's what *Los Angeles Times* marketing columnist Bruce Horivitz had to say about the Joe Isuzu liar campaign: "Joe Isuzu sells lies a lot better than he sells cars... Although the character he portrays may have scored 100 on the laugh meter, on the most important meter of them all — increased car sales — the needle didn't budge.

"In fact, it slipped backward. For the first six months of 1987, American Isuzu saw its U.S. automobile sales nudge slightly downward...about 50 fewer cars than it sold in the same period in 1986." [31]

And all the while Madison Avenue journalists were wildly applauding the creativity of the campaign.

The National Coffee Association launched a campaign to reverse slipping coffee sales. It spent some $20 million on television advertising linking celebrities' success with coffee-drinking. The campaign was halted 15 months later. "We didn't get to the ultimate goal," reported the trade association president ruefully, "We didn't sell more coffee." [32]

At the time of this writing, Metropolitan Life is four years into their licensing of the Peanuts gang as the corporate symbol. The company wanted something warm and human to pave the way for the agent's visit.

Three years later, after the expenditure of $90 million on advertising, promotion, and collateral material, what was the result?

Well, it was a mixed bag. During those first three years of the Peanuts campaign, the company's total assets did rise about 22%. But its share of total industry premium income dropped from 3.9% to 2.6%. And even its awareness score was disappointing compared to its competitors. A survey revealed that Met's aided awareness rating was about 89% — compared to Allstate's 100%, Prudential's 99%, and State Farm's 98%.

One smaller competitor who has been doing very well, Northwestern Mutual Life, believes that "the most effective life insurance advertising makes specific and unique claims." One of its well-advertised claims is superior dividend performance. Only one other company, Metropolitan, has the results to back up similar claims. But Metropolitan prefers to focus simply on having Snoopy say, "Get Met. It pays." [33]

The company and its agency argue, and possibly quite correctly, that the purpose of the advertising is not to sell insurance but simply to create in prospects a warm, friendly feeling about Metropolitan and thus pave the way for a friendly reception when the Met agent comes to call. It may be so, but we believe that Metropolitan is leaving itself vulnerable to competitors large and small who can nibble away at the Met brand franchise with more sharply focused sales arguments.

Of course we are not against image advertising when it can be proven that it has a positive long-term effect on sales. But too often this is not the case. Often it seems that companies have become so bemused by the notion of image that it has become an end in itself, quite apart from its demonstrable sales effect.

Dr. Kevin J. Clancy, as chairman of a leading marketing research firm and professor of management at Boston University, told of his astonishing discovery as a fresh Ph.D. starting out in the research department of a large agency.

He was asked to put together a collection of cases of marketing programs which had worked.

"Sure," he said, "give me a week or two and I'll put together a neat report."

But weeks turned into months as he discovered that unequivocal successes were difficult to find.

"The fact is," he now believes, "that *most advertising programs fail to show a clear effect on sales, never mind a return on investment*...My own firm's experience is that seven out of 10 new products/services taken into test markets are failures (some say the figure is higher) and of those which succeed in test (or seem to) about half are disappointments when taken national.

"The story is even more discouraging for new campaigns for established products and services. Fewer than two in ten in-market tests of new advertising programs show clearly significant effects attributable to a new program using either traditional test marketing or contemporary electronic test marketing methods."[34]

One of the reasons is sheer excess.

Studies show that the typical consumer is bombarded by 5,000 advertising messages a day, and the number of ads is expected to increase steadily. That trend has many executives in the industry worried about the cost of breaking through the growing advertising clutter.

In Baltimore, drivers can learn about Jeeps from 4,000 of the city's parking meters. Manufacturers' spiels have replaced piped-in music in 9,000 supermarkets and drugstores. Skiers at 200 resorts can view strategically placed soup ads on their way up the slopes. Even public restrooms now have ads in their stalls.

Of the 5,000 daily commercial messages — almost 2 million a year — consumers remember only 2% to 3% without prompting, according to a study commissioned by Whittle Communications.

The president of Sterling Motors was shown a reel of car advertising running on New York television stations.

He found that on a single night there were 200 different car ads costing about $10 million.

"The money being spent is ludicrous," said David Wager, director of marketing for Porsche North America. "Car advertising is becoming a continuous blur. The American consumer won't take time to keep up."

Said the *Advertising Age* story: "As the 1990 model year unfolds, that clutter is forcing auto marketers — niche players and industry giants alike — to risk new creative and media solutions to reach their prospects." [35]

Not long ago we heard a startling statement come from the lips of a top marketing executive. We were sitting in on a roundtable discussion of possible direct-marketing strategies in the conference room of a major packaged goods company. At one point, the company executive in question burst forth impatiently, "We could cut out half of our television budget tomorrow — well, maybe one-third — and it wouldn't make a damned bit of difference in our sales. When we don't have a product story to tell, we might as well save our money!"

Alvin Achenbaum (who was a leading sage and scold of Madison Avenue until he rejoined the ranks of agency executives) has pointed to market saturation as the chief culprit in the declining power of national advertising. After World War II, the incidence of usage in almost all product categories was relatively low. Over three-fourths of the population did not use a deodorant. There were no laundry softeners. It was unusual to travel by plane for personal reasons. And so on.

But 30 years later, almost every product and service category had achieved full penetration. Thanks to the massive firepower of mass marketing in the 50's, 60's, and 70's, advertisers had succeeded in getting people to use a broad variety of products and services and to use them often.

Today, with market growth limited to the increase in population, at best only 1.5% in the U.S. and even less in some European countries, in many categories marketers can gain only by stealing customers from their competitors.

And, says Achenbaum, "return on the advertising investment has naturally declined."

So your advertising has a far greater challenge than it did a generation ago, to somehow plough through the sea of advertising clutter and achieve the desired response from your prospects.

7. FEEDING THE DISCOUNT PROMOTION MONSTER

With companies under pressure from Wall Street to show ever-improving quarterly sales, "push marketing" began to boom in the 70's. Discount coupons for packaged goods skyrocketed. Everybody was happy. The consumers got a bargain. The stores got quick turnover. The manufacturers got an instant boost of sales and gained a competitive edge.

But as couponing continued to soar — from 72.7 billion coupons distributed in 1980 to 273.4 billion by the end of the last decade[37] — problems rose along with the deluge.

Counter-couponing often neutralized the advantage. Product managers became field generals, launching strikes and counter strikes against the other fellow several times a year, at a million dollars or more a pop.

Misredemption, either through carelessness or through fraud, has taken a heavy toll.

A task force study of the Grocery Manufacturers of America

and the Food Marketing Institute cautiously concluded that mis-redemption amounted to 7.1%. Given an estimated 8 billion re-demptions at an average value of 48 cents, that would mean a loss of $273 million.

The cost could be even greater. U.S. Postal Inspector Rich-ard Bowdren, after tracking coupon fraud for nearly 24 years, es-timated that one in every two coupons was redeemed fraudulent-ly in 1978.[38] If this was still true by the end of the 80's, it would mean that annual loss through misredemption was not a mere $273 million but as much as $2 billion! (Remember Dirksen's Law, named after the famous saying by the late Senator Everett Dirksen: "A billion dollars here, a billion dollars there, and pretty soon you're talking about real money.")

Then you have to count the number of coupons redeemed by current users who would have bought the product anyway. One estimate is as high as 60%. The sales manager for a system that distributes coupons at the check-out counter of the supermarket has placed the usual figure even higher, at nearly 80%.[39] Of course, these current-user redemption estimates don't quite jibe with Mr. Bowdren's misredemption estimate, since the two cate-gories then add up to more than 100%. In any case, it is certain-ly safe to say that up to several billions of dollars are spent in giv-ing discounts to current users. (Some would argue that's not all bad, of course, because it helps maintain their brand loyalty; but it's certainly not all good either.)

Other problems pointed out by experts: (1) an excess of cou-poning erodes brand loyalty by teaching consumers to buy by price rather than by brand, and (2) couponing often results only in a costly temporary blip in the sales curve.

The A.C. Nielsen Co. did a study of 862 packaged goods pro-motions and came up with some startling results. *More than 50% of the events had no impact on sales, and only one promotion in 10 generated a volume gain of 10% or more.* [40]

Meanwhile, U.S. consumers flooded with some 3,000 cou-pons per household each year are beginning to show signs of be-ing jaded. In 1989, although coupon distribution increased an-other 9%, for the second year in a row there was actually a slight decline in redemption, this time down to 7.1 billion cou-pons or just 2.6%.

Rather than learning from the painful experience of pack-aged goods manufacturers, the automobile manufacturers have put themselves in the same trap. As soon as one of them turned on the rebate faucet, most of the others followed suit and kept upping the ante. Now automobile sales are down modestly, and profit margins have been shaved almost to the vanishing point by rebates the public has come to expect.

But no matter how pointless this promotional overkill has become, there is always pressure from Wall Street for it to continue. Reported *Advertising Age:* "Wall Street's demand for better earnings from the nation's top advertisers is forcing many companies to shift the strategic focus of campaigns from long-term image-building to short-term performance gains, according to a survey by Vitt Media International."[41]

Nonetheless there is now brave talk in the trade press of advertisers kicking the discounting habit and pumping more money back into brand-image advertising. But if it is the same kind of brand advertising that has no provable profitability, as we have pointed out is often the case, there is the risk of jumping out of the frying pan and into the fire.

What we have seen so far certainly seems a rather alarming picture, doesn't it?

Advertising agencies worrying and cutting back.

Media feeling the pinch.

The mass market breaking up into small, elusive, fast-moving, hard-to-reach groups.

Network television advertising losing some of its magic and lots of its audience.

Consumers too busy to give their undivided attention to advertising and reeling from the constant bombardment of advertising messages — in the U.S., nearly two million a year.

Millions of dollars lavished on advertising campaigns which produce no perceptible effect on sales.

Discount and rebate sales promotion which erodes brand image and profits without producing permanent gains in sales.

Many consumers indifferent to brands despite the billions lavished on brand advertising.

And this picture of the U.S. market is strikingly similar in many ways to what is happening in the United Kingdom, Germany, France, The Netherlands, Italy, and other countries in Europe.

"What European countries certainly share," the 1990 London International Direct Marketing Fair was told by Stuart Heather, chairman of Rapp & Collins Europe, "are aging population, especially in the North, changing attitudes toward money and leisure time, the upsurge of the working woman, the breakdown of the family unit, and what is surprising, especially in Catholic countries, the breakdown of marriage, where increasingly it is seen as an outdated institution." And almost everywhere in the developed world there is a rising flood of advertising impressions and media clutter as the consumer-dominated economy takes over in Europe, in South America, and in Japan.

No wonder Professor Don E. Schultz calls it a "crisis."

CEO's, Marketing directors, ad managers, product managers, promotion directors, ad agency executives, and small company entrepreneurs and retailers — marketers in every country in the developed and developing world — face a formidable challenge in fighting for market share, growth, and profitability. The tools that worked so well in the past have become dull and less effective.

At the same time, as cases in this book will demonstrate, the new turnaround thinking we are proposing builds on the best of what has gone before and does not replace it.

Despite the glittering promise of glamorous new electronic media, we believe the traditional media — magazines, newspapers, direct mail, radio, and television— yes, including network television — will still be here and going strong in the year 2000.

When an advertiser has worthwhile product or service news to convey, and tells it well, television advertising will always have an awesome power to impress and impel us.

But the forms and uses of all of these established media are going to change dramatically, just as the nature of commercial radio changed after the flowering of commercial television.

Nothing we have said should be construed as a blanket indictment of discounting.

If you have a new product or a small share of market, then sales incentives may be a valuable and productive way for you to get people to try your product.

If you are marketing a service business in a field in which discount coupon wars have not yet begun, you might be able to get the jump on your competitors with tempting price-off offers.

On the other hand, if you're pouring promotion money out and not getting permanent gains back, then it's time to do some hard thinking about the alternatives we will offer in this book.

Nor are we saying that brand-building image advertising has no value. We are simply saying — and will demonstrate throughout this book — that the overall marketing strategy which includes brand-building must change and is changing to include more direct and more accountable communication with the true prospect.

As advertising professionals who spent many years in the advertising agency business, we would be the last to claim that advertising doesn't work.

Of course it works. It always has and it always will.

But it doesn't work equally well for everybody. It never has and it never will. It can't make every company No. 1, since there can be only one No. 1.

And in this present crisis, it is not working as well as it once did for a great many advertisers. For some, hardly at all.

As always, advertising is working — and will work — for those who are open to change. They will find new ways to link their advertising to the powerful new forces agency leaders formerly scorned as the "demon disciplines," sales promotion and direct marketing. It will work for those who are among the first to understand the basic turnaround in marketing now taking place, and for those who are the smartest in applying the new marketing tools demanded by this historic shift. And hopefully this book will help you join that happy band.

Note: If you work with an annual marketing budget that is only in the five-figure or six-figure range instead of tens of millions of dollars, you may wonder what many of our examples have to do with you and your problems.

You'll see. What you will soon find out in this book is that the crisis in mass advertising effectiveness we have described is beginning to cause many large advertisers to make a complete turnaround in their thinking about advertising and marketing.

And the new directions they will pursue are directions you, too, can pursue. Furthermore, you may be able to move more quickly and get there sooner because you're not burdened with corporate bureaucracy, constantly changing management, or (hopefully) the restrictions imposed by heavy debt service due to a leveraged buy-out.

2 Time for Turnaround Thinking

*The "Maginot Line" psychology...The new breed arrives...
From product development and cost control in the
60's...to the marketing concept of the 70's...to
excellence in service and niche marketing in the
80's...And now The Age of the Individual, and how to
profit from it..Why many marketers lag behind...
Breaking out of compartmentalized thinking...The ten
Turnaround Trends shaping the new thinking*

So the old ways of advertising and marketing are in deep trouble.

In our earlier book, *MaxiMarketing*, we identified and warned of troublesome developments setting the stage for the emergence of a new direction in advertising, promotion, and marketing.

Since then, with each passing year after that, the alarm bells have rung louder.

The precepts and tactics which have served America's marketers so well for so long are being swept away.

As we observed the response of many veteran marketers to the new situation, we found ourselves fascinated by the similarity to the Maginot Line psychology that gripped French military thinking in the early days of World War II.

The French General Staff had devised the ideal World War I strategy for winning World War II. They had built an impregnable line of fortifications, the Maginot Line, to withstand the German army's expected inch-by-inch frontal advance. The only problem was that, when the time came, the German panzers and Luftwaffe actually followed a totally new strategy— — pincer movements by lightning-swift mobile units. The rest is history. France fell in days.

From our vantage point, as marketing consultants and directors of The MaxiMarketing Institute, we have observed so many of today's marketers bogged down in the trench-warfare mass marketing tactics of a generation ago, at a time when a completely new kind of strategy is called for. Marketers, too, can be guilty of fighting today's battles with yesterday's methods.

ENTER A NEW BREED OF MARKETING STRATEGIST

But not all of today's marketers are trapped in yesterday's thinking. Young Turks have begun to experiment with many of the principles set forth in *MaxiMarketing*. As the previous decade wound down, we saw more double-duty advertising...more "linkage" of the advertising to the sale...more "fishing" in mass media for true prospects...more of what we called Whole-Brain Advertising...more emphasis on accountability in advertising...more experimentation with new media forms and new ways to use existing media...and most significantly, a strong turn toward a database-driven approach to marketing.

The more we observed and talked with these new innovators, the more we came to realize that there was a profound change in marketing thinking which went even further than what we had set forth in *MaxiMarketing*.

And those who persisted in playing strictly by the old rules were in danger of being left behind. But what can they do about it? What magic formula is going to rescue today's troubled marketers and bring them glorious everlasting success in the marketplace of the 90's?

Don't hold your breath. There is no magic formula.

There is, however, a way of thinking that we believe can dramatically increase your chances of gaining share and increasing profits.   We call it "Turnaround Thinking." Learning to cast off old mental sets about the marketing and advertising tools of the 80's. Learning to "think anew and act anew," armed with new marketing tools fashioned to meet a new set of challenges.

As we surveyed the wreckage in the wake of the giants who stumbled in the past decade, and observed some of the most recent astonishing successes, our vision of a new marketing imperative took shape.

We saw new technologies and capabilities being used in surprising ways and existing practices turned topsy-turvy.

We saw instances of this happening across the widest spectrum of business activity. In manufacturing companies with retail distribution. In the direct marketing world of home ordering and home delivery. In a variety of service companies. In the activities of both giant retailers, such as department stores and supermarket chains, and small "Mom and Pop" retailers with just a few employees.

We saw it happening in companies selling to the consumer and in companies selling to other businesses. We saw it happening in some of the largest multi-brand conglomerates and in the operations of successful niche marketing start-ups with less than a hundred employees.

And we saw it happening in North and South America, in Europe, in Australia, and in Japan.

What we saw was a profound shift — a great turnaround in marketing thinking — that we believe can impact both the short-term and long-term sales success of any company that sells consumer products and services, anywhere in the developed world. And it is a shift from which business-to-business marketers can learn important lessons too.

Those advertisers and their agencies who are quickest and boldest in taking advantage of what has begun to happen will emerge as the leaders of the 90's. Many already have a head start, putting to work the new turnaround marketing tools you will discover in this book — steps you can take to out-think, out-maneuver, and out-perform your competitors.

THE DECADE-BY-DECADE PROGRESSION

The opportunities made possible by The Great Turnaround we will describe do not require abandoning what already works for you. What we have found is that each decade seems to bring an overriding new insight into the secret of gaining an advantage in the marketplace while building on what went before.

The 60's was the decade of getting the product right and keeping the cost down. Those who mastered the mysteries of mass marketing, mass media, and products appealing to a homogeneous market were the heroes of the day.

The 70's was the decade of the marketing concept developed by Peter Drucker, Theodore Levitt, and Philip Kotler — and those companies who were first to pay attention to the wants and needs of a more segmented market became the big winners.

The 80's was the decade of management guru Tom Peters. With Robert Waterman, Jr., Peters preached the importance of quality and service. Companies that took their advice to heart and got close to the customer saw their sales and profits soar.

The 80's also was the decade of niche marketing, addressing ever more specific segments of the market.

What we learned in the 60's, 70's, and 80's about developing the right product, offering it at the right price, positioning it favorably in the mind of the targeted audience, and pursuing quality and customer satisfaction in every aspect of your business is as valid today as it was then. The difference today is that these great advances in understanding the marketplace are now as much the property of your competitor's mindset as they are of your own.

So how do you gain an advantage over your fast-moving competitors now? How do you determine where marketing is heading in the 90's before everyone else realizes what is happening?

THE NEXT PROGRESSION: INDIVIDUALIZED MARKETING

The answer is not as difficult or chancy as you might think. It is there for you to see in the irresistible trend which began in the 70's, picked up momentum in the 80's, and will come to maturity in the 90's.

It is the steady progression from mass marketing to segmented marketing to niche marketing to the next step, Individualized Marketing.

By this term, we don't literally mean one company addressing a special advertising message to just one individual, although in a few instances we are beginning to see this happen. But rather, *a very personal form of marketing that recognizes, acknowledges, appreciates, and serves the interests and needs of selected groups of consumers whose indidividual identities and marketing profiles are or become known to the advertiser.*

It uses the newly affordable power of the computer to target — contact — persuade — sell — and build a profitable relationship with — individual prospects and customers known to the marketer by name, address, and other characteristics stored in a database. It constantly redefines the market in terms of current consumer behavior and selects just those individuals best suited to receive the product or service message leading to the sale.

This trend toward Individualized Marketing is not an isolated commercial phenomenon. It is part of a broad societal shift in our time.

THE "AGE OF THE INDIVIDUAL" COMES TO MARKETING

John Naisbitt and Patricia Aburdene, in *Megatrends 2000*, after 300 fascinating pages, sum up what they found in seven years of research with this statement: "Recognition of the individual is the thread connecting every trend described in this book." They talk of "the Age of the Individual" and tell us that "when the focus was on the institution, individuals got what suited the institution; everyone got the same thing. No more. With the rise of the individual has come the primacy of the consumer." [1]

We chose their term for use in the subtitle of this book because everything in this book seeks to track down and trace out all the present and future manifestations of The Age of the Individual and "the primacy of the consumer" in the world of marketing.

In this new age, the smartest advertisers will establish direct contact with the consumer, whether before or after the first sale, and use that contact to gain customer loyalty and market share by building a mutually rewarding relationship.

It means placing more importance on close involvement with individual prospects and customers than is now devoted to (a) increasingly inefficient image advertising, and (b) promotional discounts aimed solely at improving this quarter's sales performance regardless of the long-term effect. This involvement covers not only direct contact and interactive communication between advertiser and identified consumers by direct mail, phone, audio and video cassette, or computer. It can also mean contact with the public through event marketing, public relations, and personal encounters between company personnel or representatives and consumers in marketplace sites such as stores and service establishments.

It means keeping and sharpening what you are already doing that works, but giving priority to direct involvement with individual prospects and customers.

THE NEW NEED FOR BEGINNING AT THE END

To win in the 90's, we believe, a basic turnaround in thinking is needed. You will no longer start by concentrating on the cleverness of your advertising message in selling your product . You will start with the end — the kind of individual relationship you want with prospects and customers — and then turn back and plan your research, media, awareness advertising, sales promotion, and dealer merchandising strategies accordingly.

It means rediscovering how to talk to individuals in a way

that many in a new generation of marketers have never learned — sensibly, persuasively, informatively, reassuringly.

And as in any good relationship, it means learning to listen as well as talk — turning the usual advertising monologue into a dialogue, finding new ways to hear what your customers are trying to tell you, and responding to them.

It means being open to the opportunities made possible by using the new electronic media and by using the established media in new ways — not just for the sake of novelty, but to locate, contact, activate, and cultivate customers in the most accountable, cost-efficient way.

What is most remarkable about this total MaxiMarketing approach as we have seen it in practice over the past four years is the two-fold impact on profit performance. First, there can be a sizeable gain in short-term profits when using targeted advertising and promotion to meet current goals. Second, the immediate sales benefits from the tactical use of one-to-one marketing can grow into a major long-term corporate strategy for anchoring the customer's loyalty and stimulating further sales.

WHY MANY MARKETERS ARE LAGGING BEHIND

The problem is, it's a whole new, unfamiliar way of operating for marketers who grew up and cut their teeth in the latter days of the mass marketing era.

Except for the best Direct-Order Marketing companies, who out of necessity have learned the art of graceful relationships with faraway prospects and customers, most companies have never had to deal with customers one by one. At least not as many of their customers as is now possible.

Many companies may have set up a toll-free call-in number or an information service department, but too often this is not the function of the marketing department, and is not included in the marketing budget. Customer service and satisfaction are seen somehow as an isolated function and are not given the same kind of top-drawer attention and strategic thinking that are lavished on advertising and sales promotion.

Another impediment to realizing the potential of marketing to the individual, rather than the mass or segments or even niches, is that it requires a different way of looking at budgeting and cost control. After a few tentative experiments, management sometimes hastily withdraws because they find making contact with individual consumers "too expensive." They turn back to the familiar world of arm's-length marketing, even though its wastefulness and inefficiency is costing them far more. Or the marketing director will make all the customary budget appropriations for all the customary programs — and then find there's "no money in the budget" for serious Individualized Marketing.

Building an interactive relationship with individual users of your product or service is not to be treated simply as an after-thought or an add-on to the advertising and promotion. In the new marketing, it takes priority over everything else you do.

Even though "the marketing concept" as a driving force in business goes back as far as the late 60's, for many companies it did not take hold until the 80's. Today almost all companies believe they are "marketing-driven," and start the selling process by targeting their prospects and asking themselves, "How can I meet the consumer's wants and needs?"

This may suffice for enabling you to keep up with your competitors, but it no longer gives you a unique advantage in the race to get ahead.

The Great Turnaround we perceive taking place in marketing today begins with "the marketing concept" and being responsive to consumer needs. But then it proposes a different way of proceeding from that point — an approach that is actually a basic reversal of what has been common practice.

THE UNFORTUNATE COMPARTMENTALIZING OF MARKETING COMPONENTS

Over the years, many marketers, especially in Europe, have become accustomed to referring to advertising in measured media as being "above the line" — and promotion, direct marketing, event marketing, and all the rest as "below the line." (Figure 1)

This terminology was expressive of a kind of secret contempt in the mainstream ad agency world for any marketing activity not devoted purely to building awareness and image. It resulted in a running battle between the mainstream advertising agencies on the one hand and direct-marketing and promotion agencies on the other hand for their share of the total marketing budget. At the annual conference of the American Association of Advertising Agencies in 1989, "members shared tactics to keep their client companies away from such demon disciplines as sales promotion and direct marketing." [2]

But by the next conference, just one year later, the mainstream agencies were singing a different tune. They were talking of putting all of these components on the same level as advertising in

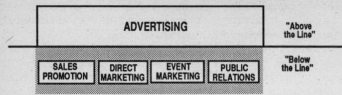

Figure 1

Figure 2

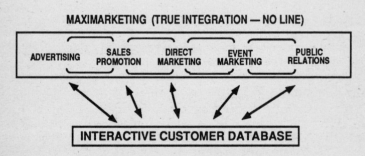

Figure 3

their thinking and organization structure. (Figure 2) Glen W. Fortinberry, in his farewell address as outgoing chairman of the American Association of Advertising Agencies, scolded mainstream agencies for their relative lack of interest in ancillary marketing services and told them that this was a problem for agencies that demanded a solution.

Mr. Fortinberry told his audience that "integrated marketing is where we believe, and where the analysts tell us, the agency business will be in the 90's....Our challenge in the 4A's is to accept this as fact and deal with it."

At the same 4A's conference, reported *The New York Times* advertising columnist Randall Rothenberg, "in speech after speech, the industry's leaders are telling colleagues steeped in the craft of television and print advertising that they ought to learn how to mount public relations campaigns, package promotional sweepstakes, and write direct-mail copy." [3]

Advertising Age added its esteemed voice in an editorial which declared: "...if clients are keen to spend money for sales promotion, direct marketing, public relations, package design, or whatever other marketplace option they choose, ad agencies must no longer resist...*No longer can they argue that collateral promotional work or non-traditional media options are beneath them.*" [Italics ours.][4]

"INTEGRATED COMMUNICATIONS" VS. TRUE INTEGRATION

The important thing, both advertising agencies and their clients must realize in the 90's, is that the so-called ancillary services (chiefly direct marketing and sales promotion) are not something merely to be added onto the agency's menu of services in order to keep the client's marketing dollars from straying elsewhere. They are, rather, elements that must be fused with the brand advertising into a unified discipline that maximizes the ability to produce sales and build relationships with individual consumers. (Figure 3) It is this new discipline—whether called by the name we have given it, MaxiMarketing, or any other name — that will lead to rethinking the very structure and function of the advertising agency as it is presently understood.

We certainly favor "integrated marketing." What we question is use of the term merely as a catch phrase to describe what Mr. Fortinberry called, in his 4A's speech, "a full buffet of services." It perpetuates the outmoded approach of dividing a client's marketing into compartments labelled "advertising," "promotion," "direct mail," "event marketing," and "public relations," rather than thinking wholistically about doing whatever is necessary to identify, contact, activate, and cultivate individual consumers and increase market share.

Another potential problem that we see lies in keeping the "buffet of services" under the mainstream agency's existing account management. Such managers tend to be steeped in the art and science of product image-making to the exclusion of almost everything else in the marketing mix. And they may have only a glancing acquaintance with the skills of direct marketing, sales promotion, and the other Individualized Marketing disciplines which are critically important today.

"The advertising industry's reluctant interest in promotional services is almost comical," say sales promotion executive search experts Steven Gundersen and Larry Levine. "Many ad execs try to learn about sweepstakes, contests, and coupons the way some children try to like spinach, peas, and broccoli. They may have intellectualized promotion's importance in the marketing diet, but they are clearly having a hard time swallowing it." [5]

Even the comprehensive framework we constructed in *Maxi-Marketing* does not go far enough today to incorporate all of the elements we see involved in the important marketing gains taking place. We now see major Individualized Marketing roles to be played by public relations, event marketing, frequency marketing, customer assistance and satisfaction programs, field marketing that builds dealer support, and inventive new point-of-sale materials. We see these activities not, as has so often been true in the past, as separate, largely unrelated activities, but as working together in a unified program to promote sales and build relationships with the most desirable and profitable customers.

Philip Kotler has described marketing as the science of customer-need satisfaction. The best marketing of the 90's will carry that science to new levels of effectiveness with a truly integrated approach to the process of bringing the producer and the user into direct contact as never before.

Both the agency and client marketing organization are evolving new structures in response to this need. When properly conceived and executed, this new approach to advertising and marketing, as you will see from the examples in this book, can have astonishing sales results.

On several occasions within the past year, one or the other of us would pick up the phone and find ourselves talking to a tough-minded marketing veteran bubbling over with uncharacteristic wonderment at results from a new Individualized Marketing program which has merged brand advertising, sales promotion, and direct marketing.

"You are not going to believe these numbers" is often the first remark — followed by excitement, tinged with amazement, at what has happened to sales when carefully selected prospects or customers were involved with the product or service in a direct way and given appropriate and attractive reasons to buy or learn more.

Some day you yourself may have just such a story to tell. The Age of the Individual is just beginning, and you will be there, helping to define the new landscape and to reap the rewards that come to those marketers who are willing to think through the new marketing in all its varied aspects.

We noted in *MaxiMarketing* that many companies in the early 80's were stumbling forward into this world of the future, by adjusting their thinking and practices in certain important ways. But we were hardly able to find at the time a single company that was doing everything well. Now, as we look around at the marketing landscape in the 90's, we see many more companies doing some of the things we spoke about, and a few who are doing it all and getting remarkable results.

In this book, we will share with you what has been happening and what we see as the next stage in this evolutionary process. We will identify the most important characteristics of the great changes taking place and illustrate them with examples that demonstrate their effectiveness. And we will suggest how you can make use of the principles underlying these changes.

THE GREAT TURNAROUND

From our own many years of experience running an international advertising agency specializing in direct advertising communication with consumers — from our present consulting work in the United States, Canada, Europe, and South America — and from our observations of and conversations with some of the most daring and visionary innovators in marketing today, we have singled out ten important current shifts away from the conventional marketing wisdom of the past.

These trends represent what we believe are the marketing megatrends of our time. Just as Naisbitt and Aburdene found a central theme in their ten societal megatrends, we see a central theme in our own ten turnaround trends: the turn away from mass marketing thinking to individualized involvement with the consumer.

Together these trends coalesce into what we see as The Great Turnaround, as great and significant a change in the marketing of goods and services as Albert Lasker's recognition of advertising as "salesmanship in print" in 1905...the emergence of commercial radio, the first universal advertising medium, in the late 1920's ...the unleashing of the power of commercial television, and Bill Bernbach's creative revolution, in the early 1950's...and the acceptance of the marketing concept as a driving force in business in the 1970's.

If you don't take seriously enough the power of the computer to create a direct exchange of information with consumers of your product or service, you may fail to realize all the profit opportunities hidden in these ten trends.

But if you are alert in your own strategic thinking to each of these great reversals, you will be in a position to greatly strengthen both your defensive and offensive marketing capabilities.

Here then are the 10 historic turnarounds in marketing that we believe are destined to play a crucial role as the shift to the Age of the Individual steadily increases. (Figure 4)

And standing behind all of these changes in direction is the consumer who is saying, "Pay attention to me! Recognize and appreciate my individuality and needs and desire for self-expression. I'll respond by buying your product and by telling you more about myself so that you can serve me better."

As you will note, there is a certain amount of unavoidable overlap among the 10 trends. Nonetheless, the arbitrary separation of the flow of developments into 10 separate and distinct tendencies makes it easier to think about them and make use of them in your own marketing planning.

And even though most of the examples will not be from your specific field, if you will look behind them to the point we are illustrating, you can adapt the experience to your own situation. Most of the examples we will present are necessarily from the U.S. marketplace which we have been closely monitoring for the past eight years. But based on our years of experience in working with clients throughout Western Europe and other parts of the world, we have also included significant marketing developments from these other areas where relevant.

So join us now as we examine the ten great turnaround trends you can use to score signifcant marketing gains in the 90's.

THE GREAT
MARKETING TURNAROUND

Means turning away from: **And turning toward:**

1 Unknown prospects ➤ Known prospects
  and customers   and customers

2 Creativity- ➤ Response-
  driven   driven

3 "Steam-rollering" ➤ Filling
  the market   each niche

4 Ad impressions ➤ New customers
  counted   won

5 Advertising ➤ Consumer
  monologue   dialogue

6 Bombarding ➤ Building
  the market   relationships

7 Passive ➤ Involved
  consumers   paticipants

8 Mass ➤ Direct mass
  marketing   marketing

9 U.S.P. (Unique ➤ E.V.P. (Extra-Value
  Selling Proposition)   Proposition)

10 Single-channel ➤ Multi-channel
   distribution   distribution

Figure 4

OUR OWN GLOSSARY OF TERMS USED IN THIS BOOK

In working on this book, we were struck once again by the widespread carelessness in which various marketing terms are bandied about, creating a good deal of confusion in marketing news reports and discussions.

For instance, a trade press story may refer to "advertising," "sales promotion," and "direct marketing" as three separate entities.

But when an advertiser runs a sales promotion offer in paid advertising space, isn't that *advertising*? When The Book-of-the-Month Club invites membership in a paid advertisement in *The New York Times Book Review*, that is what is commonly known as *direct marketing*, but it is surely *advertising* as well. And when a sales promotion offer generates a name and address that is added to a database for future direct-relationship marketing, it is certainly also direct marketing.

Therefore, for the purposes of this book, we have carefully developed and refined our own definitions of a number of terms so you will know exactly what we are talking about in the context of this book. (Of course, we would be pleased if our definitions were generally adopted in marketing. Then maybe we'd all know what *everybody* is talking about.)

Advertising or **General Advertising** is used to mean all advertising which is not specifically devoted to Direct-Order Marketing, Direct-Relationship Marketing, or Sales Promotion.

Awareness or **Brand-Awareness Advertising** is a little more specific, in our lexicon, devoted to building up public consciousness of particular advantages or benefits of using the brand advertised.

Brand Advertising is obviously devoted to building up in public consciousness a favorable attitude toward an advertised brand. There are two other terms often used in this connection which deserve comment:

Creativity-Driven Advertising means, to us, giving a higher priority to the shock or entertainment value of the advertising than to the sales strategy and actual results.

Database-Driven Advertising is direct-response advertising which seeks not only an inquiry or an order but also information about the respondent which can be stored in the advertiser's database and used to continue the relationship and stimulate sales.

Direct Mail is simply an advertising medium, not a method of advertising or distribution. This may seem absurdly obvious, but you would be surprised how many people still say "direct mail" when they really mean either Direct-Relationship Marketing or Direct-Order Marketing.

Direct Marketing. One of the most useful definitions of this much-confused and much-abused term is by Peter Winter, Vice President for Marketing Technology of the Newspaper Advertising Bureau. He has broadly defined Direct Marketing as "the distribution of goods, services, and information to targeted consumers through response advertising, while keeping track of sales, interest, and needs in a computer database." To this we would make just one small change. Instead of "goods, services, *and* information," we would prefer "goods, services, *or* information."

But there are actually two different kinds of Direct Marketing today. So in this book, we have chosen to largely but not entirely replace the term "Direct Marketing" with the following two more precise and descriptive designations. (Where we still use the term Direct Marketing, it is in a context in which the customary use makes it easier to understand what we are talking about, even though it is a rather loose description of what is really meant.)

Direct-Order Marketing (instead of "mail-order") is our term for all forms of business based on selling goods or services directly to the public, without an intermediary, obtaining orders by means of direct-response advertising in magazines and newspapers, on television or radio, by direct mail, or in any other medium, and delivering to the customer's address.

Direct-Relationship Marketing seems to us the proper term for all forms of promoting direct contact and involvement with individual consumers by marketers whose principal interest is in selling their products through retailers or other intermediaries rather than directly to the public. The use of the term "Direct Marketing" in this context is still sometimes unavoidable, such as when citing company job titles.

Direct-Response Advertising is advertising in any medium, whether direct mail, magazines, newspapers, radio, or television, which has as its *main purpose* inviting and obtaining a response from the audience. (However, a direct-response *element* may be added to *any* advertising.)

Image or **Brand-Image Advertising** is designed to create, through constant repetition over a long period of time, a favorable image of the likeability, reliability, or fashionability of the product or maker.

Individualized Marketing is the term we have chosen for any integrated program of sales communications directly from the advertiser to selected members of the public, whether by means of letters, brochures, audiocassettes, videocassettes, telephone messages, computer disks, advertiser-sponsored events, or any other means of direct contact. The individual or household may have been sifted out from the general public because of having responded to a direct-response advertising appeal, because of a known history of purchase of the advertiser's product or service, because of possessing certain favorable database indicators, or through choosing to be involved in an advertiser-sponsored event.

Promotional Advertising is paid advertising in any medium, whether magazines, newspapers, radio, television, outdoor display, or other media, that contains a sales promotion offer such as sweepstakes prizes, a discount, a premium, a free sample, or any other sales incentive designed to stimulate action leading to an immediate sale.

Response-Driven Advertising is used by us to mean direct-response advertising which has employed direct-response accountability in order to develop the best approach for maximizing responses.

Sales Promotion means all activity devoted to stimulating a sale, including sales promotion advertising in paid media, on-pack and in-pack offers, point-of-purchase materials, and even promotional discounts to dealers.

Such important issues are involved in all of these terms that we will be touching on them further in several other places in the book, especially in the discussion in Chapter Four of the turnaround trend away from Creativity-Driven advertising and toward Response-Driven advertising.

Turnaround Trend No. 1:

3 From Unknown to Identified Prospects and Customers

First came database-building by airlines and financial services ...Now company after company is joining the parade: Ford....Buick... Austin-Rover... Seagram's ... RJR...Philip Morris...Merit comes to Japan ...General Foods...Quaker Oats... Bristol-Myers... Procter & Gamble... Ukrops... Waldenbooks...Radio Shack...many small business owners

---

A phrase has entered the language, due to nightly repetition by a parade of celebrities on the local Fox television station break. As the clock approaches 10:00 every evening, you know the time has come for the celebrity of the evening to intone, "It's 10:00 P.M. Do you know where your children are?"

In the world of marketing, the time has come to say, "It is later than you think. Do you know who your prospects and customers are?" And by that we mean their names, addresses, telephone numbers, special interests, lifestyles, buying preferences, and recent purchasing history.

The ability to reach and communicate with individual consumers based on relevant information in a database — this is the big Turnaround of our time that makes most of the other Turnarounds possible or desirable.

Back in the pre-turnaround days, certain kinds of companies would save prospect and customer names on 3x5 file cards stored in shoeboxes, or typed on Rolodex cards or Addressograph plates. Other companies, such as brand advertisers receiving huge sacks of mail from rebate offers, premium offers, and sweepstakes, would simply *throw the names away* after the request had been fulfilled.

HOW THE COMPUTER IS CHANGING MARKETING

But today the computer has awesome capabilities to store millions of prospect/customer records — not only names and addresses, but age, sex, marital status and family configuration, buying habits and history, demographic and psychographic profiles. And individuals can be selected from this database by one, two, three or more of their identifying characteristics. Marketers are no longer limited to sending the same message to nonprospects, lukewarm prospects, and hot prospects alike. "Different strokes for different folks" is now well within reach.

Essentially the computer has brought to marketing three awesome powers: the power to *record*, the power to *find*, and the power to *compare*.

The computer's power to record was by itself nothing magical. It was simply good old-fashioned typing in or "keyboarding" of received data about a prospect or customer.

The difference was that, in the pre-computer days, there would have been no point in recording by typewriter or pencil literally dozens of bits of information about each customer or prospect on thousands of index cards. Without the computer, there would have been no practical way to make use of such information.

As computer data storage rapidly became faster and more economical, however, it became possible and desirable to build up and use a prospect or customer record with a staggering amount of detail.

For instance, the customer database of a company devoted to presenting business seminars has 89 "field definitions" (variable units of information about each enrollee) in its "record layout." These include: *Address Type* (home, office, or billing address?), *Agreement Date* (when was the contract signed?), *Currency Code* (type of currency with which payment was made), *Identification Number* (to indicate which one of certain code-numbered occupations), *Organization Name* (who is enrollee's employer?), *Source Code* (which mailing and which mailing list generated the enrollment?) and so on.

Now this power of the computer to record is being heightened by optical scanning of numerical or bar codes. Without the slow, costly involvement of keypunch operators, a customer's purchases or discount coupon redemptions can be automatically entered by scanning and the information appended to the customer's file.

The computer's power to find means that selections can be made from the prospect or customer file by any field definitions or combination of field definitions. For instance, in the example of the business seminars company above, if they were planning a seminar in a city in Florida on a subject that would be of special interest to certain older customers, they could command the computer, "Find me the names and addresses of *older customers* (selection 1) *living in Florida* (selection 2) who have previously indicated or demonstrated an interest in the *subject matter* (selection 3) of the seminar we are planning."

The computer's power to compare means that information about an individual recorded in two or more databases can be combined. For instance, the computer can compare a list of *older people* and a list of *golfers.* Wherever the comparison reveals the same name on both lists, it is possible to identify and record that person as an *older golfer.*

Paula Wesley, president of Wesley List Marketing, has neatly fit the possible kinds of information about an individual in a marketing database into four categories: Declared Information, Implied Information, Overlaid Information, and Appended Information.

1. Declared information. This is what the individual has directly revealed by filling out some sort of form, such as a questionnaire, a driver's license application, or a controlled-circulation magazine qualification form, or by answering questions during a phone call. (The record of a purchase or coupon would also be considered declared information since the customer is telling you something directly by taking that step.)

2. Implied information is developed by finding a high correlation between the database information and other obtainable data — for instance, if your customer is upper income and has a large family, this strongly implies that the customer must have a comparatively large house as well.

3. Overlaid information comes from comparing your individual records with adjusted census data.

In 1974, computer scientist Jonathan Robbin developed this capability to a high degree by combining census data with zip codes and consumer surveys. He programmed the computer to sort the nation's 36,000 zip zones into 40 "lifestyle clusters." For instance, residents of Zip Zone 85234, in northeast Phoenix, belong to what he calls the Furs & Station Wagons cluster. They "tend to buy lots of vermouth, belong to a country club, read Gourmet, and vote the GOP ticket." [1] He called his system PRIZM (Potential Rating Index for Zip Markets) and founded a company called Claritas to market it.

Whether you call upon this sophisticated system or a simpler public database grouping of households by estimated income or size of family or type of registered car ownership, you can "overlay" this information onto your own proprietary database and thereby transfer valuable outside information to each individual's file.

4. Appended information means matching up two or more sources of information about a customer or household file. For instance, you may have a file of customers who have redeemed a Crystal Lite coupon. Now you receive a new list of customers who have redeemed a Kool-Aid coupon. By matching the two lists, the computer can find out which Crystal Lite coupon redeemers are also Kool-Aid coupon redeemers and append that information to their files.

Direct-Order Marketing companies have been increasingly using this capability for over 20 years. And no wonder. It is their bread and butter.

But until recently, most brand advertisers, services, and retailers have been approaching it timidly. Some are still ignoring it completely.

For instance, how many restaurants do you know who keep a record of who their customers are, how often they visit, and how much they spend? There may be some, but if there are, they are few and far between. (There is a fast-food chain in Canada which is doing a superb job of this, as you will see in a later chapter.)

And when the banks began compiling databases with names of credit card holders in the late 70's and the 80's, years passed before they started linking that information with data about other accounts held at the bank and overlaying outside available data to form a true relational database.

There have been various reasons for the slow, hesitant spread of the database revolution beyond the boundaries of Direct-Order Marketing companies. The cost. The fear of being the first to gamble on an expensive, unproven marketing tool. The doubt and confusion about what to do with a database once you have built it. The human tendency to stay with the familiar while others take a chance with innovations that may flop.

Now all that is changing — with increasing rapidity. Drastically lowered cost has been a powerful stimulant. Computer cost for storage of and access to a single name has dropped from $7.14 in 1973 to well under 1¢ today.

A survey by Donnelley Marketing a few years ago reported

that nearly 50% of the nation's packaged-goods advertisers are building databases.[2]

"The days of mass markets in America are history," says John Wyek, director of strategic services at Levi, Strauss & Co. "In today's and, more important, tomorrow's market, you're going to need to market to the individual. Our objective is to be as absolutely personal as we can."

Wyek foresees the day when the company will be able to write a valued jeans customer a note telling him "we understand what you need" and informing him where he can buy it in light green, "since we know your favorite color is light green," and what the price will be. [3]

THE TRAIL BLAZED BY AMERICAN AIRLINES

One of the trail-blazing pioneers in identifying and contacting individual customers was American Airlines. Back in the 70's, airlines began to realize that 80% of their business came from 20% of their customers, the frequent-flying business traveller. But the airlines didn't know who these people were and what to do about it. They had a name on an airline ticket but no address. They kept no permanent record of the customer's destination or how frequently he or she traveled. Furthermore, government regulations forbade giving away to passengers anything of value which would upset the mandated standard pricing.

But as airlines deregulation approached, American realized the opportunity they had to identify their best customers and cultivate them with special rewards. The airline began in secret to plan the AAdvantage program, the first frequent-flyer plan with bonuses recorded and administered by means of a membership database. Introduced in 1981, it was an instant success, and it took the other airlines years to catch up. [4]

American Airlines management has repeatedly described their Frequent Flyer program as their single greatest marketing achievement of the 80's.

Once upon a time, in the 70's, the airline advertising budgets were devoted almost entirely to high-flown image-making in television, magazine, and newspaper advertising. Now the ability of each airline to talk directly to their best customers has resulted in a complete turnaround in marketing thinking from what the airline industry did in the 70's. The image advertising remains, but a significant amount of each year's budget has been shifted to communicating directly with and cultivating their best customers.

Of course, no marketing advantage lasts forever. Soon all the airlines with frequent-flyer programs were embroiled in a free mileage and price-cutting war, with each airline offering more free bonus miles than the next.

Welcome to the next phase, the Battle of the Databases, a fact of life that marketers must learn to live with and profit from in the Age of the Individual.

As one way of sidestepping the bonus mileage war among the airlines, Eastern Airlines uses the computer for *private*, selective price-cutting in which everybody wins. For a fee, travelers can join the Eastern Airlines Weekenders Club. When they sign up, they get to list the destinations that interest them. Then when a flight to one of those destinations is underbooked, Eastern sends interested members a travelgram offering them seats for a special low price.

"I don't have to advertise a low price," says Don Peppers of Lintas: USA, the agency that created the campaign. "I don't have my competitors on my tail matching the price. I've gotten more business from people who have expressed a desire to travel to specific locations."[5]

One of Pan Am's solutions has been to offer its World Pass members a special menu from which they can choose any one of nine gourmet meals before their flight.

In the mid 80's, hotel chains such as Marriott, Holiday Inn, Radisson, and Hyatt jumped on the bandwagon with their own frequent-traveler programs. Radisson research showed that 70% of all the travelers surveyed said that frequent guest programs influenced their selection of hotels. The Radisson KEY Rewards Program was said to generate $75 million in revenue in just its first 18 months.

Banks and financial services, such as Citibank, Bank of America, Fidelity Investments, and Dreyfus Corporation, began to see the advantage and the necessity of cross-selling their variety of services, and of bringing out new products aimed at customers with identifiable characteristics in their databases.

CAR MAKERS START DRIVING DIRECT TO PROSPECTS

Most automobile companies have discovered the importance of building a well-informed database of previous buyers and logical prospects. Almost every auto manufacturer in Europe and the U.S. now has customer satisfaction and customer retention programs targeted to identified owners.

Ford Motor Company has been devoting part of its $500 million advertising budget to testing various offers that feed prospect names and information to its database, and then developing programs that cultivate prospects and previous buyers within the database.

When Ford was unable to sell an expensive import from Germany under the Merkur name with brand-image advertising, they turned to direct response advertising to identify the real prospects. Ford's four-page insert with a big bold reply form and call-in number, along with 60-second direct-response television commercials, generated 30,000 hot leads and 3,000 sales, cleaning dealers' lots of cars that awareness advertising could not move.

In Europe, Systems Marketing Company, with substantial backing from Austin-Rover, forged "Superlink," Europe's largest database of identified car customers and prospects. They reported at that time that its 1.2 million car-buyer profiles were being utilized "more comprehensively than any other database in the world." In less than seven years, the program cut the cost of an incremental sale in half.[6] This was followed by a second-generation database system, Catalyst, an even more remarkable success story we will unfold later on to illustrate one of the other Turnaround Trends.

DATABASE USE BY SEAGRAM'S

Traditionally, distilled spirits would rank at the top of the list, alongside fragrances, of kinds of products supported almost entirely by image-building right-brain advertising.   So it has been surprising to see how quickly the trend to dealing individually with identified prospects and customers is taking hold in that category.

Liquor companies, struggling with a decline in consumption of hard liquor, are turning to database use to steal customers from their competitors and to deepen the loyalty of their existing customers.

Seagram's began building its user database in 1986. By 1989 they had over 6 million records and the database was growing at the rate of 20% a year. And they are using it to promote such brands as Crown Royal, Chivas Regal, and Glenlivet with direct mail pieces so beautiful, skillful, and amusing, they almost take your breath away.

One of their promotions tested an offer of free old-fashioned glasses, a calculator, or a $5 rebate as a reward for trying Glenlivet scotch. But instead of showering the entire public with the offer, as would have been done in the past, the promotion was mailed only to 500,000 people known to drink competing brands of scotch. The result was over 10,000 new Glenlivet customers. [7]

By 1990, Glenlivet was sending mailings directly from Scotland. And Chivas Regal was expanding their frequent-buyer rewards program which provides upgrades on such purchases as luxury cruises and resort visits.

In a lengthy conversation with Richard Shaw, The House of Seagram vice president for Direct Marketing, he told us: "Part of my personal crusade here at Seagram is to involve everyone in marketing in the pursuit of identifying prospects and customers. The advertising, the package, the event marketing, the in-store promotions — whatever we do must become a means of building the database."

Shaw expects the direct marketing budget at Seagram's to continue escalating every year well into the 90's. The reason why will be ever more apparent as you move through this book from Turnaround Trend to Turnaround Trend.

FROM UNKNOWN TO IDENTIFIED SMOKERS

In the tobacco industry, the first to go down the path of one-to-one prospecting was second-ranking RJR.

Early in the 80's, R.J. Reynolds reportedly spent $100 million to put together its database of about half of the 55 million people in the U.S. who smoke. In 1982 RJR became the largest client of a new company with its own set of initials — JFY Inc. Under the guidance of its visionary president, the late Harry Dale, and with the wholehearted support of his free-spending tobacco client, JFY set about building the first large-scale public database of consumer behavior.

Before long, JFY was mailing 80 million surveys a year asking America's families to tell what brands of cigarettes, pet foods, detergent, and other products they were using, as well as how often the brand was purchased. Families were asked when they expected to take their next vacation, when they planned to buy their next car, and whether it would be an imported or domestic model. There were over 200 questions, but RJR had an exclusive in the tobacco category. And the consumer proved surprisingly willing to complete and mail back questionnaires, *with name and address included*, in return for the promise of discount coupons and product samples.

Carefully managed testing programs taught RJR how to use the information they acquired through JFY and other sources to target the best prospects for new products, to practice conquest marketing aimed directly at users of competitive brands, to continually update research data, and to build loyalty among heavy users.

In 1986 RJR shifted their information-gathering to another public database company, Behavior Bank. By then they had learned through trial and error just what offer to make to win new converts to Salem and their other brands. A light smoker might get a lightweight one-pack trial offer. A heavy smoker could expect to be tempted with two free cartons or more.

THE MERIT CIGARETTES MYSTERY BRAND CHALLENGE

At first Philip Morris shrugged off what its chief competitor was doing. But then in 1987 Philip Morris began to play catch-up ball. Under the guidance of James Spector, promotion director, they launched a campaign that broke new ground.

Philip Morris ran a double-page spread with a bound-in insert card in *Time, Newsweek,* and other major publications. But there was something very novel and strange about the ads. Surely for the first time in history, here was cigarette advertising which didn't mention the name of the cigarette!

Without identifying the advertiser or the brand, the ad asked smokers to send for two free packs of a mystery cigarette. The headline put the challenge this way: "WE BET YOU TWO FREE PACKS YOU'LL PREFER THIS LEADING LIGHT CIGARETTE TO ANY OTHER BRAND. PROVE IT TO YOURSELF!"

To get your two free packs, you had to fill out a lengthy questionnaire on the bound-in reply card. There were questions like: "What brand are you now smoking? How many packs a week? Filter or non-filter? Hardpack or soft?" And much more.

Smokers who took the challenge received two packs of unmarked Merits. A follow-up mailing identified the mystery brand as Merit and asked trial users to complete a second detailed questionnaire about their reaction to the taste test. All the additional information given by the respondent was then added to the database for future use.

The trade press reported that close to *two million* smokers accepted the challenge. More than one million of them were users of brands made by competitors of Philip Morris. By the time the beautifully executed series of follow-up mailings prepared by the Leo Burnett agency had been completed, some 500,000 of the responding users of competitive brands had told the advertiser they preferred Merit to the brand they had been smoking. In additional follow-ups, Philip Morris was able to vary the promotional incentives according to the profile of each smoker revealed by their questionnaire answers and recorded in the database.

Philip Morris spent almost as much on the follow-up as the $15 million spent on "going fishing" in mass media to get the names of interested smokers. The first $15 million was advertising whose only purpose was to create the database. There was no awareness advertising purpose because the product never got mentioned in the mystery ad. The second $15 million directed toward the identified prospects created an extremely high level of awareness among the 2 million smokers who responded and the 500,000 smokers of competing brands who finally reported that they liked Merit better.

Philip Morris wouldn't say how many of those 500,000 hot prospects they have converted to regular use of Merit. But well-informed sources outside the company believed that within 15 months the entire cost of the campaign was returned in additional revenues from newly converted Merit users. And the success of the campaign was confirmed the following year when the same technique was used to introduce a new Philip Morris menthol brand.

Using mass marketing to identify and contact the ideal prospect and then focusing promotional dollars on just those people, was a complete reversal of accepted packaged goods advertising practice. With this campaign, the Philip Morris promotion director Jim Spector, one of the pioneers of Individualized Marketing, demonstrated the awesome power of database-driven advertising and promotion. Turnaround thinking paid off big for Philip Morris in '87 and '88 and has been part of their strategic planning ever since.

In *MaxiMarketing*, we urged the use of double-duty and multiple-duty advertising. We argued that "single-duty advertising may be the most costly mistake in advertising today, given the current high cost of media space and time. It is often astonishingly easy to create multi-functional advertising that works two or more ways to reduce costs and increase sales and profits."

The Merit Challenge campaign followed this precept by doing several jobs all at the same time. It got smokers to engage in a taste test in a way that was likely to make a deeper and more favorable impression than merely handing out samples. It provided information for the company database not only about one million competing brand smokers but about one million Philip Morris smokers as well. This information added to their knowledge of the cigarette market and enabled them to customize promotional follow-up. It undoubtedly uncovered hints and ideas for future product development. It even yielded as a by-product an almost unprecedented user-testimonial campaign, in which respondents were featured in ads talking about how and why they had switched to Merit after taking the taste test.

And there was another benefit. Philip Morris and its agency's direct-marketing team were able to take what they had learned to Japan and use the same individualized approach to introduce the Merit brand in the fiercely competitive market there. The only basic change was to offer just one pack free instead of two in order to conform to government regulations. More than 900,000 smokers in Japan completed and returned the insert card questionnaire. The campaign won a .7% share of the market for Merit almost overnight. This was a remarkably successful penetration of the market by a new U.S. brand. It is further evidence of our belief that unlike image and awareness campaigns, a Direct-Relationship Marketing approach usually can be transferred to another country.

NOW QUAKER OATS HAS DIVED IN HEAD-FIRST

More recently, Quaker Oats has rocked the food-marketing industry with its announcement of its ambitious plan for Quaker Direct, a program of their own proprietary coupons/promotion mailings.

We mentioned in our Introduction the big Quaker Oats cutback of $35 million in marketing expenditure in the summer of '89 and how it reflected of their concern about "dollars that were relatively ineffective." Quaker Direct is obviously the company's carefully planned response to this concern. *Adweek* saw it as "a bold attempt to back away from mass couponing in freestanding inserts. And if it succeeds, it will likely become the model for other companies seeking to establish one-on-one 'branded' media."[8] The program required three years of planning and an initial investment of $18 million. So it was clear that the company was treating it as a major departure. Industry sources said that Quaker was shifting half of its usual fsi (freestanding insert) budget into this new medium.

Essentially, Quaker Direct is a proprietary co-op with a mix of inside and outside advertising. A limited test was conducted, and then a roll-out was scheduled to be mailed periodically to about 20 million "promotionally responsive" households.

Discount coupons for Quaker products are matched to information about each household's known product-usage habits provided by Computerized Marketing Technology's Select and Save. The system is using the latest imaging technology to produce coupons tailored to specific household demographics and shopping patterns. The cents-off values can be changed from mailing to mailing to match the profile of a specific household or to acquire new customers for a certain brand.[9] Thus only households known to have dogs will receive coupons for Gaines Burgers, and people known to buy Kellogg's Frosted Flakes might get a high-value coupon for Quaker's Cap'n Crunch.

The code number on each coupon will reveal which households redeemed which coupons. Then additional couponing to the same households in subsequent mailings will make it possible to detect gains in brand preference due to the promotion and to measure the cost-effectiveness of the promotional expenditure in terms of resulting sales — at least more precisely than the old indiscriminate fsi couponing can do. Ongoing surveys will maintain a dialogue with the consumers and "help build relationships that Quaker hopes will translate into brand loyalty."

To offset the substantial cost of the program, outside advertisers are being invited to join in as co-sponsors. The plan calls for each mailing to contain ten coupon ads from Quaker Oats and six from non-competing health and beauty aids and household cleaning products. But with admirable daring, Quaker's quest for co-sponsors is roaming even further afield than that, with planned participation by such advertisers as CBS, General Motors, and Paramount.

Preliminary research on consumer interests had shown that entertainment was high on the list. So Quaker went to CBS and said in effect, "Look, users of certain products of ours are ideal prospective viewers for certain television programs of yours. So why not come in with us and do pinpoint target marketing of those programs?" For instance, kids' cartoons could be promoted along with Cap'n Crunch, and sports programs could be advertised to Gatorade households. CBS was impressed and agreed to try it.

This additional sponsorship may make it possible for Quaker to do direct-communication promotion of low-margin products that otherwise might not be affordable.

Quaker's promotion director, Dan Strunk, calls this new kind of marketing by a new name — "household marketing."

According to Strunk, "Household marketing will be one of the most important elements of the promotional mix of the future. With it, you're dealing from a position of knowledge, and you have the power to be more distinctive to a select group of consumers." [10] In another statement he went even further and declared flatly, *"Household marketing is going to be the only way a consumer packaged-goods company will be able to compete in the future."*

Participation costs four times as much as a Sunday newspaper fsi coupon and twice as much as Donnelley's Carol Wright co-op, which lacks tracking capability. But Quaker is counting on much higher redemption rates, especially among previous non-users of the promoted brand, to make the medium more cost-efficient than the cheaper alternatives. Says Strunk, "The medium will enable product managers to focus the consumer's attention, thus achieving what most consumer product marketers recognize as the key to a brand's future survival — a real one-to-one bonding with the brand's customers."[11]

It is important to note that this precedent-shattering program is *not* just "sales promotion," at least not in the usual sense of programs designed to produce a short-term seasonal boost in sales. Quaker views it as relationship-building and is in it for the long haul. Says Strunk, "Every time a coupon is redeemed, consumers participate in a two-way communication. That opens to us a number of communication alternatives. We are beginning a long-term dialogue with our consumers. We expect to improve our ability to use this program with each subsequent mailing."

IMPORTANT STEPS BY BRISTOL-MYERS

In over-the-counter pharmaceuticals, hair coloring, and toiletries, Bristol-Myers has emerged as a leader in identifying prospects, focusing on them, and adding their names, addresses, and histories to a rapidly growing relational database.

According to the cover story in the August, 1989, issue of *Direct Marketing*, more and more of the company's product managers are focusing on building a central marketing database, which at that time was said to be approaching two million names.

The article told of one ingenious promotion which added the names of some 200,000 teen-agers while performing other important functions at the same time. It was the Clairol division's Seabreeze Sweepstakes, and the grand prize was every teen-ager's dream — a separate phone, a separate line, and paid-up phone bills for a whole year!

To enter, teen-agers were told to look inside any carton of Seabreeze for the 800 number to call and the lucky number to touchtone. In addition to promoting the brand and identifying buyers, the promotion was also designed to secure preferred in-store shelf placement for 1.5 million packages of Seabreeze in 98 percent of all drugstores and 80 percent of all supermarkets.

Deep in the story was an extremely important glimpse of the company's database-building strategy, or at least the impression of it gleaned by the reporter in an interview with the Seabreeze product manager: "The long-term goal for Bristol-Myers is to build a family of loyal buyers for the company's family of products. *By tracking age, buyers can be followed during a lifetime and offered other products befitting their age group. Such a file could be used to weigh media performance, to rate store outlets, set sales goals, reward frequent buyers with cents-off coupons or participation in special events, and test the viability of new product ideas.*" [Italics ours] [12]

CONCERNED ABOUT "TV BLUR," BRISTOL-MYERS TRIES NUPRIN CHALLENGE

And here is another example of how Bristol-Myers is forging boldly ahead into the brave new world of Individualized Marketing. At a conference on direct marketing by packaged goods advertisers, Robert Merold, the company's director of established analgesics, told the story of how Bristol-Myers used turnaround thinking to launch Nuprin.

In the past, noted Merold, packaged goods manufacturers have considered that using direct marketing techniques provided too small a universe and was too costly. "We'd rather steamroll the consumer with heavy TV budgets."

But the problem with relying solely on mass TV advertising, says Merold, particularly for a mature category like analgesics, is that all the commercials sound alike. "It's one gigantic blur for the consumer — no wonder viewers are bored."

So Bristol-Myers decided to include in the Nuprin marketing mix a challenge to users of Tylenol, the category leaders, inviting them to try a sample of Nuprin and compare. An 800 number was added to a flight of Nuprin commercials, which were made 60 seconds long instead of 30 seconds in order to provide plenty of time both to tell the product story and maximize requests for the free sample.

They also used free-standing inserts and co-op mailings to promote the offer and get the names of users of competitive brands. Each free sample of Nuprin was accompanied by a questionnaire asking the requester for information which would round out the database profile.

"Thus far," Merold was quoted at the time in *Direct,* "we've received more consumer response than we expected. So our first close encounter with direct marketing tells us it *can* build share." He said he was so encouraged by the results that he planned to leverage the database he was building to promote some of the company's older analgesics, such as Bufferin. [13]

It is worth noting in the same story that Merold said the original direct marketing plan added up to being 20% over budget, but by using a zero budgeting approach, he was able to shift money from less productive brand expenditures to make up the difference. This illustrates another important facet of turnaround marketing: to start the planning process at the "back end," with the desired number of prospects to be contacted and cultivated, rather than at the "front end," with a desired number of advertising impressions to be achieved.

Procter & Gamble followed a similar approach in identifying prospective customers when they introduced Cheer-Free, a new detergent brand for people who are allergic to the chemicals found in commonly used detergents. They tested direct-response TV commercials and ran card inserts in Sunday newspaper supplements with a "Stop the Itch" message aimed at the niche market, and included a free sample offer. They got tens of thousands of itchy consumers to raise their hands and identify themselves.

When consumers called the 800 number or filled out the questionnaire in their Sunday newspaper, they were asked: Who in the family is sensitive to the chemicals in the detergent you are now using? How many washloads a week do you do? What brand are you currently using? And so on.

The number of requests received far exceeded expectations, and the new brand took off like a second-stage rocket.

THE OPPORTUNITY FOR RETAILERS

Retailers are naturally suited for leadership in the turn to Individualized Marketing because they deal with their customers personally and have daily opportunities to capture customer data.

The most advanced retailers are racing ahead of their competition by creating sophisticated database capabilities. In the early 80's, the Higbee department store in Ohio pioneered with a targeted marketing computer system which scientifically selected prospects for maximum effectiveness. They found that customers who had made a purchase in the previous 12 months were 10 times more likely to respond than those who had not purchased for more than a year.

Around 1987, the first few supermarket chains began finding out who their customers were and rewarding them for continued patronage. One of them was Ukrop's in Richmond, Virginia.

The mid-sized Ukrop's chain, with 18 stores and a 25% market share in the Richmond area, was facing increasingly tough competition. The area had experienced a 25% increase in the total number of grocery stores and supermarkets in just five years.

Looking for a competitive advantage, brothers James and Robert Ukrops were very receptive when they were approached by Citicorp and invited to be part of a test program for its new Point of Sale (POS) Information Service.

They set up a test program. A mailing was sent to households near the test store, inviting them to become a Ukrop "Valued Customer" and enjoy "Automatic Savings Without Clipping Coupons."

Members would receive a bar-coded plastic card to be presented and scanned each time they made purchases. And they would get a monthly statement listing the "electronic coupons" and rebates automatically credited to their account based on their purchases of brands offering special deals at the time — and telling them which product purchases would qualify them for additional credits. Every three months, members would then receive a voucher for credits earned, and it could be used like cash at Ukrops.

They sent out 5,000 test mailings and signed up 7,500 customers — a 150% response any direct marketer would envy! Within three months, overall sales volume in the test store had risen 10%, and two-thirds of the sales were coming from Valued Customers. [14]

Within two years Ukrops had expanded the systems to all of its (now 20) stores, and was mailing out to 196,000 members each month its newsletter, Ukrop's Valued Customer News.

"We can talk to them, tell them about new food products coming out, highlight produce that is in season, and talk about which new fish are coming in," says Carol Beth Spivey, Ukrop's manager of advertising and marketing. "We're able to pass along information in a way that is more cost-effective than anything we have ever done."

And even more important, "If a competitor opens a store in the area, we can see which customers are dropping us. Then we can write to them and invite them back." [15]

And, of course, the system offers a staggering potential for individually customized marketing offers and communications of all kinds by the retailer, the manufacturers, and others. By storing a detailed record of each customer's purchases by frequency and brand name, such systems gradually build up a remarkably detailed series of clues to the customer's habits, interests, tastes, preferences, and lifestyle. For the supermarket, it provides a powerful customer retention system. For food manufacturers, it could revolutionize new-product introduction, by permitting them to target perfect prospects for each new product with uncanny precision.   And it makes available at last the long-sought research method of tracking permanent changes in brand preferences in individual consumers as a result of their exposure to test advertising or promotion.

In 1989 Citicorp expanded the test of the program, which they called Reward America, to a number of other chains including Pathmark, Vons, and Giant Foods.

Paul Corliss of Dynamic Controls of Manasquan, New Jersey, estimates that out of 40,000 supermarkets, some 10,000 have some kind of customer card program.   But so far most of these have been limited to check-cashing cards and do not affect cash customers.   Dynamic, which began as a collection agency, has been working for years to educate supermarkets in the reality that check-paying customers are an asset, not a liability, because applying for check-cashing privilege provides extremely useful database information about each customer.

Dynamic Controls is now working to help supermarkets expand their card programs to reach their cash customers as well as those who pay by check.   The 16-store chain of King Supermarkets has launched a Signature Club which, in addition to check-cashing, gives members discounts and a monthly newsletter.   The membership application asks respondents to provide information on food expenditures, family size, dietary needs, pet ownership, marital status, and age. The database is jointly managed by King and Dynamic Controls.

WALDENBOOKS GETS EVEN SMARTER

In early '90, the giant bookstore chain Waldenbooks — which, along with its chief competitor, B. Dalton, has always been a daring and imaginative marketer in a field that has been traditionally more product-driven than marketing-driven — launched a bold counterattack against book clubs with its new Preferred Reader Program.

In full-page newspaper ads, as well as in-store promotion, members were offered an extra 10% discount, a $5 coupon automatically mailed out after every $100 spent, a toll-free number that members can use to place orders and get special treatment, and *"special newsletters with advance notice of newly published books in your own areas of interest, often at a considerable discount off the publisher's price. Included in the newsletter is information on upcoming in-store promotions as well as interviews with today's hottest authors."*

Note carefully that italicized quote from the Waldenbooks ad. What does it tell you about their plans?   It is obvious that they are going to do targeted marketing to segments of their customer database, using the knowledge stored there about each customer's previous purchases by author and subject matter. Thus, if you are an Elmore Leonard fan, they will be able to invite you to meet the author at an autograph-signing event in the branch store that you ordinarily patronize. Or, explains Ron Jaffe, senior marketing director at Waldenbooks, "we can send special discount coupons to a science fiction lover along with news about upcoming releases." [16]

And the opportunities for Individualized Marketing in retailing are not confined to the giant chains. Thanks to the personal computer and desktop publishing, the tiniest retail operation can do sophisticated customized marketing — even to a customer list of just a few thousand names.

There is a small mystery bookstore in Portland, Oregon, Murder by the Book, that has a customer database of only 1500 mystery fans. The store has found that tastes vary widely and strongly, not only by author but also by type of mystery. Some people like hard-boiled detective yarns, some prefer "police procedurals" or elegant British tales, some read only stories of spying and international intrigue, and so on. So proprietors Jill Hinckley and Carolyn Lane have divided all of their titles into the sixteen most common categories, and thanks to desktop publishing have been able to issue a separate catalog for each group.

Henry R. "Pete" Hoke, Jr., the visionary publisher of *Direct Marketing* magazine, was one of the first to see the potential the computer database offers the small retailer. He summed it up in a prophetic editorial a number of years ago:

The real challenge is converting the systems of the giants for the small retailer, of which there are 1.7 million in the U.S. Think of the potential of arming small stores with minicomputers which can maintain all names and addresses within a store's trading area. All! Then providing each store the programs by which the retailer can mark the file in four ways: (a) Customers and non-customers. Among non-customers, those who (b) have the same profile as customers; (c) those customers who have inquired or stopped-in without a purchase; (d) no activity.

Other programs could permit recording purchases in-store, by phone or mail; tracking inventory and flagging the reorder point; or the method of customer payment. Manuals, books and seminars would teach what the retailer can do with the information, how to build direct response offers and keycodes into every newspaper, shopper or radio advertisement, and how to select names and addresses off the file for special mail shots to segments of this house list. Day-end reports would show whether a prospect became a customer, and by way of which offer.

Then once a month, a subscription service might send the retailer a diskette providing the names of new move-ins, those that have left the area, or perhaps the change of address if the product line indicated the potential of national or regional mail-order business. What proved cost effective, the retailer would do more of. What didn't work would be stopped. Mindless saturation advertising would be curbed. Customer loyalty programs would reward steady shoppers. Special inducements would attempt to convert best prospects to customer status. [17]

At the time Pete Hoke wrote this, the personal computer was just becoming popular and its RAM and storage capabilities were limited. By the start of the 90's it had become possible and easily affordable for the personal computer owner to install up to 8MB or higher expanded RAM and store information on a 40MB or even 100MB removable cartridge or 600 MB CD-ROM. This makes it possible for small retailers to store and access detailed information on thousands of customers and prospects right on the desktop, and also to send customized offers to segments of the file via desktop publishing. The software to do all this is available and ready to be put to work by enterprising retailers.

Radio Shack has introduced a computer system which enters and updates each customer's record at the time of purchase. The customer's file is set up when the first purchase is made, and the computer prints out the sales receipt. Then when the customer returns for a repeat purchase, the customer file is instantly summoned by the sales clerk typing in the last four digits of the customer's phone number.

The hardware is in place, but based on our personal observations, Radio Shack stores have not yet realized what a powerful tool for upgrading purchases this system could be. Mostly they seem to be using it for inventory control, speeding up of invoice-writing, and avoiding the wastefulness of recapturing the same customer name and address over and over again. So far we have not seen one of their clerks bring up a customer record on the screen and say, "Oh, I see you bought some high-fi cables from us last time, Mr. Collins. Did you know we have a special on speakers this week?"

Treating every repeat customer as you would anyone you know well, by providing personal, individualized attention both in the store and by mail and phone, is now possible for any retailer, large or small. For those who take the trouble to do it, there are big rewards.

Do you know who your customers and prospects are? If you

don't, you'd better find out. It is later than you think.

Either *you* will be the first in your field to determine and record the identity and profile of your best prospects and customers and use this information to serve them better — or a competitor will. Here are a few stimulating questions to help you get started.

IDEA-STARTERS FOR PROFITING
FROM TURNAROUND TREND No. 1

MANUFACTURER:

✔ *How might you add a name-capturing offer to your general advertising message?*

✔ *Are you burying your name-capturing offer in tiny type or a mere one or two seconds of toll-free phone number display in a 30-second commercial? If so, how about testing a genuine direct response ad or TV commercial?*

✔ *How might you put a name-capturing offer on or in your product packaging?*

✔ *How might you add more customer-profile data to the names and addresses obtained from past sales promotion offers?*

✔ *How many different ways might you profit from your customer database? If you can't think of two or three, how about calling in an outside consultant to open your mind to new possibilities?*

✔ *How might you identify ideal prospects for you within public databases, and use this information as — or add it to — your own prospect database?*

✔ *How might you help your distribution outlets set up their own customer databases in exchange for letting you send dealer-imprinted advertising for your product to their names?*

RETAILER OR SERVICE ESTABLISHMENT:

✔ *How might you capture names, addresses, and other personal data from walk-ins as well as purchasers?*

✔ *Which computer hardware and software would permit you to do marketing to your own in-house database?*

✔ *Could you analyze your customer data to determine your ideal customer profile, then test target marketing to "clones" of your best customers selected from public databases covering your trading area?*

✔ *Are you grading your customers by the catalog marketer's Recency, Frequency, and Monetary Value of Purchases scoring system?*

✔ *How might you test and measure cost-efficiency of promotion to each decile of your customer database from most likely to least likely purchaser?*

Note: As may be true in some other chapters, these Turnaround Idea-Starters do not stand alone but should be considered in conjunction with other Idea-Starters that will come later. In other words, identifying your prospects and customers is just the first step. What you can do with this data and how you can make it pay off for you will be amplified in other chapters.

4 From Creativity-Driven to Response-Driven

The graveyard of creative excess...The new creative challenge :.."Impactfulness" vs. Response? ... The 8 forms of advertising...Untangling terminology...A common mistake advertisers make...A lesson from the 70's...Your own best mix...Limits of Image Advertising: the Benson & Hedges 'jama man...Salem makes waves...Response advertising changes its creators...Starting with the end: the Alaska Tourism story...The next wave of creativity

In the desperate struggle of advertisers to rise above the babble of the crowd, that all-time favorite buzzword, "creativity," has become more than king. For far too many advertisers and agencies, it has become a god.

The result, along with some brilliant successes, has been an advertising graveyard littered with the excesses of creativity — the campaigns that made the public laugh or gasp and cry but failed to make them buy.

This has been happening as far back as 1902. A new breakfast cereal named Force was launched at that time with full-page ads in Sunday newspapers featuring poems and drawings about a character named Sunny Jim. (He had been "a most unfriendly man" named Jim Dumps until he started eating Force for breakfast.)

The public ate it up — the concept, that is, not the cereal. Poems, songs, musical comedies, vaudeville skits were written about Sunny Jim. Soon _Printer's Ink_ reported that Sunny Jim was "as well known as President [Theodore] Roosevelt or J. Pierpont Morgan."

There was just one problem. You guessed it. The campaign failed to sell Force cereal. [1]

THE SINS OF SELF-INDULGENT CREATIVITY

Today one of the most common excesses of creativity lies in allowing the design of print advertising to become so precious that it interferes with readability and communication and becomes an end in itself. Or creating a TV commercial so clever it wins a Clio Award but viewers can't remember or don't care about what was being advertised.

You often see advertisements with a block of tiny, brief , unreadable type surrounded by a sea of space that could easily accommodate more and larger copy.

Sometimes art directors will even mandate that copy must be brief, regardless of the needs of the selling message, in order to suit the design. Worse still, copy is still seen being run in small sansserif white letters superimposed on a color halftone or black background, as if the artistic merit of the layout were more important than the legibility of the message.

Why pay copywriters in top agencies as much as $100,000 a year or more and then make their words indecipherable on the printed page?

And the television equivalent is the commercial that people rave about but don't act on.   In *MaxiMarketing* we cited the case of Heublein, who won raves from feminists for Harvey's Bristol Cream commercials in which women boldly invited men over to their apartments.   Later a Heublein spokesman admitted, "It made the brand much more visible, but *I wouldn't say it had a great effect on sales.*"

Today, for a growing number of advertisers, there is an alternative which offers some protection from unfettered creativity. And that is advertising which invites a response from its audience and is influenced by how many or how few responses are received. With advertisers beginning to see advertising as the start of a dialogue with viewers and readers, a built-in check on creative excess is coming into play. It is the stern accountability provided by adding up just how many responses are generated from a particular creative approach and by the ability to track subsequent sales.

THE NEW CREATIVE CHALLENGE

A few bold experiments at the end of the 80's gave us a glimpse of what to expect when big-budget advertisers turn around the creative process — first planning a productive dialogue with prospects, and then creating the right advertising to make it happen.

The Cheer-Free detergent test commercial mentioned earlier devoted its entire 30 seconds to singling out true prospects in the viewing audience and getting a response from them.

The commercial was all about a person making a phone call to request a sample of Cheer-Free while busily scratching the itches resulting from use of an ordinary detergent.

The casting and humor were as professionally executed as you would expect in the most "creative" commercial. The important difference is that the creativity was devoted primarily to maximizing responses from people who need the product, not just to maximizing "retained impressions" made on everybody. The toll-free number was prominently displayed again and again during the 30 seconds and not simply tacked on the end as an afterthought.

What was most striking about the commercial was how well it conveyed the product benefits story while maximizing response. It was double-duty advertising building general awareness and, at the same time, getting hot prospects to raise their hands and say, "Tell me or show me more."

Other double-duty TV advertising for Bristol-Myers' Nuprin, MCI's long-distance service, Dreyfus mutual funds, and a number of other pioneering advertisers has shown how it is possible to maintain the corporate image, build brand awareness, and trigger a torrent of response — all in as little as 30 seconds of TV time. This is the real creative challenge in The Age of the Individual in marketing, when getting closer to the right people is more important than cleverly entertaining all of the people who happen to see or hear the advertising.

THE MYTH OF "IMPACTFULNESS" VS. RESPONSE

There is a myth still rampant in advertising circles that advertising which does *not* call for a response tends to be more consistent with a quality image than advertising which *does* call for a response.

For instance, an agency art director writing in *Advertising Age* lamented that "while the execution of the creative product in direct response has improved over the years, it still seems to lag behind the impactfulness, the drama, the beauty of good general advertising...Direct response needs to change. A stronger creative product is called for. One that does not excuse itself from the standards and proven merits of top-notch general advertising."

We disagree. The problem with so much general image advertising, even though it plays a necessary role, is that its merits are
not so "proven" after all. Too often this lack of proof leads to the
self-indulgent excesses of "creativity" that we see too often in
newspaper, magazine, and television advertising.

And when the same art director writes, "How often have you
seen direct response written in a way that really stops and engages
its audience, gives them a little credit as human beings and appeals to their sense of humor, or their emotions, or their drives?" [2]
we believe he's got it all turned around — the wrong way.

It is the response-driven copy which is more likely to engage
the prospect's emotions and drives as a human being because it
benefits from direct feedback from its audience.

Do not confuse the old-fashioned mail-order advertising of a
generation ago — that went for the maximum immediate sale without regard for the long-term effect on the relationship — with today's sophisticated response-driven advertising. There is no reason to expect that adveritsing calling for a response needs to be
any less attractive than advertising not measured by responses.
In response-driven and database-building advertising, ultimately it
is the public who decides what advertising is attractive by the actions they take — not art directors.

THE CONFUSION IN TALKING ABOUT ADVERTISING

Most people, ourselves included, have often been guilty of care-
lessly using terms like "image advertising," "awareness advertising," "general advertising," and "direct-response advertising"
without dealing with the confusion and vagueness hidden in
these terms.

Traditionally most of us would say "general advertising"
when we wanted to indicate that it was not "mail-order advertising." But although by this definition "image advertising" is "general advertising," certain kinds of "general advertising" more
closely resemble "mail-order advertising" than they do "image advertising."

It is, we believe, this common confusion which muddled the
message of the art director we just quoted. While trying to say
that "direct response" needs to improve and become more like
"top-notch general advertising," actually he probably meant a certain kind of "general advertising."

Then there are the common terms "advertising" and "sales
promotion," as if they were two different things. But as we pointed

THE SPECTRUM OF ADVERTISING CONTENT AND INTENTION
and the Role of Direct Response

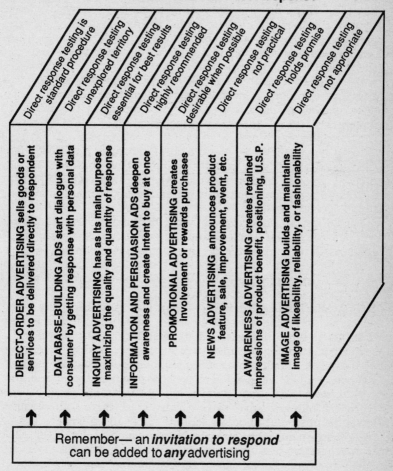

	Direct response testing is standard procedure	Direct response testing unexplored territory	Direct response testing essential for best results	Direct response testing highly recommended	Direct response testing desirable when possible	Direct response testing not practical	Direct response testing holds promise	Direct response testing not appropriate
DIRECT-ORDER ADVERTISING sells goods or services to be delivered directly to respondent								
DATABASE-BUILDING ADS start dialogue with consumer by getting response with personal data								
INQUIRY ADVERTISING has as its main purpose maximizing the quality and quantity of response								
INFORMATION AND PERSUASION ADS deepen awareness and create intent to buy at once								
PROMOTIONAL ADVERTISING creates involvement or rewards purchases								
NEWS ADVERTISING announces product feature, sale, improvement, event, etc.								
AWARENESS ADVERTISING creates retained impressions of product benefit, positioning, U.S.P.								
IMAGE ADVERTISING builds and maintains image of likeability, reliability, or fashionability								

Remember— an ***invitation to respond*** can be added to ***any*** advertising

Figure 5

out in our glossary on page 46, some promotion *is* advertising — certainly an ad in *Family Circle* containing a discount coupon is advertising, but it is also sales promotion — and some promotion is not advertising at all, but simply a discount to dealers. In an effort to clear away the confusion, not only over terminology but over aim and function as well, we have constructed a Spectrum of Advertising Content and Intention (Figure 5) based on our own definitions.

In thinking about and analyzing a great number of advertisements of all kinds, in all media, we found that almost without exception their content reflected one of eight purposes *or a combination of these purposes in varying proportions.* A direct-response element can theoretically be included in any one of the eight categories, although only three of them (Inquiry Advertising, Database-Building Advertising, and Direct-Order Advertising) have response as their main purpose.

Image Advertising is simply devoted to building up, through constant repetition, a favorable impression of the likeability, reliability, or fashionability of a product or company in the minds of prospective buyers. For example, the Prudential Rock of Gibraltar. Or "Coke, the real thing."

In its purest form, no rational argument is included. Often this is because it is for a parity product which possesses no significant rational, demonstrable superiority. How can you present a rational argument in favor of a fragrance, clothing fashion, or brand of cola?

Awareness Advertising, by our definition, wants you to remember something special about the product or advertiser, some basic advantage, benefit, sales point, or U.S.P., such as "doctor-recommended Tylenol."

News Advertising announces sale, a new product or improvement, a new location, an event.

Promotional Advertising, in our spectrum, is a very broad term for advertising intended to get its audience to take some action which hopefully will lead to their buying the product. It might be attending an advertiser-sponsored concert, entering a sweepstakes, clipping and redeeming a discount coupon, requesting a free sample, or sending off proof of purchase for a premium.

Information and Persuasion Advertising goes beyond merely selecting a single salient image or sales point to create a favorable buying attitude. It seeks to make an immediate sale by presenting many facts and arguments which might accomplish this. This kind of advertising would include but is not limited to direct-order marketing ads. Special-interest magazines about computers, hunting and fishing, home workshops, gardening, and other special interests are filled with such advertising.

Information and Persuasion Advertising, usually though not always, is used for high-ticket, high-tech, or highly unique product or service. It is very similar in purpose to Direct-Order Advertising, and for this reason its creative strategists can benefit most from studying what works in Direct-Order Advertising, as Ogilvy has said he did. This is an important point to remember. Often marketers of high-tech products, such as computer software, begin to invite direct orders in their Information and Persuasion advertising when they have trouble getting retail distribution. But they fail to use the secrets direct-order marketers have learned about what makes buyers respond.

Inquiry Advertising has as its primary purpose the offer of a promotional video, an information kit, a sales visit, or some other linkage to the sale. It is — or should be — devoted entirely to maximizing the quality and quantity of the responses generated.

We have chosen to call this category Inquiry Advertising rather than Direct Response because, as our diagram indicates, other kinds of advertising may also contain a direct-response element. The difference is that in Inquiry Advertising the main purpose is to get a response.

Inquiry Advertising may contain a great deal of information and persuasion, or it may not — inquiry advertisers have found through testing that sometimes long copy works better, sometimes not.

Keep in mind that offering product literature or "name of the nearest dealer" can be tacked onto Awareness Advertising or News Advertising. Usually it will yield few responses compared to Inquiry Advertising designed for that purpose, but it does add some double-duty function to the advertising at no additional upfront cost.

Database-Building is a new kind of advertising that did not exist ten years ago. It has as its major purpose not giving information, as most advertising does, but getting it, in the form of checked-off answers in a questionnaire or reply form to be returned. In its purest form, such as in Select and Save questionnaires inserted in Sunday newspapers or the questionnaire ads by Ford Motor Company, this gathering of consumer-profile information about the respondents for a database is the advertisement's only purpose.

Direct-Order Advertising is what has traditionally been known as "mail-order advertising." That old-fashioned term is no longer appropriate, however, in an age in which one may order directly by mail, phone, computer, or fax.

Until now, Inquiry Advertising by direct-order merchants has always been classified as "mail-order" advertising. But in our spectrum, no distinction is made between Inquiry Advertising run by direct-order merchants and Inquiry Advertising run by marketers whose goods are sold through retail outlets. After all, what difference does it make? In both cases the purpose should be to maximize the quantity and quality of responses, so the same techniques should be considered.

MORE LIKE RECIPE INGREDIENTS THAN WATER-TIGHT COMPARTMENTS

We believe that in advertising, as in architecture, form should follow function. So in sitting down to create an advertising message, the first question should always be, "What function are we fulfilling here?"

However, these eight categories are not water-tight compartments and not even a continuous spectrum flowing from one to the other. One advertising effort can serve a number of different purposes. A better way to think of the advertising content mix might be as a recipe with the right combination of ingredients for best effect.

For example, a highly informative and persuasive long-copy advertisement might also build up a very favorable image of the company or product. An outstanding example of this has been the delightful campaign for Ballantine's Scotch in which each two-page spread was divided into three sections: Everything You Need to Know About Scotch in 30 Seconds (very short copy), Everything You Need to Know about Scotch in 15 Minutes (slightly longer copy, proposing sipping the product for 15 minutes), and Everything You Need to Know About Scotch in 17 Years (a leisurely essay on Scotland, scotch, and the brand).

Even though what Ballantine's is selling comes close to being a parity product, the ads were very informative and persuasive about the brand as they built up an awareness of Ballantine's special qualities and an image of Ballantine's as a fine scotch.

We pointed out that three of these eight kinds of advertising have response as the main purpose — Inquiry Advertising, Database-Building Advertising, and Direct-Order Advertising. In these three cases, the desired effect is different from that of the other kinds of advertising, and it calls for the use of different creative principles than those of general advertising. We use the following two terms to keep this distinction clear.

"Response-Driven Advertising" means to us that the style and content of the advertising is influenced or dictated by the number of responses various approaches have generated during testing. In other words, just about any Inquiry Advertising or Direct-Order Advertising.

Can Awareness Advertising also be response-driven? Most advertising professionals have a hard time accepting the idea. But as David Ogilvy reminded us in his *Confessions of an Advertising Man*, when the Dove toilet bar was introduced, his agency compared responses to the same standard "buried" offer in varying Awareness Ads in order to uncover the most effective promise. Thus the final Dove Awareness Advertising was "driven" to feature the winning promise that emerged from this testing process: "Creams your skin while you wash."

"Database-Driven Advertising" signifies that an important purpose of the campaign is to get certain information from qualified prospects, add the data contained in (or implied by) their responses to an in-house database, and continue the dialogue based on the information obtained. (The response might be to fill out and return a questionnaire or it might be simply to request a free sample — after all, when people request a free sample of an arthritis remedy, they have in effect told you that they have arthritis.) The content of the advertising is planned to achieve that purpose.

The Nuprin, Cheer-Free, and Merit Cigarette campaigns to which we have referred are all examples of turnaround thinking in which the demands of database-building and dialogue, rather than the demands of building image and awareness, are given top priority.

They are part of a visibly increasing trend toward turning around the usual creative process — toward starting with the desired kind and quantity of advertising responses and then working backward to plan the advertising accordingly, rather than starting with a "catchy" idea or theme and going on from there to create the campaign.

A COMMON MISTAKE — FAILURE TO MATCH CONTENT TO PURPOSE

We believe that throughout the 90's an increasing number of advertisers will turn away from admired "creative" advertising which produces no visible effect — and toward response-driven and database-driven advertising which establishes immediate contact with, dialogue with, and traceable sales to real live customers.

During this transitional period, when the pressure is on to make every advertising dollar count, advertisers can afford less than ever to make one of the most common mistakes in advertising. And that is using the wrong type of advertising for the problem at hand or failing to use a proper mixture.

For example, pure Image Advertising may be the best thing for a parity product for which no rational argument can be presented. But many unique products and services have a compelling story to tell yet fail to use Information and Persuasion Advertising to tell it, opting for feeble Image Advertising instead. And even parity products sometimes could, but neglect to, pre-empt a fascinating product category argument which their competitors could also use but don't.

Bertolli Olive Oil showed how this could be done in a very nice ad for their olive oils which combined Awareness, News, Information and Persuasion, and Inquiry stimulation. It was headed: "FOR YEARS, BERTOLLI HAS SAID OLIVE OIL CAN LOWER YOUR CHOLESTEROL, BLOOD PRESSURE AND BLOOD SUGAR. LAST WEEK, MEDICAL SCIENCE SAID WE WERE RIGHT." And the text made no claims at all for Bertolli's own particular make of olive oil other than to mention that it is "delicious." Instead it pre-empted and backed up the claim that mono-unsaturated fats "such as olive oil" can reduce the "bad" LDL cholesterol and protect the "good" HDL cholesterol. Then it offered to send more information about the health benefits of olive oil.

On the whole, what Bertolli has done here seems fairly sound and effective. But it is possible that Bertolli and others doing similar direct-response advertising could make it even more effective by using the most precise as well as the most neglected copy research tool in advertising.

A MAGIC PILL FOR DOUBLING AND REDOUBLING RESPONSE

Until the 80's, almost the only advertisers asking for a direct reponse were the Direct-Order companies (what was then called mail-order). Now, in the 90's, when so many advertisers are turning to some form of direct response for the first time, they could access a vast body of knowledge about what works and what doesn't.

The trouble is that too often the new users of direct response in combination with awareness advertising turn to unprepared awareness advertising specialists at the advertising agency rather than listen and learn from direct-response specialists.

What the best direct-response specialists have is an accumulated body of techniques and instincts based on the collective observation of results from hundreds and even thousands of split-run tests for nearly a century.

In a split-run test, two different advertising approaches, Ad A and Ad B — it might be a test of just one variable, such as a different headline, illustration, or offer — are given simultaneous equal exposure, with the reply forms in each ad separately coded for tracking and comparison.

This simultaneous equal exposure can be accomplished on-page in magazines and newspapers that offer split-run service (evenly intermixing copies with Ad A and copies with Ad B). Or, by evenly intermixing advertiser-supplied magazine or newspaper inserts at the printing plant, more than two ads can be tested — as many different inserts can be tested simultaneously as the size of the publication circulation makes advisable. Or by testing the control ad against a different new approach in different regional editions of TV Guide, theoretically as many different ads could be tested in the same issue as would yield a statistically significant response. (In direct-response television testing, roughly the same aim can be achieved by rotating spots and markets.)

At Rapp & Collins, we relied heavily on simultaneously testing half a dozen ads or more, a technique that we called telescopic testing. (We don't claim to have invented it, only named it — the technique had long been used in direct mail testing by sophisticated mailers like Reader's Digest.)

We called it telescopic testing because through testing a number of approaches simultaneously in print media, we could telescope what would have been a series of A-B splits — Ad A vs. Ad B, the winner vs. Ad C, etc., spread out over a year or two — into a single test.

Again and again it quickly led to breakthrough results in which the winning approach would produce twice or three times as many responses as the old advertising.

Based on research into the marketplace and the agency's creative thinking, we would come up with perhaps ten different advertisements, each one expressing a different well-conceived hypothesis or copy platform.

There was no other copy research method then, and we believe there is still none today, which could reliably predict which copy alternative would yield the best response. (In *MaxiMarketing*, we told what happened when at Rapp & Collins we had an opportunity to compare the ranking by predictive research of eight different direct-order advertisements for the RCA Record Club and the actual ranking based on responses. Figure 6 shows how far off the predictive research was.)

So we would give all ten of the advertisements, including the existing or control advertisement, equal simultaneous exposure, with the reply forms individually coded for tracking.

The results were usually humbling. Although our years of experience with split-run testing had given us a far keener instinct for which hypotheses deserved testing, even we were often wrong about which ad turned out to be the winner. And even with the most carefully prepared rationales, an average of only

A comparison of consumer-interview predictive research and actual split-run results, RCA Record Club, 1981

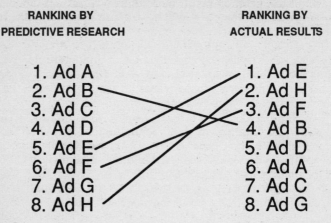

RANKING BY PREDICTIVE RESEARCH

1. Ad A
2. Ad B
3. Ad C
4. Ad D
5. Ad E
6. Ad F
7. Ad G
8. Ad H

RANKING BY ACTUAL RESULTS

1. Ad E
2. Ad H
3. Ad F
4. Ad B
5. Ad D
6. Ad A
7. Ad C
8. Ad G

Figure 6

one out of seven new approaches tested would produce a "break-through" — an increase in response of 50% or more.

Using this technique, we worked with Richard Cross, then associate director of Consumers Union, to triple the response to subscription promotion advertising for *Consumer Reports* magazine. This was an important factor, along with constant testing and roll-out in direct-response television, in building the circulation from 1.5 million to over four million today.

Today, as a steadily increasing number of advertisers of all kinds are turning to direct-response advertising in order to locate and cultivate prospects, it seems extremely wasteful for them not to make use of this precision instrument of research.

As indicated in our diagram, a direct-response element can be included in almost any kind of advertising.

And frankly, we think that in publication advertising it very often should be.

After all, this offers you a chance to identify, learn about, and communicate with people who are most keenly interested in what you are advertising — at no additional upfront media cost!

WHO SHOULD DO SPLIT-RUN TESTING?

Whether direct-response testing via split runs should be used as a copy research tool in every kind of advertising is quite a different question. As our diagram indicates,the feasibility and desirability of this increases as we move across the spectrum from right to left.

Starting on the right side of the diagram:

RESPONSE TESTING OF IMAGE AND AWARENESS ADVERTISING?

Using responses as a research method to determine the best approach to pure Image Advertising is usually not appropriate. For example, it would be almost impossible to use direct response to test the value of the symbol of the Rock of Gibraltar for Prudential in comparison with some other symbol. And we would be the first to agree that a buried offer in different Pepsi ads would not be a very good way to measure the effectiveness of different approaches to Pepsi image-building.

Moving left in the diagram: when it comes to Awareness Advertising, the value of split-run testing as a copy research tool would probably be hotly contested by most creative directors and advertising research executives.

Yes, there are instances of Awareness Advertising that simply don't lend themselves to this kind of testing. But as the Ogilvy experience with Dove indicated years ago, it is not out of the question. Yet the possibility of using responses as a way of evaluating Awareness Advertising has been studiously avoided by most brand advertisers for the last sixty years or so. Ogilvy's Dove tests, and perhaps other tests he hasn't told us about, would be the rare exception.

But as direct-response advertising increases as a means of building a database, more advertisers and agencies may want to experiment with split-run testing of Awareness Advertising as a copy research method. It could hardly be more faulty and unreliable than some of the other copy research methods being used, as we pointed out in *MaxiMarketing*.

NEWS ADVERTISING GOES BY TOO FAST

News advertising — the announcement of a sale, a new product, a new improvement, a new retail location — certainly doesn't lend itself to gradual improvement through direct-response testing, since news advertising is basically a one-time event. By the time you finish your testing and are ready to incorporate the results in your advertising, it is too late.

PROMOTIONAL ADVERTISING CRIES OUT FOR TESTING

On the other hand, certain kinds of Promotional Advertising seem to be crying out for split-run direct-response testing. Of course, if the purpose of the advertising is a discount coupon to be presented to a retailer, it takes so long for the coupons to travel down the "pipeline" from consumer to redemption reports that it is difficult to test one discount-coupon ad against another. (Increasingly, "single-source research" using supermarket scanners to track changes in individual shopper buying habits may be making discount-coupon ad testing possible for heavily advertised supermarket products.) But in promotional advertising calling for direct responses that can be measured immediately at the fulfillment center, such as a premium, free sample, or rebate offer, it is wasteful not to do multiple direct-response testing to determine which approach will yield more responses and sales for the same amount of expenditure.

SPLIT-RUN TESTS INVALUABLE FOR INFORMATION AND PERSUASION

In Information and Persuasion advertising, which and how much information and persuasion should be included and what should be the main appeal? Here split-run direct-response testing can be invaluable in providing the answer. Many in-depth information advertisements in special-interest magazines are already inviting responses anyway (and sometimes, quietly, orders as well). So they might as well start comparing the number of responses from different approaches and incorporating whatever they learn from this in their future advertising.

A "MUST" FOR MAXIMIZED INQUIRY ADVERTISING

Next in the spectrum diagram, we come to Inquiry Advertising, the main purpose of which is to maximize the quality and quantity of the responses generated. Here the folly of failing to test one approach against another in the crucible of real-world advertising insertions is self-evident. (Or at least it ought to be!)

We have often observed, in our own direct-order marketing advertising agency experience over many years, that the difference in the volume of response between the best and the worst of a number of different expressions of the same appeal can vary as much as five to one. This means that inquiry advertisers who are "flying blind," without split-testing, may be investing up to five times as much as is necessary on advertising to get the same quality and quantity of responses. Think of that — spending $5 million on inquiry advertising instead of $1 million! Or put another way, neglecting an opportunity to get $40 million worth of advertising for only $8 million.

WHY NOT SPLIT RUNS FOR DATABASE-BUILDING ADVERTISING?

Moving along in the diagram to Database-Building Advertising:
we have indicated in our spectrum diagram that the use of split-
run testing here is "unexplored territory." To the best of our
knowledge, it has never been done — yet! But when you think
about it, this certainly seems like something that deserves to be
tried sooner rather than later.

As an increasing number of advertisers turn toward Database Marketing, consumers will be deluged with an increasing
number of database-building questionnaires, just as they were
deluged starting in the 70's with discount coupons. And they will
necessarily become more resistant to responding.

Then more study and testing will have to be devoted to the question of which is the best way to maximize the number of returned
questionnaires. A cash reward? A gift? If so, what kind of gift?

Split-run testing is an ideal way to find the answer, for it
measures not what people in an artificial copy research environment claim they would do or seem like they might do, but rather
what they actually do in a real marketplace situation.

SPLITS OBLIGATORY IN DIRECT-ORDER MARKETING

In Direct-Order Marketing, "there oughta be a law" requiring sci-
entific A-B split-run and telescopic testing of new campaigns or
new additions to successful long-running advertising. Certainly it
is almost universal practice when direct mail is the medium used.
But in other media, both print and broadcast, too many people
in a new generation of direct-order marketers, both on the client
side and the agency side, have forgotten the importance of this remarkable research tool.

DETERMINE YOUR OWN BEST MIX

Obviously much Image and Awareness Advertising is brilliant and
effective, sometimes breathtakingly so. It has been demonstrated
again and again that skillful dramatization of a product theme or
personality or product positioning or U.S.P., repeated often
enough, can affect public buying attitudes. The question is
whether — when — and to what extent — you should be relying
on this as the *total* answer for your advertising.

We say you should think about and determine your own
proper mix of image...awareness...news....sales promotion... information and persuasion...inquiry advertising...database-building...

and direct-order marketing.

Your mix should be based on the special needs of the product or service you are selling, including the competitive and product life cycle situation at the time.

If you have a broad enough market and deep enough pockets, then your image advertising unquestionably has an important role to play.

Even if it does not win you new customers, it will help you keep the ones you already have.

But note those "ifs."

Remember the agency executive we quoted in Chapter One who said, "I can count the clients on the fingers of one hand who spend enough on advertising to be effective."

And he made it clear that "enough" meant at least $8 million to $10 million a year (for a national brand advertiser). Often it takes more like $15 to $20 million to make a perceptible difference in public attitudes.

Remember that the same executive also argued, with some justice, that advertisers who spend "only" $3 million to $4 million are "wasting their money."

And even big advertisers with big budgets for image advertising, we have noted, can't always prove that it pays. Huge, highly touted image campaigns are a kind of high-stakes roulette game in which big advertising dollars are gambled and don't always get back big winnings to show for it.

Compare Philip Morris's highly accountable Merit Challenge advertising results that we described in Chapter 3 with the experience the same company was having about the same time with its image advertising for Benson & Hedges cigarettes.

Philip Morris was having trouble with the brand and was losing market share because the brand's elitist image wasn't strong enough to counter the trend to more mainstream, lower-priced brands.

The Benson & Hedges brand spent $55 to $60 million a year on one of the most talked-about campaigns of the time, the "For people who like to smoke" ads.

One of the advertisements was the famous ad that showed a bare-chested man wearing pajama pants standing in the door of the dining room and chatting with the people gathered around the dining table for what seemed like brunch — a group of women and an older man.

Remember?

Speculating on what was going on in the picture became such a popular guessing game among magazine readers that the company finally capitalized on all the curiosity by running a contest with prizes for the best explanations submitted.

And yet, reported *Advertising Age*, "Despite all the hoopla it created, the 2-year-old-campaign has failed to spur sales." The brand's market share slipped during that time from 4.3% to 4.1%. [3.] By the beginning of this decade, it was down to 3.7%. [4]

This doesn't necessarily mean that the campaign was a failure. The fact is, it may have slowed the decline of a very profitable premium brand by bolstering the loyalty of the remaining users. But at the same time, it was another jolting example of the limits of highly creative, highly praised image advertising.

HEDGING YOUR BET WITH AN IMAGE/DATABASE MIX

For all these reasons, we believe this decade will see a steady trend toward advertising budgets which will provide for a mix of image/awareness advertising and response and database driven advertising — that is, advertising which is crafted primarily to create interaction with prospects and feed information to the advertiser's in-house database.

Sometimes there will be two separate campaigns. Sometimes both purposes will be achieved in the same advertisement or broadcast commercial.

Although our main point is the need for awareness advertisers to include more direct-response in their marketing mix, the need to find and use the proper mix is one that applies to *all* advertisers, including direct-order marketers. The latter often can benefit from some image advertising in their mix as much as image advertisers can benefit from direct response.

Centraal Beheer, a Direct-Order Marketing insurance company in The Netherlands, provides a striking example of an effective use of awareness advertising by a direct-order marketer.

The company has grown to be the fifth largest insurance company in Holland by getting all the essentials of direct-order marketing right and at the same time becoming one of the best-known and most talked-about television awareness advertisers in that country.

One-third of their total advertising budget is devoted to building the company's image with 30-second commercials that do not include any request for a direct response.

As a result of this image advertising, in just three years the spontaneous top-of-mind awareness of the company shot up from 58% to approximately 82%. And their direct-marketing sales shot up as well.

The slogan at the end of each commercial is "*Even Apeldorn bellen,*" which translates as "Just call Apeldorn" (the town where the company is located). This supports and stimulates the responses to their full-page direct-response advertisements in Holland's leading magazines and newspapers.

For large advertisers addressing a broad market, designing a mix of awareness and direct-response can be a way of hedging their bets, by diverting some of the usual awareness advertising money into measurable advertising which singles out and concentrates on known prospects and customers.

For many smaller advertisers and niche products, the turn to direct response will become a dire necessity — often almost the only way to spend advertising money efficiently and with predictable results in the face of rising media costs and the demassification of the market.

For such clients, the primary challenge to advertising agency creativity will be not how to devise the cleverest, most unforgettable TV commercial or the most beautiful print ad.

Rather it will be how to maximize responses and database information input consistent with corporate or product image guidelines, and then how to make the most effective and imaginative use of the buried treasure of information stored in the resulting database.

A NEW KIND OF ADVERTISING AGENCY REQUIRED?

This new creative challenge may demand and result in the development of a new kind of advertising agency — peopled with, in the words of *Adweek's* Laurie Petersen, "agency executives who consider their role *the solving of marketing problems — not the creation of television advertising or the perfect direct mail letter or sweepstakes.*" [5] [Italics ours]

One such agency she describes is Cramer-Krassert. Its president, Peter Krivkovich, deliberately built "a staff with an ability to think outside a specialty without any danger of losing compensation or status within the agency."

He is, says Petersen, "as passionate about the database marketing used to sell Allen-Edmonds shoes as he is for the award-winning creative execution of 'Do the Twist' TV commercials for Skil Tools." [6]

Another effort to create the advertising agency of the future is FCB/LKP Integrated Communications Group.

There a direct marketing person, a sales promotion person, and a general advertising person literally sit next to one another and interact to solve problems.

SALEM MAKES WAVES WITH A TOTAL MIX

One of the results of this new way of working was "Salem Sound-Waves," the advertising agency's daring $35 million test program for RJ Reynolds that is reported to have boosted the market share for Salem cigarettes by 2.5% and more in six test markets.

In recent years, the cigarette market has been shrinking, and companies and brands can only grow by stealing customers from their competitors. Toward the end of the last decade, RJR found that Salem, one of the three major menthol brands, was losing ground, with its market share declining from 7.3% to 6.2% in one year.   And a single market share point is worth $358 million. [7] The problem was to change the image of Salem with young menthol smokers ages 20 to 24, who tend to prefer Newport.

"We were convinced that creating a one-time promotion would never meet the objective," says Larry Gershman, executive VP of FCB/LKP. So they persuaded the client to test an elaborate multi-faceted ongoing program built around a basic interest of young men in the target age group — the "new music."

The campaign kicked off with a database-building four-page magazine insert with an offer of a free TDK blank audio cassette and a free copy of *Salem SoundWaves* Magazine. The ads carried an 800 number to call, permitting operators to capture for the database the name, address, smoking preferences, and other data about the callers. Some 200,000 smokers called and received, in addition to the audio cassette, a free membership card, a free subscription to the bimonthly *Salem SoundWaves* magazine, and an opportunity to order from the hottest "new music" records, tapes, and CDs of the month from Express Music at a special price.

To help offset the cost of the magazine, advertising was sold to non-competing manufacturers such as Hitachi, Jovan, RC Cola, and Coors Light. The magazine also sells Sweatshirts and other Salem SoundWave specialty merchandise. Every shirt or travel bag sold with the Salem name emblazoned on it becomes a walking billboard for the brand.

About twice a month in each test market, Salem Sound-Waves was the host at each market's hottest clubs. There are radio tie-ins with the appropriate local music stations, and the radio station dee-jays appear at the club events. Winners of contests at the clubs are then promoted on the radio station programs. [8]

"I honestly don't think 'Salem SoundWaves' could have happened anywhere but here," says FCB/LKP's Gershman. "When we all got together in a room, it just grew and grew."

WILL CREATIVE ATTITUDES ALSO BE AFFECTED?

Does all this mean that the very nature of advertising will change in the future? Perhaps. As a new generation of creative people starts doing advertising which communicates directly with prospects and customers, something interesting may happen. They may find that the feedback provided by the number of responses their ads generate will begin to alter their creative convictions about what constitutes good advertising in general.

For example, listen to Mike Slosberg, partner and creative director of Bronner Slosberg Associates.

He was a rising star in creative management at Young & Rubicam when he was selected by the agency in 1978 to become CEO of one of its most important acquisitions, the leading direct marketing agency Wunderman, Ricotta & Kline (now Wunderman Worldwide).

It was a problem, he now confesses, to make the transition from what he calls general advertising's creative arrogance and subjective evaluations.

"Being measured continually is a tough lesson," he says. "In direct, it's cost-per-lead or cost-per-sale, not some art director's squinty-eyed aesthetic standard that counts. And you learn very quickly that you can be wrong about how you think people will react. When you put it on the line this way, *you become a different kind of creative person*." [9] [Italics ours]

DAVID OGILVY'S WISDOM ABOUT "CREATIVITY"

In his first book, *Confessions of an Advertising Man*, David Ogilvy presented his own definition of a good advertisement as "one which sells the product without drawing attention to itself. It should rivet the reader's attention on the product. Instead of saying, 'What a clever advertisement,' the reader says, 'I never knew that before. I must try this product.'

"It is the professional duty of the advertising agent," he goes on to say, "to conceal his artifice. When Aeschines spoke, they said, 'How well he speaks.' But when Demosthenes spoke, they said, 'Let us march against Philip.' I'm for Demosthenes.

"If my new recruits," said Ogilvy, "boggle at this stern definition of good advertising, I invite them to return to their previous incarnations, there to flounder in silliness and ignorance.

"My next step," he said, "is to tell them that I will not allow them to use the word creative to describe the functions they are to perform in our agency."[10]

Yet in terms of taste, imagination, good design, and persuasiveness, the ads created under Ogilvy's direction were distinctly "creative." It was just that he insisted on putting these qualities at the service of the selling needs of his clients.

He was able to do this because he, almost alone among general advertising leaders of his generation, believed passionately in the importance and value of getting direct responses from his audience — a precursor of database-driven advertising. These responses told him when he was on the right track. And his earlier experience doing readership studies for George Gallup had taught him that pictures and captions and readable, uncluttered type would help him maximize the message-retention and responses.

HOW GETTING RESPONSES MAY ALTER
THE NATURE OF ADVERTISING

Now the rise in Individualized Marketing is putting pressure on advertisers to call for a response in order to feed data into the database. Once that happens, many of them are going to start scratching their heads and wondering why the same invitation to respond in different advertisements produces widely different results. And they may start asking their agencies to create advertising which, as long as it serves their other objectives and reflects the corporate or product image, also includes the tested elements which have been proven to encourage response.

The jolting impact of getting measurable responses to advertising is already beginning to influence media selection.

Buick had always based its media selections on the assumption that it was selling an "older person's car." But to their surprise, they found that their direct-response advertising was getting a good response from a publication aimed at the 30-to-35-year-old. Ron Fusile, manager of sales promotion and direct marketing of the Buick Motor Divison of GM, told us, "We will be directing our ad agency to begin taking into account how responsive a publication or TV program is to our inquiry offer — and not just make decisions on the basis of media impressions."

The next inevitable step for any direct-response advertiser will be to start observing how many responses one piece of copy or headline produces compared to another, and then taking this into account in the creation and roll-out of campaigns.

We said in *MaxiMarketing* that, we believed, when advertisers start tabulating and comparing responses, "reality begins to intrude and may change the entire character of the advertising."

This will surely happen more and more during the spread of the new marketing revolution.

SOME EXAMPLES OF STARTING WITH THE END, NOT THE BEGINNING

There are still very few examples of what we call DPA — database-driven promotion and advertising. With DPA, as in the Salem example cited above, the marketing strategy starts with whom you want in the database and what you are going to do with them after they get there. Then you decide what promotion to use and how to position the advertising. It is a complete turnaround from putting image and awareness advertising first and then thinking about promotion and direct marketing as separate elements later.

One of our favorite models of database-driven advertising has always been the direct-response advertising of the Alaska Division of Tourism. The advertisements include just enough attractive photography to kindle your interest in Alaska and remind you that you have always hankered to vacation there.

But the headline — "100 PAGES OF FREE ADVICE FOR ANYONE READY TO DISCOVER ALASKA." — and the text are devoted to the main purpose of the ad, which is to obtain your name, address, and vacation-travel profile for their database and their follow-up promotions.

In the booklet mailed out to inquirers, there are all the opportunities for creative design an art director could wish for, and much more creative text than a page ad in a magazine could ever include. (And this is only the beginning. Alaska Tourism makes the names and addresses of inquirers available to Alaska cruise lines and vacation resorts who also mail out their own voluminous material.)

But all this follow-up advertising is sharply focused on prime prospects who have been attracted and identified by the direct-response inquiry advertising, not squandered on prospects and non-prospects alike.

The Nuprin, Cheer-Free, and Merit Cigarette campaigns to which we have referred are all striking examples of advertising by mass marketers in which the demands of direct response and database-building come first. Then it is time to turn around and plan the response advertising which will achieve the desired goal.

The most productive response-driven advertising and sales promotion of all, as we shall see later in this book, is that which is designed as the first step in building a long, profitable, interactive relationship — a true community of interest between the advertiser and the customer.

More and more, the word "creativity" is going to take on a new meaning in the advertising of the future.

It will no longer be just a matter of advertising which wins awards and makes people laugh or talk about it. It will come to include advertising communications most creatively devised to attract, identify, contact, involve, activate, and cultivate your most promising prospects.

IDEA-STARTERS FOR PROFITING FROM TURNAROUND TREND No. 2

MANUFACTURER:

✔ *What form of advertising, or combination of forms, do you use? Could you change the mix to increase overall effectiveness?*

✔ *How might you use split-run testing of direct-response advertising to increase the impact of your next campaign?*

✔ *How might you include a direct-response element in your print advertising? Offer a free sample? Background booklet? Toll-free number to call for location of nearest dealer? A 900 number interactive information service billable to callers?*

✔ *How about asking your ad agency's art directors if they can use their creativity to give the response element in your print ads more prominence and legibility without sacrifice of the overall effect?*

✔ *Is your ad agency's prejudice against direct-response advertising keeping you from contacting your best prospects?*

✔ *Do you hide your offer in hard-to-read type or split-second TV exposure and then wonder why you don't get many responses?*

✔ *If you include an offer in your advertising, have you decided what information you would like to capture in your responses and how you plan to use the data strategically?*

✔ *If you are planning a premium promotion campaign, could you do split-run testing beforehand to determine the best premium and the best way to advertise it?*

✔ *If you have often wondered whether your image/awareness advertising is really worth all the money you pour into it, why not split off part of your usual advertising budget for a database-driven or response-driven campaign with fully accountable results?*

✔ If you are already running highly informational advertising, why not do split-run testing of copy and art alternatives to find out if there is a better way to tell your story?

RETAILER OR SERVICE ESTABLISHMENT:

✔ Could you use your sales flyers and catalogs as a split-run test vehicle, then apply lessons learned to your other advertising?

✔ Even if the aim of your advertising is store traffic, could you include a direct-response element to monitor its effectiveness and to capture names of prospects not yet ready or able to visit your store?

✔ How might you do your own database-building advertising? How about inserting a questionnaire in the shopping bag with each purchase and offering a very attractive gift or discount to customers who fill it out and return it?

✔ How might you establish a frequent-buyers club to build and retain the loyalty of your customers and to obtain buying behavior information you could use in individualized future promotion?

Turnaround Trend No. 3

5 From "Steam-Rollering" the Market to Filling Each Niche

The birth of "computer communities"...4 ways to reach them...The coming of customized, personalized magazines...Time Inc. enters The Age of the Individual.... The great public databases...Sears' new retail-customer database....Marriott's segmentation strategy ...Northwest Airlines...Casinos gamble on database targeting...Barnes & Noble slices it thin

We are all members of countless invisible, unrealized brotherhoods and sisterhoods and personhoods. You may be part of the personhood of brunettes or golfers or computer fanatics or dieters or senior citizens or all of the above.

Advertisers have always addressed themselves to these separate communities, whether it was a cosmetics firm's message to women worried about their complexions or an auto maker talking to people in the market for a new car.

Until recent times, the audiences of prospective users were so broad and accessible that the advertisers could afford to address their prospects in mass media which reached everybody. "Everybody" needed toilet soap and almost every household did some home baking and could use baking powder.

But then the mass markets of the 60's splintered into the segmented markets of the 70's and then the even finer niche markets of the 80's.

Today, niche marketers flood the marketplace with highly

specialized products and services for special needs. Sharply targeted messages attempt to seek out the prospects for whom the product or service has been created. The turning away from "steam-rollering" the entire market and toward wooing the niches grows stronger each year.

However, as media costs continue to soar, it becomes increasingly uneconomic to spend all of your advertising money talking to everybody just to reach the niches you really want.

Now the computer, by capturing, storing, and combining bits of information about who we are, where we live, what we like, what we need, what we buy, is making countless niches in the marketplace identifiable and accessible — creating what economist Robert J. Samuelson has dubbed "computer communities."

The nation's community of golfers (or a great many of them) can be singled out by direct-response advertising and/or computer selection and addressed privately. Or even senior citizen golfers who drive luxury sedans and are in the market for a new one.

And even in public advertising in the mass media, as Samuelson points out, "Magazine and television audiences are dissected by the same computerized scanning to determine which are best for cameras and which for beer." [1]

Today the number of existing "computer communities" or niche markets where people with common characteristics or interests can be found or assembled is mind-boggling. To name just a few: new move-ins, pregnant women, single-parent households, Scotch drinkers, smokers, theatre lovers, "snow birds" (Northern retirees who spend summers in the North, winters in the Sunbelt), tall people, overweight people, tall overweight people, working mothers, empty nesters, new immigrants, and on and on.

The world is moving so rapidly that all this may seem old hat already. But many advertisers have yet to make the corresponding turnaround in their thinking which calls for a different way of measuring the connection between their advertising dollars and the niche market of consumers they are trying to reach. (More about this later.)

There are essentially four ways to reach a niche market to which you would like to advertise and sell.

1. ADDRESS A NICHE MARKET IN MASS MEDIA

This is a time-honored method of "fishing" for customers when you don't know who or where they are or how better to reach them.

A TV commercial for denture cream, seeking to snare the

small percentage of denture wearers out of the total viewing audience, is no different in marketing strategy from the one-inch magazine ad headlined "ULCERS?" that would run in popular magazines month after month, "fishing" for ulcer sufferers, half a century ago.

This way of communicating with everyone in order to reach your special niche market is still alive and well, and perhaps it always will be. But there is an unmistakable trend, noted throughout this book, toward using this communication not simply to send an awareness message, but to get a response so you can identify these elusive prospects and then cultivate them intensively with direct communication.

Today there is a real question of whether there will be such a thing as universal mass media in the future. Within the span of two generations we have seen the great mass medium of network radio shattered by the arrival of the great mass medium of television, and splintered into literally thousands of shards of special-interest radio stations. We have seen the great mass magazines such as *Life, Look, Collier's,* and *The Saturday Evening Post* fall before the onward rush of thousands of special-interest magazines — Gulliver tied down and made helpless by a swarm of pygmies.

Today network television is threatened by the continued fragmentation of its audience, steadily being nibbled away by cable TV, videocassette rental, and coming up fast on the outside rail, pay-per-view movies.

Perhaps some form of network TV as a mass medium will still be here by the year 2000. But as their audiences shrink, the networks must raise their rates to maintain their quality of service (as they have been doing) or even, some day, cut their rates and cheapen their product.

It is not exactly a win-win situation. If they continue to increase their rates faster than the rate of inflation, media alternatives competing for advertising dollars become more tempting. But if they cut rates and cheapen product, this also makes competing media buys more attractive.

Meanwhile, network advertisers will feel the economic pressure to get more for their money, to make their television advertising do double duty — not only to build image and increase awareness, but to get responses to feed their databases with the names, addresses, and other data about the special community of people within the viewing audience who are their true prospects.

In Chapter Ten, we will look at the emergence of what we have termed Direct Mass Marketing — using the mass media to go fishing for prospects, then pulling them out of the "ocean" with an offer which makes it possible to identify them by name and address and cultivate them further.

2. RUN A NICHE-MARKET MESSAGE
IN NICHE-MARKET MEDIA

This, too, is nothing new, but it is a trend which is accelerating with breathtaking swiftness. Today, in addition to some 12,000 magazines, mostly for special interests, there are exotic new kinds of media such as gymboards in over 1,000 schools, sponsored music videos on videocassette for showing in campus cafeterias and student lounges, Whittle Communications' magazines for doctors' waiting rooms and advertiser-sponsored books, and so on.

There are radio stations and television programs that approximately match the psychographic profile of your ideal prospect. Campbell's Soup claims to have discovered that "Search for Tomorrow" fans buy 27% more spaghetti sauce than average but 22% less V-8 juice. [2]

A comprehensive survey of these targeted media should also include rentable direct-mail lists, which can put you in direct contact with individuals in literally thousands of different "communities" of interest, ranging all the way through the alphabet from Accountants and Aerobic Exercise Video Buyers to Zen Students and Zoo-keepers.

An ingenious example of using the pinpoint targeting capability of direct-mail list rental was provided by a promotion designed by Lipton Communications Group for Andrew Jergens Co. The aim was to introduce and promote their new product, Actibath carbonated bath tablets, which produces a carbonated effect similar to the hot springs found at health spas. So they sent a clever mailing aimed directly at 6,400 female health-spa enthusiasts whose names appeared on spa catalog and spa vacation lists. Inside the mailing, there was a 50¢ discount coupon, a selling letter, a free sample, and a bathroom door hanger that says, "Leave me alone. I'm at the Spa. Actibath."[3] What a refreshing improvement over the usual mass marketing promotion broadcast to the whole wide world, including to people who don't even know what a spa is.

Now the magazine publishing industry is poised on the threshhold of an extraordinary new era in printed communication — the age of the customized magazine. In such a magazine, you can not only buy the slice of circulation that contains just the segment you want, you can personalize your message to those subscribers by name and the reader's individual interests.

The magazine that led the way was *Farm Journal.* Born in 1877, the magazine continued to grow until by the 1940's it had become *The Saturday Evening Post* of farming, with 3.2 million circulation. Then came television, with devastating effect on advertising sales. Large general advertisers like General Motors and Westinghouse decided it was cheaper to sell their products on television than in a general-interest farm magazine.

Farm Journal realized that the only way it could survive was to serve serious farmers exclusively and do a better job of it. In 1958 they bit the bullet and weeded out subscribers who were not serious farmers, even refunding their subscription payments. Based on intensive subscriber research, they developed special sections on hogs, cattle, or soy beans to compete with more narrow-focus farm magazines. Because farmers don't have much time, they tried to make each issue as sharply focused as possible. But it still meant sending out a magazine with a soy-bean article to a farmer who was raising hogs and couldn't care less about increasing soy-bean yields.

Then in 1982 came the big breakthrough.

R.R. Donnelley & Sons developed a method of computer-collated binding — they call it Selectronic Binding — that enabled *Farm Journal* to put together customized contents to match each of its 825,000 readers' special farming needs and interests, based on information gathered in periodic telephone surveys.

Now each issue of *Farm Journal* comes out in 2,000 to 3,000 different versions — the record so far is 8,896 different versions of a single issue. [4] And whenever the advertiser chooses, the advertising is matched to the customized editorial content and the individual subscriber profile. So makers of hog-farm equipment and supplies can talk just to hog farmers, with no waste circulation.

Soon *Games, American Baby,* and *Modern Maturity* followed with their own experiments with selective binding, though not on anywhere near as ambitious and daring a scale as *Farm Journal.* *American Baby*'s 1.1 million readers can be divided into new parents and parents-soon-to-be (including the expected date of birth), based on information provided by new subscribers. Gerber's has run different personalized advertising messages in *American Baby* for mothers of two-to-three-month old infants and mothers whose babies are now three-to-four-months old, with the appropriate product for each age group featured.

Then, at the beginning of the 90's, Time Warner jumped into selective binding and imaging with both feet, offering advertisers a chance to insert and personalize ads that reach only certain selected subscribers to *Time, Sports Illustrated, People,* and *Money.*

Right on press, computer-driven technology can select just those ads to be seen by specified individual subscribers with desirable characteristics, such as high-income senior citizens or mail-order buyers or people who have moved recently. And with selective ink-jet imaging, the advertisers can alter the on-page copy to reflect the information about the reader available in the Time Warner subscriber database.

Naturally there is a premium. But if one of those groups is your target audience, it is better to pay a little more per thousand readers and buy an ounce of pure gold, rather than paying less per thousand readers and getting a ton of ore.

On January 15, 1990, subscribers to *Time* were surprised to find a bound-in card inviting the reader by name to test-drive a new Isuzu and providing the address of the nearest Isuzu dealer location. In addition, two million newsstand copies, which obviously could not be personalized by the reader's name, nonetheless did list the nearest dealer based on matching the zip codes of Isuzu dealers and newsstands.

Joanne Lipman, writing in *The Wall Street Journal* about this historic turn in advertising, reported that Isuzu first tested the personalized ad a few months earlier in 400,000 copies in the Boston area. At the Auto West dealership in Westwood, a Boston suburb, about 40 people brought in the personalized card and took a test drive, according to Alexis Breese, office manager. "At least eight bought cars, and several other sales are pending."

At another dealer in Massachusetts, ten cardholders came in during the first week, and four of them bought cars. "This promotion really worked," said Bob Scena, the owner, "I think they should do it a lot more." [5]

One month after Isuzu's January insertion in *Time*, Chrysler followed with their own personalized card insert and in March it was Volkswagen's turn.

Bruce Judson, director of marketing for the Time Warner Company, told us, "The future of marketing will be more and more characterized by the ability to create a relationship with your customer. The magazine can become the primary vehicle for making this happen."

Reportedly Time Warner spent two years assembling the equipment and gaining the database management expertise needed to bring a new era of personalized advertising to fruition.

The next step could be to go beyond ad customization and ad personalization, and to start customizing the editorial content for the reader as well. Further down the road, *Time* has hinted, lies at least the possibility of creating a customized magazine which would be part *Time*, part *Sports Illustrated*, part *People*, part *Money*, and part *Entertainment Weekly*. In conversations with *Time* magazine management, we heard over and over that the move to selective binding and selective imaging was a decision taken at the highest corporate level in order to position Time Warner publications as leaders in the new era of Individualized Marketing.

Thorough customization and personalization of magazines requires costly research and development and a fairly large general circulation rate base.

Many smaller special-interest magazines may argue that they are already specialized and targeted sharply enough. But the *Time* move is handwriting on the wall in magazine publishing, one great step toward treating each subscriber as individual and special.

Time Warner has put up big bucks to be ready to meet what they see as a shift to a more personalized form of marketing in the 90's. And they have put pressure on other major magazines to follow suit.

3. FIND YOUR NICHE MARKET WITHIN A PUBLIC DATABASE SERVICE

In the late 70's and early 80's, a big step forward in targeting was the manipulation of census and other data to group all the U.S. households in 36,000 selectable zip zones and 206,000 carrier routes by type of neighborhood. Database services sprang up to offer this new capability to direct-mail users.

Today this technology has been refined even further. Equifax's MicroVision system can now slice census-block groups even finer, by dividing America into 19 million ZIP+4 residential neighborhoods, each containing only 12 to 15 households. [6]

But this system can only make certain assumptions about individuals within a neighborhood based on the averaged profile of all the households in that type of neighborhood.

Then in the late 80's we saw an even more important development, the emergence of giant marketing databases crammed with detailed profiles of American consumers and households by name and address and available to advertisers. Companies like R.L. Polk, Computerized Marketing Technologies, CCX Network, May & Speh, Donnelley Marketing, TRW, Demographic Systems, Equifax, and National Demographics and Lifestyles began to combine demographic data, credit data, and public records like automobile registrations with consumer answers to detailed questionnaires about product usage, interests, and lifestyle.

From all this they have been able to construct and offer to advertisers computer databases containing impressively specific profiles of the consumers in millions of households. This means that advertisers can now send direct mail to millions of sharply defined prospects targeted with pinpoint precision.

For instance, Equifax's Consumer Marketing Database contains nearly 100 million consumers, with as many as 340 items of information about each of them, including age, marital status, history of moves, credit card activity, buying activity, number and type of credit relationships and bankruptcies, liens, and other public records. Infobase boasts files on 179 million individual consumers, with up to 160 different data elements on each.

Porsche Cars North America has shown how this treasury of information can be used to zero in on ideal prospects. Its direct-marketing agency, Rapp Collins Marcoa, spent eight months and $250,000 narrowing down a universe of 80 million car-owning households to just 300,000 carefully screened, affluent prime prospects, who were then invited by mail to take a test drive. The first step in this elimination process was to reduce the list to 15 million households by keeping only names and addresses matching a composite of recent Porsche buyers. Then demographic, psychographic, and lifestyle attributes were used to screen the list further, bringing it down to two million names. These were then ranked in order of desirability, and the top 300,000 selected for the mailing. Porsche expected the program to help sell 1,200 cars, about one-tenth of its projected volume for the year.

This example also demonstrates how the information in public databases can be used to develop one's own proprietary database. Porsche now has its own prime prospect database which can be viewed, updated, and used for customized correspondence at any time. [7]

Of course when it comes to more personal information about brand usage and lifestyles, these systems can't provide equally detailed information on every household because not everybody in America is willing to fill out and return a questionnaire — some of them can take as long as 15 or 20 minutes to complete! But still the numbers are impressive.

CMT's database contains more than 1,000 pieces of individual data on more than 25 million "promotionally-responsive" families, including what brands they use in various categories and whether they are heavy or light users. Here is a typical profile sketched in the company's promotion:

Name: Mary Anderson
Address: 100 Main Street, Anytown, CA 90001
Brand used: Brand A
Usage frequency: heavy
Status: married, home owner
Age: 35, spouse 40
Children: 1, age 7
Occupation: office worker

Interests: sailing, gourmet foods
Affluence: microwave, VCR, computer

Periodically, each household within the database receives a different package of coupons in the company's direct mail co-op, Select and Save, customized according to its individual profile. This means, according to a company spokesman, that an advertiser "can send dog food coupons only to dog owners, nasal spray coupons only to that 18% of the population that suffers from sinus problems, and a Glenlivet scotch promotion only to drinkers of Cutty or Dewar's."

Brand advertisers can use one couponing strategy for current users, another for competitive users, a third offer for heavy users, a fourth for light users, and so on. Or they can heavy up in geographical areas where dealers need a boost.

Then since each coupon has its own individual household code number, through CRT's Performance Tracking System the advertiser can determine redemption by audience segment and evaluate individual household responsiveness. Certain households can be selected for a follow-up mailing based on how they performed the first time.

Of course the cost per thousand is much greater than it would be for steam-rollering the entire market with a Sunday newspaper fsi. But the redemption rate is three to four times as much and the wastefulness of rewarding current users can be controlled or eliminated as the advertiser pleases.

4. ASSEMBLE AND COMMUNICATE WITH YOUR OWN NICHE MARKET DATABASE

Your company can assemble its own database from responses to your advertising and sales promotion offers — product warranty names — personal data bits gleaned from questionnaires included in your advertising and sales promotion or with your product warranty literature — information gained from phone interviews with people who respond to an offer by calling your toll-free number — and information from outside lists and databases. From this database the computer can then identify and select niche markets as desired, such as blue-collar housewives or Sunbelt senior citizens,

As many companies are ruefully discovering, an unplanned, undifferentiated in-house database, accumulated as a by-product of other efforts, must be extremely large in order to be able to select useful niche markets out of it. What good is it to you as a national advertiser to select from your database those people suspected to be elderly overweight joggers if the total comes only to 500 individuals?

But a special-purpose database, planned from the beginning to target a clearly defined niche market, can be relatively small and still be highly productive. For many kinds of products and services, it represents the new frontier of marketing.

And a big advantage of the in-house database, as opposed to a public database, is that you own it, you can expand it, refine it, enhance it, update it, constantly add to it, and use it as often as you like.

As we discussed in Chapter Three, database services can overlay a great deal of additional outside information onto the record of each individual in your file.

For example, Infobase Services maintains a multi-source database of all households with discretionary income. It combines the resources of R.L. Polk, Lifestyle Selector, Database America, and Smart Names. Infobase can match names in your file with names in files of theirs that contain a great many details about each individual — hobbies and interests, number and ages of household residents, income range, occupation, value of car(s), marital status, credit cards, whether mail-responsive, kinds of charitable or political donations, and so on.

Overlaying this kind of information onto the individual prospect or customer files in your own database obviously can increase its value and usefulness greatly. To help pay for the cost, you can even rent it out to non-competing advertisers.

May & Speh Direct offers not only database enhancement services but also a database management system to guide companies in establishing and using an in-house database and tracking the results.

Companies like Seagrams, General Foods, Marriott, General Mills, Quaker Oats, Amana, Sprint, MCI, Bristol-Myers — in fact, probably more than half of the companies selling consumer goods and services — are now building their own proprietary databases. And the new frontier of marketing lies in figuring out creative and profitable ways to make use of this important new asset.

Sears Merchandise Group, which operates the company's network of retail stores, has been engaged in constructing a massive retail-customer database covering about 30 million households, roughly a third of all households in the U.S. (This system is apparently kept separate from the Sears Direct Response Group database, which covers some 24 million shop-at-home customers who get nearly two billion direct mail pieces a year. It is possible that attempting to combine the two would present a horrendous problem and not serve a sufficiently useful purpose.)

The Sears retail system can now link the customer name and address file with transactional data captured when a customer buys in a Sears store and charges the purchase with a Sears or Discover credit card.

"The retail store customer's product needs have become increasingly more specialized," says Ron Meyers, manager of marketing services. *"We found that 90% of the advertising reaching our customers was discarded because it didn't apply to their interests."* [Italics ours]

Meyers indicated that Sears believes the future of successful retailing lies in targeting specific niches with specific offers. He said the project's ultimate objective is to divide Sears customers into household groups sharing common traits. Then meaningful advertising programs can be tailored to each group's demographics and lifestyle.

"The system produces a well-defined picture of who the customers are for any of our vertical businesses (automotive, fashion, bed and bath, etc.), the departments within those businesses, and the product lines within those departments."

He said the system was helping them get incremental sales by a process we refer to elsewhere in this book as "cloning" — noting the characteristics of a group within the database on whom a promotion works best and then finding more people who have that group's characteristics and also promoting to them.

The database tells Sears the percentage of their customers who are shopping, the average dollars they are spending, and the average number of shopping trips they are making. By analyzing this data and obtaining reports by geography and types of merchandise, the company can monitor the business with a new precision and track important changes in shopping dynamics.

They can use the database to test media — to determine which worked better, a postcard mailing or a 36-page flyer. [8]

Sears took some hard knocks from critics when their dramatic switch to "everyday low prices" in 1989 failed to produce the expected reversal of declining retail sales. But with the wheeling up of this powerful new weapon, you can expect the company to move toward regaining its title as retailing champion of America.

Of course, the granddaddy of all the company-owned niche-marketing database was surely the Frequent Flyer programs of the airlines, beginning with the American Airlines AAdvantage Program, as we discussed in Chapter Three. The niche in the market they pursued was the business traveller who made up only 20% of all passengers but was yielding 80% of the sales volume.

Soon their competitors jumped in, of course, and eventually neutralized their advantage.

Along the way, the airlines began to discover and cater to even smaller niches within the niche market of frequent flyers.

For instance, if Pan Am observed or learned that certain frequent flyers loved to ski or often traveled to ski resorts, the next WorldPass communication sent to those members might include information on ski packages to Chile, Austria, and other ski resort areas.[9] And Delta Airlines developed a club for families who fly with their kids.

From all this and more, it is clear that an increasing number of advertisers either will not or cannot any longer devote their entire marketing budgets to "steam-rolling" the market.

Whether by fishing prospects out of the mass media audience with a direct-response solicitation — reaching them through media with a richer concentration of prospects — sending direct mail to precisely profiled households in a public database — or building and segmenting a proprietary database — advertisers are turning away from talking to the public at large. They are turning toward private, personal communication with each member of the groups representing their best prospects and customers.

WOOING MARKET NICHES BY CHANGING THE PRODUCT

You can change the message and change the media to reach the market niche for your special product or service. Or you can take the next step and reshape the product or service itself to suit the special needs of an important niche in your market.

Recently Northwest Airlines seemed to be moving toward taking that next logical step, under the leadership of Albert Checchi and Frederic V. Malek.

As executives of the Marriott Corporation in the early 80's, they were widely credited for their role in increasing the company's profit.

Through customer surveys and interviews, they developed the "Marriott formula" of different hotels for different types of business travelers.

They found that some travelers just wanted a good night's sleep and a quick breakfast. Some wanted economy. Some wanted lavish entertaining facilities for colleagues and guests. Some wanted a home away from home.

So the Marriott chain developed five different kinds of hotels: the Courtyard for the average business traveler; Residence Inns, with suites for long-term guests; Fairfield Inns, for the budget-minded traveler; Suites by Marriott, for travelers who like to invite guests up to their living room; and Marriott Hotels, for those who demand full-service luxury hotel attention. Their competitors were doing the same: Holiday Corporation now markets six different product lines and Quality Inns has five "brands."

To satisfy the most common demands of business guests, Marriott's Courtyards installed better mattresses, quieter air-conditioning, automatic check-out, and guaranteed delivery of breakfast in five minutes.

Then in July of 1989, Checchi led an investor group that took over Northwest Airlines. He moved in as CEO and brought with him Fred Malek as president. Together they began to study how the "Marriott formula" might be applied to the airlines industry.

As they had done at Marriott, they began customer surveys to determine the different kinds of travelers and what their needs were.

With that information, they then planned to lay out different sections of the passenger cabin for different groups — such as one section for people who just want to work in a quiet, well-lighted area, another section for people who would like to be entertained with television and hi-fi, and so on.

"As the airline industry moves beyond the immediate adjustment that it had to make after deregulation, you're going to see the same kind of segmentation of travelers that we saw in the hotel industry," said Checchi. "You are going to see a different kind of physical configuration of the aircraft with different kinds of services being provided." [10]

When Checchi and Malek were at Marriott, the hotel chain conducted a very vigorous and innovative frequent-guest program. By 1986 the company had enrolled over a million members and was mailing out more than five million pieces of mail per year to the membership.[11] It seems highly probable that if the two men are able to apply the "Marriott formula" to the configuration of the aircraft, they will also follow the "Marriott formula" of constructing large computer communities of each segment of their airlines market and cultivating the customers in it continuously.

Within the large all-inclusive proprietary database, there are many hidden smaller markets to be ferreted out by the power of the computer to search, match, and select.

These hidden niche markets can be served by reselling them with customized messages — by selling them other suitable products and services that happen to be available — by creating new products and services to answer their special needs — or by reshaping the existing product to offer it in different forms or with extra benefits at extra cost.

NICHE MARKETING BY GAMBLING CASINOS

One of the most surprising yet logical places for sophisticated marketing to niche markets within a house database that we have observed is in the $7 billion gambling casino industry. Faced with fierce competition in a crowded industry, the smartest casinos are blazing new trails in building a database and using it for niche marketing. In exchange for filling out detailed questionnaires, guests are given discounts on service or the chance to win a cash prize

"In these questionnaires, they want to know everything — your age, how often you come to gamble, what you play, where you like to stay, how you travel to the casino, what your budget is," says Marvin Roffman, a casino-industry analyst at Janney Montgomery Scott. "They even want to know about your cars, pets, and favorite sports." In addition some casinos can track players' activity by encouraging them to use magnetic-strip plastic cards that register their plays, and this information too is fed into the database.

Then the casino can devise specific promotions for different customer segments within the database. For example, if you are a slot-machine or blackjack player, you may receive an invitation to a slot or blackjack tournament. If you are a fan of boxing or of Frank Sinatra, you'll be notified when there's going to be an event that you'll love. If you're a big spender, you may receive a birthday card (just so you'll know they really care).

The databases also tell the casinos where their customers come from and how they travel. By analyzing which zip zones have the most customers, the casino can get a better fix on where advertising should be concentrated and where bus service needs beefing up.

Now casinos are working on using their databases to reach beyond the 10% of their customers who are the high rollers and to identify, cultivate, and build casino-specific loyalty in a much larger market niche, the middle-market recreational gambler.[12]

HOW BARNES & NOBLE CUTS FINE DATABASE SLICES

Barnes & Noble, the large bookstore chain, has shown how finely a customer database can be sliced. Their database segmentation system was developed for their direct-order marketing division, but its principles could be adapted to brand manufacturer, service organization, or retailer databases.

The 750,000-name database was converted first from a 300-

byte fixed record to a 900-byte record, then to a variable format which reserves 400 bytes for name, address, and demographic data, and allows an unlimited number of bytes for further purchase history and segmentation analysis. This means that some segments in the file have as little as a few hundred people in them. A typical cell might be defined as "a travel product space ad multibuyer from the first half of 1986 who has purchased three times to date at $15 or more on the last order," a description which 1,400 customers fit. [13]

Doing special promotions to such finely sliced niches is not only possible, it is the future of marketing. And it is a game that anybody can play.

The small business may even have an advantage over the lumbering giants. For in many large companies, a promotion proposal may take months to work its way through the committee approval system. If there are dozens or hundreds of minor promotions in the works, they can clog the pipeline. The small business owner, on the other hand, can get an idea this week for a special promotion to a customer database segment, then use desktop publishing and personal-computer addressing to be in the mail next week.

The proliferation of new products and services, each appealing to its own niche market, is a basic trend of the 70's and 80's that is continuing into the 90's. Selling to these niche markets calls for a complete turnaround in marketing thinking from the mass media techniques of the past. It has been said that all you need to know to be successful in retailing is Location! Location! Location! What you will need to know and pay attention to in the 90's is Database! Database! Database!

Fine-tuning individualized messages to identified, profiled prospects and customers is in. "Steam-rollering" the market is out. By concentrating on one niche market after another and then adding the results together, tomorrow's MaxiMarketers will get to the big numbers with a cost-effectiveness beyond the reach of what have become wasteful mass marketing practices.

IDEA-STARTERS FOR PROFITING FROM TURNAROUND TREND No. 3.

MANUFACTURER:
✔ *How many promising market segments for your product — newlyweds, empty nesters, new movers, frequent travelers, single women, new parents, newly promoted executives, etc. — can you think of?*

✔ How could your product or service be modified or what benefit could be added to make one or more of these niches your private domain?

✔ Have you consulted a list broker about database enhancement overlays which could add details to individual files in your prospect/customer database and extract the most promising and useful segments from it?

✔ What kind of direct mail offers could you devise for each of these segments with built-in cost-effectiveness yardsticks?

✔ How might you test altering or customizing your core product or service to appeal to different segments of your database?

✔ Do you have a customer information questionnaire in your product package? And if so, are you giving buyers enough incentive to fill it out and return it?

✔ Have you spoken to a representative from Time or Newsweek about how you might experiment with preparing personalized advertising aimed at your special niche market and buying only the subscribers you want?

RETAILER OR SERVICE ESTABLISHMENT:

✔ (If your in-house database is large enough), how might you use computer overlays of outside lists to reveal the demographic and psychographic profiles of the best customers in the database?

✔ Have you tried using overlays to identify, extract, and mail to your best prospects out of phone directory lists in your trading area?

✔ Could you devise an offer to appeal to a specific promising segment of your local area market, and use the responses to build a special database subgroup?

6 From Ad Impressions Counted to New Customers Won

_Limits and failures of traditional copy research yardsticks.
...Lee Jeans and Burger King: "operation success but
patient died"...the growing acceptance of the Lifetime
Customer Value concept...Finding the right
offensive-defensive mix...Campbell's Soup and LTV...Tom
Peters' $180,000 forehead... Importance of thinking Ad
Cost per Incremental Sale...When "expensive" is a
bargain...Applying past and future thinking to Oldsmobile_

How much advertising is enough? Is it paying for itself? And how do you decide?

In Chapter Four we discussed how the content of advertising is changing due to the demand for responses and their impact on creativity. In this chapter, we want to look at how the measurement of advertising effect is changing.

In the early days, measuring the effect of advertising was pretty much seat-of-the-pants. "We ran a big ad on Sunday, and the store was jammed on Monday."

Then as advertising grew and planning became more advanced, many advertisers would arbitrarily budget a percentage of the previous year's sales, say 5%, for advertising. Thus as sales increased, so did the advertising budget. This meant, in effect, that they advertised because they made sales, not that they made sales because they advertised.

Advertising research has tended over the years to measure

the effect of the advertising on the audience rather than on sales. Agency research departments would measure things like basal skin response, brain waves, eye movements, pupil dilation, unaided and aided recall, awareness of the brand, changes of attitude toward the brand, expressions of buying intention. (One novel research technique involved putting panelists on stationary bicycles; the faster they pedalled while looking at an ad, the better they were supposed to like it.)

Of course efforts are often made by the largest advertisers to try a new campaign in regional test markets before rolling it out. But this is a costly, time-consuming procedure and may still not answer the ultimate question, "How much is enough to create profitable sales?" or "How much can we afford?"

AGENCY PRESIDENT CONFESSES RESEARCH LIMITS

As president of Grey Advertising, Edward H. Meyer recently gave an insightful talk in which he recalled wryly the limitations of agency research in its glory days.

> The advertising agency business had its own bout with technological blindness. During the golden age of research, those were the days when Nielsen audience numbers and copy test scores were new and fascinating.
>
> Just imagine it, there we were, pretty much groping along on instincts and sales reports, when the Nielsen people walked in and told us precisely what percentage of new mothers in Cleveland had seen our baby powder commercial the night before. Well! Talk about excitement. The mind reeled. All of a sudden, we could be absolutely certain our commercials were being seen by the right audiences. And not only that. Another new tool, the copy test was telling us whether consumers understood our message. Outstanding.
>
> There was just one missing ingredient. *Neither measurement could tell us whether consumers gave a damn about what we said. Nor could they tell us how to make consumers care about what we said.* [Italics ours.]

Yet many advertisers and their agencies continued to cling, and still do, to measuring and treasuring the cost of "retained impressions."

It is astonishing how much trade press coverage and how many awards are given to campaigns without regard to measured sales effect. Either a campaign is admired for its "creativity," or if it is a sales promotion campaign, it may be saluted for the number of "gross impressions" it has achieved through advertising, promotion, and publicity. Thus the Lever Brothers "Singing in the Tub" on-air radio competition in 30 markets, admittedly a very imaginative promotion, was hailed in *Adweek's Marketing Week* for gaining 87 million gross impressions — no mention of whether the Lever brands scored any permanent marketing gains. [1]

If you get enough people to see and hear your name per advertising dollar spent, then the advertising must be a success, right?

Not necessarily.

LEE JEANS: "OPERATION SUCCESS, PATIENT DIED"

Consider the rather startling statement made by an executive of the advertising agency for Lee Jeans a few years back.

"Any advertising management," he declared," has an obligation to ask, 'What are we getting for our money?' Efficiency is one measure. Market performance is another."

Why is this startling? Because in the story which followed, it was revealed that the agency's Lee Jeans campaign that same year *had succeeded in "efficiency" but failed in market performance.*

According to *Adweek*, the campaign "scored among the most efficient of all TV campaigns last year, at a cost of $4.43 per thousand retained impressions...Lee took honors in a segment where CPM was generally low [intended meaning, "poor"]. Levi's CPM for retained impressions was $7.47. Wrangler came in at $9.16, and Chic spent $11.90."

However, the story goes on to say, "the operation was a success but the patient died." Lee's sales during the year actually slipped 12%, and its market share, which had been growing 1% to 2% a year since 1981, remained flat. And Lee moved its account to a new agency. [2]

There appear to have been a couple of glaring fallacies in the idea of using the concept of "retained impressions" as a measurement of the Lee campaign's advertising efficiency.

One is that the yardstick presumably measured the impressions made on the entire viewing public rather than on the true jeans prospects within that larger group.

And the other is that retained advertising impressions, even on prospects, don't necessarily translate into sales.

SOMETIMES AWARENESS GAINS AS SALES DECLINE

Measuring public "awareness" of their product or claim and "share of mind" has been another favorite yardstick of big advertisers and their agencies. Thus in April of 1988 Burger King announced proudly that its two-months-old "We do it like you do it" campaign had gained four percentage points in top-of-mind awareness and was winning the awareness battle. Burger King said its surveys had revealed heightened awareness of flame-broiling as the company's competitive advantage and that 54% of adult fast-food hamburger patrons associated the slogan with Burger King. "If we know that more than half of the TV viewers can associate the slogan with the product in just 30 days, then we have scored an important victory," proclaimed an executive of Burger King's agency at the time.

Unfortunately, during the first month of the campaign sales sank 3.5% lower than they had been in the same period a year earlier . It was an even greater monthly decline than in the two months before the campaign began. Meanwhile McDonald's was showing sales gains during the same period.[3] And Burger King fired the agency that had scored such an "important victory."

Then came Burger King's next campaign, its ninth in 13 years. They spent $150 million making the public aware that "Sometimes you just gotta break the rules." The public was made aware of it all right, but instead of helping sales, it actually caused problems. Said one franchise operator: "Some people believe [it means] they can get anything they want, and for free."*

Yet with that big an advertising budget, you'd better believe that a hefty sum must have been spent on advance market research which assured management, "No problem. This time we're really going to win the battle against McDonald's for share of mind."

Chevrolet's "Heartbeat of America" campaign has scored No. 3 in *Adweek's* "America's Favorite Print Campaigns." But Chevrolet's share of the American car market declined from about 15%, when the campaign began, to only 13.6% after it had been running for three years.[4]

And then there was Joe Isuzu. In Chapter One we pointed out how despite the widespread public awareness of Joe and his amusing lies, sale of Isuzu cars actually declined. It was almost an exact replay of the case 80 years earlier of the wild public popularity of the advertising character Sunny Jim and the failure of the campaign to sell Force cereal.

When will they ever learn?

Not quite yet. The battle for retained impressions and share of mind is still treated as big news in the advertising trade press.

Adwatch, a joint project of *Advertising Age* and the Gallup

---

* For some good news about Burger King, you will read in Chapter 8 about their first foray into relationship marketing, with what seems to be a startling difference on results compared to all the efforts at building share of mind.

Organization, regularly questions a national sample of one thousand adults about which recent advertising campaigns first come to mind in various categories, and the winners are given a big play in *Advertising Age.*

Adweek's Annual Effectiveness Ratings employs similar research by Opinion Research Corporation, but then correlates the retained impressions score for each brand with its brand advertising expenditure to calculate for each brand an "EQ" or Efficiency Quotient — the cost of producing 1,000 retained impressions in the minds of consumers. A recent issue of *Adweek's Marketing Week* devoted eleven pages to summarizing the results.

We are not saying that creating and retaining share of mind has no value. In many product categories, it probably does an important job in helping to hang on to and reinforce the loyalty of existing customers, although it's hard to prove. But as a way of winning and keeping new customers, the truth is that increasing top-of-mind awareness has proven to be woefully unreliable. And over-emphasis of the importance of "victories" in this struggle can distract marketers from what is really important.

The real advertising challenge is not to maximize retained impressions. It is not even to increase sales during the current season — sales promotion has demonstrated it can do that easily, though often at the expense of profitability.

The real challenge is to win the most and best customers over the long haul. And that calls for a new way to measure the effectiveness of advertising expenditure, a method which will in turn help determine that expenditure. There is such a method, and it is now receiving increasing attention. It comes from the world of Direct-Order Marketing.

BORROWING A FINANCIAL MEASUREMENT CONCEPT FROM DIRECT MARKETING

Companies that market their products or services directly to the public, and get orders back by mail or phone (or new communications channels such as fax and computer), are spared this distressing vagueness in advertising measurement.

They can tabulate precisely not only the immediate sales resulting from each dollar of advertising expenditure, but also the long-range profit.

Before the computer, they had to make these computations laboriously with a calculator, a pencil, and a stack of index cards.

Today, with every advertising expenditure and every customer payment fed into the computer, they can determine the Advertising Cost per Response from each source — the Advertising Cost per Initial Sale — the number of subsequent sales to the same individual — and the total long-range profit contribution or *LifeTime Value* (LTV) per customer.

The LifeTime Value is calculated simply by multiplying the margin or markup per unit sale (the difference between the cost of producing the unit, including overhead, and the income received from its sale) by the number of likely averaged sales per customer within a reasonable time frame. The length of time depends on the customer attrition curve.

This calculation in turn permits Direct-Order Marketers to establish an Allowable Advertising Cost Per Order. Or, to put it another way, out of the total revenue expected from keeping an average new customer supplied for the selected period of time, after subtracting the cost of the merchandise and your usual amount for overhead and profit, how much is left over to invest in the advertising which will make it happen?

Along with other Direct-Order Marketing tools that the Maxi-Marketing concept brings to retail-distributed products and services, this method of measurement has significant potential application outside of the field of Direct-Order Marketing.

What we are talking about here is more than just another method of measurement. It is the start of a complete turnaround in attitude concerning accountability for many advertisers of retail-distributed products.

What we will see during the 90's is a turning away from counting ad impressions and toward counting customers. The tools and techniques to make this possible are already partially developed. Soon the remaining pieces will fall into place.

THE SHARE POINTS YARDSTICK VS. LTV

Until now, most advertisers of branded products and services have tended to pursue one of two policies in evaluating the effectiveness of their advertising.

1. They launch a new campaign and immediately measure its effect on share of mind, rejoicing when it increases. Then six months later they look at sales to see if "the needle has moved."

No allowance is made for the LTV of each customer gained. That has seemed too much like "pie in the sky." And it would not impress the security analysts on Wall Street.

2. Or they doggedly stick with the same unresultful advertising month after month or even year after year, out of blind faith in

something called "cumulative effect."

We believe the leaders in The Great Marketing Turnaround will be those companies that take into account the concept of LTV. And for those who do, it will permit looking at advertising expenditures and media in a new light.

For instance, it will help justify marketing expenditures heretofore considered "too expensive" — private communications with identified prospects and new customers — as it becomes clear that the carefully forecast income from such individuals will more than pay for the cost of the communications within a reasonable time. In such a context, "retained impressions" becomes irrelevant.

ONE BUDGET FOR GAINING NEW CUSTOMERS, ANOTHER FOR KEEPING THE OLD?

In this new perspective on advertising expenditure, we suggest that most consumer goods marketers should plan two advertising budgets, or at least one that is divided into two parts.

One part of the budget would be devoted primarily to creating or maintaining public awareness of the virtues of your product, including conveying associative values, announcing improvements, or hammering home your U.S.P., as so much brand advertising has always done. This would help you hold on to the loyal customers you already have and favorably influence the awareness and attitude of potential new customers.

Despite the limitations of — and frequent incidence of failure in — such awareness advertising, as we have pointed out, there is some evidence that it is a valuable tool for retaining existing customers.

Martin Block, director of the graduate advertising division at Northwestern University's Medill School of Journalism, is one of a number of business academics who have been seeking to extract conclusions from "single-source data." *

He was reported to have found hints that (awareness) advertising works better on consumers who don't use a product category than on those who do.

Then when he focused on people who do use a product category — the group he chose was users of spaghetti sauce — he concluded that advertising was probably better at holding onto existing

* Single-source research data is provided by tracking what individual consumers watch on television, including commercials, electronically tracking what they buy at the supermarket, and then in effect combining the two sets of data to observe what effect the advertising for a particular brand had on the actual sales.

customers for the brand than at getting them to switch. "It's a better defensive tool than an offensive tool," he said. [5]

The other part of the budget would go on the offensive with a campaign primarily intended to attract, identify by name and address, cultivate, and win over new customers identified by name and address — either first-time users attracted to the product category or switchers from competitive brands.

DETERMINING THE RIGHT MIX

And how should the advertising funds then be divided up? How much should be set aside for the Awareness Advertising part of the budget before planning a Direct-Relationship Marketing campaign to be funded by the remainder?

It all depends on so many things, as every ad manager knows so well:

- whether your product costs 59¢ or $590
- how widely it is available at retail
- whether it is a casual impulse purchase or a carefully considered purchase
- whether it is a unique product or a parity product
- whether it is a brand-new brand or a mature brand in a declining market
- whether it has a 2% share of market or a 40% share
- whether the Customer LTV is $4, $400, or $4,000
- whether the competing brand uses advertising and promotion aggressively or conservatively

Some advertisers are successfully devoting all of their budgets to database-driven advertising and promotion, as we will see later on.

On the other hand, if you are dealing with a $1.99 product that people buy only a few times a year, then you might be better off with a 100% expenditure for awareness advertising.

But regardless of what portion seems advisable for pure awareness advertising, the rest of the budget, the second part, would be devoted to gaining, tracking, cultivating, and keeping identifiable new customers (and perhaps also retaining old customers, as in the case of frequent-buyer programs).

How? By designing database-driven advertising and promotion to get direct responses, and then deepening the advertising effect on those individuals who do respond by means of additional two-way communication.

Then the concepts of LTV and Allowable Advertising Cost per Sale can be brought into play. And they will make possible a degree of measurability which, as we have pointed out, is so often sadly lacking in pure awareness advertising.

The advertising cost per response can be measured.

The percentage of responders who convert to users can be measured.

How many new users remain loyal, for how long, can be measured with follow-up research. Or today, in the case of supermarket products, by tracking the purchase patterns by brand of customers who are enrolled in a shoppers' club and who present a magnetic-strip membership card when checking out.

Thus the LifeTime Value of each new customer can be measured, and assessed in light of the total advertising and follow-up cost.

CAMPBELL'S SOUP USING LTV THINKING

In 1989, Campbell's Soup appeared to be edging in this direction, in a rather startling turnaround from conventional marketing thinking.

Reported *Advertising Age:*

Campbell's traditionally defined soup purchasers as consumers who spent about $200 annually on the product, a level the company determined was too low to merit additional individualized marketing programs such as direct-response efforts.

But Campbell's has expanded its view, looking at consumers' soup purchases over a lifetime and making it cost-effective to allocate more marketing resources to these consumers.

Each of these 'core soup buyers' contributes $8 to $10 in profits annually to Campbell's bottom line [says Tony Adams, vp-market research]. 'Clearly, these are consumers we want to know. We can select [consumer] targets that are more worthwhile to spend higher cost per thousand levels against.'

Mr. Adams says vehicles such as network TV likely will be used 'only for new products to get awareness,' and will be supplemented by more individualized media such as direct mail and in-store efforts closer to the point of purchase.[5]

This provides a telling rebuttal to pre-turnaround marketers who insist they "can't afford" direct-mail contact with identified prospects and customers because it is "too expensive." (It costs a minimum of $250 for an advertiser to send a message by direct mail to one thousand people vs. around $5 to $7 via television or a Sunday newspaper free-standing insert.)

If you look, as Campbell's is doing, at the LTV of your customers, then you, like Campbell's, may find it "cost-effective to allocate more marketing resources to these consumers."

WHY THE NEED FOR LTV THINKING IS GROWING

How many other packaged goods manufacturers, as well as advertisers in other fields, are secretly planning a similar strategy? Based on published case histories and reports of intense database-building by a great many brand advertisers, it seems likely that there are — or soon will be — a rapidly increasing number. (A Donnelley Marketing survey published in 1988 indicated that 92% of all $1 billion+ companies already were building a consumer database or anticipated doing so.) However, we have a word of warning for these companies: unless you face squarely the issue of LTV, you may find yourself with a database "all dressed up and nowhere to go."

In the marketing of services, the importance of Customer LTV can be of enormous importance. There it bears a critical relationship not only to how much can be spent on advertising to obtain new customers but also how much can be spent on improving the service in order to keep the customers you have.

In *Thriving on Chaos*, Tom Peters points out, "When the Federal Express courier enters my office, she should see '$180,000' stamped on the forehead of our receptionist. My little twenty-five-person firm runs about a $1,500-a-month Fed Ex bill. Over ten years, that will add up to $180,000."

And, he points out, this is only the tip of the iceberg. If a delighted customer persuades just one potential customer of the value of the service, the regular customer's value doubles. "And that sign on my receptionist's forehead should now be read by the Fed Ex person as $360,000 rather than $180,000."[6]

THE MATH OF THE COST PER INCREMENTAL SALE

There is another vital consideration in considering the importance of Customer LTV and its effect on the Allowable Advertising Cost per Sale. It is the hidden cost of *incremental* sales — those additional sales you squeeze out with the last, most questionable dollars in your advertising budget.

If you increased your advertising and promotion budget by

10%, you would not automatically get a 10% increase in sales. In actuality, as you well know, your rate of increase in sales would likely be substantially less. Otherwise, the job of a marketing director would be quite simple — you could increase your sales by any percentage you desired simply by increasing your ad budget by the same percentage. But in the real world, you find that if you divide the cost of any additional Awareness Advertising by the number of additional sales it produces, the average cost of those incremental sales may be, let's say, four times as high as the overall average.

This same factor is at work even if you do not increase your annual budget. Hidden in your total budget are always certain advertising expenditures which are less productive than the overall average. These "last" dollars you spend are producing incremental sales at a far higher Advertising Cost per Sale. And failing to recognize this can keep you from spending those "last" dollars more effectively.

Suppose that last year your company sold 20 million product units at a retail price of $5, for a total volume of $100 million. And you spent 5% of sales revenue, or $5 million, on advertising. Your average Advertising Cost per Sales was 25¢. But your advertising cost per *incremental* sale might have been as high as $1.00.

Now suppose you test a Direct-Relationship Marketing campaign with trackable results, and you find that the average cost per resulting sale is not 25¢ but 50¢. That means the campaign is a failure, right? No, only if you compare the result with your average Advertising Cost per Sale. If you compare it with the incremental cost of $1.00 that you might have to pay to score an equal gain with your usual advertising, you might find that your Direct-Relationship Marketing test is actually a howling success.

This is the arithmetic of the Cost per Incremental Sale that we suspect many advertisers overlook. If you are not mindful of it, you run the risk of rejecting an opportunity to spend the final 10% or 20% of your ad budget in the most cost-effective way. The cost of interactive direct communication with identified prospects and customers may make it seem "expensive." But it may actually be a bargain compared to squeezing out more sales by simply pouring on more Awareness Advertising or the usual short-term promotion.

APPLYING INCREMENTAL SALE COST LOGIC TO AUTOS

A savvy free-lance consultant named Robert Roderick, working with executives of Patlis Advertising, once showed how this might work in automobile marketing, in a marketing proposal they made to Oldsmobile.

For many years, Oldsmobile enjoyed the third-highest customer loyalty rates in the U.S. auto market. An estimated 48% of Olds customers would buy another Olds when it came time for a new car.

But in 1986 they found that their retention rate had been slipping and they invited proposals from direct-marketing experts.

Patlis learned that in 1984 Olds had spent more than $42 million on advertising to sell one million cars. Sales promotion and other merchandising activities accounted for another $10 to $15 million.

This meant that the company's advertising and promotion cost per sale was $50 to $60.

Since their average profit per car sold was $2,000, why not simply spend more per car on advertising and promotion?

The answer, based on the hypothetical example that we gave previously, is that they undoubtedly were already spending much more per sale than $50 or $60 to push out the last few percent of cars sold. Not just $50 or $60 per car. Instead, maybe as much as $1,000 per car, cutting into the profit margin. Otherwise, no problem. Olds could just double the advertising and promotion expenditure, and the sales would double accordingly.

But the Patlis proposal argued that through offering various incentives such as sweepstakes, premiums, and rebates, a direct-mail campaign to four million previous buyers of Oldsmobile could bring as many as 30% of them into the dealer showrooms to take a look at the new Olds.

Not counting customers who would have bought a new Olds anyway, Roderick estimated that a series of such mailings would generate nearly one million additional showroom visits.

If just one person out of a hundred of these incremental showroom visitors actually purchased an Olds, it would add up to 10,000 additional sales. Multiplying this by the average profit per car results in an additional profit contribution of $20 million, at an estimated direct-mail campaign cost of $11 million, for a net gain of $9 million.

That was the conservative estimate. On the optimistic side, the additional showroom visits might result in a 4% conversion to sales, for an additional $80 million in profit minus the direct-mail campaign cost.

Note that the advertising cost of cars sold via the Patlis proposal might have been $110, roughly double the average Advertising Cost per Sale. But that would presumably have still been far less than what would possibly be the $1,000 Incremental Cost per Sale achieved via additional mass advertising.

THE DUBIOUS $30 MILLION OLDS/MCDONALD'S TIE-IN

Contrast this proposal with the lavish cross-promotion campaign that Olds did with McDonald's from April 1 to June 9 in 1988. Visitors to McDonald's could obtain a key giving them a chance to win one of hundreds of free Olds Cutlass Supremes. Visitors to an Olds dealer could obtain a Big Mac discount coupon. At a cost to Oldsmobile of $30 million, the campaign was said to have drawn some 750,000 to Olds showrooms.

But what was the result? Not much, according to a story in *Adweek's Marketing Week:*

> On a recent visit to a New York City dealership, this scene was witnessed: A woman walked into the showroom. A salesman reached into a drawer, handed her a chance card to win a new car, and she walked out. No words were exchanged. "She's come in here every day since the promotion started. I could set my watch by her... that's the kind of people it has attracted," said the dealer.
>
> An Ohio dealer said most of the people coming into the showroom for game cards couldn't even afford to buy an Oldsmobile. "It was all a lot of nothing," beefed the dealer. "Most came in looking for coupons for Big Macs."
>
> ...The Cutlass was the only GM10 car (the others were the Pontiac Grand Prix and the Buick Regal) that showed a sales decrease during the first five months of the year.[7]

The time has come to face the fact that top-of-mind awareness of a brand or manufacturer's name is no longer synonymous with sales.

What counts is not what people *think*, but what they *do* — and not just next month, but for the next three, four or five years.

Involving identified prospects and customers in an interactive two-way communication is not only essential in breaking through the deluge of advertising clutter. It is also a way to bring a new accountability to advertising expenditure, by measuring the worth of a customer over the long haul and calculating the advertising expenditure that this makes affordable and advisable.

IDEA-STARTERS FOR PROFITING FROM TURNAROUND TREND NO. 4

MANUFACTURER:

✔ *Can you calculate the LTV of a newly-acquired loyal customer for your product or service? (Net Margin for Advertising and*

*Profit per Unit of Sale x No. of Sales per Year x No. of Years Select-
ed x Attrition Rate)*

✔ *Based on past ad expenditures and sales, what do you
think your Advertising Cost per Incremental Sale would be if you
increased your budget by 10%?*

✔ *What do you really know about the effectiveness of the advertising you are currently running? If you cut or increased expenditures in one region, could you detect the long-term difference?*

✔ *Have you considered a Direct-Relationship Marketing program designed to cultivate prime prospects? How would the advertising cost per converted customers compare with the incremental
cost per new customer gained through conventional advertising?*

✔ *How might you lengthen the "lifetime" of your present customers through a Direct-Relationship Marketing program?*

✔ *How many impressions has your advertising created each
year over the past five years? How does it correlate with sales increases or decreases during the same periods?*

RETAILER OR SERVICE ESTABLISHMENT:

✔ *Can you determine from your present record-keeping system the average length of time a new customer continues and the
average expenditure per customer?*

✔ *If you can't answer the above, how might you set up a system which would give you this information?*

✔ *Could you start or test a Customer Club concept and measure its success by comparing the cost for advertising and follow-up
against the forecast average contribution to advertising and profit
per enrollee over 2 years — 3 years — 5 years?*

✔ *How might you design an "ice breaker" promotion which
would permit you to identify new customers who respond and to
track their continued patronage? How much could you afford to
spend per new customer based on the average projected LTV?*

7 From Advertising Monologue to Consumer Dialogue

60% of consumers say they want to be consulted...Benefits of Dialogue ...Nestlé France and Gerber hotlines...How Lands' End listens and Stash Tea corresponds...the Nuprin dialogue strategy...Call Commodore for what?...Two Cheers for Louis Kemp Crab Delights...Really Sharp service

---

Recently we saw full-page newspaper ads for a new deluxe JVC videocassette recorder, the HRS-10000.

Actually they did a pretty good job of conveying a number of worthwhile facts about the machine.

Hm-m. It has "comb filters." And "a multi-purpose Jog/Shuttle control." What are they exactly? And what's good about them? Are they worth the extra money?

But JVC doesn't make it easy to find out. They don't include an address or phone number we can use to get more information.

This is still true of most national advertisers. They conceal their whereabouts from the public! You can't inquire. You can't request. You can't complain. You can't challenge. You can't suggest. All you can do is sit there and be bombarded by their advertising monologue.

A recent ad for Bayer Aspirin proclaimed, "TO HELP PREVENT SECOND HEART ATTACKS, DOCTORS CHOSE BAYER 4 TO 1. FOR THEMSELVES." Very interesting.

You mean they chose Bayer over generic aspirin? Why? It doesn't say.

How many doctors? It doesn't say.

How was the survey conducted? It doesn't say.

Where can we write and inquire? It doesn't say.

This is yet another example of the frustration of monologue advertising.

Mona Doyle is president of The Consumer Network, a consumer research firm that polls 2,000 consumers monthly. Here's what she says they are telling her on this subject: "To relieve their frustrations with products and packages, consumers agree strongly that 'every product should have a toll-free number so the manufacturer has a direct line with consumers in the real world.' A few feel that the numbers don't really help, or that they are too often busy or that they are only reaching complaint clerks when they would like to reach decision makers."

She quotes one consumer who found another fruit product inside an incorrectly labeled can of Libby's Lite Pears: "There was no 800 number on the can, and Libby's had no listing for one. I will never buy that canned fruit again." [1]

The smartest advertisers today are listening. They are picking up on a trend that began in the 80's. It's good business now not only to permit but to encourage two-way communication with prospects and customers.

NO MORE SILENT GUINEA PIGS

Consumers are not satisfied to be silent guinea pigs any more. They want to be vocal partners in the process of providing satisfactory goods and services.

Grey Research surveyed 1,000 households and talked at greater length to 152 household heads. These people were asked how likely they would be to answer specific questions by an advertiser. About 60% said they would when inquiring about goods or services. Up to 34% would be willing to answer questions in any situation. Most of the people indicated their belief that companies need to listen to customer feedback.

It is extraordinary how willing, even eager, people are to be heard. Mel Poretz of The Fulfillment House has estimated that 9 out of 10 people responding to an offer of a rebate, refund, or premium do answer the questions on the order form.

Select and Save is able to add to their Behavior Bank database detailed information on 10 million consumer households a year by getting people to fill out a questionnaire with as many as 250 items. They get people to tell them things like: "Which pastas do I use regularly? How many individual batteries are used in my home per month? Which long distance companies do I use for calling outside my area code? Do I plan on moving to a new residence this year?" And on and on.

Dialogue with the consumer offers many valuable benefits.

It can tell you when you're doing something wrong and how to do better.

It can give you ideas for new products and ways to present existing products.

It makes the prospect more interested and less wary, less annoyed and frustrated.

It makes the customer feel more loyal and more committed to doing business with you.

It can provide impressive customer endorsements for your advertising.

It yields an extra dimension of value to your product or service.

Since 1987, Procter & Gamble has listed on its products toll-free numbers consumers can call with questions. The company handles around half a million calls a year. When are they going to take the next step and put the number in their advertising as well? (Granted that this may not be practical in a 15-second commercial, but it can certainly be done in print advertising and promotion.)

Procter & Gamble took another big step in the direction of consumer dialogue with their ground-breaking introduction of non-allergenic Cheer-Free detergent. Respondents to their free sample offer were asked questions like, "How many wash loads do you do a week?" and "Who in the family is sensitive to the chemicals in detergents?" And they were put on a mailing list to receive appropriate additional information.

DIALOGUE WITH PARENTS WHO BUY BABY FOOD

In France every Sopad Nestlé Baby Foods product carries a phone number. Mothers can call "Allo Diététique Nestlé" any time 10 hours a day, six days a week, to talk to one of Nestlé's four licensed dieticians about Baby's eating needs. The dietician will stay on the phone as long as Mother likes, answering questions about what to do and what not to do to meet her child's nutritional needs. Every phone call and mail contact is summarized for storage and analysis in Nestlé's computer. And there are birthday cards for Baby and Mother's Day cards for Mother.

Nestlé receives 500 thank-you calls a year from appreciative customers. Does it pay to invest so heavily in consumer dialogue?

The proof is in the numbers.   Between 1985 and 1989,   Nestlé made a whopping gain of 10 points in the French baby food market, from a 20 share to a 30. It rose from No. 3 to No. 2, outdistancing Gerber. And the managing director of Sopad Nestlé gave credit to their consumer dialogue and other relationship-building activities for at least 25% of their growth.

In the U.S., Gerber Products has set up a similar service. Every ad and piece of literature put out by Gerber encourages parents to call Gerber's 800 number for more information about the care and feeding of the baby. Gerber's receives some 1,200 calls a day.

The program grew out of a long company tradition. In 1938 Mrs. Dan Gerber, the wife of the company founder, set up a consumer relations department which personally answered every consumer letter.

The service offers a striking example of the value of the feedback obtained through dialogue with the consumer.   So many callers asked about the edibility of half-eaten jars of baby food that the company decided to bring out smaller jars, so infants could finish a jar in a single feeding.

It also demonstrates the speed of in-house consumer research that the hot-line makes possible. For instance, when the CBS program, "60 Minutes," broadcast a report that touched off nationwide alarm about contamination of apples by the pesticide alar, within days Gerber was able to start monitoring customer reaction on its hotline. Meanwhile, the company rushed to prepare new labels and point-of-sale materials that would assure consumers that Gerber apple products were safe. But an analysis of discussions with callers about the problem led Gerber to decide that no such reassurances were necessary, saving the company a significant amount of money. [2]

When Avon launched their Deneuve fragrance, they applied the lessons learned by observing the pioneering marketing practice that had led to the meteoric success of Giorgio. Avon's first step was to build up retail demand with massive Direct-Order Marketing. During this direct-marketing phase, the company discovered, as had Gerber, an additional benefit of dialogue with customers: guidance in new-product planning. "With retail sales, you don't know who your customers are," said Betty Faden, marketing director. "We collected names and addresses when people placed orders and later mailed them questionnaires asking what other Deneuve products they'd like.   That helped us develop a bath line." [3]

Although direct sales of Deneuve were fairly satisfactory, sales at the retail level did not meet Avon's target because the drawing power of the French film star Catherine Deneuve was not as great as anticipated. However, Avon was able to use what they had learned from the Deneuve experience, including dialogue with Deneuve customers, to make their next new fragrance Red a solid success.

Every month *The Morris Report*, a magazine published for cat-lovers by 9 Lives Cat Food, receives thousands of letters, poems, photos, and cartoons from its readers. Just think what an emotional bond this creates between 9 Lives and its customers.

A key factor in the phenomenal growth of mail-order catalogs and other Direct-Order Marketing ventures is that they are in a constant daily dialogue with many of their customers. This provides instant, continuous monitoring of customer satisfaction and dissatisfaction, whether in the form of letters and phone calls or simply in the form of ordered and returned merchandise.

LANDS' END CUSTOMERS TALK BACK? GOOD!

Lands' End is one of the meteoric successes in Direct-Order Marketing, with a database of 4 million customers and a growth rate of 30% a year, with 1989 sales over $500 million. "Our customers are literate, educated people," says Terry Wilson, vice president for customer relations. "They are not reluctant to tell us what they think. When we do well, they share their praise with us. When we screw up, they're the first to let us know."

The catalog often prints "Letters to the Editor" which encourage the dialogue between advertiser and customers, strengthen the bond between them, and add to the company's knowledge of customer likes and dislikes.

Not all of the letters printed are completely favorable. For example, one customer wrote,

> The blouses you feature on pp. 4-7 are indeed pretty and good-looking. However, the prices seem way out-of-line. $38.50-$44.50 for a cotton or cotton-poly blouse made me stop and wonder
>
> Your top-of-the-line Pinpoint men's shirts are $35.50, with vast descriptions of the "69 separate sewing steps and 72 separate inspections." Nowhere in the catalog could I see a man's shirt costing more than $39.50 with monogram.
>
> Certainly a well-sewn and tailored men's shirt requires more work — and fabric! This

disparity in pricing prompts this query.

Of course this gave the editor a perfect opening to explain to that customer and to all the other readers all about the extra pains that go into a fine women's blouse as well:

> Features which contribute to the cost of our women's blouses include details like a pleated front, covered front placket, fagoting on the collar and front placket, or embroidery on the collar.
>
> Blouses may also often have pleated or gathered fullnesses at the shoulder or sleeve, fabric-covered or pearl buttons, waistline darts for a better fit, or a fancier, more expensive fabric like piqué or damask.
>
> Our Women's Oxford Shirt may be a good alternative for someone who wants a simpler, less expensive blouse.

This interchange illustrates another important point about consumer dialogue — if you get into "conversations" with your prospects and customers, you'd better have some genuine merit to talk about, as obviously Lands' End does.

Often Lands' End will act on a customer complaint by making system-wide changes. Says Wilson, "Our buyers know what they like and don't like, and we're usually able to put their suggestions to good use." [4]

Katie Muldoon, a leading catalog marketing expert, has speculated that the success of companies like Lands' End is related to a widespread need to feel good about something in this dreary world.

"Obviously," she writes, "the consumer is looking for a bond, for someone they can trust...Perhaps one of the reasons that Lands' End sales continue to climb is that the company makes a sincere effort to establish a relationship with its customers. Lands' End pulls customers in as part of a special family and gives them the support and warmth that many consumers feel they are missing. And it's so strong that this bond transcends long distance." [5]

THE TWO-WAY STREET BETWEEN STASH TEA AND ITS CUSTOMERS

But you don't have to be a Direct-Order Marketing company or division to get the benefit of this kind of two-way communication. The essential requirement is not direct distribution but simply direct contact and establishment of direct communication channels between the advertiser and the prospects or customers. And as you will learn throughout this book, there are many ways this can be accomplished that do not involve giving up your distribution through dealers and retailers.

Stash Tea Company sells its products every way it can — to restaurants, in supermarkets, in specialty and gourmet food shops, in natural food stores, and via its own mail-order catalog. The company has been growing steadily ever since it was launched in an entrepreneur's garage, and at last report was enjoying a growth rate of 20% to 30% a year.

Recently the company made a fascinating discovery about consumer dialogue which has important implications for many other advertisers.

Printed on every Stash Tea bag packet is an offer of their free catalog. In this way, they receive some 3,000 requests per month for the catalog and these requests have played an important part in their growth.

Many of the letters they receive include one or two personal details, such as how the inquirer happened to discover Stash Tea.

So Stash decided to experiment with sending such inquirers a computer-typed letter with standard paragraphs but also with customized sentences such as, "We enjoyed hearing about your trip on the Mississippi Queen." They found that even after allowing for the increased cost of this kid-glove treatment, there was a sharp increase in the net profit from sales to inquirers who received the customized responses, compared to those who received merely a well-written form letter.

You may say that "the numbers are too small" to mean very much. But just one fiercely devoted customer has the strength of ten, and is the unpaid agent of the most powerful advertising medium of all — word-of-mouth.

A DIALOGUE MODEL BY
CATALOG MERCHANT JOAN COOK

Direct marketing expert Dick Hodgson has called attention in his monthly column to the superb job catalog merchant Joan Cook does to cement a bond with customers through encouragement of dialogue. A merchandise package received from Joan Cook contained the following dialogue marketing components:

1. A warm personal letter. It does such a wonderful job of reaching out and touching the customer that it deserves quoting in full. Inside a folded note with "Can We Talk?" written on the outside was the following typewritten communication:

Dear Customer:

You and I rarely get to meet each other, doing business by mail as we do. And so I'm never really sure how well we're treating you as a customer.

I know when you're satisfied, because you order from us regularly. And of course we hear from you when you're dissatisfied!

But what if you feel "lukewarm" about this order? It's okay, but not great? Probably, you won't contact us — not for an adjustment, and certainly not for another order.

If that's the case, we've done a poor job. We won't stay in business with one-time customers. We need to satisfy you so completely that you'll feel confident in ordering from us regularly.

I hope you'll tell me if you have even the slightest complaint. The special phone number and mail address are below. I won't answer directly, because my Customer Service Office has all the records, but I will get a report on your call or letter.

Thank you again for your order.

Sincerely,

(Signed: Joan Cook)

2. An appealing customer response device. As customer questionnaires begin to multiply like rabbits, as they are sure to do in the Age of Individualized Marketing, it will become harder to make your questionnaire stand out and get your prospects or customers to fill it out and send it back. Joan Cook dealt with this by making it seem like a game with the customer's future satisfaction as the prize. The envelope containing it was labelled: "Twenty Questions. Clue: a game that guarantees you are the winner!" Inside, another note from Joan Cook says:

Dear Customer: And a winner you are when you shop with us. I hope you're delighted with this purchase. But if not, just let us know, and we'll fix things. These twenty questions are designed to help us change the rules of the catalog game, so you come out a winner.

The questionnaire then asks about demographic details such as male or female, type of residence, age category, sports, hobbies, magazines read, etc. And there is also a section in which the customer can rate Joan Cook on everything from helpfulness of customer service to an evaluation of the merchandise and timeliness of delivery.[6]

We are reporting this approach in considerable detail because it provides a model of good consumer dialogue technique that companies not engaged in Direct-Order Marketing can profit from. Our personal experience in responding to offers by brand advertisers is that too often the company communications we subsequently receive are cold, stiff, or awkward by comparison.

With these messages, Joan Cook is killing not just two birds with one stone but three. (1) By virtually begging for complaints, no matter how mild, the company can smoke out trouble spots in their products or service and correct them. (2) In expressing such eagerness to hear of customer troubles, Joan Cook builds an image of itself as a warm, caring, trustworthy catalog merchant. (3) By selling the customer on how much Joan Cook cares, the promotion increases the number of replies containing valuable information for the company's customer database.

IS CONSUMER DIALOGUE "TOO EXPENSIVE"?

You may also argue that giving prospects and customers this kind of personal attention is "too expensive." We refer you to the discussion of the Lifetime Value of a Customer a few pages back.

If you are marketing a 79¢ product that users purchase an average of twice a year, you may be right.

But what if your average customers have an LTV, like Campbell's Soup, of some $200 a year — and, to paraphrase Tom Peters, can be viewed as having $200 x 10 years or $2,000 stamped on their foreheads? Then it will pay you to treat each communication from a prospect or customer not as a nuisance, but as an important opportunity to engage in a mutually rewarding "conversation."

Think for a moment of your own experience as a consumer. If you have ever struggled to master a new piece of computer software, for instance, you undoubtedly have your own Winners and Sinners list of companies as far as customer support is concerned. Some companies are coy about it and put their phone number and offer of support in the user's manual either in very fine print or not at all. Others feature it fairly prominently in the manual and are extremely warm and friendly when you call.

You know which of these two kinds of company you will rave about when your friends ask for your advice on software, and which kind you will recommend avoiding.

If you encourage consumer feedback through questionnaires, calls to your 800 and 900 phone numbers, letters to the editor of a customer magazine or mail-order catalog you may launch, or queries inspired by invitations on your packaging, you will come to know your prospects and customers not as faceless members of the crowd but as individuals. And if you respond appropriately to what each one tells you, you will forge important bonds of friendship and kinship.

By inviting communication from the public, and by customizing your responses — which the computer makes possible and affordable today — you can show that you are listening and that you understand and care.

Says Grey Advertising president Edward H. Meyer, "We wanted to get Tylenol users to try our product [Nuprin]. And we wanted to use the moment of trial to bond consumers to Nuprin. Interactive direct marketing seemed to be the best way to do that. Through Nuprin fulfillment mail, we could thank consumers for their response, offer our samples, and at the same time get a dialogue going about them, their kind of pain, when and why they used Nuprin, and how it worked."

Bravo!

It is important to note that Bristol-Myers committed itself wholeheartedly to this strategy. They devoted the entire 30-second TV commercial to the direct response sampling offer, and they accompanied the sample with a questionnaire and an incentive for filling it out and sending it back.

HALF-HEARTED INVITATIONS WON'T DO

By contrast, half-hearted measures don't accomplish much. And we are seeing a great deal of that sort of thing. We see 800 numbers flashed on the screen for literally one second during a 15-second commercial, making it almost impossible to respond. Or print ads in which the use of an 800 number is poorly planned and poorly displayed.

If the advertiser is really fearful, for budgetary reasons, of getting too many responses from the public, why bother at all?

One of our colleagues has inelegantly but aptly described it as the C.Y.A. Strategy, i.e., Cover Your Ass: put an 800 number in your ad like everybody else seems to be doing these days, just so your boss won't ask, "How come we don't include an 800 number in our ads the way everybody else seems to be doing these days?" But never mind thinking seriously about why the number is included, and never mind treating the calls that come in very seriously.

In a recent issue of *Newsweek*, there was an eight-page ad for the Commodore Amiga computer with just such a feeble invitation. Six of the eight pages were devoted to six profiles of six different kinds of delighted user. At the end of two of them appeared this signature paragraph:

> The Amiga allows you to fly faster than you thought you could. Without spending a lot of money. Without waiting around another 50 years. Amiga from Commodore. Why not give us a call at 800-627-9505?

Give them a call and *what*? The advertisement suggests no partricular reason for calling.

The last page lists 60 dealers in our New York area (a good use of the regional edition of *Newsweek*) and heads it with: "You could be next. Call the Amiga dealer nearest you or 800-627-9595."

Call for more information? Then why not say so? And not only say so, but make the offer of information so attractive that readers are highly motivated to call?

When we called, we were asked for our address and simply given the name of the nearest dealer. The operator did not volunteer to send any additional information, and only agreed to do so when we specifically requested it.

(A year or two earlier, Commodore had produced and offered a superb video which brilliantly demonstrated the Amiga's unique capabilities. But the video was promoted somewhat half-heartedly, and was probably viewed by the company simply as sales promotion — i.e., a temporary sales stimulant for that season — rather than as a continuing opportunity to engage in a serious "conversation " with serious prospects.)

In the same issue of *Newsweek*, there was a page ad for Louis Kemp Crab Delights, which of course are not crab at all but imitation crab. It is apparently a product found in the frozen food cabinet of the supermarket, although that was not very clear. The ad provided several serving suggestions, and under the logotype at the bottom it said, "Recipe Hot Line 1-800-222-1421."

A daily recipe over the phone? No, just a way of calling to request a recipe folder. Then why in the world not show and describe the recipe folder in the ad? Could it be because Louis

Kemp doesn't want *too many* requests? Then it would be too much trouble? It would cost too much? Or could it be just another case of C.Y.A., and nobody had really given it much thought one way or another?

We don't mean to single out these two advertisers for special criticism. They are merely a couple of examples chosen at random out of literally hundreds to which we could point.

In the Great Turnaround, the mere fact of dialogue, however feeble, is not enough. It must be *good* dialogue in which the advertiser really sounds interested in hearing from people, really pays attention to responses, and really responds intelligently and well.

In the same magazine, in refreshing contrast to two examples cited, an advertisement for Sharp products Authorized Service Stations carried a simple, pleasant, thoughtful, reassuring, reasonably well-displayed signature line, "If you have a question regarding any Sharp consumer product, please call 1-800-526-0264."

Wouldn't we all be better off, advertisers included, if every advertisement carried such a line? The day may be approaching, but there's still time for you to grab a place near the head of the line.

IDEA-STARTERS FOR PROFITING FROM TURNAROUND TREND No. 5

MANUFACTURER:

✔ *Could you put a hot-line number on all your packages?*

ALL:

✔ *Would it make sense to put a hot-line number in all your ads and customer communications?*

✔ *Do you provide a clear reason when you invite hot-line calls? More information? Advice? Enrollment in customer club? Nearest dealer location?*

✔ *Are your hot-line operators trained in courtesy, knowledgeability, and helpfulness? Do you ever pretend to be a consumer and call your own hot-line number to monitor your service?*

✔ *Do you record, summarize, and analyze content of hot line calls for danger signals and product/service ideas?*

✔ *Are you capturing information from your hot-line calls for database-building?*

✔ Have you considered customer dialogue possibilities? Newsletter or magazine with Letters to the Editor? Call-backs? Correspondence? Questionnaires?

From Bombarding the Marketplace to Building Relationships

8

Hard-sell vs. "invisible cloud"...Today's third way...Burger King's first step...the Woolworths Kids Club in the U.K. ... Clubs by Miller Lite, McCormick, Hallmark. Other approaches by 9 Lives Cat Food ...Pfaltzgraff ...Huggies ...Pampers...John Deere...Kohler...General Mills ...Garden Way...Did Brown-Forman give up too soon?...American Airlines in Europe..Barbie Doll....the Venture Capital Club...The Disney Magic Kingdom Club....the Relationship-Driven 90's

---

As the resistance on the part of consumers to being bombarded into buying grows, the wildly escalating cleverness of so much advertising seeks somehow to break through the clutter — but often, as we have seen, to no avail.

And the alternative — fighting for customers with discounts and rebates — has also been too often counter-productive, merely producing a temporary and unprofitable blip in the sales curve.

Now, for many advertisers, a third way is coming to look more and more attractive: using the advertising to begin, and the sales promotion budget to continue, a long-term relationship with prospects or customers.

Part of the secret of its effectiveness is that while the advertising is convincing some prospects to apply for a direct relationship, a great many others are receiving advertising impressions which may move them later on. And once the relationship is joined, it gives a new, more important, more productive role to sales promotion. The power of sales promotion can be concentrated efficiently on a highly receptive target audience, and used not just to stimulate sales temporarily but to win and keep loyal customers.

This represents an important turning away from a point of view almost as old as advertising itself — the idea of bombarding the marketplace with your advertising in order to form and shape a favorable public awareness of your product or brand.

The ad man probably most deserving to be called father of brand-awareness advertising was Theodore F. MacManus, author in 1915 of perhaps the most famous advertisement of all time — the Cadillac ad of 1915 headed, "The Penalty of Leadership."

As advertising historian Stephen Fox characterized the McManus approach: "Surrounded by what MacManus called 'an invisible cloud of friendly, favorable impressions,' the product would all but sell itself at the proper time." [1] And this concept is still alive and well. The good-will built up over many years around such familiar names as "Colgate" or "Goodyear" or "Ivory" can be worth literally billions of dollars, as has been proven by the value accorded to brand franchises in leveraged buyout deals.

In 1960, onetime Ted Bates chairman Rosser Reeves, best remembered today as the father of U.S.P. (the Unique Selling Proposition) carried thinking about the shaping of buying attitudes a step further. In his brilliant little book, *Reality in Advertising*, he argued persuasively that

> ...there is a limit to what a consumer can remember about 30,000 advertised brands. He cannot remember all the advertising he reads, any more than he can memorize the Encyclopaedia Britannica. ...It is as though he carries a small box in his head for a given product category. This box is limited either by his inability to remember or his lack of interest. It is filled with miscellaneous data, and when a new campaign forces more in, some data is forced out and the box spills over.[2]

At Ted Bates, Reeves and his colleagues developed the concept of the U.S.P. as a simple, memorable claim, repeated over and over, that would push awareness of your product into the category box in the consumer's mind. It would crowd out or squeeze down awareness of competing products.

Today, more than three decades later, *Reality in Advertising* still reads very convincingly. And in the battles between the giants of brand advertising for share of mind and share of market, it undoubtedly still has validity.

Indeed, two researchers who analyzed 1059 commercials for 356 brands concluded in their 1984 report: "Many years ago Rosser Reeves argued that every commercial should include a unique selling proposition. Our results would seem to suggest that he was right." [3]

WHY THE ROSSER REEVES "BRAIN BOX" CONCEPT DOESN'T ALWAYS WORK TODAY

But as we have seen in the cases of Isuzu, Burger King, and Lee jeans, an increase in Share of Mind, even when awareness advertising is able to make that happen, does not necessarily translate into sales.

Sometimes while the Share of Mind is increasing, Share of Market and sales are actually slipping.

Why should this be? A number of possible reasons come to mind:

A. *Advertisers think they are using Reeves' principles when they really aren't.* Against his advice, they change their U.S.P. frequently (Burger King changed their campaign theme nine times in 13 years), leaving the public confused about what their unique claim really is. Or they fall victim to what Reeves calls "vampire video," in which the attractiveness of the presenter or presentation draws attention away from the product itself.

B. *It's a far different society today.* In an era in which people are too rushed to eat while sitting down — product proliferation and niche marketing have vastly increased advertising clutter since Rosser Reeves' day — and a network television program watched by 15% of the nation's households is considered a success — it requires heavier advertising expenditure than most products can afford to break through and achieve a significant increase in share of mind.

C. *Public attitudes toward advertising have changed.* In the early days of television, Ted Bates created Anacin commercials showing a pounding hammer, a coiled spring, and a jagged bolt of electricity inside boxes in the head of a headache-sufferer. They were, Reeves later conceded, "the most hated commercials in the history of advertising." But in eighteen months they raised Anacin sales from $18 million to $54 million.[4]

However, the Baby Boomers who grew up with this kind of advertising hated it even more and developed a resistance to the hard-sell claim.

To appeal to them, advertisers have often swung too far in the other direction, with terribly entertaining, lovable, clever advertising with no memorable U.S.P. or powerful association and sometimes no effect on sales.

MUST YOU CHOOSE BETWEEN
ENTERTAINMENT AND IMPACT?

A 1985 study by the Ogilvy Center for Research and Development seemed to strongly indicate that people who like commercials are more likely to be persuaded by them.

When people were shown 73 commercials and asked to rate how much they liked or disliked each of them, 16.2% of those who said they liked the commercial a lot also said they would be more likely to buy the product advertised. In contrast, an average of only 8.2% who were neutral about a commercial had their brand preference increased by it.

Alas, note that this measured only a favorable buying inclination in a laboratory situation, not actual sales. The commercials featuring Joe Isuzu, the amusing liar, that we cited in Chapter Two were certainly very amusing, entertaining, and likeable. It is possible that these commercials would have scored as "very enjoyable." Some viewers interviewed in a research pre-test might have claimed they would be more likely to buy an Isuzu car because of the commercials. But as we pointed out, despite the entertainment value of the advertising, Isuzu sales went down while it was on the air.

So many brand advertisers today are caught on the horns of a dilemma: whether to go for hard-sell, repetitive, but dislikable advertising or soft-sell, lovable, but often ineffective advertising. And while brand-building image advertising is still valuable and often essential, its current limitations raise serious questions about major brand advertisers putting all of their eggs in this one basket.

CAN YOU AFFORD THE IMAGE-BUILDING GAME AT ALL?

And for lesser brands and lesser advertisers, working with national budgets of "only" a few million dollars, there is an even more serious question of whether or not they should be in the television image game at all — or whether perhaps they should be spending their limited marketing resources in entirely different ways.

The truth is that, brilliant as Reeves' theorizing was, it is not only dated today in many ways, it is also relevant to a narrow spectrum of the more than $100 billion spent annually on national advertising.

His ingenious measurement tools of "penetration" and "usage pull" really apply only to directly competing products on store shelves.

And there are thousands of advertisers who just don't have the kind of big bucks required to fight Reeves' Share of Mind war — but who can still, with shrewd and careful planning, make effective use of their comparatively limited advertising dollars.

In preparing marketing budgets, the alternative to fighting for share of mind with awareness advertising has always been sales promotion. But this too has its problems, as we discussed in Chapter One. When a product is new and novel, sales promotion can be powerfully productive. But in a mature market, saturated with discount promotions by all players, it can be counter-productive and lead to erosion both of brand franchise and net profits.

NOW— THE THIRD WAY

Now a number of innovative companies are exploring the third way to spark sales and build a brand — relationship marketing.

It depends neither on "an invisible cloud of friendly, favorable impressions" nor on the jump-start jolt of a seasonal sales promotion. Instead it seeks to build and maintain a lasting, mutually rewarding relationship between the advertiser and the customer.

Share of Mind advertising asks, "What shall we say to the people we want as customers?" Direct-Relationship Marketing asks, "What shall we do for the people we want as customers?"

It doesn't depend on forcing a favorable awareness of the product's unique value into a little box in people's heads and hoping that the memory of the advertising message stays there for days, weeks, or months.

Instead it buttonholes the most likely prospects as they go hurrying past — or seeks them out — and draws them into a mutually rewarding, long-term, interactive relationship.

The consumer gets extra attention and special rewards. The seller gets a promotional arena in which to sell existing products and to introduce new products exactly suited to the customers the seller has gotten to know so well.

It is not a path for the timid, the changeable, or the impatient.

It is not just traditional sales promotion — and in many cases it is a great mistake to turn it over to sales promotion experts. Many of them may have the skills needed, but are not prepared by their experience and way of thinking to deal with this long-term method of marketing. (There are some conspicuous exceptions.)

For instance, in the new Direct-Relationship Marketing, the role of warm, intimate, sparkling direct mail letters can be an important part of the program — but this is a skill that has been almost the exclusive property of the Direct-order Marketing experts. The sales promotion people never thought it was important and never bothered to develop it because it was never demanded of them by their clients; thus sales-promotion fulfillment houses have mailed out rebates, refunds, and premiums by the millions with a curt, cold form letter or no letter at all.

But now the winds of change are ruffling the field of sales promotion too. "The aim of promotion will continue shifting toward continuity of purchase and away from mere one-shot efforts," writes Laurie Petersen, the perceptive editor of the promotion marketing supplement to *Adweek's Marketing Week*. "Marketers will be thinking about their promotions as a way to achieve a goal. Instead of just saying, 'What promotion are we running in the third quarter?' the questions will be, 'What is it we are trying to accomplish? How can we best do that?'"

Relationship Marketing is antithetical to the short-term thinking that has often put American business at a disadvantage in competing with the Japanese. This makes it easy prey to the committee system of management.

Smart people often become dumb committees. The patient work of years can be swept away in an instant by bottom-line managers looking for something easy to cut out of the budget.

So it is with Relationship Marketing. There is the ever-present danger that the program will be cut short by bottom-line management before it has had time to develop into a clearly accountable source of profits and growth.

Another problem is job-hopping. A brilliant director of marketing launches a dazzling long-range program — and then a year later moves on to an even bigger and better job, leaving behind associates and successors not as committed to the program and not as clear about how it must be conducted.

Despite these obstacles, there is not a doubt that more companies are establishing direct relationships involving regular communications with the end-users of their product or service. It is a growing trend.

A POWERFUL NEW VEHICLE — CUSTOMER CLUBS

As we write this, Burger King is taking its first steps into what appears to be a serious entry into Direct-Relationship Marketing. Their new Kids Club has lined up different premiums for each season of the year. But Burger King is not just handing them out to everyone. Kids have to sign up to become members of the club. This means the start of a Burger King database that can pay off big later on.

The Burger King Kids Club seemingly will go beyond just a calendar of premium promotion for kids. Children who join the club receive a "Super Official Totally Secret Membership Kit." This includes a personalized membership card and letter, stickers, a poster featuring Kids Club characters, and the Club's official iron-on transfer. At Burger King restaurants, kids will be able to get a four-page color newspaper, published five times a year and with games, puzzles, film and video reviews and previews of upcoming premiums.

A newsletter will encourage feedback from club members and seek to build a relationship between them and the restaurant.

It is interesting to note the contrast between the franchise operators' reaction to the new Burger King image campaign launched about that time — with the theme, "Sometimes you just gotta break the rules" — and their feelings about the Kids Club.

The operators grumbled that customers didn't understand what "break the rules" meant. Or wanted to take unfair advantage of it, like the customer who wanted to break the rules by getting six packets of barbecue sauce with his 69¢ bag of fries.[5]

But the operators loved the Kids Club. After three and a half months, one operator said that children's meals were now accounting for 6% of his sales, compared with 1% before the program was launched. Another said that about 50% of the kids who had come in since the program was launched had filled out membership applications. Within six months, nearly one million kids had walked into a Burger King restaurant and signed up as members.[6]

The Burger King Kids Club began as a promotion by an enterprising West Coast sales manager, Sharon Fogg, and was so successful that the idea was snapped up by the parent company.[7] It is a striking example of what Ries and Trout called "Bottom-Up Marketing," in their book by that name, in which a tactic that works is found and built up into a company-wide strategy.

The Woolworths Kids Club in the U.K. It is interesting to compare the Burger King Kids Club with the Woolworths Kids Club in the U.K. (perhaps that's where Burger King got the idea).

The Woolworths club, for kids up to age seven, was launched in 1987 and within two years had enrolled over 450,000 members.

Parents enroll their children by filling out an entry form giving the child's name, address, and date of birth. Within a month the child receives the new-membership pack. It contains a badge, a membership card, a stationery pack, a comics and games newsletter, a game board, a calendar, and catalogs.

The child's friends at the Kids Club headquarters are ladybug characters, led by Dotty, the Club mascot.

Every four months a new comic book is mailed out to members. This 12-page publication contains photos of club members, their artwork, sometimes letters to Dotty. (Notice this important interactive aspect.) It also has features on toys sold at Woolworth such as Masters of the Universe and Barbie.

On Christmas and on birthdays, members receive greeting cards from Dotty and the other ladybugs. Just think what a thrill that must be to a small child — not every kid on the block gets mail from an attractive ladybug — and how pleased parents must be that Woolworths is so thoughtful.

And the parents are not forgotten, either. Three times a year they receive their own adult newsletter. It tells them about seasonal sales and special discounts for members. They are given their own parent/guardian membership card to establish their eligibility for the discount offers. [8]

Major advertisers in the U.S. who are now running clubs include General Foods, McCormick-Schilling, Miller Brewing, The House of Seagram, Warner-Lambert, and Hershey Foods. [10]

SOCIETIES OF MILLER LITE, MCCORMICK, HALLMARK CUSTOMERS

The Miller Lite Club is called the Lite Beer Athletic Club. It is targeted to ages 21 to 25. The Club's members (75,000 in 1988) pay $3 dues the first year, $2 thereafter, and receive a jocular quarterly magazine which, among other things, promotes Miller-sponsored events.

Says Charles Copin of Rogers Merchandising, "Our aim is to sell beer by influencing the prospective customer's attitude about Miller Lite." No proof of purchase is required, but Miller-Lite sales jumped up when the club was promoted in radio spots in Los Angeles, Dallas, Chicago, and Boston. When was the last time Miller Lite had an immediate lift in sales from introduction of a new awareness ad campaign theme?

McCormick-Schilling started the Society to End Dull Meals Forever, according to Mary Randisi, director of consumer affairs for the company. McCormick's research showed people were cooking home meals from scratch less often and with fewer ingredients. So in addition to updating its packaging, McCormick launched what is essentially a consumer education campaign to "renew the taste buds" using 400 "tip cards" with ideas for preparing fast, nutritious meals that use spices. The Society is a vehicle to market those cards.

Promoted nationally through free-standing inserts in Sunday newspapers and in mailings to food editors and extension home economists, the year-old Society attracted the interest of close to 200,000 cooks. Respondents who sent in their name and address started receiving a quarterly newsletter mailing and 12 tip cards every six months.

The Society is also promoted in McCormick's Ye Olde Tea House restaurant, next to its factory in Baltimore's Inner Harbor. The tip cards and other McCormick-developed educational materials are used in many university home economics classes, whose students were made members in a further effort to promote McCormick as a consumer educator.

Randisi says McCormick plans to use the Society's membership list to deliver future coupon offers and product samples. [9]

Hallmark started its Keepsake Ornament Collector's Club to keep its members (76,000 in the first year) informed about new trends in collecting and new products. Members are given the opportunity to collect special editions available only to members. These special orders must be picked up at the nearest Hallmark retailer, thus generating store traffic.

Mattel has launched a club to stimulate the sale of genuine Barbie Doll fashions. Over the years, sale of the dolls had increased as they became more interesting, but Barbie fashion sales declined due to competition from generic Barbie fashions by other makers. To join the Barbie Pink Stamps Club, members just send in $2 and a filled-out copy of the membership forms enclosed in Barbie merchandise. Television support advertising tells young viewers to look for their membership application in specially marked packages of Barbie fashions.

New members receive hair accessories, a Barbie fashion poster, a Barbie Doll T-shirt, and the 36-page Barbie Fashion Guide. It contains beauty tips, stories, games, puzzles, and a section of mail-order premium items such as a Barbie telephone or pink fur coat. Children can order the items and pay for them either with the pink stamps they earn with their store purchases of Barbie fashions or with part cash.

"Previously, Mattel never knew who its customers were," says Marc Reines, Mattel's manager of Direct Marketing. "The company just assumed they were kids between the ages of 3 and 11." Now, through the club, they intend to start building a database showing not only the names and ages of the young members, but their purchase behavior, their parents' names, and the names and ages of other children in the household. [10]

In Europe, the club concept has been ingeniously applied to the venture capital field.

A company called 3i offers a distinctive blend of financial and industrial skills in helping to develop successful businesses. They invest in people and companies ranging from small start-ups through young businesses to major national and international concerns. They are the biggest and most successful company in the world providing venture capital.

But how does such a company find the right people to whom it makes good sense to turn over millions or tens of millions of dollars so they can realize their dreams?

One of the imaginative ways 3i is doing it is with a Direct-Relationship Marketing program limited to 5,000 club members. They are all managers who have been identified with direct response advertising and a follow-up questionnaire as having the potential to start up, build up, or buy into a major business in the next few years.

In this exclusive club, members meet people with similar ambitions, attend seminars, and participate in an ongoing dialogue with 3i leading up to the day they are ready to take the plunge and 3i is ready to back them with venture capital.

Many of the events provided in the program are paid for by the members themselves to help defray the costs. It is a win-win situation, with both sides coming out ahead when everything goes right. And that's just what Direct-Relationship Marketing is all about.

In Japan, an important secret of Shiseido's success in selling $2 billion worth of cosmetics annually to Japanese women is the Shiseido Club of ten million members. In it Shiseido uses a number of the MaxiMarketing techniques we have been pointing out.

Members can obtain a Shiseido Visa card which entitles them to special membership discounts with participating retailers, hotels, theatres. There is a continuity purchase rewards program, with points earned by members when they buy designated Shiseido products. Members' monthly credit card statements contain enclosures selling everything from apparel accessories to floral arrangements.

From time to time, members receive a questionnaire in the mail surveying their buying behavior and attitudes.

Shiseido also publishes its own magazine. It is sold to the retailer, who in turn distributes copies of it free to store customers. It is a general interest woman's magazine, touching on a wide range of subject matter consistent with Shiseido's image and identity. And, of course, the magazine includes a discreet and appropriate presentation of Shiseido products.

Everything in the Shiseido programs supports their multi-channel distribution through not only their independent dealers but also their own chain of Hanatsubakai retail outlets. It is all coordinated by the Shiseido Business Center — an outstanding example of truly integrated marketing.

Of course a relationship marketing program need not be a club, although that is a common form. The important thing is simply to develop a method of continuing direct communication with prospects or customers which is attractive, appealing, interactive, attitude-shaping, and sales-producing. There are a number of other ways this can be accomplshed. Here are some of them:

A company magazine with "advertorial" information about company products and services. The Austin Rover customer magazine *Catalyst*, the *Nintendo Power* published for Nintendo game enthusiasts, the *Morris Report* published by 9 Lives cat food, the *Poolife* magazine published for swimming pool owners by Olin Chemical, the desktop publishing magazine published by Aldus for buyers of its software, the *TroyBilt Owners News*, the quarterly magazine for baseball card collectors that Topps chewing gum is now publishing, — these are just a few of a growing number of advertiser-created publications that are changing the way companies communicate with their customers and sometimes their prospects.

Mattel Toy Company has licensed Welsh Publishing Group to publish *Barbie*, the magazine for young Barbie Doll fans. It now has some 600,000 subscribers, and Mattel is beginning to see the enormous possiblities in combining the resources of the magazine and the Barbie Pink Stamps Club in a powerful integrated marketing program.

The possibilities offered by this new medium are impressive. They include:

• creating editorial copy that is responsive to the special interests of readers who match the profile of the company's best customers and prospects. By identifying the advertiser/sponsor with the reader's own lifestyle, a community of interest is created between sponsor and reader.

• running conventional company advertising at a lower cost per thousand than regular magazines — and partially or totally offsetting the cost by charging for subscriptions or by accepting paid advertising from other non-competing advertisers

• running advertorials with far more depth of information, interest, and credibility than is possible in the constricted format of paid magazine and newspaper advertising

• binding in questionnaires and inviting letters to the editor to get valuable feedback from readers as guidance for future product development

• building consumer confidence in a multi-brand company's name and overall reputation as well as in the individual brands

• heightening reader interest and appreciation by having the readers generate all or most of the content, as *Musenalp* is doing in Switzerland and Germany. (This remarkable success is a publication entirely written by the teen-agers who read it! It has a circulation of 300,000 in the German-speaking Swiss market and 1,200,000 in Germany. Bound into each copy is a catalog of products available through the magazine's Junior Discount Club — home computers, camping equipment, pocket calculators, radios, even vacations — at discounts averaging 15%. [11] The magazine also carries advertising by companies like Sony, Atari, Agfa-Gevaert, and Visa.)

When selling a high-ticket item, such as an automobile, the costliness of this way of keeping in touch can easily be justified. Other ways such a publication can be made affordable include

(a) selling "upgrades" directly to the customer, a common practice in the computer software field,

(b) getting other advertisers to take out space in your publication, thus paying for part or all of the cost, as Olin Chemical Co. does with its *Poolife* magazine to swimming pool owners,

(c) selling subscriptions to your magazine, as 9 Lives Cat Food does with its magazine for cat lovers, *The Morris Report.* Subscriptions are offered for $6 per year, and subscribers receive at least $6 worth of 9 Lives coupons to offset the cost. "Traditional mass marketing is an inefficient means of reaching the one-third of all households that own a cat," says Eric Brown, product manager. "*The Morris Report* enables us to reach those households by effectively managing a cat-owner database."[12]

Anyone interested in seeing Direct-Relationship Marketing developed as a fine art would do well to study the *Troy-Bilt Owner News*. This is a tabloid newspaper mailed out four times a year to several million owners and prospects by the Garden Way Manufacturing Company, founded by marketing genius Lyman Wood to make Troy-Bilt Rototillers and other lawn and garden products and sell them direct to the consumer. Each issue is filled with product ads, maintenance tips, recipes, letters to the editor, and gardening advice. It also carries an earnest, homey, down-to-earth editorial by Dean Leith, Jr., the sales manager, whose smiling face appears in various features and product plugs throughout the newspaper.

Over the years, this interactive relationship marketing vehicle has built an almost fanatic loyalty to Troy-Bilt products. And we are sure that if Dean Leith appeared unannounced at a reader's door, he would be instantly and warmly invited to step inside for a cup of coffee.

A customer newsletter. The editorial, printing, and mailing costs are of course much lower than for a magazine, and an occasional special offer can help pay the cost.

Pfaltzgraff dinnerware found that an increasing number of their dealers were reluctant to carry as many as 100 different items in a given pattern. So they started permitting customers to order direct when they wanted to round out their collections with pieces not available at their dealers. Out of this grew a very successful newsletter. Writes Katie Muldoon, president of the company's catalog advertising agency:

> The creation of a newsletter that specifically encouraged a two-way dialogue between the consumer and the direct marketer (Pfaltzgraff) resulted in a phenomenal success story from the first mailing. Further, the consumers never seem to tire of the communication with Pfaltzgraff; they continually suggest new products and clever uses, share recipes, etc. If at all possible, Pfaltzgraff actually produces these suggested products, further creating a trust and a type of brand loyalty that is seldom seen today. [13]

An educational program. When Kimberly-Clark launched Huggies disposable diapers, they built a database program which could identify by name and address 75% of the 3.5 million new mothers each year. Even before the baby was born, the mother would start receiving a series of warm, helpful, educational pamphlets and letters about what new mothers need to know...plus, toward the end of the series, cents-off coupons for purchase of Huggies.

The program reportedly cost Kimberly-Clark $10 million a year. That's roughly four dollars per prospect, compared to around less than a penny for thirty seconds of network television advertising.

But think back to what Tom Peters said about the value of a Federal Express customer. In this case, Kimberly-Clark sees $1300 on the mother's forehead, for that is how much she will spend on diapers in the first two years of her baby's life. And this database program has played a big part in their capturing and holding one-third of the market in disposable diapers.

(Procter & Gamble has responded by choosing the company magazine route to promote its competing product, Pampers. A recent list-rental advertisement offered rental of more than eight million young mothers who have filled out and returned a coupon entitling them to a free seven-issue subscription to Procter & Gamble's Pampers *Baby Care* Magazine. The list-rental income could easily be several million dollars, and could underwrite a good part of the cost of the program.)

Mail-order catalogs carrying "free" advertising for your retail-sold products. An outstanding example of this approach has been provided by Deere & Co., makers of John Deere lawn and garden products.

In casting about for ways to diversify, Deere discovered that they had an important hidden asset. They already had a fulfillment operation that supplied its dealers with replacement parts within two days of receiving orders. Why not use the same fufillment capability to start a mail-order catalog business?

This is what they did in 1987, selling by mail home and garden products which are in keeping with the John Deere image but which are not anything like the tractors, lawn mowers, and other farm and home equipment John Deere is famous for. Therefore catalog sales do not compete with John Deere dealers for customer dollars.

On the contrary, each catalog carries half a dozen pages of advertising for dealer-sold John Deere products such as lawn tractors. At the bottom of each ad there is a phone number to call for the name of the nearest dealer.

The catalog goes out about four times a year to 600,000 prime prospects, home owners age 35 to 55, with incomes of $30,000 and up.

Do you see what a win-win situation this is? The long-respected heavily-advertised John Deere name lends credibility to the catalog. And the catalog builds a personal relationship through frequent direct contact with the recipients, and carries advertising for dealer-sold John Deere products directly into the homes of prime prospects. Each advertisement, while not strictly speaking free, costs only a penny or two for printing the catalog page on which it appears.

This approach makes so much sense, it is really surprising that so few other advertisers have adopted the idea. If Deere chose, they could even use the catalog as an advertising research laboratory, by doing split-runs of two or more different versions of each John Deere equipment ad in the catalog and seeing which one pulls the greater number of responses. Then the winning ad could be rolled out in the magazines and newspapers they normally use.

McCormick & Co. has taken a slightly different approach to catalog sales. In addition to its Society to End Dull Meals Forever which we mentioned earlier, McCormick has its own mail-order catalog, "American Accents," offering attractive, unique, appropriate non-McCormick products for kitchen, dining room, and garden. And right there on the back cover is a full-page ad offering for mail-order purchase McCormick spice racks, filled with the same McCormick spices which are also available in stores. This performs double duty, making direct sales while supporting the brand and the products at retail.

Theoretically they ran the risk that retailers might grumble at McCormick competing with them for sale of McCormick spices; but with 17,000 products to worry about, it's not likely that supermarket buyers will find time to worry about what McCormick is doing here. (And even if they did, McCormick should be able to prove that such promotion helps, not hurts, retail sales.)

KOHLER AND BROWN-FORMAN CATALOGS— REALLY A MISTAKE?

Kohler Co. the leading maker of luxury bathroom fixtures (sinks, tubs, faucets, etc.) also experimented with a mail-order catalog of related merchandise. The bath-related items offered were not Kohler products, but Kohler did purchase and inventory them. The catalogs also contained photos of new Kohler products and explained how to decorate with Kohler Color Coordinates, a system for matching its products with those of other companies.

"Consumer awareness of plumbing products is very low," said Janice Baiden, direct marketing manager at the time. "Bathroom remodeling is very costly and is usually a one-time activity. The more the consumer likes what we have to offer in the catalog, the more likely he or she will consider Kohler when redoing a bathroom."

Kohler found a way to measure the impact on its retail sales by offering a rebate tied to invoice amounts for Kohler plumbing products purchased.[14] After a few years, for corporate reasons the Kohler catalog was discontinued. The profit per catalog was improving, but the catalog was still not breaking even. But while they operated it, Kohler was getting awareness advertising to a highly targeted audience in their own private advertising medium, where the reader would be undistracted by the ads of Kohler competitors. The riddle is whether the money lost on the catalog operation was still not a better investment in brand-building and sales promotion than the same amount of money spent on conventional awareness advertising.

It is interesting to note the difference and the similarity between Kohler and McCormick. McCormick sells a very low-cost product, perhaps $1.95 for a bottle of tarragon. Kohler sells a very high-price product, bathroom tubs and fixtures costing hundreds or even thousands of dollars. But the point of similarity is that in both cases it is hard to make advertising affordable — McCormick because it is dealing with a low-priced product and low LTV, Kohler because it is selling products that may be purchased only once in a lifetime. The mail-order catalog with "free" advertising for the brand offers a way to stay in touch with prospects and customers at a cost which is at least partially amortized by the mail-order sales.

Another discontinued mail-order catalog by a branded product was the Paddle Wheel Shop catalog, begun in 1981 by Brown-Forman to promote Southern Comfort liquor. Three mailings a year were sent to one million targeted customers and prospects, offering items inspired by the South such as Victorian lamps, plantation hats, wicker rockers, glassware and bar accessories. Only about a dozen of the catalog items bore the Southern Comfort name. But there was additional soft sell for Southern Comfort in the catalog editorial message: "As you examine the selections, you may note that some items bear the name of a unique liquor of Southern origin. It, too, is part of a venerable tradition, dating back more than a century."

Said Gail Koach, the direct marketing manager for Southern Comfort, "We did a standard telephone research study of customers. We found *even with the receipt of one catalog it did enhance brand imagery.*"[Italics ours.] And David Higgins, senior brand manager, agreed: "Our research showed the catalog positively changed the attitude toward Southern Comfort." But "we couldn't control cost of the catalog. Also, the catalog should go to Southern Comfort customers, and we found the demographics of our mailing lists didn't fit." And, he went on, "we're not in the mail-order business, we are a distilled spirits business." And so the catalog bit the dust in 1986. [15]

From our point of view, they came close to a breakthrough in Direct-Relationship Marketing and probably abandoned the experiment too soon. The catalog combined the advantages of partially self-financing advertising with the advantages of brand-name exposure on glasses and other items paid for by the consumer.

We believe that the catalog could have found more exposure among Southern Comfort customers if they had promoted it with a free-catalog offer printed on "bottleneckers" or hang tags attached to each bottle or displayed on the carton or on a package insert, a strategy that packaged goods manufacturers with mail-order catalogs seem reluctant to pursue.

Looking at the situation from the outside, it would appear that Brown-Forman made the mistake of confusing Direct-Relationship Marketing with Direct-Order Marketing ("mail-order") and ended up with neither clearly contributing to the bottom line. It may have been another case of compartmentalized thinking in which each separate marketing arm — awareness advertising, sales promotion, direct marketing, specialty advertising — each was pursuing its own end, with no one to pull it all together into an integrated strategy.

Also, given the progress that has been made since then in profiling individual America's households by marketing database services, it is possible that Southern Comfort might have made a different decision on the fate of the catalog if they had possessed today's more advanced database thinking and capability.

By expanding overt advertising for Southern Comfort in several pages of the magazine, something which was not done at all until the last issue, they could have increased the favorable effect on brand imagery. And by mailing catalogs to households that were demographic and psychographic "clones" of identified Southern Comfort devotees, they could have influenced more of their target audience. It is true this might have worsened the financial picture for the catalog as a separate profit center. But even if it then lost as much as $1 million a year, that $1 million might have been better spent in this way than the same amount of money spent on bland reminder advertising for Southern Comfort in magazines and newspapers.

Most such ventures are evaluated by the company as a separate profit center rather than an integral component of the marketing strategy. But the trouble with that is that it may take a catalog years to start turning a profit, and even then the profit may be extremely modest compared to the company's main business. This makes such a project easy prey for elimination at board meetings, where decisions tend to be made from a financial rather than a marketing point of view.

HOW ABOUT A PROFITABLE "LOSS CENTER"?

We would like to propose a daring new Relationship-Marketing concept — the idea of operating, instead of a profit center, a "loss center."

The loss center would be a mail-order catalog like Deere, Kohler, McCormick, or the Paddle Wheel Shop, which promotes the brand while selling non-brand merchandise and possibly runs up a modest annual loss instead of a profit. This loss would be treated as a brand advertising expenditure, and the resulting brand exposure and good will would be compared with the impact of spending the same amount of money in print advertising or television. Any catalog profit would be ploughed back into extending its reach.

We believe that in such a perspective, the mail-order catalog as a vehicle of relationship marketing would have a much better chance of surviving, thriving, and becoming a powerful brand-building force.

A frequent-buyer rewards program. This is what General

Mills does with its Betty Crocker catalog offering premiums on some 200 products and General Foods is doing with its Wacky Warehouse catalog of wacky premiums for kids who drink Kool-Aid. After years of coasting along in the backwaters at General Mills, the Betty Crocker catalog has been rejuvenated. Today it is offering items obtainable with a combination of cash and proofs-of-purchase, and now it is not only encouraging purchase of over 200 General Mills products, it is producing a catalog sales profit as well.

Of course one of the greatest breakthroughs in frequent-buyer rewards program was the original American Airlines frequent-flyer program, AAdvantage, so successful that it was soon copied by almost every other U.S. airline and is today an important part of every airline's marketing budget.

By the end of the 80's, American was extending its service to Europe, and along with the new service they extended the AAdvantage program to the U.K., France, Germany, and other countries. Using double-duty advertisng which reflected the airline's positioning in the European market, they used direct-response advertising to build their frequent-flyer membership to impressive numbers in each new market almost overnight. Outstanding awareness advertising combined with outstanding relationship-building built their marketing success against the tough competition offered by the national airlines of Europe.

A toll-free hotline, such as Nestlé's "Allo Nestlé Diététique" in France for new parents and Clairol's toll-free hot-line in the U.S. for women who need advice and assistance on coloring their hair. A limitation of this approach, of course, is that it puts the advertiser only in contact with customers who voluntarily call rather than with the entire market of users. But whether used alone or in combination with other relationship marketing techniques, it is still an extremely valuable tool. And with today's sophisticated automated call processing technology, you can set up a hot-line service which can handle millions of calls and provide detailed customized responses to the caller without the use of live operators or risking the vexation caused by tied-up phone lines and busy signals.

Building relationships through third-party selling. In our personal lives, we often gain a new friend through being introduced to one another by a mutual acquaintance. In marketing, forging a link between buyer and seller can be accomplished the same way, through the helpfulness of a third party.

The third party, which might be a labor union or a trade association or a record club, will send out the direct-response invitation of the marketer to its own roster of names with a covering letter of endorsement. Sometimes this third-party assistance is granted in return for a percentage of the income generated; sometimes it is done simply in order to be able to offer the members, customers, or employees a good deal such as special discounts or special benefits.

Prudential markets insurance directly to the 20 million members of the American Association of Retired Persons through AARP communication channels and with, in effect, the AARP endorsement. (Ironically enough, AARP was originated many years ago as a senior citizens group invented by another insurance company, Colonial Penn, to reach that market; then over the years, the organization took on an impressive life of its own, and now the contract to be the official insurance company of AARP is put up periodically for bid.)

One of the most remarkable third-party programs in the U.S. is Walt Disney's Magic Kingdom Club. It was originated in 1959, two years after the original Disneyland had opened in Anaheim, California, and, hard to believe, was faltering.

Walt Disney came up with the idea of going to nearby companies and offering to enroll their employees in Walt Disney's Magic Kingdom Club. Members could obtain ticket books at a single price which represented a substantial discount off buying the tickets separately.

In 1971, Walt Disney World opened in Orlando, Florida, and the program went nationwide with dramatically increased benefits, including group travel packages, discounts on car rentals, special hotel rates, a newsletter, and much more.

Today club membership is free, and the Club has enrolled as members some six million employees of 30,000 companies. Disney's communication is primarily with the companies and only secondarily with the members themselves. A very sophisticated computer program permits them to select and track the most promising companies for each park location. The companies do not pay for participation (unless they are very small, and then only a small administration fee). Disney provides each company with a variety of collateral materials — newsletters, membership guides, brochures, posters, etc.

Other parts of the Disney empire are involved through giving Club members in the database the Disney mail-order catalog, a 10% discount at Disney stores, special offers on Disney videos, and so on. It is a prime example of synergistic interaction among many different divisions of the same enterprise. Every Disney division is directed by corporate headquarters to work in concert with all the others to maximize the benefits of dealing directly with identified individual customers.

Now the Disney formula for relationship marketing is being

transported to Europe, for use after opening of the Euro Disney theme park outside Paris in the spring of 1992. Millions of employees among the 350 million people in the Common Market population of 350 million will be enrolled in the Magic Kingdom Club of Europe, and will help build the expended attendance of 11 million visitors

Bob Baldwin, the national director, told us that the Club operation "is not a major part of the marketing group budget, but the effectiveness and revenues are huge."

You may be certain there will be other modes of relationship marketing in the future that no one has thought of yet. If you don't want to be left behind, you'd better start thinking now about how you can start building a mutually rewarding interactive relationship with your (or your client's) prospects or customers before the competition finds a way to cozy up to them.

Just as the marketing concept of the 70's became the rallying cry of the marketing-driven companies of the 80's, so will the one-to-one relationship concept pioneered in the 80's by companies like American Express, Fidelity Investments, and marketers cited in this chapter provide the formula for success in the 90's.

Being marketing-driven will no longer be enough. The new leaders will be relationship-driven.

IDEA STARTERS FOR PROFITING FROM TURNAROUND TREND No. 6

MANUFACTURER:

✔ *Can you "force fit" your product or line to any of the most common forms of Relationship Marketing: club...customer magazine... customer newsletter...educational program...mail-order catalog...frequent-shopper rewards program and catalog...toll-free hot-line?*

✔ *Can you evaluate the comparative financial desirability of each "force fit," using on the Allowable Cost per New Customer and LifeTime Value concepts?*

✔ *Is there any way you can combine the forms: e.g. magazine plus educational, magazine plus catalog, frequent-shopper rewards plus newsletter, etc.?*

RETAILER OR SERVICE ESTABLISHMENT:

✔ *What special privilege could you offer shoppers or homeowners in your trading area that might interest them in becoming steady customers?*

✔ *How might you insure the loyalty and increase the patronage of your best customers with some form of "inner circle" recognition?*

✔ *Could you identify important segments within your customer database and send out a monthly customized message to each segment, perhaps as a billing statement enclosure?*

✔ *Instead of just saying, "We care about you," as so many do, can you think of some way to prove it? Send a Valentine to your customers? Offer a birthday gift to those who will tell you their birth date?*

✔ *Could you do something special for special customers; not just a ho-hum customer discount, but really special, like give a party?*

9 From Passive Consumers to Involved Participants

The revolt against "couch-potato" consumerism: non-database one-to-one marketing...the Henninger Beer game cards ... Dewar's Profile parties ... Miller Lite throws "The Biggest Party in History" ... A tiny Wisconsin brewery shows how to compete ... Liz Taylor's Passion ... KLM boosts traffic to U.S. 30% ... Kransco Power Wheels blitz shopping malls...Why kids in 150 schools saved 6 million Care*free gum wrappers...Buick combines involvement with database

---

The American consumer is getting numb from the bombardment of 5,000 commercial messages a day and 2,200 discount coupons a year. Looking ahead to marketing in the Year 2000, Professor Robert Blattberg of the University of Chicago foresaw, "There will be a boredom level to overcome — a cents-off boredom." [1]

And consumers are not only turning off to the avalanche of rebates, giveaways, and discounts.

They are also numbed by the incessant pounding from advertising which keeps turning up the power in order to break through the commercial clutter in our society.

What can you do about it?

In addition to the direct-response and database-driven marketing methods we describe in this book, there is another way to break through the boredom, one which does not necessarily depend on direct response and database-building.

It is not entirely new, but it is assuming new forms and a new importance. We call it Involvement Strategy.

You could argue that it is a kind of sales promotion, but "promotion" has too often largely come to mean the same old tired discount coupons or Hawaiian vacation sweepstakes resulting only in a temporary blip in the sales curve.

You could call it a kind of event marketing, but it is more focused, involving, and measurable than the usual vague good will engendered by a brand sponsoring a sports event or concert. And getting half a million people to call you up or send in a game entry is not exactly an "event" in the commonly used marketing sense, yet it goes far beyond the passive indifference that greets so much of today's monologue advertising.

Whatever you call it, it is an outgrowth of an important society change. There is growing evidence that the 70's and 80's view of consumers as passive receptacles waiting to be won over by pouring in a specific number of advertising impressions is no longer accurate.

Sure, there are still plenty of "couch potatoes" out there soaking up impressions emanating from the ever-glowing TV tube.

But there are millions of others who are saying: if you, the advertiser, want us to hear you above the deafening roar of today's hawking and bargaining, give us a piece of the action.

Consumers welcome it. They want it. They enjoy it. And they respond to it with their purchases and brand loyalty.

We have already touched on some of the ways this can be accomplished through two way communication with a customer database, such as *The Morris Report* magazine published for cat lovers by 9 Lives and the Wacky Warehouse catalog for kids who drink Kool-Aid.

But what was startling to us was the number of demonstrably successful one-to-one marketing strategies which do not necessarily involve building or using a database. And we decided that any review of promising marketing trends we might undertake could not afford to ignore these accomplishments and what they can mean to you. Recent stories of the growth of this approach are fascinating.

THE HENNINGER BEER SOCCER GAME CAMPAIGN

Henninger, Southern Germany's No. 2 beer, was looking for a promotion which would capitalize on the soccer fever stirred up by the upcoming annual European Cup matches. Working with their promotion agency, they developed a two-player rub-off game card to be hung around bottle necks and passed out at pubs and restaurants.

The game involved a simulation of real soccer strategy skills. If you rubbed a spot and no soccer ball appeared, you had to wait for your opponent's next shot. Then you could change direction and rub again.

The first one to reveal a soccer ball inside the goal won the game. Then prize winners were selected in a random drawing from all of the mailed-in game cards.

The prizes were modest. The Grand Prize was a gold Henninger cup or the Deutschmark equivalent of $500. Ten First Prizes were weekends for two, including tickets to the finals, in the European Cup city of the the winner's choice. One hundred runners-up received soccer balls. The total cost of prizes was about $10,000.

Over 140,000 game cards were mailed in (that would amount to 700,000 in terms of U.S. population), and over 70% of the restaurants and pubs in the market area participated. Sales were reported to be dramatically up for the period. [2]

One striking aspect of the promotion is that it moves up from the mild interest in a typical rub-off card promotion to the more intense involvement of a two-player game card.

Another is that it demonstrates that the consumer does not have to be bribed with lavish prize structures if you make it fun to participate and the prizes are appropriately keyed to the fun. And sometimes news coverage doubles and triples the impact of the promotion at no additional cost.

One characteristic of this imaginative Involvement Strategy is its recognition that a promise of emotional pay-off can be more powerful and motivating than mere material reward. People can get much more excited about a chance to be "famous for 15 minutes" than about winning a Hawaiian vacation for two.

Another aspect involves the brand acting as a kind of matchmaker, bringing people together to share a rewarding experience.

Here in the U.S., Dewar's White Label Scotch managed to combine both of these appeals in an ingenious newspaper ad campaign headed, "You can appear in a Dewar's ad. Watch for Dewar's Profile Parties at these Manhattan locations." A sidebar showed a kind of generic Dewar's Profile ad and was headed, "This could be you in (newspaper logotype)."

The ad explained that at the listed restaurants and nightspots, on the dates indicated, candidates for subjects of the famous Dewar's Profile ads would be selected.

The ad would have been much stronger if it had explained what was going to happen at the Profile Parties and how the selections would be made. But it still sounded like a tempting way for a yuppie couple to spend an evening out on the town...an evening in which Dewar's figures very prominently.

National Patent Medicals offered parents a chance to make their kids "famous for 15 minutes" and in doing so managed to carve out a 5% share of market. In a national freestanding insert, the company announced a contest in which parents were asked to send in photos of their kids using its Mickey & Pals adhesive bandages. The winner was promised a part in a TV commercial for the product, and thousands of entries poured in.

Yes, running this kind of event takes a lot more planning and administration than just giving away a T-shirt premium or a cents-off coupon. But as we have already indicated, gaining an advantage in the 90's is not simple.

MILLER LITE'S "BIGGEST PARTY IN HISTORY"

In Texas, Miller Lite threw a Texas-size party that carried Involvement Strategy to new heights. It lasted for 16 months. [3]

Texas is Miller's No. 1 market. One-sixth of all of its sales come from there.

When their sales in the state were down for two years in a row, the company was understandably concerned. So they decided to throw "The Biggest Party in History" to boost their market position.

What followed was a 16-month involvement extravaganza that could only happen in Texas. And only a giant like Miller could afford to pick up the tab.

But it is almost a textbook example of how many different pieces of a promotion can be made to work together, developing a synergistic effect that puts the marketer at the center of the human experience.

The campaign kicked off in May of 1988 with commercials in which the actor Randy Quaid decides to throw a party and invite two million of his friends. Live entertainment events throughout the state were planned. The headline act in Dallas and Houston would be The Who singing group, concluding their national tour there.

This was followed by radio spots in which Quaid enlists the aid of a senator (this was at the height of the 1988 presidential campaign) to run an election to pick the "Party President" for a "party" with live entertainment in each of half a dozen Texas markets. All of these goings-on were, of course, sponsored by Miller Lite.

Disk jockeys were the candidates and listeners cast their

votes at in-store displays. You can imagine how much free air time that produced.

Then in another TV spot, Quaid tried to order 500,000 egg rolls at a Chinese restaurant. This led to thousands of fortune cookies being distributed to radio stations, who held "practice parties" at which listeners could win prizes based on the messages in their cookies.

Then there were the in-store life-size cut-outs of Miss Texas, Quaid's date for the party. They had to be carefully guarded because they kept disappearing.

To add to the emotional satisfaction of participants in the event, various tie-ins were developed to benefit Texas Special Olympics, which stages athletic competitions for the handicapped. Miller guaranteed a donation of at least $1 million.

It was a costly bash, but in the first four months of 1989, the number of Miller Lite barrels sold in Texas increased by nearly 72,000 — 6.4% over the same period a year earlier.

So how do you use an Involvement Strategy to compete with a giant like Miller's if your entire production is maybe 1% of Miller sales in Texas alone? Believe it or not, it can be done. You may not make Miller tremble — but you can still carve out and enlarge your own tiny niche in the market. Consider the following story.

HOW A TINY BREWERY IS GROWING 30% A YEAR

One new phenomenon in the fragmented markets of today is the springing up of micro-breweries. From just a handful in the early 80's, little local breweries producing fewer than 15,000 barrels of beer a year have grown to more than 125. Altogether they account for only .1% to .5% of the total beer market.

One of them is Capitol Brewery of Middletown, Wisconsin, which produced about 5,000 barrels in 1989.

"We can't afford to blanket the market with ads," says sales director Larry Christensen. So what could they do that would make a big splash on a small budget?

Their solution was to stage the Great Taste of the Midwest, a beer-tasting festival which offered samples not only of Capitol's own four beers but also those of 20 other Midwestern micro-breweries as well. And because it wasn't just self-serving hype for Capitol, they were able to get a local radio station to co-sponsor the event, thus building attendance and receiving 200 free on-air plugs for their Garten Brau beer.

"Instead of taking away from our sales, I think showcasing

micro-breweries creates more excitement for our market niche," says Capitol president Richard King.

Another low-cost way of creating excitement that Capitol uses is to send its brewmaster, Kirby Nelson, to liquor stores to greet customers and talk about the beer.

"The brewmaster is the biggest celebrity in the brewery, and people are impressed that he came to their liquor store," Christensen says. "How often does the brewmaster for Miller do something like that?"

As a result of imaginative shoestring Involvement Strategies like these, Capitol has been able to increase its production about 30% a year.[4]

Involvement is a two-way street. People seem to like a chance to participate in the action, and they seem to like having the advertiser personally involved too.

In the first full year that Elizabeth Taylor's Passion fragrance was on the market (at $175 an ounce!), the brand racked up $35 million in sales. And the following year sales almost doubled to $60 million.

Of course part of the reason was simply the wide appeal of Elizabeth Taylor, which Parfums International had carefully researched before they chose her to sign a new fragrance. Part of it was brilliant PR, as when the invitation to the press conference announcing the fragrance came in a purple envelope with the words "Top Secret" across it. (All the major networks came, and so did 17 foreign film crews.)

But an important ingredient was Elizabeth Taylor's own involvement. When the product was introduced, she went on a five-week, nine-city promotional tour. The company estimated that 700 to 1,000 people would show up at Neiman Marcus in Dallas. It turned out to be more than 10,000. And in each store, the star met personally with the beauty advisors who would be selling her products, and afterwards sent them thank-you notes. [5]

KLM airlines managed to increase overall air traffic to the U.S. by 30% in a single year with a carefully integrated program called "America Now or Never." A special magazine, *Amerika*, partially subsidized by co-op ads, was created and given free to travel agents, who could sell it to their customers for about $1. A tie-in was arranged with Postbank, and about two million of their account holders received an insert with a coupon good for a free copy of the magazine from their local travel agent. But the centerpiece of the promotion was 17 local "circuses." At each, there was a theatre showing films from America...live TV direct from America...films about American football...Disney films were shown and Donald Ducks given away. There was a street parade with musicians, cheerleaders, break-dancers, and Walt Disney characters. Local publicity and direct mail drew thousands to each fair.[6]

Just think how hard it would be for mere "image" advertising to equal the impact of these lively fairs.

KRANSCO'S POWER WHEELS
AND THE MULTIPLIER EFFECT

At the heart of any Involvement Strategy is a multiplier effect. By making something happen, and making the consumer part of the happening, you achieve an impact far beyond what you could buy through seeking advertising impressions alone.

Suppose you were the maker of a kind of kiddie car that tots sit in and drive. And suppose you had a budget of just $75,000 to promote sales. How much of an impression could you hope to make on the parents of America with awareness advertising using a trifling budget like that?

Kransco had just such a problem marketing its toy vehicle, Power Wheels. So through its agency, Very Special Events of San Diego, it used its paltry $75,000 to make something happen. And part of the solution was — would you believe? — a sweepstakes prize that parents and children alike were dying to win and yet cost nothing to provide!

The secret was arranging to become exclusive sponsor of the holiday promotion at 63 shopping malls during the Christmas season. Children entering the sweepstakes had a chance to win the honor of being named one of "Santa's official escorts" and driving a Power Wheels vehicle in a mall parade celebrating Santa's arrival. Through the program, Power Wheels is said to have reached 46 million shoppers, picked up $656,000 worth of advertising from participating malls, garnered free publicity estimated to be worth $8,000 per market, and gained a number of new toy store outlets. It is hard to imagine anyone getting more mileage out of $75,000. [7]

CARE*FREE GUM CHARMS SCHOOLS
FOR ONLY $45,000 PER MARKET

Chewing gum is a modestly priced commodity that doesn't offer much advertising+promotion+profit margin for the manufacturer to work with. Would you really ask kids to save up gum wrappers they could exchange for a cassette player? By the time they saved enough wrappers, they wouldn't be kids any more.

But what if you could offer something that kids would really get excited about? Something that would involve them working together and talking about and using your product over a period of time? And something which, like the Power Wheels winners in the Christmas parade, would win your product even more attention and favorable publicity during the big pay-off?

Planters Lifesavers Company and its agency, Campus Dimensions, found the answer for Care*free Sugarless Gum in a $400,000 campaign which offered junior high and high schools in each of 9 target markets a chance to win a live rock concert and a check for $1,000. The school that turned in the most Care*free gum wrappers (or facsimiles) in each market would get a free concert by the British rock group, The Escape Club.

The contest was publicized with radio spots on the Top 40 stations in each market, a mailing to each school, and a toll-free hotline to call for more information.

In all, more than 150 schools participated and more than six million wrappers or facsimiles were redeemed. Display space given to Care*free gum increased by 10% to 20% in each market.

Then the nine concerts in each of the winning schools attracted local television and press coverage — and Care*free banners were conspicuously displayed above the musicians' heads.[8]

Thus, in effect, the young customers were made partners in the promotion and not just passive subjects. Contrast this with the comparative ineffectuality of the likely result if the company had chosen instead to spend just $45,000 per market on advertising simply urging kids to chew Care*free!

DARE FRAGRANCE COMBINES INVOLVEMENT, DIALOGUE, AND THE MULTIPLIER EFFECT

With a modest $500,000 budget, Quintessence Inc. launched an ingenious campaign for their Dare fragrance, one of the best examples we've seen of what happens when the multiplier effect of an Involvement Strategy is combined with the benefits of one-to-one Dialogue Marketing.

The theme of the campaign was "Daring Adventure." In 25 top markets, women were asked to submit accounts of their most intimate, daring trysts by letter or phone to designated radio talk shows.

The event was publicized by point-of-purchase displays, counter cards, and radio talk show mentions. A number of the stories were then to be selected and woven into a romance novel for Bantam Books by author Nora Roberts.

Wait! They're not finished. As a final flourish, the book was to be offered as a gift with the purchase of a Dare product.[9]

Victor Zast, the company's senior vice president for corporate marketing, has informed us that even before the point-of-purchase materials reached the stores, the company was flooded with "daring" stories. Over 750 women saw advance publicity about the promotion in *U.S.A. Today*, purchased a bottle of Dare as required for participation, did some research to find out where the company was located (since the newspaper story didn't say), and sent in their personal stories.

This sounds like just the beginning of a brilliant Involvement Strategy marketing triumph, filled with possibilities for a multiplier effect and continuing dialogue with the women who responded.

THE BUICK OPEN — THE POWER OF MARRYING AN INVOLVING EVENT TO INDIVIDUALIZED MARKETING

Effective as an involving event can be as a selling tool even without the use of database promotion, it can double in potency if the two are used in tandem.

For many years there has been a kind of event marketing which has suffered from a lack of accountability and linkage to the actual sale. An advertiser "sponsors" a sports, cultural, or charitable event, and donates financial support, free merchandise, or both. In return, the theory goes, the advertiser gets lots of reminder advertising from frequent name exposure, and lots of good will benefit — the public thinks warmly of the advertiser for supporting such a worthy event, and therefore is more likely to buy what the advertiser is selling.

The trouble is, too often this vague good will dividend does not translate into sales. Or if it does, it is very difficult to detect and measure, just as we have seen is true of so much image and awareness advertising.

But what if you could combine the impact of event marketing with the power of Individualized Marketing, in a campaign in which the database direct mail promotion builds up interest in the event and at the same time incorporates an event-related sales promotion offer? Then you would achieve a powerful synergistic effect.

That is exactly what is being done at the Buick Motor Division of General Motors, with spectacular results, according to Ron Fusile, the company's manager of sales promotion and direct marketing.

When Fusile took on his job in 1987, he brought to it an unusual background and point of view for someone in automobile marketing. A decade earlier he and his wife had started an upscale clothing store in the Washington, D.C., area, and had used targeted direct mail to build it up into a successful venture. This experience became part of the arsenal of skills he brought to his new position at Buick. And he soon made an interesting discovery.

"When I took my job," he writes, "I was sitting in my office and, just 12 miles south of that office, was an event that took place in Grand Blanc, Michigan. It was called the Buick Open. The strange thing was, I didn't realize at the time that the event was going on. As far as Buick Motor Division was concerned, it was a public relations event. The Buick Open was 23 years old. It was the oldest PGA event in existence. But not many knew it. Not our employees, not our franchise customers and, obviously, not our retail customers." [10]

At the same time, Fusile found, his company was facing a formidable marketing challenge. The U.S. demand for automobiles was level, but production was increasing and U.S. car makers were losing share to imports. In response, companies were engaged in an incentives war, with inducements ranging from 1.9% financing to rebates of up to $2,000. Of course, the end result of the rebate war simply was to neutralize any advantage and increase the cost of doing business.

CORRECTING A COMMON WEAKNESS IN EVENT MARKETING

Fusile felt there was a real opportunity to rise above the noise of the marketplace with a new kind of event marketing which would build a profitable relationship with owners and prospects. The weakness of so much event marketing, he concluded, was that marketers failed to leverage the event by investing in related promotion linked to measurable dealer traffic and sales.

He decided to use the next Buick Open as a peg on which to hang an elaborate total marketing program. It would have as its objectives the building of awareness and a relationship — increasing event attendance and TV viewership — showroom traffic-building — strong dealer tie-ins — directly influencing identified prospects through all stages of the buying cycle from early interest to the actual purchase — integrated media support — and measurable sales results.

Extensive demographic research studies of the database of Buick owners had established a profile by age, education, and income. When this was matched against the profile of enthusiasts of the top 40 participatory sports, golf ranked as having the highest concentration of "Buick types." Golf also ranked highest among prime Buick prospects in event attendance, TV viewing, and personal participation. And it had an upscale image that harmonized with the brand positioning that Buick wanted to maintain.

HOW ALL THE PARTS WORKED TOGETHER

The campaign that was developed was a model of how all the elements of a marketing program support each other in the Maxi-Marketing concept. (Figure 7)

Each of the two-hour television broadcasts of the event carried 32 commercial spots for Buick.

On-course signage linked Buick to the event in the minds of both viewers and attendees.

The tournament program was turned into a souvenir program with worthwhile coverage of the history of golf, the history of the Buick open, and Buick products.

The dealer kit built up dealer enthusiasm for the promotion and provided suggestions for local dealer tie-ins. Buick even created a video for dealers designed to explain exactly how the program worked, and to show their sales people everything they needed to know to cooperate and to benefit from the program.

The heart of the program was the direct mail campaign with three compelling elements — a traffic-building golf sweepstakes, a test-drive incentive, and a purchase incentive. The mailing also encouraged TV viewership by printing the tournament's TV schedule .

The involvement device in the sweepstakes was a golfer's "driving contest" with a different "yardage" figure in each mailing package: recipients would take the entry to the dealer and win a prize if their yardage number matched a prize number. The grand prize was $180,000, the same amount awarded to the winner of the Buick Open. Other prizes ranged all the way down to 10,000 videotapes of Ben Crenshaw on "The Art of Putting," retail value $89.95.

The test-drive incentive was a reward of a sleeve of Buick Open golf balls just like the ones used at the tournament.

The automobile purchase incentive was an additional discount of $300.

This mailing was sent to 3.8 million people, a target audience made up of Buick owners, selected owners of competitive cars, and demographically desirable golf fans selected from lists of golfers and subscribers to golf magazines. Thus Fusile zeroed in on just the right prospects he wanted to reach — "demographically bound to Buick but also very closely associated with the world of golf."

The Buick Open golf tournament sweepstakes campaign

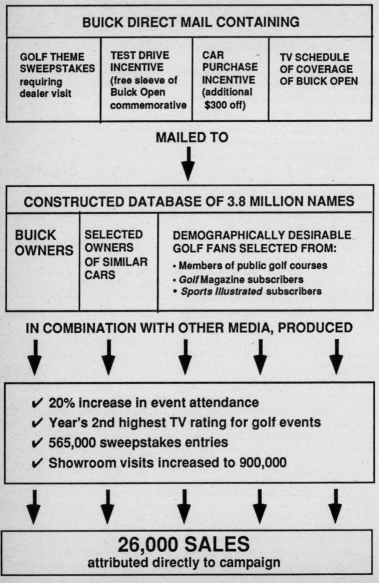

BUICK DIRECT MAIL CONTAINING			
GOLF THEME SWEEPSTAKES requiring dealer visit	TEST DRIVE INCENTIVE (free sleeve of Buick Open commemorative	CAR PURCHASE INCENTIVE (additional $300 off)	TV SCHEDULE OF COVERAGE OF BUICK OPEN

MAILED TO

CONSTRUCTED DATABASE OF 3.8 MILLION NAMES		
BUICK OWNERS	SELECTED OWNERS OF SIMILAR CARS	DEMOGRAPHICALLY DESIRABLE GOLF FANS SELECTED FROM: • Members of public golf courses • *Golf* Magazine subscribers • *Sports Illustrated* subscribers

IN COMBINATION WITH OTHER MEDIA, PRODUCED

✔ 20% increase in event attendance
✔ Year's 2nd highest TV rating for golf events
✔ 565,000 sweepstakes entries
✔ Showroom visits increased to 900,000

26,000 SALES
attributed directly to campaign

Figure 7

The promotion resulted in 565,000 sweepstakes entries and 900,000 showroom visits. Sales people were tied in with an incentive program which awarded prizes to those who signed the back of winning sweepstakes forms. For example, the salesman who signed the form of the winner of the grand prize of $180,000 received a prize of $10,000.

A total of 26,000 sales was traced directly to this campaign. Fusile told us, "It was more sales than any other program run for Buick had ever produced." He said they were planning to expand the next mailing from 3.5 million to 5.5 million, and expand the event marketing portion from one tournament to two.

Nor is the campaign over when it's over. Fusile told us that every response is tracked indefinitely. If someone does not buy a Buick, an effort is made to learn whether some other make of car was bought, or, if no purchase was made, whether the prospect intends to buy a car later. Buick expects to reactivate the "lost" sale prospect two or three years later.

The Buick Open promotion offers an inspiring example of what can be accomplished by changing an advertiser-sponsored event from merely a source of amorphous "good will" into a powerhouse of a wholistic Individualized Marketing program.

The relationship Buick has begun to build with America's community of golfers matches the personality of the brand with the lifestyle of the prime prospects. As Buick has demonstrated, the likelihood of making a sale is greatly enhanced when seller and potential buyer have a common interest and can become involved in sharing it.

THREE COMMON DENOMINATORS

Three common themes run through many of these examples of the trend toward personal involvement with consumers.

1. Reach out and move someone. Each of these campaigns includes direct contact between the marketer and the customers in a way that leads to some response action by the customer in addition to purchase.

2. If it works, don't stop. The Kransco promotion described above had been successfully done for four years when we learned about it. (The endless quest for novelty and "excitement" causes many worthwhile promotions to be discarded too soon.)

3. Work every angle. The most successful involvement promotions often use an artful blend of advertising, promotional incentive, publicity, and sometimes dialogue to leverage their expenditures.

Involvement Marketing may not be as predictable, measurable, and trackable as a database-driven relationship marketing program. But when imaginatively planned, it can stir up huge amounts of public attention, product-related activity, publicity, and good will, and sometimes can be the best way to make a big difference with a small budget.

And it needn't be just the short-term one-time event that too often it is visualized to be. If you capture the names, addresses, and other relevant data about people who participate in your promotion, they can be cultivated further in other ways long after the event is over.

IDEA STARTERS FOR PROFITING FROM TURNAROUND TREND No. 7

✔ *Do you watch Advertising Age and Adweek's Marketing Week for news of prize-winning promotions? Have you considered seeking out and talking to the agencies that created the ones which impressed you most?*

✔ *If you do couponing, how about diverting part of your usual couponing budget into a carefully planned experiment in Involvement Strategy? Then do a research study comparing the effectiveness dollar-for-dollar with your usual couponing .*

✔ *Could you plan your next promotion in a way that will Make Something Happen — something that will get people involved, will reflect favorably on your company, and can leverage your promotional investment with lots of free local-media coverage?*

✔ *What kind of promotion could you run that would make people come together or work together in a way that would encourage sales, good will, and retail tie-ins for your company? Could you bring together customers in your database, as American Express does with its theatre parties for Gold Card members?*

✔ *Where does your product usage pattern overlap the lifestyles and interests of your best customers? Think how "Miller Lite" was combined with "party," and try force-fitting your own product positioning to a common pastime of your best prospects.*

10 From Mass Marketing to Direct Mass Marketing

The shocking cost of mass marketing in the Age of the Individual...The paradox of "Direct Mass Marketing"..Zero-base budgeting...The Benadryl breakthrough...Need for bridge between advertising and sale...Alaska Tourism's 2-track campaign... Computer-disk Softads for Buick, Ford...Video follow-up comes into its own...How Claude Hopkins sold beer 80 years ago...The Canon Camcorder offer...Air France's videos...Citibank makes house calls...Place of linkage in product life cycle....The five levels of ad impact on actual prospects

In our classification of advertising content into eight kinds in Chapter Four, one of the eight was Inquiry Advertising, which has as its prime purpose getting the most likely prospects in the total advertising audience to identify themselves through a mail or phone response. (In this broad sense, an offer of a free sample would be considered Inquiry Advertising.)

Information and Persuasion Advertising is often very similar in purpose and function. It may do as much of the selling job as it can within the limits of the mass media advertising unit purchased, and then complete the sale, for those who are still not convinced, by inviting them to write or call for even more information.

This first step, in the mass media, is only half of a total marketing process which is gaining new importance as a revitalized form and use of mass marketing. We have termed it Direct Mass Marketing.

THE ESSENCE OF DIRECT MASS MARKETING

In Direct Mass Marketing, *you use mass marketing to catch the eye and learn the identity of your true prospects, and then direct additional communications to them alone.* The means of accomplishing this, of course, is to make an offer and to invite a response by any appropriate means -- mail, phone, fax, computer — and tomorrow, who knows, by Nintendo game machine or interactive cable TV? Then the advertiser uses this response to build a bridge between the advertising and the sale — whether by naming the nearest dealer, sending out information or a free sample, offering membership in an affinity group or customer's club, or any other advisable means.

For more and more advertisers, this is becoming an economic necessity. Increasingly fragmented product lines, markets, and media have made it steadily less efficient to reach your targeted prospects by spending all of your advertising dollars blanketing the entire market with a saturation advertising campaign.

It would be a gross overstatement to claim that traditional awareness-fostering mass marketing is going to disappear in the forseeable future, especially for certain kinds of products.

Every advertised product or service is an answer to a need. But it is often not possible to know, despite the best efforts of market research, exactly who out there has the need at the moment.

For instance, the best research, at least so far, can't tell you who is most likely to catch the flu, and who is most likely to have a miserable case of it right now.

So there will always be mass advertising that stands on a soapbox and calls out, "Hey, is anybody here who already has or is coming down with a bad case of the flu? If so, listen up — I have an important message for you." The choices and forms of media may change, but broadscale, buckshot dissemination of such messages will continue.

And yet it is so horrendously wasteful to bombard 1,000 viewers with denture cream commercials over and over again in order to wear down the sales resistance of the 25 or 50 viewers who wear dentures.

Think of the advertising dollars wasted by automotive manufacturers bombarding TV viewers and enticing magazine readers with saturation advertising, since four out of five car owners are not ready to buy at the time the ads are running, and most of the public seeing the advertising couldn't be less interested in the particular model car or truck being advertised.

THE TRUE COST OF MASS ADVERTISING

In television, there are almost always more non-prospects than true prospects watching the commercial.

And the higher the ratio of non-prospects to prospects, the greater the true cost of the advertising.

A common figure used as the average cost of a 30-second prime-time commercial is $7 per thousand impressions— i.e. .7¢ each. Sounds like quite a bargain.

But if only one out of ten viewers is really a prospect, then your true cost is $70 per thousand or 7¢ per impression. And if it takes viewing the commercial five times to make a retained impression, we are talking about 7¢ x 5 or 35¢ to influence a prospect.

Or what if only one viewer out of a thousand is a true prospect, as when selling sophisticated computer software or business services? Then your true cost of a retained impression zooms to $35, compared to perhaps 80¢ for a beautiful high-quality direct mail package with first-class postage sent to a sharply targeted prospect. The television spots may still be worth it, but the true cost raises serious questions as to whether at least some of the money could not be better spent on targeted direct communications. And the same arithmetic holds true in other media as well.

So it is important to examine the true cost of influencing prospects, not just the cost per thousand viewers or readers.

People who don't and won't ever use your product category are not prospects.

People who use your type of product but are firmly wedded to a competing product are not prospects.

People who don't care about brands in your category and just want the cheapest product may be prospects for a bargain deal, but are not very good prospects over the long run.

People who may be in the market for your product some day but not right now – they're not very good prospects right now either, although you may want to invest in them for the future.

In sales promotion couponing, as we pointed out earlier, it is a similar story.

Billions of dollars are lavished on distributing hundreds of billions of discount coupons to non-users, loyal users of competing products, brand-indifferent bargain hunters, and downright cheaters just to reach and try to win over that rare true prospect.

Another problem with mass advertising and promotion is that while it gives non-prospects too much, it often doesn't give true prospects enough, whether it's information or a convincing sample or a trial. It employs a kind of hit-and-run tactic that leaves the prospect in a mildly interested but also slightly dazed and bewildered state.

In print advertising, narrow niche products and services are able to effectively reduce the wastefulness by reducing the size of the ad. But then there is the grim law of compensation which dictates that the impact is also reduced.

So Direct Mass Marketing offers a happy solution, a much longer, deeper sales message for true prospects than is economically feasible in mass media but without a proportionately increased cost.

Instead of running a 30-page ad in *Newsweek*, you can run a one-page ad in *Newsweek* and send 29 more pages of advertising (or the audio/video equivalent) to the truly interested people who respond and want to know more — at a total cost that is considerably less than 30 pages of paid advertising space!

Of course the above is only a manner of speaking to make the point. The ad making the offer could be any size proven most suitable for the purpose, and the follow-up might be not 29 pages (or any other number) of additional advertising but maybe a free sample, a phone conversation, or any other sales conversion tool.

It is important to note that Direct Mass Marketing cannot be simply added on to an already standardized mass marketing budget, as some marketers made the mistake of thinking in the 80's. If that is done, then the question inevitably arises, "Where's the money going to come from? Who's going to pay for this?" And our experience has been that each fiefdom, whether that of the product manager or the sales promotion manager or the newly installed direct marketing manager, fiercely defends his or her own turf (budget allocation).

USING ZERO-BASED DIRECT MASS MARKETING

Instead, Direct Mass Marketing must start with zero-based planning and budgeting. In the Nuprin case cited earlier, the marketing manager said that the original plan ran 20% over budget, but by using a zero budgeting approach, he was able to reallocate money from stagnant ad programs to the Nuprin direct mass marketing program. "First and foremost," he said, "we looked for what would work best and then chose what was most affordable." [1]

This zero-based approach flows logically from the answers to certain critical questions:

- **How broad is your market?** The narrower it is, the more wasteful your mass advertising.
- **How large is your share?** The larger your share of market, the greater the need for maintenance advertising, but the higher the incremental advertising cost per new customer if you want to increase your share.
- **How intense is your market?** The more intensely people care about their problem or your solution, the more likely they are to respond to your offer and identify themselves.
- **How much persuasion would a follow-up add?** For example, would a free sample provide convincing proof of desirability or superiority? If you have an inferior product, offering and sending out free samples may only make matters worse. On the other hand, if people who try your product are impressed, then one sample may be worth 1,000 words. Even if you have only a parity product, not much different from your competitors', we pointed out in *MaxiMarketing* how enhanced sampling — surrounding your free sample with a favorable climate or attractive package or persuasive copy, not unlike what was done in the Merit Cigarette Challenge — may make your free sample seem even better.
- **How high is your Customer LTV?** The higher the potential lifetime value of a new customer, the more you can afford to spend on follow-up advertising and cultivation.
- **What is the right mix for you?** What proportion of your total advertising budget should be devoted to brand image and awareness building, what proportion to reaching out and getting in touch with prime prospects, and what proportion to interaction with them once they are known to you by name and address?

THE BENADRYL BREAKTHROUGH

Warner Lambert, makers of the allergy remedy Benadryl, has provided a dramatic demonstration of what can be done in Direct Mass Marketing for a low-priced product.

In 1989 they commissioned their advertising agency, Sudler & Hennessy, to create a commercial which would offer information about allergies and get many of the 15 million allergy sufferers in the U.S. to "raise their hands" and identify themselves. The phone service provider that was chosen, Touchtone Access Systems, suggested that the commercial invite allergy sufferers to dial an 800 number and find out the latest pollen count in their zip code area. This could be done by using the new automated voice response technology which marries the computer to the telephone. Thus viewers calling one toll-free number could branch to the specific recorded information for their area without the involvement of human operators.

The plan was adopted and a network of Pollen Information Centers was established in the 16 test markets to feed updated pollen counts to Touchtone every week.

This information would be converted by computer to digitized voice recordings. Then a caller simply punched in his or her five-digit ZIP code to hear the pollen count report for that area.

The television schedule provided for achieving 30 Gross Rating Points in the 16 markets, representing 25% of the country, over a 16-week period. It was estimated that the client would do well to get 35,000 calls altogether.

That proved to be wrong. They received that many calls in just the first *two weeks*.

"What followed was a logistical nightmare, as we raced to expand our capabilities in order to handle the mounting number of calls," we were told by Kathleen Campbell, associate media director of Sudler & Hennessy.

But to the credit of both the client and the agency, they didn't back off. They never cancelled a single TV spot because the program was "too difficult" or "running over budget," as a more timid or conventional advertiser might have done.

The agency argued that this was a breakthrough opportunity to reach out and get involved with prime prospects. And the client had the flexibility and imagination to seize the opportunity and start shifting dollars from other programs to handle the flood of responses.

By the time the first campaign was through, Touchtone had recorded an astounding 500,000 calls. Sixty per cent of the callers were repeaters. Some people called as many as 30 times. (In the second campaign, repeat callers were automatically identified so that only new caller names would be added to the database.)

Warner Lambert had started out with no intention of building a database of callers. Midway through the campaign, it was decided to start capturing names and addresses. In 55% of the calls, ANI (automatic number identification) was able to determine the caller's phone number and look up the corresponding name and address. (Now, whenever a caller's address cannot be retrieved by the system, the call is instantly switched to an alternate message asking the caller to leave name and address in order to receive information and coupons, and about half of these callers are also identified.)

In the first campaign, nearly 16,000 names and addresses were captured and became the foundation for the database. These people were mailed helpful information about allergy along with Benadryl cents-off coupons. The rate of redemption of these coupons ran 800% ahead of normal redemption rates!

The following year, 1990, Warner Lambert extended the program to 50% of the country, aiming to attract one million calls and follow up with additional allergy information and discount coupons. At last report, the number of calls were running ahead of schedule and they were capturing 70% of the names and addresses.

They tested using a 900 number and charging $1.50 for the call instead of the toll-free 800 number. Results dropped off by 90%. So they decided to stick with the 800 number — after all, they are in the business of selling Benadryl, not information.[2]

We were not able to learn the cost of the program or what percent of the total advertising budget it represented. But we understand that it represents a minimal portion of the total expenditure, yet has produced results far beyond the modest cost.

Warner Lambert does not yet have a precise measurement of the effect on sales because they have not yet been able to separate it from the effect of all their other marketing activities. As we write this, they are just now putting research tools in place to make this possible.

But even without knowing the end to the story, there are strong hints that the program is having a "very favorable" effect on sales. It is obvious that Warner Lambert is onto something big — a way to locate, identify, and conduct a mutually rewarding dialogue with allergy victims. It's a Direct Mass Marketing success story in the making.

WEICHERT REALTY MAKES A "TURNAROUND" TO DIRECT MASS MARKETING

Weichert Realty has proven itself to be in the vanguard of turnaround thinking with not one, but two daring probes into the future of marketing. And the fact that they abandoned the first for the second only means they deserve to be commended for having the courage to experiment.

In their first experiment in breaking through the clutter of real estate advertising for fine homes, they launched a weekly interactive television program, "Home Shopper's Showcase," in New

York and Philadelphia. Each program took viewers on a quick television tour of some 90 homes. But then viewers with touch-tone phones could call and get user-specific answers to questions about financing. Callers could touch-tone choices in down payment and financing options, and the telephone-answering system would automatically calculate monthly payments and relate them over the phone via voice synthesizer. [3]

But a year later the company reported that it had moved on to what appeared to be an even more efficient selling method, one using true Direct Mass Marketing. They cancelled the television program and started running space ads in 200 newspapers offering the "Home Shoppers' Showcase" on a free videocassette.

A Weichert executive explained the advantage of the new system in a news story in *Direct*. "According to James Murray, Weichert's senior vice president, marketing, the company [had been] paying for broadcast time, an 800 number, and outbound telemarketers who spent much of the time informing callers that the company didn't serve that particular area...[And] only 18% to 20% of those who called the interactive 800 number left their name and address. Now, with the video, everyone who calls is required to leave this information."

Do you see what Weichert has done? Now, by doing mass advertising in geographically selected areas, they can target the right audiences. And then, by offering the video homes showcase, they can pull out of the total audience just those people who are shopping for a new home, obtain their names and addresses, and then focus incredibly powerful advertising on just those comparatively few prime prospects.

WHEN SHOULD YOU "TELL ME MORE"?

Sometimes what is being marketed cries out for providing the consumer with additional information. In other cases, it doesn't make much sense.

Do we really want more information on Charmin toilet tissue or Nabisco Oreo cookies before making our buying decision? (Although if we haven't tasted an Oreo since childhood, we wouldn't mind a free sample.)

On the other hand, if the purchase to be made is of some financial and emotional importance, then a 15-second commercial or a one-page advertisement simply may not be able to tell all the things a prospect hungers to know.

Often this poverty of advertising information leads to intense frustration and even anger on the part of some of your best prospects. Listen, for example, to this frustrated consumer's letter to the editor of *Video* Magazine:

> Last month I was looking for a VCR with at least one hour of battery backup. Most salespeople I spoke with didn't know what battery backup was. One told me even his $1,300 top-of-the-line unit had only five minutes. Another said manufacturers have stopped putting battery backups on new machines. Some thought there was no such thing. In desperation, I spent hundreds of hours over a ten-week period persuading salespeople to let me search through the manuals. Some manuals said nothing about battery backup, others said the VCRs had two minutes, a few said 30 seconds. Most frustrating were manuals that said if 12:00 a.m. was blinking on the clock, the power had been out longer than the battery backup. Useless information, for sure.
>
> Service representatives promised to call back, but never did. Others switched me from rep to rep trying to find one who "might know better." I received such conflicting information that I had to call some companies four times to find out which answer was correct! [4]

In cases like this, it makes eminent sense for the advertiser to locate and identify the true prospects and focus on them the additional information and persuasion they need and want.

This offers a way to make the advertising more cost-efficient. You can set aside at least part of your usual awareness advertising budget of past years to run "public" advertising which will maximize responses from your true prospects and then follow up with "private" advertising focused just on them.

In *MaxiMarketing*, we called this Linkage Advertising because it provides a link or a bridge between the advertising and the sale. You might also think of it as *extended* advertising — extending or expanding your 30-second television impact into as much as thirty minutes of follow-up discussion, or expanding your one-page advertisement into as much as twenty or thirty pages of persuasive follow-up.

A SEPARATE CAMPAIGN FOR LINKAGE?

One "upfront advertising" campaign or two? Separate campaigns for building awareness and pulling in responses? Or combine both functions in the same upfront advertising? Or maybe even forget about upfront awareness advertising altogether and go all-out for the responses and the follow-up promotion?

It's hard to say. Each case is different. But we can say that if you treat the direct-response part of your campaign casually or contemptuously, with just a brief mention of an offer or a reason for responding (and believe us, it does happen, more often than we care to think about), you may as well not bother with it at all.

The Alaska Tourism Marketing Council, to which we referred earlier, has chosen the route of separate campaigns. In their fiscal year 1990, they had a budget of $7.9 million. Out of this, $1.2 million was said to be allocated for ads in such publications as *National Geographic Traveler, Outdoor, Travel and Leisure,* and *Reader's Digest,* offering their vacation planning kit ("linkage" advertising). Presumably most of the remaining $6.7 million was spent on their TV image advertising.[5]

Alaska's image advertising on TV and vacation planner kit advertising in magazines provides a kind of double whammy -- first they make you want to visit Alaska, then they offer to help you plan the trip.

But if we were running the Alaska campaigns, we would certainly want to look at the possibility of increasing the present ratio of direct-response to image advertising — for instance, by "wrapping" the vacation planning kit offer around the image advertising spots on television. We would be encouraged in this direction by a fascinating case history in the tourism advertising field that we stumbled upon while writing *MaxiMarketing*.

Two marketing scholars at the University of South Carolina had made an exhaustive analysis of that state's tourism advertising. Like Alaska, the state had been doing both beautiful full-color image advertising (with a brief information offer added on) and smaller, hard-working black-and-white direct-response ads devoted entirely to soliciting requests for their travel information kit.

The professors found that respondents in each of the two groups spent about the same amount of money if they actually visited the state.

But because the cost-per-inquiry of the direct-response ads was so much lower, the Return on Investment produced by each dollar spent on them was $56.53, compared to only $11.80 R.O.I. from image ads with an offer included. (Of course, this is not an entirely fair comparison; the image advertising may have stimulated responses to the vacation kit direct-response ads. And it may also have generated additional travel activity from tourists of whom there is no record, since they didn't respond to any of the ads. Still, the figures do provide food for sober thought.)

Another noteworthy aspect of the Alaska vacation kit campaign is that it provides the state tourist bureau with so much "free" advertising in the follow-up. One look at the beautiful 9x12 booklet mailed out to all inquirers, the *Alaska 1990 Official State*

Vacation Planner, suggests strongly that the net cost to the State of Alaska may well have been nothing. Instead, the cost would seem to be well underwritten by paid advertisements for cruises, car rentals, lodges, etc., ranging all the way from classified ads up to two-page color spreads with bound-in reply card by advertisers like Princess Cruises and Holland-America Westours.

Apple Computers is one of the few other national advertisers we have found who appear to have consistently followed the Alaska strategy in consumer advertising for a high-ticket sale. They didn't bury an offer of "more information" about the desktop media capability of the Macintosh in awareness ads. They made the offer of a free booklet the main theme of a vigorous campaign, with ads headed, "It takes quite a booklet to show you all the terrific ways Apple Desktop Media can help you express your ideas," and a picture of part of the booklet above the headline. And they have used the same response-driven approach to offer explanatory videos.

Not only can this kind of linkage marketing provide more information and persuasion than is possible in mass advertising, it can do it better. Theoretically there are no limits of time, space, or format, as there are in a broadcast commercial or a publication advertisement. And while practically there is always a cost limitation, you can obviously afford to spend much more per individual in converting true prospects into customers than you can in spraying advertising "impressions" on the public at large.

This means that you (perhaps with the financial assistance of third-party co-advertisers) can splurge on a computer disk, an audio tape, video tape, book, sample, or other powerful means of sales conversion. These are some of the exciting media opportunities that are available today for building a bridge between the direct-response advertising and the sale.

LINKAGE ADVERTISING VIA VIDEOCASSETTE

One of the most powerful new media of all is advertiser-created videocassettes.

According to a study by the Wharton School of Business, video brochures increase memory retention by approximately 50% and expedite buying decisions by 72% compared to print advertising. The study also found that three times as many people are likely to request a video as ask for print information and six times more people will respond to an offer made in a video brochure than to an offer in a printed ad.[6]

Although our research has uncovered a number of examples of all-advertising videos, we were amazed at how few examples we could find of the two-step process — using inquiry advertising which has as its main purpose the attracting and identifying of prime prospects, then using follow-up video as a way of focusing powerful advertising on these prospects.

(And by the way, the cost per cassette may be less than you think. A political consultant, Vic Kamber, reported he had created a short video for a candidate and had been able to order videocassettes of it in quantity for barely more than a dollar each.)

Both Apple and Commodore have made extensive use of videos to dramatize and demonstrate the capabilities of their computers more effectively than could be done in any other way.

For several years, Air France ads offered videocassette previews of such travel packages as its tour of Paris and the Riviera.

Now in this case it is true that a completely free offer would probably attract too many costly inquiries from frivolous non-prospects. So Air France dealt with this problem in an ingenious manner. When you requested one of the videos, you were asked for your credit-card number. Then you could either return the video within 14 days and pay nothing — or you could keep it and your credit-card account would be automatically billed for $29.95.

At one time, Air France had produced nine different videos and was receiving 2500 requests for videos per week, 20% of which were converted to a purchase of an Air France tour package.

LINKAGE ADVERTISING VIA COMPUTER DISK

Nowadays the cost of duplicating a computer disk is so modest, as low as $1 each, that many advertisers can afford to send it out "cold" to lists of carefully targeted prospects. This is especially true in business-to-business advertising.

But in marketing consumer goods and services, it makes more sense to use a disk or video as bridge or linkage advertising in a two-step inquiry and follow-up process. If people have requested such an item, they are much more likely to use it when they receive it. Obviously, however, a computer disk probably should be used only for selling a product or service of some costliness and complexity, one which lends itself well to interactive self-education at the computer keyboard.

A computer wizard named Paula George started a company called SoftAd to create just such interactive software. Her company creates SoftAds on floppy disks for advertisers who want to target the 14 million Americans who have personal computers. This radically new kind of interactive advertising makes it possible to have what is literally a separate, unique communication with each individual in an enjoyable way, just as a computer game does. Besides Paula George's "SoftAd Group," other "software ad agencies" include Einstein and Sandom, SAGE Worldwide, and Creative Media Group.

By 1990, advertisers were spending about $10 million a year on disk ads.[7] A spokesperson for The SoftAd Group has said that a typical program takes from three to six months to develop and costs between $40,000 to $100,000 for everything — concept, design, copy graphics, animation, the master disk, dupes, and packaging. (Of course a large number of disks would require an additional per-disk cost.)

THE BUICK COMPUTER DISK BREAKTHROUGH

The Buick division of General Motors Corporation was one of the first advertisers to discover the power of this new form of linkage advertising.

The Buick automobile in America has a comparatively low share-of-mind among readers of computer magazines. Upscale Americans prefer BMWs to the best General Motors can offer.

So in 1987 Buick ran a page ad offering a free SoftAd to readers of *MacWorld* magazine, the leading magazine for owners of the Macintosh computer, with circulation of about 200,000.

The SoftAd offer got a phenomenal response of 17% of the *MacWorld* circulation, and the home computer demonstration and interaction brought hundreds of buyers into Buick showrooms — prospects who had never thought of owning a Buick automobile before. And 84% of them said they would show the disk to a friend. Ten percent of them said that they would buy a Buick.

In the first year, Buick distributed 67,000 disks, and it has repeated and expanded the program in subsequent years.   In the second year, it expanded distribution to 170,000 disks, this time offering an IBM as well as Macintosh version. The disk came with a $400 "diskount" which could be redeemed at a Buick dealer during the following six months.

You really have to boot up the Buick SoftAd and run through its interactive adventures to appreciate its power and fascination. Through animation and choices, it opens up a door to a new way of looking at a product, one that would simply not be possible in another medium.   The Macintosh version even includes sound effects such as car doors closing and dogs barking. And, reported Nancy Newell, a marketing manager at Buick, "What we found is that the innovative, high-tech feel of the disk carried over into people's image of Buick." [8]

American International Group Insurance Co. has used Soft-Ads to communicate with more than 1,000 CEO's. Squibb gives one to business school students whom the company wants to recruit. Smith Kline & French gives doctors a SoftAd disk enabling them to compare one of its antibiotics to a competitor's in a variety of medical situations.

Coca-Cola in Sweden uses SoftAds to sell companies on the benefits of installing Coke dispensing machines in a country where coffee is preferred by 90% of the population. When the disk is booted up, carbonated bubbles fizz on the screen and animated graphics explain the ease of offering a choice of beverages from vending machines in the workplace. By punching in answers to questions, each company can create a customized consumption profile based on the number of its employees, the number of visitors, and the number of workdays in a typical month. On the screen then appears a recommendation of the appropriate vending machine for that company.

Another company working with SoftAd, The Robeco Group of The Netherlands, is the first mutual fund company in the world to market financial products to consumers via interactive computer disk. Instead of sifting through the fine print of glossy brochures and noodling arithmetic on a scratch pad, prospects can simply insert the disk into a computer. Then, in response to their input, they get personalized suggestions and recommendations to help them select the portfolio strategy best suited to their desired levels of risk and return.

For computer software producers and computer-accessed information services, a floppy disk demonstrating their program or service has become an especially powerful selling tool.

For their advertisement in *Forbes*, Nexis bound right into 200,000 copies of the magazine a disk demonstrating how easy it is to use their information service.

If you are a software maker working with a small budget and think you can't afford the development cost involved in having a demonstration disk created, think again. Sage Software/Polytron Corp. has come out with a $199 software program called DEMO II that enables you to do it yourself. [9]

The touchtone telephone and automated call processing technology have transformed the lowly telephone of yesterday into a highly sophisticated and versatile medium for interactive one-to-one communication, free from dependence on human operators and consumer impatience with busy signals.

We described how Bristol-Myers has used this new capability to capture the attention of some 200,000 teen-agers with their instant-winner sweepstakes for Seabreeze. And how Warner Lambert is serving the 15 million potential users of Benadryl who suffer from allergies by providing a phone information service which reports local pollen counts on a given day. All handled by digitized voice communication at a fraction of the cost of a live operator.

The advertising possibilities of automated call processing (which permits callers with push-button phones to give and get personalized information without a live operator) are endless.

It can be used to build a database rapidly by simultaneously and inexpensively receiving and capturing data from hundreds of thousands of calls.

It can expand on points in a printed advertising message.

It can provide local dealer names and addresses.

It can do an instant survey.

It can provide callers with local endorsements using the real voices of satisfied customers.

It can offer a choice of languages for foreign-born consumers not skilled in English.

It can provide customized insurance quotes and mortgage payment schedules. Plus many other possibilities too numerous to list or not yet invented.

And the use of the 900 number — in which the caller's phone bill is charged for the actual phone-company charge for the call plus, if the advertiser chooses, a stipulated additional charge — has opened up new vistas in promotion.

A marketing director once confessed to us that he has withheld his database-building offer from television out of fear that it would be "too successful."

What he meant was that not only would the flood of responses now include prospects who were possibly less qualified than from other sources — more important, the cost of fulfilling the huge number of requests would break the pre-set budget limits for that.

But by inviting a response via a 900 number at a modest caller charge of perhaps $1, to be split with the phone company, he could both cut down on qualified responses and generate enough income to pay for fulfilling the expected flood of requests.

IS MAKING A PROFIT ON LINKAGE ADVISABLE?

Shortly after Buick offered a free SoftAd for Macintosh owners, Ford put together a SoftAd of their own for IBM computer owners.

The *Ford Facts and Fun* offer appeared in *PC World* magazine. Ford charged $4.50 for their disk-- and actually made a $250,000 profit by the time the promotion was over.

However, we think it was a mistake for Ford to have made a profit of $250,000, which is little more than carfare and lunch money for their marketing executives. The objective should have been to maximize circulation among targeted prospects. And the fact that the offer was in computer magazines, and required a certain amount of effort for someone to respond, should have made it selective enough without imposing the additional burden of a charge for the disk — which we know from direct marketing experience will drastically cut response.

If you think of advertising costs in the traditional marketing way, then a costly follow-up is simply an additional marketing expense, and an opportunity to recoup some of the cost of the follow-up by charging for it can seem like welcome news.

But if you view marketing expenditures in terms of cost-per-response and cost-per-customer, which is essential in The Great Turnaround, then you get quite a different picture. You see that instead of gaining by charging for your follow-up, you may lose. (It is true that you gain in selectivity by weeding out frivolous inquiries, but if it is a serious offer in a serious publication, is this really a serious consideration?)

Let's round off the numbers to keep it simple and consider the following example. Suppose you run an ad for $50,000. The ad offers a SoftAd or other intriguing follow-up for $5. Actually fulfilling the inquiries costs you $3. You receive 2,000 responses, bringing in a total of $10,000 in payments and costing you only $6,000 to fulfill. So viewing it from a traditional marketing perspective, you've made a nice little $4,000 profit which can now be subtracted from the original marketing expenditure of $50,000. Thus your net media cost is only $46,000. That should look very good in your annual marketing summary.

But now let's look at it the other way, the Turnaround way. You received 2,000 inquiries which cost you $56,000 to obtain and fulfill, or $28 per individual. But suppose you eliminated the $5 charge and found that your number of responses zoomed up to 10,000. "That's terrible," you say to yourself, "now, instead of giving me a $4,000 profit, the follow-ups are costing me $30,000 in additional marketing expense. So I'm actually $34,000 worse off."

However, if you add your direct-response medium cost of $50,000 to your follow-up cost of $30,000, for a total of $80,000, and divide by the number of inquiries (10,000), you see that your total cost per *individual*, for inquiry generation and fulfillment is now only $8 instead of $28! By eliminating the $5 charge, you have spent less than a third as much per respondent to identify and influence each individual who responded to your offer.

Even if one argues that the prospects who respond to a free offer are simply not as good quality as those who must pay something, the difference in cost-per-prospect between the two ways in this hypothetical case suggests strongly that you can afford to attract more non-serious prospects with your free offer and still come out ahead of the game.

This same arithmetic can be applied to advertising extended by videocassette, which is much more common and useful than by computer disk, since far more people actually use their VCRs daily than use a home computer.

In some cases, it makes a lot of sense to do as Lincoln-Mercury did in 1989 — simply send a video free to the very best prospects, and offer it free to other prospects who are almost as good. The company created a 7-minute video introducing the 1990 Lincoln Town Car and mailed it directly to 100,000 Lincoln Town Car and Continental owners and 75,000 high-end Buick and Oldsmobile owners. They also offered the video in a mailing to 300,000 Cadillac owners and got an 8% response. The entire program was said to cost around one million dollars — mere pocket money in the megabucks world of automobile advertising.[10]

THE RISE OF "VOLUNTARY ADVERTISING"

Another way to look at linkage is as "voluntary advertising." Or what Lester Wunderman, chairman of Wunderman Worldwide, has termed "consumer-initiated advertising." In a world in which consumers are becoming numb and indifferent in the midst of a blizzard of advertising clutter, one way to break through the clutter is with advertising which people actually request.

Billboards, p.o.p. displays, storecasting (voice messages delivered over a store's loudspeaker system), outbound telephone solicitation, advertising on the movie theatre screen — these are not voluntary. They are inflicted on us whether we are interested or not.

Traditional mass advertising in the major media — magazines, newspapers, radio, television, direct mail — are what might be called semi-voluntary. One can always turn the page, twist the dial, flip to another TV channel, toss aside the unwanted direct mail to escape the advertising message.

Voluntary advertising fits right in with the concept of Individualized Marketing in that the individual selects or requests the advertising suited to his or her current individual needs or interests. It might be a brochure, an audiocassette or videocassette, a recorded telephone message, a mailing of requested discount coupons, or a "take-one" in a supermarket information rack.

Yes, don't overlook that humble advertising servant, the take-one. Did you know that about $600 million is spent by advertisers printing take-ones? Supermarket Communications Systems of Norwalk, Conn., supplies and stocks literature racks for more than 7,000 stores in 35 states. Some 15,000 people a week shop at an average supermarket, which multiplied by 7,000 comes to 15 million shoppers.

Of course most shoppers won't take or even look at any of the 30 or so offers on the rack. But studies show that about 10% glance at the rack on the way out, and about 1% actually stop and study the offers. Now we are talking about making an impression on 150,000 actively interested people at a cost of $3.25 per month per store. And because each card must be picked off the rack by a truly interested prospect, the efficiency is very high and there is very little waste.

Dennis Hatch, editor and publisher of the newsletter *Who's Mailing What*, has pointed out the attractive potential of these supermarket take-ones as a direct-response copy test medium. For example, Headline A could be boldly displayed on your literature in half of your run and Headline B in the other half, and the comparative pulling power of each determined for considerably less than what a direct-mail test would cost. [11]

POTENTIAL OF LINKAGE FOR MAKING A PRE-EMPTIVE CLAIM

For certain kinds of high-ticket products and services, the contemporary form of "two-step" advertising — direct-response advertising followed up by linkage material sent to those who respond — is a woefully neglected opportunity.

For instance, in the camcorder field, more than a dozen brand names and literally scores of different models are vying for the purchase of the bewildered consumer.

A Sony or Canon could blow competitors out of the water by giving up their generic, interchangeable advertising and feeble preemptive claims and devoting most of their advertising dollars to ads offering a blockbuster video devoted to describing and explaining their various camcorder models.

Almost anyone who would request such a video would have to be sincerely interested, a prime prospect. And the video could crowd the competition's products out of the prospect's mind by explaining the brand's different models and features, interviewing delighted owners, demonstrating ease of use, showing prize-winning examples of home videos made with the product, and so on.

This is the huge opportunity for "pre-emptive claim" advertising in the 90's — home video advertising, not imposed on a captive audience as advertising on movie videocassettes is, but *requested* advertising with the wealth of information and persuasion that might bore the non-prospect but will fascinate and convince the true prospect.

HOW CLAUDE HOPKINS PRE-EMPTED
THE CLAIM OF PURITY FOR A BEER

Nearly a century ago, the legendary copywriter Claude Hopkins used the art of the pre-emptive claim to sell Schlitz Beer, which was then in fifth place.

"All brewers at that time were crying 'Pure,'" wrote Hopkins later in his classic memoir, *My Life in Advertising*.[12] "They put the word 'Pure' in large letters. Then they took double pages to put it in larger letters. The claim made about as much impression on people as water makes on a duck."

So Hopkins went through the brewery. There he saw plate-glass windows where beer was dropping over pipes. They explained to him that those rooms were cooled with filtered air, so the beer could be cooled in purity. He saw great filters filled with white-wood pulp. They showed him how they cleaned every pump and pipe twice daily, to avoid contamination. They showed him how every bottle was cleaned four times by machinery. They showed him artesian wells which went down 4,000 feet for pure water.

Then they took Hopkins to the laboratory and showed him their original mother yeast cell. It had been developed by 1,200 experiments to bring out the utmost in flavor.

They told him that all of the yeast used in making Schlitz Beer was developed from that original cell.

Hopkins came back to his office amazed. He said to his client, "Why don't you tell people these things? Why do you merely try to cry louder than others that your beer is pure? Why don't you tell the reasons?"

"Why," they said, "the processes we use are just the same as others use. No one can make good beer without them."

"But," Hopkins replied, "others have never told this story. It amazes everyone who goes through your brewery. It will startle everyone in print."

And so, he wrote, "I pictured in print those plate-glass rooms and every other factor in purity. I told a story common to all good brewers, but a story which had never been told. I gave purity a meaning. Schlitz jumped from fifth place to neck-and neck with first place in a very few months."

The principle that Hopkins describes here is timeless. Only the media tools and techniques have changed.

USING VIDEO FOLLOW-UP TO SPELL OUT
THE PRE-EMPTIVE CLAIM

Today video communication can achieve the effect Claude Hopkins was striving for, with an awesome power to communicate and persuade that he never dreamed was possible.

But it would be neither practical nor sensible to attempt to "spray" this kind of advertising at the entire general public, prospects and non-prospects alike.

For certain kinds of products and services, though, it is practical and sensible to attract, identify, and cultivate prime prospects by offering powerful video advertising for their home viewing at their own request.

Most of today's camcorder advertisements, for example, make claims similar to those of their competitors about "6:1 zoom lens" or "4 lux minimum illumination" or "flying erase head."

But none have thought to *pre-empt* the leadership position with a powerful video which does for the camcorder what the Hopkins ads did for Schlitz Beer, and then to design an ad campaign which would maximize the number of requests for free copies of the video from true prospects.

However, we were pleased to note that Canon at least took a promising step in this direction with a two-step campaign in the fall of 1989. Large ads headed "How to choose a video camcorder" provided more information than most competitive ads do. Then a reply coupon offered a free booklet, "The Canon Guide to Better Home Video."

But for our money the Canon approach still didn't go far enough toward demonstrating how a camcorder works, reassuring prospects who are wary of them, and convincing them that Canon is the right brand choice. Only a video could truly do that for today's television generation. The booklet we received when we answered the ad was a fairly modest effort, with 20 black-and-white pages. In the back, were postage-stamp sized illustrations of the 4 models of Canon 8 camcorders, each with a small-type list of features but with no suggestions on how to go about choosing from among them.

(And, of course, no letter! Again and again we found that brand advertisers sending out material either include no letter at all or else a short, stiff note. A great leap forward in Direct-Communication Marketing will take place when advertisers learn to include in their fulfillment mailings the kind of long, warm, chatty, informative, hypnotically readable letter that has earned fortunes for so many companies in Direct-Order Marketing.)

We think Canon would have done better if they had put that ad headline over an ad offering a video on the same subject. Too expensive? Then how about selling it for the cost of a blank video-cassette, and telling readers they can erase it or record over it after they have viewed it — or can return it for a refund if they prefer?

Audiocassettes can also be used for linkage instead of video, and at less cost. It all depends on what you are selling and how much order margin you have to play with.   Financial service is not essentially a visual product, making audiocassette instead of videocassette linkage a sensible choice. Fidelity Investments and other investment services have offered audiocassettes effectively.

Of course for the right product there is still nothing wrong with offering a booklet or brochure which will extend your advertising message far beyond the limits of a magazine or newspaper page or a brief radio or television commercial.

BERTOLLI OLIVE OIL'S PRE-EMPTIVE DIRECT MASS MARKETING

Bertolli Olive Oil advertising seems to be moving in the direction of Direct Mass Marketing, offering printed follow-ups, and pre-empting the health benefit claims of olive oil that any olive oil brand could rightfully make. We mentioned earlier the Bertolli ads offering more information on the medical benefits of consuming olive oil.

Another recent Bertolli newspaper ad carried two coupons, one to use for ordering an olive oil recipe booklet and another to present to the retailer for a 50¢ discount.

And yet to our way of thinking, this second Bertolli ad fell between two chairs — neither presenting a compelling pre-emptive claim for the nutritional value of this near-parity commodity product nor working hard enough to maximize requests for the recipe booklet.

The ad appeared on Valentine's Day and carried the perhaps too-clever headline, "WHEN IT COMES TO AFFAIRS OF THE HEART, NO ONE KNOWS MORE THAN BERTOLLI." Get it? Yes, you get it if you have time to kill and are willing to take the time to study the ad, associate the headline with the picture of olive oil bottles just below the headline, and read the copy. But we talked in Chapter One about the increasing demands on people's time. This means that often the hard-pressed consumer has better things to do than stop and figure out the message of a leisurely non-compelling advertising essay.

The coupon for ordering the recipe booklet is headed, "FREE! THE BERTOLLI LIGHT AND HEALTHY RECIPE BOOKLET." The copy states: "Over 30 easy-to-fix recipes that are low in cholesterol and high in flavor. Facts on olive oil, cholesterol, and healthful eating, too. A $2.95 value plus $1.50 in money-saving coupons for Bertolli olive oils."

Not a bad offer. Except right below this, in much smaller type, it says, "Send your $1.00 check or money order (for postage and handling) to Bertolli Recipes," etc. *What* dollar? This is the first mention of any dollar. And why charge a dollar? The charge is not really needed to qualify responses -- almost anyone who takes the trouble to answer is a prospect for more use of olive oil. The gain in income derived from the dollar charge is picayune, and is, we are sure, wiped out by the higher advertising cost per response caused by imposing the charge.

It is not fair to single out Bertolli for special criticism, and that is not our purpose. If anything, Bertolli deserves praise for moving in the right direction, however cautiously.

The Bertolli ad is no better and no worse than dozens of similar awareness/sales promotion ads appearing around the same time. But that's just the trouble. There are too many ads like this that are making an effort, but only a half-hearted effort, to go beyond the immediate advertising impression and start a meaningful dialogue with the most interested prospects. Such ads seem to be caught in the grip of the short-term sales promotion mentality and mass advertising copy techniques of the past rather than seeking to "think anew and act anew" in the dialogue marketing mode of the future.

If we were to apply direct-marketing and MaxiMarketing thinking to this Bertolli ad, we would try to make it more like the Alaska tourism ads to which we have referred.

We would throw out that vague, feebly clever headline and make the recipe booklet offer the main headline. We would eliminate the $1 charge. We would provide more powerful motivation for sending for the booklet by tempting the reader with mention of a few mouth-watering recipes, such as *Broccoli Stufati Al Vina Rosso*, Smothered Broccoli in Red Wine, or *Polpettone de Fagiolini alla Genovese*, Green Bean and Potato Pie, Genoa Style. (We had to borrow these recipe ideas from Marcella Hazan's classic Italian cook books, since we don't know what's in the Bertolli booklet.)

Also, like so many of the ads of the kind we are talking about, the Bertolli ad coupon says, in extremely tiny type, "Please allow 6-8 weeks for delivery." Why? *Why?* (Why does it take six to eight weeks to deliver 95% of promotional offers in the United States? Are they using the Pony Express? When will advertisers recognize that frustrating respondents in this way is being penny wise and pound foolish?)

And if we were Bertolli, we would preview in the ad some of the important nutritional information to be provided, such as the fact that today some experts believe exclusive use of polyunsaturated fats is as bad for you as too much saturated fat, and what medical studies this is based on.

We would split-test various copy and headline approaches in the direct-response advertising, and then roll out with the ad that maximized responses in a way that was consistent with the overall image we desired to project for Bertolli.

That would be true Direct Mass Marketing.

Whether you choose a booklet, a computer disk, a videocassette, or an audiocassette, we strongly advocate once again that you prepare and test various advertising approaches designed to maximize requests for the follow-up material. In this way, you will achieve the lowest advertising cost per inquiry, and thereby (assuming a constant conversion percentage) also achieve the lowest advertising cost per sale.

Of course, it is possible that in one ad version you will find your offer is too "wide open" and attracts too many curiosity-seeking non-prospects, in which case your percentage of conversion to sales will drop. But by tracking respondents all the way to the cash register, you should be able to determine how "tight" or "loose" your offer should be for maximum sales and profitability.

PLACE OF LINKAGE IN THE PRODUCT CATEGORY LIFE CYCLE

Another consideration in the planning of linkage advertising is where the prospects are in the life cycle of the product category. Unfortunately they are not all in the same place at the same time.

Everett Rogers has calculated that 2.5% of consumers are Innovators, 13.5% are Early Adopters, 34% are in the Early Ma-

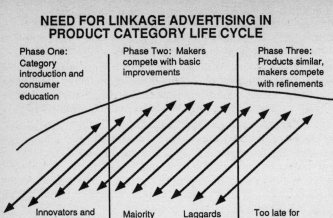

**NEED FOR LINKAGE ADVERTISING IN
PRODUCT CATEGORY LIFE CYCLE**

Phase One:
Category
introduction and
consumer
education

Phase Two: Makers
compete with basic
improvements

Phase Three:
Products similar,
makers compete
with refinements

Innovators and
Early Adopters
Need Linkage

Majority
Needs
Linkage

Laggards
Need
Linkage?

Too late for
Linkage?
Not always

Innovators   Early Adopters   Early Majority   Late Majority   Laggards

**THE SPECTRUM OF CONSUMER DARING
(based on Everett M. Rogers, *Diffusion of Innovations*)**

Figure 8

jority, another 34% constitute the Late Majority, and 16% are the
Laggards.[13]

As the diagram in Figure 8 depicts, when an important new
kind of product or service, such as a camcorder or a financial
management account or a Frequent Flyer program, is introduced,
the Innovators and Early Adopters are seizing on it while the Laggards are not even aware of it. Linkage advertising can hasten
this early adoption process and give an important edge to the
marketer who pre-empts this opportunity.

Later, when the market is well established and a number of
competing companies are battling for it by introducing and promoting important improvements or advantages, linkage can still
play a valuable role in educating the Late Majority and Laggards
who are just beginning to get interested in the category and in
touting the superiority of the marketer's product or service to
members of the Early Majority.

By the time the category has become a commodity largely
sold on price and even the Laggards are climbing on board, as is
the case with VCRs, it may be too late to justify the investment in
linkage advertising. But don't be too sure. In the welter of claims

and counter-claims by commodity products, it may still be possible for one marketer to command a leading position with powerful pre-emptive linkage promotional material.

Direct-Order marketers who use two-step selling — inquiry advertising and sales conversion follow-up — have learned that the conversion material is like *smorgasbörd*. The more there is spread out on the table, the better people seem to like it and respond to it. But most will not consume it all, just as most *smorgasbörd* restaurant customers will not sample every dish in the buffet. Each individual will take from the total just what he or she wants and needs to satisfy individual appetites and concerns.

So even in the late stages of a category life cycle, it may be a mistake to assume that "everybody" understands all the basics of the category's benefits and is only interested in the latest minor improvement. In some cases, as with credit cards, this is undoubtedly true. But in other instances, it may pay to do inquiry advertising and linkage follow-up which starts from the beginning and assumes that most people don't know very much at all.

For instance, a cruise line following this strategy might headline their advertising, "FREE BOOKLET (OR VIDEO) FOR PEOPLE WHO ARE INTERESTED IN TAKING A CRUISE BUT AREN'T SURE WHAT IT WILL BE LIKE."

Such an approach might scoop up the Laggards and the Late Majority before the competition gets to them. And it might even succeed in re-selling some of the Early Majority and Early Adopters who have already taken at least one cruise but are now considering other travel options.

DIRECT MASS MARKETING AND LINKAGE COME TO BANKING

This way of thinking is very relevant to the marketing strategy involved in the advertising and selling of competitive advantages on consumer banking. Some banks started introducing innovations like a consolidated statement and banking by home computer as early as the mid-80's, but only the Innovators and Early Adopters showed eager interest. Now banks are fighting fiercely to win over the Early Majority, the Late Majority, and the Laggards.

And it is noteworthy that Citibank, which has always been marketing oriented, has run response-driven full-page newspaper advertising using Direct Mass Marketing and follow-up education by means of linkage advertising on video. One ad was headed, "NOW CITIBANK MAKES HOUSE CALLS," and like the Alaska vacation kit ad, the subject of both the headline and the text is the follow-up material (in this case the video) that they want you to obtain through a phone call or visit.

Of course, the body copy which is devoted to selling you on the contents of the video is also selling you on the bank features that the video will demonstrate, so the advertising does double duty. Nonetheless, like the Alaska tourism and the Air France ads, the Citibank ad is rare and remarkable in that the main purpose of the advertising is to get you to send for more advertising. And someone in Citibank marketing seems to have figured out that if this is the purpose of the ad, then it makes sense to maximize responses by emphasizing the offer in both the headline and the body copy.

HOW ABOUT "SENDING" A VIDEO FOLLOW-UP VIA CABLE TELEVISION?

What if you could deliver a 30-minute video advertising follow-up to interested prospects without the cost of manufacturing and shipping videocassettes, and reach a lot of other people at the same time?

This is the still largely untapped power of the so-called long-form television advertising – a documentary-style 30-minute television advertisement, either on a broadcast station or a cable channel. If such advertising is supported by tune-in advertising using radio, television, direct mail, newspapers, *TV Guide*, or any other appropriate method, as we argued for in *MaxiMarketing*, then the audience of interested prospects should be greatly enlarged.* Thus the Advertising Cost Per Prospect could be comparatively low even though the gross rating points were unimpressive. And even more important, prime prospects would be exposed to long-form advertising that is 10, 100, or 1000 times as powerful and persuasive as a 15-second or 30-second commercial.

For example, suppose Ford Motor Company ran ads in *TV Guide*, local cable magazines, and the television listing pages of local newspapers, urging readers, "If you are thinking of buying a new car, be sure to tune in our program on Channel 42 at 8:00 P.M. Friday."

---

*As you may recall, the sweepstakes mailing for the Buick Open Golf Tournament that we described contained a TV schedule specifying the network and times to watch the tournament on the air — which, in effect, is what we are talking about. It was a kind of direct-mail support for long-form advertising in the shape of a sponsored sports event. And the result was the second highest TV rating for a golf broadcast that year.

The *percentage* of all television viewers watching that show would be tiny. But the actual *number* of watchers who would be hot prospects for Ford would be impressive in marketing terms. They would include not only people who saw and responded to the tune-in advertising, but also viewers who were flipping around the dial and whose attention was caught because they too happen to be interested in cars. And of course a 30-minute infomercial with a powerful offer would attract a powerful response from the viewers.

It would be an interesting variation of the standard Direct Mass Marketing Sequence we described earlier in this chapter. Instead of :

Direct-response Advertising → *Responses* → *More Information in Follow-Up,*

The sequence would now be:

Tune-in Advertising → *More information on television* → *Responses* → *Still more information in Follow-Up.*

It is also worth noting that such an approach to informing and persuading prospects faced with an important buying decision would also fit our description of "voluntary advertising." Prospects watch long-form television advertising because they *want* to, not because they can't escape it

In 1984, in the midst of the Reagan era of deregulation, the FTC lifted the restrictions on the amount of commercial minutes allowed per hour over the air, and long-form advertising began to experience explosive growth.

Probably the king of today's long-form advertising is Tim Hawthorne, the founder and president of Hawthorne Communications. He says that in that first year of deregulation, his company had sales of about $20 million. By 1989, sales had risen to $350 million.

And just as mail-order commercials improved in quality and finesse over the years, incorporating many of the slick production values of the most expensive brand awareness commercials, so has the long-form infomercial progressed from schlock to quality presentation.

"Long-form is changing," says Hawthorne. "The environment is becoming so competitive that it's forcing the quality of production to go up. We're getting away from the talk show formats that have been popular in the past and we're going to documentary formats. More and more celebrities are being used. And a wider range of companies are beginning to include long form in their marketing mix."

And as Hawthorne pointed out, "If you've got a [response from] a person who has watched 20 to 30 minutes of a long-form commercial, you've got an incredibly qualified lead."

For this reason, Hawthorne predicted, major advertisers will start trying long-form for lead generation.

"There's no reason," he says, "why Chrysler can't develop a long-form commercial that showcases its new models, and use that commercial to generate customer leads. I think many advertisers just aren't aware that long-form is out there." [14]

BEYOND LINKAGE

The deepest level of Direct Mass Marketing is Customized Continuing Database Marketing (Relationship Marketing), in which the responses are not only fulfilled with linkage advertising but the information about each respondent is added to the in-house database and used to conduct continued and customized communication in the future.

We have been observing these days a good deal of thoughtful, intelligent direct-response advertising and linkage follow-up — which then comes to a dead stop. Incredible as it seems at a time when there is so much talk about database marketing, our distinct impression is that a great many companies are still fullfilling requests for samples or more information -- and then throwing the names away! (We base this conclusion on the personal experiences both of us have had of answering an ad, hearing from the advertiser once -- and then never again.)

This is often outrageously wasteful. Admittedly there are instances involving low-price low-intensity products in which it is simply not economic for the advertiser to attempt to continue the relationship. But where there is sufficient emotional involvement and Lifetime Customer Value, there is no excuse for not continuing to seek the sale or loyalty of the person who has responded.

And by continuing the relationship, you can reinforce the enthusiasm of new customers, cross-sell other products, and build a ready-made market for new products.

Putting it all together, it can be seen in Figure 9 that there are actually five different levels of impact on actual prospects, from indiscriminate Mass Marketing — to Targeted Marketing — to Targeted Direct-Response and Linkage — to Maximized Responses — to Continuing Database Marketing.

How much emphasis you should place on activity at each level depends on the size of your budget, the breadth or narrowness of your market, the intensity of consumer interest in your product or category, and the Lifetime Value of a new customer.

But as a marketer, you should certainly be asking yourself,

5 LEVELS OF IMPACT ON ACTUAL PROSPECTS

1. Mass marketing in mass media chips away at everybody

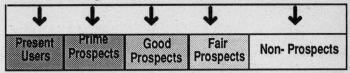

2. Sharp targeting of message and media makes deeper impression on actual prospects (and users)

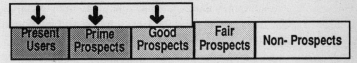

3. Direct-response advertising and linkage follow-up makes even deeper impression on best prospects (and users)

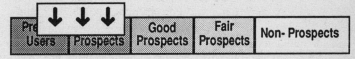

4. Maximizing responses via split-run testing widens the reach of linkage follow-up

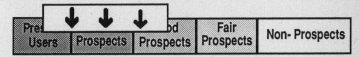

5. Maximized responses and *customized continuing database marketing* combines width and depth of impression on best prospects (and users)

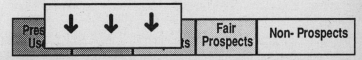

Figure 9

"Shouldn't I be extending my hand in at least some of my advertising to my true prospects, leading by the hand those who do respond, taking them closer to the first sale, and then continuing the relationship?"

IDEA-STARTERS FOR PROFITING FROM TURNAROUND TREND No. 8

✔ *Does your product or service have more of an advantage than you are able to convey in your media advertising?*

✔ *Is your advertising seeking a serious and costly purchase that could benefit from direct-response advertising and linkage follow-up building a bridge between the advertising and the sale?*

✔ *Could you use linkage advertising to pre-empt the copy story common to your product's category and tell it in fascinating, compelling detail (the same way the competing brands could but don't)?*

✔ *Could you develop an audiocassette, videocassette, or a computer disk to bridge the gap between your advertising and the sale?*

✔ *If you are charging the consumer a higher rather than a lower amount for requested follow-up material, have you tracked and computed whether the additional revenue is more than consumed by an increase in the advertising cost per response?*

11 From U.S.P. to E.V.P.

The growing parity products problem..The Extra-Value Proposition solution...The product as service...Sopad Nestlé's spectacular service for new mothers in France...Cadillac's Roadside Service ...The Oldsmobile Edge...Printed instructions, the "black hole"...E.V.P. for packaged goods, service companies...How Amex leapfrogged the service competition stalemate...A sweetheart of a bank in Chicago...The role of Direct-Relationship Marketing...How Apple adds service to its marketing...Learning from Lands' End, L.L. Bean, MacWarehouse., C & R Clothiers..How PACE Warehouse serves small businesses

We discussed earlier both the virtues and the limitations of the brilliant Rosser Reeves concept of the Unique Selling Proposition.

The concept is still alive and well. You can still see examples of advertising that reflects a U.S.P. on your television set nightly. Such as the headache remedy that "more doctors recommend," Tylenol.

But in a mature market, where competitors are able to quickly imitate any special advantage you may introduce, competing products move ever closer to parity and it becomes ever harder to carve out the perception of a unique difference.

So where do you go from here? How do you make the perception, or better yet the actual value, of your product or service, superior to that of your competitors?

The answer lies not in turning away from the idea of U.S.P. but in adding to it — in turning to the E.V.P., the Extra Value Proposition. This is becoming increasingly essential, for manufacturers and retailers alike.

In the 90's, an E.V.P. can be the best way to have a unique advantage.

Wrote marketing critic Alvin Achenbaum in *Advertising Age* in 1988: "As manufactured products manifest a marked similarity, service could well become the differentiating feature in the sale of merchandise as it moves through its distribution channels. And it opens up a whole new arena of opportunity for communications aimed at consumers."[1] We might add that retailers, fastfood companies, and other service companies can also benefit from this same opportunity.

"When the 'Marketing Mix' was propounded back in the 50's," muses that wise observer of the Japanese market, George Fields, "we learned to consider the interactions of many elements — 'product,' 'price,' 'sales,' 'distribution,' 'packaging,' 'advertising,' etc. But somehow in the original mix, 'service' was left out. The idea that even manufacturers are selling a service and not just a product is now well understood, or is it really?"[2]

Once marketers realize that they are selling a service as well as a product, wonderful new opportunities arise. It becomes possible to construct a supplementary service proposition that might even go so far as to shine even brighter than the product itself in the consumer's mind. What is important is that it creates a favorable mindset leading to more product purchase and loyalty.

NESTLÉ BABY FOODS E.S.P. IN FRANCE

The success of Sopad Nestlé in France illustrates how E.V.P. can lead to greater customer satisfaction and sales.

Sopad Nestlé in France was in a poor third place position behind Gerber in the baby food sector.

Both Gerber and Nestlé produce a top-quality line. Both have strong brand recognition and run powerful awareness advertising campaigns.

Management at Nestlé knew they had to do something dramatically different to set themselves apart. So they turned to an individualized marketing strategy built around several E.V.P.s.

First of all, as we described in Chapter Seven, Nestlé advertising and packaging now prominently displays a toll-free phone number. French mothers can call "Allo Diététique Nestlé " any time 10 hours a day, six days a week, to talk to one of Nestlé's four licensed dieticians about Baby's eating needs.

These helpful conversations with a real expert are as much a part of the Nestlé baby foods product as the fruit and vegetables, the glass containers, and the labels.

The dieticians answering the calls immediately establish a warm, reassuring presence and make a powerful contribution toward creating an appealing corporate and product personality in the minds of the callers. Nestlé receives 500 thank-you calls a year from appreciative customers. (How many thank-you calls from customers does *your* company receive in a year?)

Allo Dietétique Nestlé is not just a toll-free number on the product label. It is an Extra Value Proposition which has become an intrinsic part of the argument for using the product.

Another part of the Sopad Nestlé E.V.P. strategy goes even further to set Nestlé apart from their competitors in the public's mind. In cooperation with a diaper brand called Lotus, Nestlé comes to the rescue of parents who are traveling along the highways of France in the summertime.

They have erected Relais Bébé waystations, where Mother and Dad can pull off the road and tend to baby's needs. When they enter the building, a hostess greets the couple with a Nestlé baby food menu from which a delicious meal can be chosen for Baby. There are high chairs for the infant and comfortable seating for the parents. And, there are fresh diapers and a changing table where the parents can make the little one comfortable.

More than 120,000 cars stopped at Relais Bébé during the first summer of operation. At many of the stops, there was a line of cars waiting when the doors opened at 6:00 A.M. Word of this great convenience provided by Nestlé spread like wildfire to friends and neighbors from those who were the first to use the Relais Bébé facilities.

Is this any way to sell baby food? You bet it is. The proof is in the numbers. Between 1985 and 1989, Nestlé made a whopping gain of 10 points in the French baby food market, from a 20 share to a 30 share. It rose from No. 3 to No. 2, outdistancing Gerber. And Jean Semah, the managing director of Sopad Nestlé at the time, told us that he credited the extra value added by the phone-in service and the roadside service for at least 25% of their growth. Those 2.5 share points more than paid the cost of the Extra Value Proposition. And who can estimate the long-term value of the word-of-mouth advertising and the good will generated by Nestlé's turnaround marketing approach?

CUSTOMER SATISFACTION CAN
BOOST REPURCHASE 25%

Listen to these words of wisdom from Daniel P. Finkelman of the consulting firm of McKinsey & Company:

> Every business has ample opportunity to create a higher level of customer satisfaction.
>
> According to Jan Carlson, chairman of Scandinavian Airlines System, each time a customer is greeted by a salesman or voices a complaint, and every time a customer brings a product back to the service department, it is a moment of truth for the entire company — an opportunity to develop a long-lasting relationship.
>
> Unfortunately, few businesses capitalize on these moments — and it costs them dearly.
>
> Satisfying customers is not just another platitude. Increasing a customer's level of satisfaction pays off by building loyalty and increasing the likelihood that a customer will repurchase a company's product.
>
> For example, the Ford Motor Company reports a 23 percentage point difference in the level of repurchase between its customers who are very satisfied with their dealers' service and those who are very dissatisfied with their dealers.
>
> Another large manufacturer of consumer durable goods found that among its retailers that failed to satisfy their customers service requirements, product-repurchase loyalty was only 20 to 25 percent. By contrast, those retailers that generated high levels of customer satisfaction had a repurchase loyalty that averaged more than 50 percent.
>
> The evidence is clear: satisfying customers, which includes repairing their product and responding adequately to complaints, can generate increases of 25 percentage points or more in repurchase loyalty. In addition, it is harder and much more expensive — in some industries as much as six times as expensive — to wrest a customer from a competitor than to win a new sale from a current customer.[3]

But it would be a serious mistake to think that service is crucially important only in selling services and hard goods. A can of Campbell's Chicken Soup is a service. It performs the service of filling your belly. It also performs the service of saving you the trouble of buying your own chicken and making your own soup.

(And it would perform an even greater service if Campbell's would promote wider distribution of its great little book of recipes using Campbell's soup as an ingredient. Pillsbury has a series of cooking booklets which are sold right at the check-out counter in supermarkets.)

Viewed in this way, it can be seen that the value of the product can be increased not only by improving the product itself but also by offering extra value in the form of an extra element of service. One-portion cans of soup, for example, for people living alone. Or smaller cans of pet food for people with smaller pets, so that leftovers need not be stored in the refrigerator and re-used.

There is another component of value in product selling, and that is what computer software producers call "support" — meaning, "What are you going to do to help me get the most out of your product after I buy it?" And in that respect, a point must be chalked up in Cadillac's favor for the campaign they have run headlined: "CADILLAC ROADSIDE SERVICE, ANOTHER REASON WHY CADILLAC OWNERS ARE THE MOST CARED-FOR IN THE WORLD." Listen to what it promised:

> Professional help is a toll-free phone call away — 24 hours a day, 365 days a year.When you phone the Cadillac Roadside Service Hotline at 1-800-882-1112, you speak with a phone advisor who knows your Cadillac intimately. The advisor will ask specific questions to help diagnose the problem and, in many cases, give you instructions over the phone to get you back on the road...

> On-the-spot service when you need it the most — nights, weekends, holidays. If necessary, a service advisor will dispatch an authorized Cadillac dealer technician in a specially equipped vehicle, well stocked with special tools and genuine GM parts. The dealer technician will even provide you and your passengers with courtesy transportation to your home, a hotel, or another local destination if more extensive service is required.

That's a pretty impressive and appealing promise. Hidden inside it is a second promise, a promise of excellence: only an excellent product could afford to make an offer like that. And in case readers were skeptical, the newspaper ad backed up the service claim with equally impressive testimonials like these from delighted owners:

> "It was the Fourth of July when Roadside Service provided the help I needed."

> "With the advisor guiding me on my portable phone, I corrected the situation — in an evening gown."

> "I was very impressed with the quick service and relieved at having the repairs made right away without the trouble of having my car towed, as well as the inconvenience of being without a car."

We were also pleased to note that the newspaper ads included an

800 number to call for "product literature." But we were not so pleased at that mundane description of what was being offered. Think how much more provocative the invitation would have been — and how many more responses Cadillac would have received — if instead the offer line had said something like: "Call this toll-free number for two free booklets: (a) "Cadillac Roadside Service, The Whole Story" and (b) "The Cadillac Catalog: Every Model and Every Option." And then added enticing descriptive copy to make you want the booklets.

About the same time, General Motors also made news by announcing that *any buyer of a new Oldsmobile who was dissatisfied for any reason within 1,500 miles or 30 days could return the car for a full credit toward the purchase of another Oldsmobile.*

"Promises of quality don't do it any more; you don't get away with words," said Oldsmobile's director of customer services. [4] Oldsmobile has added this satisfaction guarantee to its own 24-hour Roadside Assistance and GM's 3-year, 50,000-mile Bumper-to-Bumper Plus warranty to create a complete E.V.P. package they call the Oldsmobile Edge Customer Satisfaction Program.

A buyer research study by the company showed that over 10% of all the sales of the 1990 model Oldsmobiles in the first months could be attributed to the program. And out of 94,388 eligible cars sold, only 536 or just .6%, were returned to their dealers. Most of these returns were for customer preference reasons such as a desire for more options, different seats, or a more expensive model, rather than performance-related reasons.

The Roadside Assistance service had received 1,286 calls, only 27% of which had been for mechanical problems. About 62% were from buyers seeking trip route assistance, 5% for help with a flat tire, and 4% for lock-outs.[5]

This surely represents an impressive new chapter in wrapping a product in a service. Imagine having included with your automobile purchase an opportunity to get help with routing your trip or fixing your flat tire!

Sharp electronics products has provided an admirable example of not only providing what sounds like superb back-up service but encouraging its use. Their two-thirds page magazine ad is headed: "SHARP SERVICE. EVERY SHARP PRODUCT COMES COMPLETE WITH DENISE MARTIN." Beneath a photo of Denise and two other Sharp hotline staffers, the copy goes on to say, "If you have a question or problem with an electronics product, who do you call? If it's a Sharp consumer product, you can call Denise Martin, Mike Bosanti, Paul Moore, or another of the professionals standing by in the Sharp Consumer Information Center. They're trained to have the answers you need. And authorized to resolve problems quickly. How to install a CD player. What a VCR limited warranty does and does not cover. Where to find a replacement battery charger for a laptop computer...If you have a question regarding any Sharp consumer product, please call 1-800-526-0264."

In the electronics field, where products often seem so similar and there is a strong inclination to buy by price alone, doesn't advertising like this make you feel a little more like insisting on a Sharp? If only Sharp would follow up each call with a really nice personalized letter, a catalog of Sharp products, and information on how to find them at retail, they would double the value to the company of this outstanding service set-up.

PRINTED INSTRUCTIONS — THE "BLACK HOLE" OF HIGH-TECH OR UNASSEMBLED HARDGOODS

How much longer must we consumers suffer with confusing, poorly written, poorly illustrated instructions for setting up and using a high-tech item that is either high-ticket or comes unassembled? At last report, Sony had 554 product-information specialists fielding some 500,000 calls for help per year from customers, a good number of them needing help on setting up and using the Sony product they had just purchased or been given.[6] Of course, it is commendable that Sony is providing such help. But one can't help wondering why Sony is receiving so many calls for help, and whether better instruction manuals wouldn't cut down on the number of calls.

Which manufacturer is going to be the first to win the undying gratitude and loyalty of its customers by demanding that every bit as much communications talent and brilliance as is used in making the sale must also be used in the printed instructions that accompany the product? A consumer affairs feature story in *The New York Times* verified the widespread existence of this problem:

> Each year, thousands of Americans are baffled by the ever-more complicated electronic devices they receive as holiday presents or are tempted to buy at sales. Service centers say they are flooded with calls from customers who cannot set up or operate their gifts or purchases.
>
> Dan Siegel, an 82-year-old retired salesman, was at home in Largo, Fla., when a blackout erased the programming on his brand-new, 27-inch color television set. He found the diagrams in the owner's manual indecipherable. Putting the machine back into working order re-

quired five telephone conversations with the dealer who sold it...

"I tried to follow the instructions, and I'm not an ignorant man," Mr. Siegel said. "But I absolutely could not figure out what to do. They make those instructions so complicated, it's worse than the I.R.S."...

The telephones ring all day at McCann Electronics, a service center in Metairie, La. Many of the callers have working televisions and video-cassette recorders, but cannot understand how to operate them...

Confusing instruction manuals are often to blame for consumers' difficulties, said Gary Walker, a spokesman for New York City's Department of Consumer Affairs. "They often tend to speak in tongues as far as most of us are concerned, or it may be a manual written in a foreign language and then badly translated into English," he said.

The problem is particularly acute with computer software, which in many cases is now accompanied by a manual of several hundred pages. Software producers know that success in using the product is as important as the virtues of the product itself, and they have tried desperately hard to make their manuals understandable. The best producers have succeeded pretty well, and makers or importers of high-tech products in other fields would do well to study these outstanding manuals and learn from the models of explanation and reassurance that they provide.[7]

The bottom line is that in cases of tricky assembly or use, outstanding instructions add enormous value to the product. And poor, confusing instructions are a form of negative advertising that subtracts from your company and product reputation.

Some day, a few smart marketers are going to not only include brilliant instructions with their products but feature that fact in the product advertising. Then they can stand back and watch hordes of eager customers come charging up to their front door. Furthermore, they could invite customer comment on the clarity (or lack of it) of their instructions and then make the instructions even better by incorporating what they learn from these comments.

Are you ready for a really daring thought? What electronics company will be the first to do a television commercial showing how simple it is to hook up their latest VCR to your cable system and then set it to record on-air programming? Or how about enclosing with each new VCR a videotape demonstrating these points?

ORTOFON USES SERVICE TO GROW IN A SHRINKING MARKET

At a time when the market for recorded music was inexorably shifting from LP records first to audio cassettes and then to compact discs, how would you have liked the job of building sales for upscale record turntables selling for $199 to $875?

That was the formidable task that confronted Kevin Byrne, president of Ortofon, when his company bought the rights to distribute and market Dual turnables in the U.S. But while U.S. turntable sales overall have been declining, Dual's have grown almost 25% a year.

How has Ortofon turned things around? By an ingenious combination of upscale image-building, through advertising in audio buff magazines, cross-promotion with high-quality record manufacturers, and a unique E.V.P. customer-service program. The latter has been devised to bring in and resell the thousands of Dual turntable owners who still have and cherish a large collection of LP records.

Each year Ortofon puts on about 25 free in-store turntable and cartridge clinics at dealers in major cities around the country. The dealers promote the clinics locally, partly with co-op ad money supplied by Ortofon. Company representatives set up Ortofon-built test computers in the stores, and customers bring in their Dual turntables and Ortofon cartridges for a free check-up. Each customer gets a printout showing the findings and any recommendations for new equipment that might be necessary.

Most of the problems that show up require only simple adjustments and calibrations, and the Ortofon representative performs these free of charge. You can imagine what a warm glow this gives the customer. About 25% of the customers who participate end up buying a new Dual turntable or Ortofon cartridge.[8]

It's a wonderful example of "doing well by doing good," of winning the hearts and minds of customers by wrapping an Extra-Value Proposition around the product.

E.V.P. FOR PACKAGED GOODS

Although packaged-goods manufacturers have by and large been slower than high-ticket high-tech hardgoods makers to appreciate service as a significant factor in the buying decision, the smartest ones are showing that they understand.

Bristol-Myers builds Extra Value into its Clairol hair coloring products by providing a toll-free service number in each package and receives 500,000 calls a year from people wanting help or advice. And we have just discussed how in the baby foods field Sopad Nestlé is offering an E.V.P. through heavy investment in maintaining a telephone hot-line for parents.

When you buy any one of more than 200 General Mills products, the Extra Value Proposition is an opportunity to save up to 77% on Oneida flatware and enjoy attractive discounts on many other kitchen and household products in the Betty Crocker catalog.

Hy Gottesman of the public relations agency Ruder-Finn has pointed out that much of the best promotion today looks beyond mere short-term sales. "This means giving the consumer added value, something to remember the brand long after the coupon is redeemed and the product purchased. It could be something tangible like the Glad Bag-a-thon where whole communities pitch in to clean up, or an intangible, like the feeling you get when you contribute to Ronald McDonald House." [9]

SERVICE BUSINESSES NEED E.V.P. TOO

Of course, if what you are selling is services, the need for superior service is glaringly obvious. But as always, some service companies race ahead by offering better services while their competitors bring up the rear.

We have noted that the Burger King E.V.P., their Kids Club, got rave notices from their franchisees and brought droves of kids into Burger King.

Fidelity Investments, one of the pioneers in mutual funds since the early 70's, has always recognized that although yield, safety, and growth are important, so is the E.V.P. They were among the first to offer check-writing, a huge choice of different types of fund, phone switching from one fund to another, round-the-clock phone service, walk-in investor centers, a comprehensive monthly investment statement, a free investment magazine, etc. They have invested heavily in phone capacity to lessen the likelihood that you will ever get a busy signal when you call. [10]

The National Westminster Bank announced that it would start giving $5 to customers who are treated rudely by bank employees and $50 to anyone who failed to receive a fast response to a loan application.

AT&T has promised business prospects rebates and free calls if their AT&T incoming toll-free lines were out of order for more than an hour. [11]

HOW A SMALL CHICAGO BANK DOUBLED ITS ASSETS

A small bank in Chicago, the Cosmopolitan National, one out of 400 banks competing in the city, doubled its assets through its innovative additions to their basic banking services.

For instance, they ran ads in local legal publications offering lawyers a free safe-deposit box for one year.

They made it possible to open a checking account at the bank's automatic teller machines simply by viewing an explanatory video and then putting an envelope with $100 or more in it into the machine.

And to stir up excitement during the slow month of January, the bank created and offered the "Sweetheart CD": if you bought one for $2500 or more, the bank gave you a Valentine's Day package which included flowers for your sweetheart from a local florist, dinner for two at a local restaurant, a show at a local comedy club, and a night at the recently opened Swiss Grand Hotel. The bank got the local merchants involved to donate the gifts in exchange for the advertising provided.[12] Cosmopolitan National has discovered the secret of adding E.V.P. to make the bank unique.

HOW MARKETING AND SERVICE ARE INTERTWINED

It follows that if service is a valuable component of the product, then marketing personnel should be involved in management decisions about service. The marketing director is in the best position to know or find out what added service can best strengthen the marketing message.

When the mutual funds company, American Capital Management and Research, faced slowing sales and back-office snarls in the mid-1980's, they hired Don McMullen of Mellon Bank to revamp both marketing and service. "Because," said McMullen, "when it's all said and done, the quality of your service has a lot to say in how well your product sells." Under his supervision, the company started new training for phone clerks, an automated telephone order system, and computer equipment so clerks could call up customers' records instantly, spending about $1 million for equipment alone.

LESSONS IN SATISFACTION FROM DIRECT MERCHANTS

Catalog merchants live or die by the degree of satisfaction experienced by their customers. You might return to a department store because of its convenient location even if you had been treated discourteously by a sales clerk there. But with dozens of specialty mail-order catalogs to choose from, you are not likely to re-order from a catalog company from which you have received bad service.

So the smartest ones have realized that the Extra Value they can and must provide is absolutely superior service and satisfaction and attention to every aspect of the customer relationship. You can profit from their experience by closely observing their customer-satisfaction techniques even if your company is not involved in direct marketing

The legendary L.L. Bean, now with annual sales of $650 million, has built its business in part on its very simple, powerful, unequivocal guarantee: *"All of our products are guaranteed to give 100% satisfaction in every way. Return anything purchased from us at any time if it proves otherwise. We will replace it, refund your purchase price, or credit your credit card, as you wish. We do not want you to have anything from L.L. Bean that is not completely satisfactory."*

Lands' End has a similarly emphatic guarantee: *"Our guarantee has always been an unconditional one. That's why we can boil it down to just two words. 'Guaranteed. Period.' If you're not completely satisfied with anything you order from us, at any time, for any reason, send it back and we'll refund your money. No ifs, ands, or buts."* That means you can return an item two years, three years, or five years later and get your money back if it disappointed you.

Lands' End piles service on top of service on top of service. Their operators are well-trained, friendly people who will "give you good service, and good advice if you have questions about sizing, colors, anything." If you do have special questions about sizing, wardrobe coordination, etc., you can ask for a Specialty Shopper who will gladly provide assistance free of charge. They even have a special number and Telephone Device for the Deaf (TDD) to assist people with hearing impairment. They frequently devote a full page of the catalog to the people that serve you, with fascinating stories about their everyday lives and the care they take in doing their jobs.

Animal, a catalog of pet care products, blazoned on the front cover an ingenious way to dramatize the speed of their order-filling service: "We guarantee to ship within 24 hours or we'll send you a free $50 Gift Certificate."

THE SPECTACULAR COMPUTER SOFTWARE DISCOUNTERS

In the computer software field, most retailers simply can't or won't handle most of the tremendous number of software packages available. So they have virtually abandoned the field to mail-order discounters.

But because the largest mail-order discounters are battling

among themselves for supremacy and need every competitive advantage they can get, they are providing inspiring models of what service should be.

For one thing, they offer breathtaking speed of delivery. On several occasions we have ordered software by phone in the afternoon and received it by noon the next day for only $3 shipping cost (that's total, not extra).

The most recent MacWarehouse catalog we saw went even further and offered next-day delivery on items ordered as late as midnight. Compare this with the typical contemptuous fulfillment of a sales promotion offer, which usually arrives six to eight weeks later in a battered brown envelope.

What these software discounters are doing goes beyond mere efficiency and speed. They convey an attitude that is so often sadly lacking in both brand promotion and retailing.

A MODEL OF WARMTH AND REASSURANCE FROM MACWAREHOUSE

For instance, enclosed with a recent shipment from MacWarehouse was the following memo. It is worth quoting in full because that is the only way to convey its delightful tone.

It is "from the desk of" Kerry (handwritten name) and is headed with more handwriting which says "Hi! Thanks for choosing MacWarehouse!" Then this typewritten message follows:

> It's great having you as a customer, and your satisfaction with our products and services is very important to me, and to all the MacWarehouse staff.
>
> If, for any reason, you're not completely satisfied with the products you purchased, or the service you received, please call our toll-free number right away: (800) 255-6227.
>
> If you have to return a product, we want to process your return quickly and efficiently! We'll give you a Return Merchandise Authorization (RMA) number, and instructions for returning the product. (You'll find some handy information about returning products on the back of your packing slip -- but be sure to call us first.)
>
> I know you'll want the copy I've enclosed of the latest MacWarehouse catalog. It features over 1200 of the newest and best-selling products. If

you want an extra copy for a friend, just call, and I'll be happy to send one out right away.

If you need more information about a program, or if you'd like to place an order, remember you can call toll-free: (800) 255-6227. There's never a charge for the call, and our team of Mac fanatics is standing by, waiting to hear from you.

And don't forget -- you can talk to me or any of the MacWarehouse staff in the Electronic Mall on CompuSERVE. The MacWarehouse GO code is GO MW. You can count on fast, courteous service, and over-night delivery to most areas -- for only $3.00!

Now get to that computer and enjoy all your new Macintosh products.

Sincerely
Kerry (signature)
Customer Service Director

P.S. I'd love to hear about your favorite Mac pro-grams and how you use them. Why not drop, fax, or CompuSERVE me a line?

MacConnection, another outstanding direct merchant of Macintosh Software, devoted two expensive pages in Macintosh magazines just to promoting its customer-satisfaction policies. These include next-day delivery for just three dollars on orders placed as late as 8:00 P.M., unlimited toll-free technical support for customers, and a 30-60 day money-back guarantee and 120-day warranty.

C&R CLOTHIERS DEMONSTRATES E.V.P. IN RETAILING

In the retail field, C&R Clothiers, the men's apparel chain in Los Angeles, is demonstrating how E.V.P. can put it a step ahead of its competitors. As advised by its forward-looking advertising agency, Admarketing, C & R stores now open at 8:00 A.M. on weekday mornings. For an extra fee you can get 24-hour "express tailoring" service for repairs and alterations. Their E.V.P. also includes lifetime free alterations on any clothes you buy there. And you can join the C&R Executive Club, which offers benefits like free pressing of your suit in the middle of the day.

These C&R innovations provide a fascinating glimpse not only of the retailing of the future but also of the advertising agency of the future. What Admarketing is doing for C&R is a long step forward from the traditional agency service of simply seeking to provide the most clever, memorable, attention-getting advertising.

PACE WAREHOUSE SETS THE PACE WITH EXTRA SERVICE TO SMALL BUSINESSES

In the membership warehouse industry, PACE Warehouse found itself in fierce competition with the three other top clubs — Price Club, Sam's Wholesale Club, and Costco. Despite this, in six years the company rose from a one-warehouse operation generating $15 million in sales to a 41-store business with over $1.2 billion in sales in 1988.

PACE's secret has been to cater to small businesses in each trading area — not just serve them, but provide Extra Value in the form of special shopping hours and free seminars for its small-business members. The seminars are often held in the PACE warehouse and give small businesses an opportunity to network as well as learn management techniques. PACE also works with the local chambers of commerce to attract, keep, and assist small businesses in the area. It's a win-win situation: the more PACE can help their small-business customers succeed, the better PACE customers they will be.

Most of the PACE Warehouses keep in touch with their members with newsletters distributed by mail or in-store. [13]

BORROWING A CONCEPT FROM DIRECT-ORDER MARKETING

In Direct-Order Marketing, we frequently refer to what we are selling as a "proposition." By this we mean, "If you (the consumer) will do such-and-such for me, I (the advertiser) will do this-and-that for you." In this sense of the word, The Book-of-the-Month Club selling offer is a proposition. In effect it proposes to prospective members, "If you'll agree to let us send you a Club selection or other book every month unless you tell us otherwise, we'll agree to send you this sensational introductory bargain, to sell you books at a saving, and to send you an informative club magazine every month." It turns a product — books — into a proposition.

This is a useful concept in drawing the distinction between a mere sales incentive and an E.V.P. and in thinking about how to add E.V.P. to your product or service. If you pack three cans of soup in a carton and sell them for the usual price of two, you could argue that this is offering extra value. But that's not what we are talking about, that's merely a promotion scheme to generate a temporary spike in the sales curve. An Extra Value Proposition is a *proposition*. It proposes to the consumer, "If you'll agree to buy our product, we'll agree to do the following to help you get more out of it and get more out of life."

HOW INDIVIDUALIZED MARKETING CAN HELP DEVELOP AN E.V.P.

In developing an Extra Value Proposition, Individualized Marketing may not always be essential, but often it can play an extremely important role. By relating directly to prime prospects, you can both create an E.V.P. and measure its appeal.

For example, Apple Computer frequently sends out direct mail enclosing a Pre-Approved Credit Certificate, permitting the purchase of up to $3,500 worth of merchandise with no money down. To make this offer to everyone, in newspaper advertising, would clog the dealer showrooms with unqualified prospects who would have to be rejected. The act of mailing it to carefully selected prime prospects with a personalized certificate to be presented to the dealer both helps make the service possible and yields measurable responses.

To dramatize that its Ultimate Lead-Free gasoline burned more cleanly, Amoco announced it would pay customer repair bills if fuel systems were damaged within 75,000 miles. [13] The cynical reaction of many customers might be, "You mean your regular Amoco was damaging my fuel system all these years and you didn't tell me?" Testing the concept through Relationship Marketing would have revealed better than opinion panels whether consumers really bought the idea.

And through direct feedback from respondents, you can monitor the continuing effect of Extra Value additions with real-time research involving real customers.

Later on, we will explore some detailed case histories in which you will see how some of the marketers of tomorrow are using Individualized Marketing to build an E.V.P. into their products or services.

Yes, these extras may add to the product cost, but this extra cost can be recouped through a higher Lifetime Customer Value and a lower Advertising Cost per Sale. And the more precise accountability of Relationship Marketing can make it possible to prove that this is so.

IDEA-STARTERS FOR PROFITING
FROM TURNAROUND TREND NO. 9

MANUFACTURER:

✔ *How might you develop and promote an 800-number or 900-number customary advisory service?*

✔ *Can you understand and follow the instructions that come with your product? (Can you read them in a dim light?)*

SERVICE ORGANIZATION:

✔ *How can you build more service into your service? (e.g., auto rental is a service — they have built in more services such as automatic check-in check-out.)*

ALL:

✔ *Have you ever invited typical customers and prospects to sit in on discussions of how to make your product or service better?*

✔ *Do you "WITSO" (Walk In The Shoes Of) the person in your target market one day a month and ask yourself: what might I do to make what I am selling more accessible, more satisfying, more distinctive, more enjoyable, more important, less frustrating?*

✔ *Could you organize a special-interest club that would give your product or service extra value?*

✔ *If you and your competitors are in a stalemate, how might you offer more to the customer without simply starting another price war?*

✔ *How can you use Direct-Relationship Marketing to develop, provide, and publicize your E.V.P.?*

✔ *Have you ever tried being your own customer and finding out what it feels like?*

12 From Single-Channel to Multi-Channel Distribution

The pressure towards direct distribution...The two kinds of Direct Marketing...The decade of delivery: Gevalia coffee...Doorstep Diets...Perform Dog Food...Dial-a-what?...Groceries by Phone...The Giorgio precedent...Starbucks Coffee expands retail via catalog... Williams-Sonoma moves both ways...Michael Anthony Jewelers helps retailers go direct...The Pfaltzgraff fix for a too-complete line...How Stash Tea built 3 channels...Dr. Cookie is flying high

---

In our Spectrum of Advertising Content in Chapter Four, we placed Image Advertising at one end of the spectrum and Direct-Order Advertising at the opposite end.

The first extreme says, in effect, "Think of me kindly when the time comes to buy some day," and the second extreme says, "Buy me right here, right now!"

If you look again at the spectrum diagram on Page 73, you will see that there is a certain logical progression in the various categories leading from one extreme to the other.

So the most extreme marketing turnaround of all is not merely to turn away from passive image-building as an advertising method, but also to turn away from it as a selling method. And to turn toward not just communicating directly with prospects and customers but selling directly to them.

Your first reaction to this subject may be to snort, "Ridiculous! Doesn't apply to our business at all!" and turn the page.

But before you do, pause to consider: an astonishing number of companies who have always sold through intermediary distributors, and who themselves would have snorted "Ridiculous!" just ten years ago or twenty years ago — are singing a different tune today.

They are finding ways to market directly to the consumer which are completely compatible with their previous selling methods and their overall corporate aims. And that is what we want to examine in this chapter.

Sometimes, in the 1970's, when direct marketing first began to boom, visionaries in the field would get carried away and would predict that by the year 2000 direct distribution from seller to buyer, bypassing stores, would be the dominant mode of delivery.

Today it is recognized that this was an unrealistic expectation. The physical marketplace shopping experience has played an important role in society for at least several thousand years and will undoubtedly continue to be the dominant mode for quite some time to come. Going shopping is a vital social as well as functional activity.

On the other hand, there are certain powerful social forces pushing us toward shopping in the home and getting delivery to the home.

• There is the squeeze on personal time which makes it harder to find time for shopping and cooking.

• There is the increasing annoyance and wastefulness of having to battle automobile traffic and shopping crowds when you need something.

• There is the boredom of going out and buying the same "replenishables" and lugging them home over and over again.

• There is the frustration of not being able to find what you are looking for in stores due to their spotty, incomplete, and poorly maintained inventory.

• There is the widely noted deterioration in the quality of service in retail stores.

So as the importance of the prospect/customer database continues to grow, it is logical and inevitable that this direct channel is being increasingly used not only for communication but also as a convenient distribution channel.

Buying books, records, or clothing directly and having them delivered to the home is certainly nothing new. But coffee? Dinner? Pet food? Groceries? Computers? Pharmaceutical drugs? Cake? Clearly something new is happening.

Some of these forays into selling direct to home shoppers are by major manufacturers of branded products distributed through retailers. They are experimenting both with new products created especially for the home delivery market, as Carnation is doing with its Perform dog food, and with ways that makers can sell their retail products directly without upsetting retailers, as Hanes does with catalog sales of some of their pantyhose and underwear products. The databases they are building serve both of these purposes and provide some built-in protection against excessive dealer demands.

At the same time, some leading specialty Direct-Order catalogs are elbowing their way into the retail marketplace and stealing customers out from under the noses of complacent, staid retailers.

There are huge differences of opinion about the extent of direct marketing today. One reason is that it is very hard to measure the total annual expenditure.

This is complicated by the fact that the term "direct marketing" has come to be used broadly and loosely to refer to two quite different forms of activity, with some shading in the middle. But until now this has never been sufficiently noted, creating considerable confusion. In our Glossary, we spelled out our proposed way of keeping the two kinds of direct marketing clearly separated. It is an important point that deserves repetition and further clarification.

THE TWO KINDS OF DIRECT MARKETING

The two categories are Direct-Relationship Marketing and Direct-Order Marketing. (See Figure 10.) As we define them —

Direct-Relationship Marketing has as its main purpose the stimulation of sales at retail by establishing direct contact with prospects and customers in their homes. Some direct selling may be involved, but its purpose is not to produce a significant profit from such sales.

Yes, Nintendo sells $15 subscriptions to its magazine *Nintendo Power* directly to its game users, but the real purpose of this is to stimulate sales of Nintendo games, not to make money out of the magazine business. In its first year and a half, the magazine built up an astounding circulation of close to 3 million. But the gross revenue from magazine subscriptions amounted to less than 2% of the company's total income. So it might be said that they are using Direct-Order Marketing techniques to offset the costs of their relationship marketing program but are not really running a Direct-Order Marketing business.

And this is true of many other companies. For instance, the Betty Crocker catalog now offers products which can be purchased by a combination of cash and proofs-of-purchase, but any

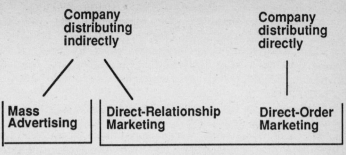

Figure 10

profit to General Mills will be a trivial addition to the General Mills bottom line.

Direct-Order Marketing, on the other hand, differs from Direct-Relationship Marketing in that it depends for its income primarily on purchases which are made from the home and delivered to the home.

People still use the clumsy, antiquated term "mail-order sales" even though the order may come by phone, fax, or computer and the delivery may be made by United Parcel, Federal Express, or the seller's own delivery service.

Lands' End refers to themselves as "direct merchants," a very useful description.

However, "mail-order" is still the most common and convenient shorthand term for home ordering and home delivery because everybody knows what you are talking about.

But would you really describe Doorstep Diets of San Diego as a mail-order company? Yet it is an extremely ingenious example of the trend toward home ordering and home delivery. Customers pay $63 a week for fresh, low-calorie meals delivered to their homes or offices five days a week. It is obviously a godsend for busy, weight-conscious singles and couples.

"We're entering the decade of delivery," according to a report on prepared foods published by FIND/SVP. Michael G. Mueller, a restaurant analyst at Montgomery Securities, agrees: "This trend toward home delivery fits right in with the whole couch-potato phenomenon of people tending to stay home more."

General Mills has been experimenting in suburbs of Minneapolis with a project called Order Ann, which delivers restaurant-style meals in about 20 minutes. [1]

Even though enterprises like these may seem a far cry from

"mail-order" selling, eventually the increasing competition will force them to pay attention to the principles of effective direct-response direct-order advertising evolved by mail-order sellers.

For when you start selling and delivering directly, your "store" is the advertising itself, and certain advertising messages, techniques, and offers will produce measurably more "store traffic" than others.

"Creativity" in the advertising won't be enough unless it is validated by a satisfactory level of measured response.

This subtle influence of the demands of accountability is clearly visible in the advertising for direct-sold Perform dog food. Their four-page ad in *TV Guide* had three of the pages devoted to copy with a distinct direct-response copy orientation -- fairly long, clear, persuasive, reassuring copy that includes a free trial offer and a money-back guarantee, strikingly different in approach from the usual "image" advertising.

Another company whose advertising has been shaped by its distribution method is Dell Computer Co., which grew in five years from a dormitory-room operation to a $260 million company selling its IBM-clone computers entirely by direct-order marketing.

As the founder, Michael Dell, recently named one of the 100 richest people in Texas, puts it, "We do not have any physical locations, so the advertising strategy has been very, very key for us. Advertising is our store. It is also the communication vehicle to attract and gain a customer base...We use advertising for both lead generation and brand-building. I suppose [competitors] may use advertising to build traffic in their stores, but they are much less direct-response oriented."

Of course, distribution need not be a question of either-or. Many companies are finding there is a synergistic effect derived from opening up multiple channels of distribution, whether it is a retailer starting a mail-order catalog, a mail-order catalog merchant starting a chain of retail shops, a brand advertiser turning to direct-order to supplement retail sales or force retail distribution, or a manufacturer opening its own flagship store.

So the real Turnaround Trend is not just toward direct-order and home delivery, but toward multi-channel distribution.

In our earlier chapters on Consumer Dialogue and Building Relationships, we have already observed a number of striking developments in Direct-Relationship Marketing. Now we would like to explore the trend toward Direct-Order Marketing and its interaction with retail sales.

Altogether, we have been able to count at least a dozen ways in which manufacturers, retailers, and entrepreneurs are joining the trend. Undoubtedly there are even more. But here is our list.

1. START FROM SCRATCH AND CREATE A WHOLE NEW DIRECT-ORDER DIRECT-DELIVERY BRAND, SERVICE, OR SUBSIDIARY

If your company is blocked from starting or expanding retail distribution or increasing share of market at retail — or if your product or service just isn't well suited to retail distribution — or if you simply want to tap into the huge new demand for home shopping convenience — then why not start from scratch with a new operation that deals directly with the end user?

The fastest-growing segment of the $6 billion pet-food market is the "superpremium" products sold in veterinarians' offices, pet shops, and food stores. Now Carnation Co. has invaded this market with their new pet food product called Perform — "the high-performance pet food that delivers." Pet owners are invited to order direct from direct-response ads and direct mail, and the product is delivered to the home. No problem with dealers getting upset because there aren't any dealers. [2]

General Foods has been able to expand its share of the coffee market with its mail-sold Gevalia Kaffee. Extrapolation from the information on a list broker's Gevalia data card hints that there are 700,000 to a million subscribers in the automatic shipment program, with an average annual sale to each of $60, suggesting an annual gross of perhaps $40 million.

Yes, that's pretty small potatoes in the $6 billion U.S. coffee market. But gourmet coffee is booming, from 3.6% of the marketing in 1983 to over 11% in 1990. Selling Gevalia direct permits General Foods to get in on the ground floor just in case that is where the market is going.

They don't have to worry about lavish television advertising to create share of mind or slotting allowances to dealers and cents-off coupons to consumers. And it is the attractive nature of automatic-shipment programs that, although naturally there is a constant attrition of subscribers who must be replaced by additional advertising, the hard core of steady customers continues to grow. Since the advertising cost of acquiring these hard-core customers has already been paid, and no dealer discounts or allowances have to be subtracted from the selling price, the profit per unit to these continuing customers should be much higher than from a comparable product at retail.

New delivery techniques and telecommunications capabilities are spawning new kinds of direct-order business that would not have been possible before.

For example, there is now a dial-a-cake service. By calling the 800 number of Telecake International, you can have a cake delivered anywhere in the U.S. or Canada within 24 or 48 hours, whichever you choose. The company's five-pound cakes are baked on the West Coast and shipped frozen via Federal Express, so they are still chilled by the time they arrive.[3] (To prove our point about the term "mail-order" as convenient, universally understood shorthand for home ordering and home delivery, the news item about Telecake was headed "Cake Company Turns to Mail" even though actually the U.S. Postal Service was not involved.)

A boring, expensive product like prescription medicine is a natural for direct-order distribution. Nobody ever had fun going to the drugstore to get a prescription filled. So direct sales of both prescription and over-the-counter drugs are growing by leaps and bounds. They added up to a total of 5.6% of all pharmacueticals sales in 1988 and are expected to hit $9 billion a year by 1995, according to a study by Find/SVP. One of the leading companies argues that through 24-hour toll-free phone service and an extensive tracking system, consumers have greater contact with and get more information from most direct-order pharmaceutical firms than they do from their local retail druggist. [4]

2. CREATE A DIRECT-ORDER MARKETING CLEARING HOUSE TO ACT AS AGENT FOR LOCAL RETAILERS

Instead of delivering its own meals to the home, a Chicago company called Roomservice Deliveries is linked by computer to eight restaurants. It has ten delivery trucks equipped with refrigeration and heating equipment, and its drivers are dressed in tuxedos and bow ties.

In Austin, Texas, EatOutIn operates in a similar way; its 25 employees take telephone orders and deliver moderately priced dinners from five restaurants, tacking on a $3.50 delivery charge. [5]

And Jeno Paulucci, the unquenchable entrepreneur who built and sold off Chun King Chinese foods and Jeno's pizza, recently started over again at the age of 71 with Groceries by Phone. Consumers phone a local number that automatically switches calls to a Groceries by Phone operator. After choices are made from a list of 40,000 items, the order is electronically transmitted to a local supermarket and are delivered by Groceries by Phone employees in as little as six hours with no markup in prices. The service will be offered by only one supermarket chain in each city, which will pay a one-time equipment charge and a fee for each order.

An important potential of the system is that operators can interact with the customer, and may be able to get promotion money from manufacturers in exchange for suggesting to callers brands, new products, deals, and sale items.[6]

In Los Angeles, a company called Dial-n-Save has experimented with providing callers with a recording that lists stores featuring a sale. Some hospitals are now advertising one number to call for referral to the appropriate medical specialist.

3. USE DIRECT-ORDER MARKETING TO FORCE RETAIL DISTRIBUTION OF A NEW NATIONAL BRAND

New-product introduction has become fearfully expensive and risky. It requires a bare minimum of $20 million to fan the flames of national retail demand with an advertising blitz. And that's quite apart from the problem and the cost of persuading retailers to make room on their already jammed shelves for still another new brand. Even then, your product may flop. But a couple running an elegant boutique in Beverly Hills proved that there is another way to gain national distribution and success, one that doesn't require that kind of megabucks investment.

In 1981, they introduced their own fragrance, Giorgio of Beverly Hills, at $150 an ounce. It sold very well in the boutique. But when they approached department store buyers to seek wider distribution, they were brushed off due to lack of customer demand and limitations of floor space. So they began to sell Giorgio directly, in both direct mail and upscale magazine advertisements, using a Scentstrip to permit readers to sample the fragrance. By 1983, they were doing $15 million in volume, two-thirds of it by direct order. Then, according to a company executive, "The demand triggered by Giorgio's magazine exposure brought retailers to Giorgio's door in hordes."[7] By 1985, Giorgio's products were being sold in 250 retail outlets, and total annual sales were over $100 million. In May of 1987 the company was sold to Avon Products for $165 million.

Avon had obviously been impressed by how Giorgio had accomplished this, and followed a similar strategy when it introduced its Red fragrance.

4. ADD A DIRECT-ORDER OPTION TO YOUR NATIONAL BRAND ADVERTISING AND RETAIL DISTRIBUTION

This is a strategy that makes cold beads of sweat pop out on the brows of national advertisers who distribute through retailers, for the advertisers are usually petrified at the thought of possible dealer resentment and revolt. But as we pointed out in *MaxiMarketing*, if such advertising is visualized as a mixing faucet, it is possible to control dealer reaction by controlling the amount of emphasis flowing from the first faucet ("go to our nearest dealer") and the second ("or order directly from us").

Adding a direct-order option is a stratagem now very commonly employed by computer software makers, particularly the hundreds of smaller companies who are fighting a losing battle for shelf space in computer stores anyway. And you are beginning to see it used, ever so timidly, by certain kinds of packaged goods marketers. For instance, we answered an ad by Foltene, the hair thickener, that offered the option of ordering direct. But the offer was so poorly displayed, and the follow-up was so feeble (no re-sell and no re-order form enclosed, for example) that it makes one wonder why Foltene bothered to do it at all.

We believe that this fear of dealer revolt against a direct-order option in the advertising is out of step with the realities of today's marketplace. Store buyers today are far more concerned with dealer allowances, point-of-sale support, merchandising promotions, and inventory control over thousands of products than they are about a single manufacturer's advertising practices. Especially if the product thus advertised is bringing in eager buyers.

And the direct-order option, if handled properly, can generate enough additional income to make a larger ad campaign affordable and in this way build an increase in retail demand and an eagerness on the part of dealers to keep the products in stock. This is undoubtedly true, for instance, of the smaller computer software makers who are running ads in computer magazines with a direct-order option.

This leads to an important principle of adding the direct-order option: *if you don't have many dealers to lose, why worry about losing them?* The chances are you will end up gaining more dealers than you lose. The direct orders you receive will help pay for the advertising, permitting you to run more advertising than you could otherwise afford, thus building up more retail demand.

Here is another example of a national product using a direct-order option to supplement its limited retail distribution.

Philip Morris has a deluxe brand of cigarettes, Cartier Vendome, packed in oval boxes bearing the House of Cartier's logo. They cost about twice as much as regular cigarettes. It would be very costly to build up national retail demand through awareness advertising, and probably wouldn't pay, since the sale of luxury tobacco products is less than 1% of U.S. cigarette sales. So Cartier Vendome cigarettes, previously sold only in Europe, were introduced in the U.S. in the late 80's as a niche market product offered only in upscale hotels, restaurants, and tobacco shops.

But will Philip Morris stop there? No, as you might expect from one of the leading MaxiMarketers of the 90's, the company also indicated plans to offer "home delivery"of Cartier Vendome to credit card holders. This would provide national distribution without a massive national campaign, and, if successful, might pave the way for national retail distribution later on just as the Giorgio direct-order advertising did.[8]

5. AS A RETAILER, USE DIRECT-ORDER SELLING TO EXPAND YOUR MARKET

You'll benefit in two ways: first, by stimulating store visits, and second, by making additional sales to people who can't or won't come in to see you. But a retailer promoting mail and phone orders skillfully is a rule more honored in the breach than in observance. Most retailers still either stubbornly ignore the opportunity, or even if they do launch a "mail-order catalog," fail to measure its full value by tracking the effect of the direct-order promotion on increased store sales.

The experience of Starbucks Coffee Co. of Seattle shows what can be accomplished. Starbucks has 29 gourmet coffee stores, most of them in the Northwest. In 1988, after having received repeated demands for a catalog from customers calling the 800 number printed on each package, they decided to take the plunge and issue their first mail-order catalog. They printed 280,000 copies and mailed catalogs not only to their 5,000 most frequent buyers but also to all the people who had requested a catalog and to other likely prospects chosen from lists of mail-order buyers in each store's trading area. Each catalog had the name of the nearest retail location on the cover to stimulate retail traffic. The catalog showed a profit in its first year and also helped Starbucks double overall sales in its retail outlets. [9]

Until 1986, the Laura Ashley stores, with sales totalling $197 million the previous fiscal year, derived only 3% of its sales from its mail-order catalog but spent 75% of its advertising budget on it. That tells you something about how important they consider the catalog as a store-traffic builder. The company's marketing director revealed that they were moving to two catalogs, one to build traffic and another to push harder for mail-order sales.

6. AS A DIRECT MERCHANT, USE YOUR CATALOG AS A LAUNCHING PAD FOR RETAIL SHOPS

The Sharper Image and Williams-Sonoma have been two of the most conspicuous successes with this approach. Thanks to the "free" advertising provided by their catalogs, when companies like these open up a new shop, they find eager customers waiting in line at the front door...without any additional advertising!

Ironically enough, Williams-Sonoma began as a little store,

used the store as a launching pad for its mail-order catalog, and then the mail-order catalog built up a demand for more stores.

In 1955 Chuck Williams bought an old hardware store in Sonoma, California, and turned it into a gourmet cookware and housewares shop. Later, when he moved it to San Francisco, he called his store Williams-Sonoma so his old customers would know it was he. Then after twenty years or so, he found he had accumulated a customer database of some 10,000 people who had bought from him but lived outside his trading area. So to accommodate them, he created his first mail-order catalog, and then started mailing it to outside lists as well.

In 1978 the firm acquired a new marketing-minded part owner and CEO, Howard Lester. Under his firm direction, the company acquired other catalog operations, started opening more stores, and by 1987 had grown in annual volume from $4 million to $139 million, half catalog sales and half retail. By 1988 there were 55 Williams-Sonoma stores around the country, and its catalog is said to penetrate one out of seven households in the U.S. [10]

Part of the importance of the Williams-Sonoma story is not only that it demonstrates the synergistic effect of operating both retail stores and a catalog, it is a rare case of a company that has quantified this effect and been willing to talk about it.

In a trade conference panel discussion in 1982, the company's vice-president for mail-order sales, Pat Connolly, told of their studies of the effect of catalog mailings on retail sales. "We found," he reported, "that we can get about a 30% lift [in retail sales] if we mail our catalog in a store area." [11]

This success story has been repeated again and again. For every one or two who eventually ran into trouble trying to run both a catalog and retail stores, such as Royal Silk and The Banana Republic, there are many more like Williams-Sonoma, The Sharper Image, Eddie Bauer, Talbot's, Brookstone, and Laura Ashley who have enjoyed continued success from the synergy of the dual distribution.

7. HELP YOUR RETAILERS DO THEIR OWN
  DIRECT-MARKETING OF YOUR PRODUCT

If you are a manufacturer and you still insist that you would never touch direct distribution with a ten-foot pole for fear of alienating your retailers, then here's a way you can have your cake and eat it too: do direct marketing *with* and *through* your dealers. That way, everybody wins, everybody is happy.

James S. Porte was an I.B.M sales representative when he made a sales call on Michael Anthony Jewelers, a manufacturer.

He was so impressed with the possibilities he saw in the jewelry manufacturing business that he left I.B.M and joined Michael Anthony as marketing director. He wanted to get into something entirely different where he could apply what he had learned about the power of the computer.

Porte told us that the marketing of jewelry has traditionally been product-driven — you create an outstanding product, place it in jewelry stores, and wait for customer to come in and discover it. All that is changing now. The jewelry business has become more fiercely competitive, and small jewelers can no longer afford to sit back and wait for customers.

Porte spent three years visiting 500 jewelers in 40 states. He persuaded 350 of them to sign up for a program which taught them to capture shopper names and personal-profile data and send them to Michael Anthony, who would then set up and maintain a separate customer database just for them. This database would then be used for mailings which are sent to the dealer's own list and which bear the dealer's own name and address.

This is an extremely exciting, sophisticated marketing program from which there is much to be learned. We will be examining it in greater detail in the next chapter.

8. START A MAIL-ORDER CATALOG OF OUTSIDE MERCHANDISE AND USE IT AS A VEHICLE FOR "FREE ADVERTISING" FOR YOUR RETAILER-DISTRIBUTED PRODUCTS.

We have pointed to John Deere and McCormick as two of the few manufacturers who have stumbled onto this secret.

You might even be able to build up a list of catalog customers without doing any catalog request advertising or mailing to outside lists.

Stash Tea has managed to do this by printing their offer of a free catalog on the foil packets containing the tea bags that are provided to restaurant diners (and now also to purchasers of Stash Tea in supermarkets). They have built a database of 150,000 direct-order buyers this way, and used it as a lever to pry open additional supermarket outlets. We will be telling more of their story in the next chapter.

If we were McCormick, we would consider putting those little bottles of cooking herbs and spices in individual cartons. Then each carton could contain a leaflet which could both offer cooking suggestions (and a cookbook?) and a reply coupon for requesting a free copy of their catalog.

Manufacturers who distribute tens of millions of packaged goods items a year are overlooking a gold mine. They disregard the fact that any product which is or could be packaged in a carton is a potential direct-response advertising medium with a circulation far larger than *TV Guide* or *Reader's Digest*. A free catalog offer advertised in this way, printed on the outside of the carton or on a package enclosure, starts off with a powerful financial economic advantage that most catalog merchants would die for — namely, the acquisition of the names of genuinely interested, responsive customers at no advertising cost.

The response from what Stash Tea's Susan McIntyre calls "package-based solicitation" can be significantly increased by going even further and enclosing a postpaid business reply card in the carton. We have seen this done only once, inside a carton of Tabasco Sauce imprinted with an offer from Hosiery Corporation of America of free pantyhose (plus 2 more for $1) plus $1.25 in coupons for other Tabasco products. We once suggested the idea to Susan McIntyre, and she informed us recently that she has started enclosing a reply postcard in retail gift packs, with "very good response."

But whether you build your catalog database this no-cost way or take the more conventional route of mailing out catalogs to rented lists of mail-order buyers, you will then have created a potential advertising vehicle for your main line of business that is extremely cost-effective — perhaps even paying its own way entirely.

9. FILL IN THE GAPS IN YOUR NATIONAL RETAIL DISTRIBUTION

If you put dots on a map of the United States representing your retailers and then drew a trading-area circle around each dot, what would the result be? For many manufacturers and service-providers, the resulting map would show a number of scattered circles, many overlapping of course, with great empty areas outside the circles.

Those blank areas represent a whole new market which you might be able to reach and serve through direct-order marketing.

That's how Sears' Nationwide Insurance once got into direct marketing. They simply sent direct-order insurance offers into counties where they had no agents and no over-the-counter store sales of insurance.

10. SELL DIRECT TO THE PUBLIC MORE OF YOUR FULL LINE THAN RETAILERS ARE ABLE OR WILLING TO CARRY

Pfaltzgraff dinnerware offers a comparatively small number of patterns but as many as 50 or 100 different matching pieces. Customers get hooked in collecting them, acquiring more and more items in the pattern they have chosen. But retailers were reluctant to carry 100 items in each pattern. Pfaltzgraff began getting letters from collectors asking where they could buy more pieces and if they could purchase them directly from the company. So Pfaltzgraff finally created its own highly successful direct-order catalog, filling it out with other handcrafted items and mailing to all known Pfaltzgraff customers.

11. OPEN UP A NON-COMPETING DISTRIBUTION CHANNEL AS A NON-COMPETING PROFIT CENTER

Stash Tea is a classic example of opening up a second channel of distribution without disturbing the first. They started by selling their herb teas to restaurants. The restaurants certainly didn't mind if the foil tea packet carried an offer of a free Stash Tea mail-order catalog — it wasn't taking any business away from the restaurant, and indeed in due time might make the restaurant a little more appealing to Stash Tea fans.

Then Stash decided to attempt to gain shelf space in supermarkets — a tough challenge for a tiny regional marketer. They used computer print-outs of mail-order customers within a supermarket's trading area to persuade the supermarket to start carrying the Stash Tea retail line. The retail line was deliberately priced lower than the catalog line to give the retailer a sales advantage over the catalog and bring local Stash loyalists thronging to the store.

So Stash ended up with three distribution channels which not only don't conflict with one another but actually support one another. That's quite an accomplishment. But it shows what turnaround thinking can achieve when a manufacturer is open-minded about multi-channel distribution.

A tiny cookie company, Dr. Cookie Gourmet Cookies, is pulling itself up by its bootstraps using elements of the Stash Tea success formula.

The company was started in 1985 by two doctors, Dr. Marvin Wayne, an emergency-room physician, and Dr. Stephen Yarnall, a cardiologist, to market individually wrapped, low-cholesterol, low-salt, high-fibre cookies.

The product didn't lend itself to supermarket selling because it uses no preservatives and has a short shelf-life (to say nothing of the difficulty of a small new brand breaking into the overcrowded shelves of this market).

To attempt to set up their own retail outlets would have been an overwhelming undertaking. So they approached airlines with the idea of including their cookies in onboard meals, and signed up United, Northwest, Horizon, U.S. Air, and Qantas.

Soon, in this way, more than 8 million air travelers were sampling Dr. Cookie Gourmet Cookies. And on each wrapper is a toll-free number and a fax number which pleased travelers can use to order cookies directly, charging the purchase on their Mastercard or Visa.

This approach started generating 1,000 calls a month. Callers spend an average of $16 to $50 each and tend to be repeat customers. At last report the company had 30,000 names in its customer database and was planning to launch a catalog. [10] Note how Dr. Cookie, like Stash Tea, used one distribution channel as a springboard for entry into a second, non-competing channel. The airlines certainly didn't mind that Dr. Cookie was inviting direct-order customers on the cookie wrapper. [12]

Note also that Dr. Cookie, like Stash Tea, is using its packaging as an effective direct-response advertising medium.

Now movie studios are pulling a triple-play of their own, adding to their theatrical release and video release businesses with mail-order catalogs of movie memorabilia and collectibles based on their own logos and movies. Paramount, Warner, and Walt Disney are all now putting out catalogs with merchandise featuring logos, titles, or famous movies and movie characters. "For years we'd been denying requests for Warner Bros. products from around the country," says the president of their merchandising division. "When we began to realize there was an appetite for exclusive merchandise, we also realized that we were a sleeping giant."

In a prologue added to two Warner home videos, Bugs Bunny offered a free catalog. Within weeks they had 500,000 requests for catalogs. In one of their Christmas catalogs, in one week they sold out 50 sets of marble sculptures of Batman and the Joker at $495 the pair!

12. START A MAIL-ORDER CATALOG OF COMPATIBLE NON-BRANDED MERCHANDISE TO REINFORCE YOUR BRAND IMAGE

This is very similar to Method No. 8. The difference is that the catalog becomes a vehicle for strengthening overall brand image rather than awareness of specific retail products, as John Deere does in its direct-order catalog.

Even though the Kohler bathroom accessories catalog has been discontinued, it was a trail-blazing experiment which pointed the way to an entirely new method of brand-building — whether as a profit center or as a "loss center," which we recommended earlier. A homeowner is unlikely to buy plumbing products more than once or twice in a lifetime. The Kohler catalog offered a way to meanwhile keep the public reminded of Kohler quality by widely distributing a catalog of items that lived up to the Kohler reputation for quality and excellence.

Said a Kohler executive at the time, "The more the consumer likes what we have to offer in the catalog, the more likely he or she will consider Kohler when redoing a bathroom." It was a judgment call whether the money the company was losing on the catalog could better be expended on image advertising. Kohler finally called it one way by discontinuing the catalog; you might have called it the other, in favor of continuing this self-amortizing private advertising to their target audience.

In Chapter Eight, we told how the Southern Comfort mail-order catalog of Old South nostalgia items demonstrably enhanced brand image and consumer attitudes for Southern Comfort, even though the advertising for the brand in the catalog was very soft-sell and indirect. This venture too was eventually discontinued for financial and organizational reasons — Brown-Forman was undergoing a major reorganization at the time. But we believe we will see more brands following the trail blazed by Kohler and Southern Comfort with a direct-order catalog that supports and strengthens the brand image.

If this is the age of "getting close to the customer," you can hardly get closer to your customers than by taking orders directly from them no matter how far away they are. In the past, you may have concluded that this way of operating just doesn't apply to your kind of business. If so, it's time to think again.

When someone in your company tries to brush off a suggestion to explore alternate distribution channels because it will endanger your primary distribution, it's because their thinking is still stuck in the groove of the 60's and 70's. Today, as you have seen in this chapter, there are many variations of direct-order selling which can open up new ways to have a direct relationship with your customers that won't harm and may actually support your primary distribution channel.

IDEA STARTERS FOR PROFITING
FROM TURNAROUND TREND NO. 10

MANUFACTURER:

✔ *How about creating a separate line of branded goods exclusively for home delivery?*

✔ *Could you force retail distribution of a new product by selling it directly first?*

✔ Would it make sense to add an "order direct" option to your product awareness advertising?

✔ Does your product line lend itself to home shopping to be offered by your retailers? Could you set up a program that would help them do that?

✔ Could you offer your small retailers a service in which they would send you filled-out customer questionnaires and you would set up and maintain a separate customer database just for them?

✔ How about starting a mail-order catalog that sells other people's merchandise and using it as a vehicle for free advertising for your own products?

✔ Could you round out your distribution with a catalog which would be mailed to geographic areas in which you have no distribution or which would feature additional items in your line which your retailers are not able or willing to carry?

✔ Could you print an offer of related merchandise or a free direct-order catalog on your product packaging or on a package insert?

RETAILER OR SERVICE PROVIDER:

✔ Are you doing enough about home delivery for busy working singles and couples who don't have time to visit your establishment?

✔ Does your kind of business fit selling off-site via catalog?

✔ Do you capture and store in a computer the names and addresses of all who visit your establishment? Other data? How could you use this information to expand your sales and profits?

ENTREPRENEUR:

✔ What kind of 800 number service could you start that would receive and farm out dial-a-product orders or inquiries for local retailers or services? How about a phone service to take orders for a group of merchants appealing to the same target market?

13 The Best and the Boldest

The big turnaround in thinking at Kraft General Foods ... Nintendo's "Secret Weapon"...Stash Tea's no-cost advertising triumph...Automobile marketing in The Age of the Individual: Austin Rover in the U.K., Volkswagen in France...Michael Anthony Jewelers shows how manufacturers can boost their retailers... How Steinway & Sons in the U.S., Roland in Italy, identify music lovers... Pizza Pizza and the phone number all Toronto knows by heart... The U.K.'s catalog of the future...Lessons from Toddler U... Murphy Realty turns home selling upside down

In surveying the ten trends that make up The Great Turnaround, we have provided a great many references to what is happening, mainly in U.S. companies. Now we'd like to move in for a closer look at a handful of especially noteworthy examples of marketers, not only in the U.S. but around the world, who are combining a number of principles of turnaround thinking to achieve outstanding success.

This is by no means a definitive list of the very best turnaround thinking being done today. Too much is happening, on too many fronts and in too many countries, to attempt any such assessment. Very likely, many more spectacular MaxiMarketing programs are being prepared by major marketers and innovative entrepreneurs as these words are written, and may have burst on the scene and swept the field by the time you read this book.

There is not even any guarantee of continued success by the marketers we describe. There never is in marketing. You never know when a sudden new burst of energy by the competition with a new product breakthrough or a new marketing direction will alter the balance of power — or a leveraged buyout will starve a worthwhile marketing program of needed funds as the company staggers under its new debt burden — or a suddenly receding tide in public taste will leave a company stranded on the beach.

However, we believe the programs we are going to describe demonstrate convincingly that what we have been advocating works extremely well in the crucible of the marketplace. We also believe that as these companies come under competitive pressure, they will have the advantage of a distant early warning system available in the dialogue they maintain with their best customers.

Each of the following programs deserves special mention for some outstanding characteristic, some feature that breaks new ground in the application of Individualized Marketing and has broad application to other marketers and other kinds of products and services. Much of the information in this chapter is based on our conversations and interviews with the advertising managers, promotion managers, and marketing directors involved, bringing to light some aspects of the programs not previously made public.

Each program is, in its own way, a breakthrough, providing an opening through which you may find new opportunities of your own. And each usually illustrates the use of not just one but several of our Ten Turnaround Trends. We have pointed this out in a number of places, but in other instances we have left it to you to make the connection. By your stopping to think in each case about which of the Turnaround Trends are being employed and how this is being accomplished, it will help drive home the points of the book in your own mind.

Here, then, is our parade of some of the Best and the Boldest of the new breed of turnaround marketers.

THE BIG PACKAGED GOODS BREAKTHROUGH
AT KRAFT GENERAL FOODS

America's largest single advertiser is Philip Morris Companies, with all of its divisions at last report racking up over $31 billion in sales worldwide and spending over $2 billion annually on U.S. advertising and promotion. Of this, the largest chunk was accounted for by its Kraft General Foods division. They recently reported combined sales of $22.5 billion and expenditures of $940 million a year on advertising and $760 million on sales promotion — more than Procter & Gamble or General Motors.

When a huge ocean liner of a company like this begins to slowly alter its course, the turning might not be obvious at first glance. But after a while, the change in direction and destination becomes unmistakeable, and it pays to sit up and take notice.

Philip Morris Companies, a titan of the age of mass marketing, is visibly moving in a new direction — toward finding out who their prospects and customers are and dealing directly with them as individuals.

We commented earlier on the success of the Philip Morris ice-breaking Merit Cigarette Challenge campaign. What followed was an intensification of the Philip Morris commitment to become heavily involved in building and using a customer database.

Now we want to take you aboard the Kraft General Foods division of Philip Morris Companies and see some of the wondrous things happening there.

If you still have doubts about which way the ocean liner is turning, this close-up look should dispel them.

The company's slow but steady turnaround toward one-to-one marketing is apparently due in large part to the vision of several top executives there, including William Shaw, now Promotion Director for Maxwell House Coffee, Eric Strobel, Senior Vice President for Corporate Marketing Services, and James Morgan, Senior Vice President of Philip Morris Companies. They foresaw the rapid approach of the day when all American households would be profiled in remarkable detail in various proprietary marketing databases. And they seem to have realized that the leaders will be the companies that "git there fustes' with the mostes'" and do the best job once they get there.

General Foods* (which was soon to become Kraft General Foods) started to move in a new direction back in 1985, at the time we were writing *MaxiMarketing*.

They created a new position, Director of Direct Marketing, and hired John Kuendig to fill it. Kuendig had made a name for himself at Avon Products with direct marketing programs to reach

---

*General Foods had for some time been experimenting with Direct-Order Marketing. We mentioned in Chapter 12 their Gevalia Coffee program. In addition, they have experimented with selling a line of Thomas Garraway gourmet foods directly, and long before that had sponsored an ambitious but disappointing home handicrafts direct-order venture called Creative Village. But Kuendig's mandate was quite different in scope — not to pursue Direct-Order Marketing of non-retail products, but rather to explore Direct-Relationship Marketing put to the service of retail distribution brands.

millions of women his research showed Avon had been missing.

The building of the database. When he arrived at Kraft General Foods, Kuendig began to draw together into an organized master database all of the loose threads of household and product usage data derived from the company's many products and promotions, and to test programs designed to make profitable use of this treasury of information.

They ended up with, in effect, two databases. First came the "overall" database with information on a total of more than 35 million households. But they found that this was too unwieldy and costly to maintain as a dynamic, relational database. So they pared it down to a functional, on-line database profiling 25 million households. **(Trend No. 1, Known Prospects and Customers)**

When we asked Kuendig how expensive it had been to create the database, he told us that it had cost them relatively little. KGF already had the hardware in-house. They bought a software package for about $500,000. They were already keypunching all of their premium requests and sweepstakes entries. It cost "next to nothing" to turn this information into a usable relational database, he said.

Now, as they receive and enter data on a new household, they overlay information (demographics and lifestyle) from Polk-NDL. Then they record additional behavioral data as time goes on if the same household responds to additional KGF offers and promotions.

They also use Donnelley Cluster Plus to add demographic information.

And they are working with Citicorp POS Services and Catalina Marketing to collect relevant data from supermarket check-out database programs recording weekly purchases.

Still more information is obtained and entered by including a questionnaire in all promotional offer fulfillment packages. (An astonishing 20% to 25% of recipients complete and return the questionnaire, even without an incentive.)

The cost of maintaining and updating the database is not considered a substantial item in view of the widespread use of the data. The cost of keypunching is minimized by getting compilers to handle it in exchange for making some of the information available to them.

There is an important lesson here for multi-brand advertisers who have been timidly nibbling at "direct marketing" with a brand-by-brand approach which is left entirely in the hands of the individual product manager.

A database simply consisting of the names and addresses of people who have responded to various promotional offers is of limited value. Yet to build a large, useful relational database, one that both includes a major portion of the total market and is rich in detailed information about each household, can be quite a serious undertaking.

The KGF approach presents a persuasive case for a corporate commitment at the highest level to create a permanent company-wide asset, one that is as important and valuable as a vast production plant yet considerably less expensive.

Here, the economies of scale work to the advantage of the megasized packaged goods conglomerates who are wise enough to see the opportunity. What is surprising is how slow some of them have been to move in this direction.

At the same time, we have seen how smaller entrepreneurial companies, unburdened as they usually are by a cumbersome committee approval system, can build databases of their own and use them to gain on their giant competitors.

In-house co-ops. Kuendig can put together his own direct-mail co-op cheaper than by going to Carol Wright — and his past history of each household is more relevant. "By putting a value-added offer into my co-op package, I can build good will for KGF while delivering my promotional incentive," says Kuendig. "After a while, the consumer will look for my packages because they offer what she wants and needs, and because the value-added extra is custom-tailored to her lifestyle and shopping habits." **(Trend No. 3, Filling Each Niche)**

"Everything I direct to the consumer reflects the fact that my database knows about her or him," says Kuendig. "I can create co-ops that make sense." For example, he has run a "light foods" co-op featuring 13 different brands appealing to health-conscious families. "Then," he points out, "I can continue the dialogue by asking for additional meaningful information." **(Trend No. 5, Consumer Dialogue)**

One of the new frontiers we explored in *MaxiMarketing* was the effect of a targeted promotion on consumers who do *not* respond. Kuendig says that all KGF redemption promotions can now take into account the promotion's effect on the subsequent buying behavior of coupon non-redeemers. They measure share-of-mind impact on the total audience contacted, not just the respondents, just as they would do for an awareness advertising campaign.

Custom publishing. One of the most promising avenues of communication with households in a database is the use of custom publishing to produce the company's own magazine. KGF has moved strongly in this direction with several in-house publications based on natural groupings of households in the database.

What's Hot for Kids is a magazine aimed at households with children ages five to ten. It is published by Field Publications for KGF, and filled with advertorials and ads for such KGF products as Cool Whip, Jell-O, Kool-Aid, Post cereals, and Tang.

Food Extra is a thrice-yearly magazine of menus and recipes for the 1.5 million people who have responded to recipe promotions, with participation by all KGF brands that use recipes.

On Our Own is a magazine for 18-to-25-year-olds who have just moved into their first home of their own. Early cultivation of such households obviously represents enormous LifeTime Value potential.

Cross-promotion.   Psychographic information about the customers in the database makes it possible to target users of one product as likely prospects for another. For instance, a mailing to Crystal Light customers may include a coupon for Light 'n Lively Ice Milk, based on the likelihood that fans of the first product are good prospects for the second.

Multi-product promotion.   An early roadblock to database marketing development in multi-brand companies has been the traditional brand management structure, with each product manager defending his or her own turf and budget and reluctant to cooperate in a joint promotion.   KGF moved to push aside this barrier after Kuendig had been with the company for four years, by expanding his duties to include cross-brand promotion. He is now in charge of all "group events," multi-product promotions that go beyond the brand manager's individual responsibility.

Kuendig sees a growing trend in the direction of promoting groups of products rather than individual brands. He says the economics of supporting with direct communication a single product that sells for $2.50 and has a frequency of purchase of three or four times a year "just isn't there." But the cost efficiencies of grouping line extensions and/or brands in promotion that goes to a target audience within the database who have similar characteristics has been shown to work again and again.

The Crystal Light Program.   The longest-standing successful ongoing program at KGF is the Crystal Light frequent buyers club.   It has been a critical test of whether continuing, rather than one-shot, direct mail to the same users of a packaged goods product can justify its cost with sufficient payback.

Crystal Light is a popular low-calorie artificially-sweetened drink powder. It sells for $2.89 a box, and a heavy user will buy ten or more boxes during the warm-weather months.

There are between 750,000 and one million members in the club program at any given time. This is obviously not the total market by any means. But what is important about them is that they have been identified as the medium-to-heavy users. We are back once again to the marketing textbook's classic of going after the 20% who do 80% of the buying. The aim of the program is to preserve and increase usage in this core market.

Four times a year members are mailed a package that contains a club newsletter on diet and fitness, discount coupons for General Foods products, a cover letter, and a small catalog. The catalog reinforces the brand image and encourages frequent buying of Crystal Light by offering workout suits, stopwatches, mugs, etc., all bearing the Crystal Light Logo. Each item can be obtained with cash plus a specified number of "foil seals" from cans of Crystal Light. **(Trend No. 6, Building Relationships)**

Each year, Kuendig told us, marketing research measures the impact of the program, both with volumetric research and with attitudinal research that measures brand awareness and intent to buy. The results have clearly shown a profitable payback on investment year after year.

The Wacky Warehouse venture. If you have a product in a mature and declining market segment, one way to do better is to encourage more usage from the customers you already have. This was the challenge faced by KGF's Kool-Aid, in a market dominated by Coke and Pepsi, and it provided a perfect opportunity to prove the value of Individualized Marketing.

For five years prior to 1987, Kool-Aid sales had been in a steady decline, being beaten back by the incessant, massive, trendy advertising of Coke and Pepsi. The basic problem was not to get more Kool-Aid users, but to get existing Kool-Aid users to choose it more often.

The Kool-Aid target is the child between four and nine years old, who on the average, let's say, might consume 20 packages a year for a total sale of $5. That doesn't provide enough working margin to invest heavily in getting and keeping the average user. But of course heavy users consume far more than that. So a program to increase usage, if successful, would be clearly affordable.

The first experimental probe in this direction was a four-page, coupon-filled newsletter called *Funday Times* sent to parents in known Kool-Aid user households. The coupons performed twice as well as expected and up to eight times as well as traditional mass coupon-delivery. Research showed that the program helped get light users to purchase Kool-Aid more often and heavier users to buy more with each purchase.[1]

The encouraging results from this first step led the Kool-Aid category manager, John Vanderslice, in 1987 to expand a premium promotion program called the Wacky Warehouse and to start promoting it with awareness and direct-response advertising.

The Wacky Warehouse is a mythical place run by The Kool-

Aid Man and crammed with appealing kid merchandise like Wacky Suspenders, Kool-Aid Man Comic Shorts, and the Wacky Skateboard — all of which can be earned with Kool-Aid proofs of purchase or "points" plus shipping and handling costs. A special comic book was created, *The Adventures of Kool-Aid Man.*

A prospect database of nearly four million households was assembled. They were mainly blue-collar families with children aged 3 to 12. It combined the in-house list of known Kool-Aid buyers, users of other beverage-type General Foods products, users of a competitive powdered soft drink, and users of General Foods heavily pre-sweetened cereals. **(Trend No. 1, Known Prospects and Customers)**

Two different direct-mail packages were tested, one to Mom and one to the kids in the household. The direct mail to Mom enclosed Kool-Aid coupons, coded for tracking by optical scanner, and urged her to use them so the kids could earn premium points. The direct-mail to the kids showed the keen things they could get with Kool-Aid purchase points and alerted them to the fact that Mom was getting a mailing explaining the program.

The Wacky Warehouse is featured in TV advertising, in free-standing inserts in Sunday newspapers, in children's magazines, and in direct mail. Almost every month, during the warm-weather season, there is a Wacky Warehouse promotion breaking.

One of Vanderslice's most interesting innovations has been to bring Kool-Aid purchase rewards down to the level of the child's own neighborhood, with such offers as free toys in exchange for points at a nearby movie theatre, or free admission to a nearby attraction such as the Mystic Marine Aquarium or the Riverside Amusement Park. He argues that many children are not accustomed to frequent transactions by mail and that rewards tied to their own local experiences are often more meaningful. He once ran in Sunday newspapers a free-standing insert for Kool-Aid that was published in 77 different versions in order to be able to offer free admission to a local attraction in each of 77 market areas.

Vanderslice and his associates at General Foods have demonstrated beyond dispute the power of targeting, involvement, and building relationships to move the needle for a package selling in the supermarket for as little as 25¢.

Vanderslice told us that since the program began, the decline has been reversed. Sales have increased each year. Previously the preference of kids was 60% for Coke and Pepsi to 40% for Kool-Aid. Now those percentages have been reversed — a rare and startling reversal in the annals of "marketing warfare."

Today Kool-Aid has an 83% share of the powdered drink market. Obviously their sales gains can't go on forever. But the

Wacky Warehouse Individualized Marketing program has demonstrated so much strength that now KGF can always use it simply to maintain share, the role traditionally played by a great deal of awareness advertising. The program appears to be getting about 70% of the brand's advertising and promotion dollars.

This represents a complete turnaround from the awareness advertising-driven and discount-driven selling that had been the approach used before, when the brand was in the doldrums.

The next frontier.   Current thinking at KGF makes it clear that Individualized Marketing is not and must not be limited to influencing only the consumer.

The next great challenge in packaged-goods retailing is creative communication with the database of dealers and distributors.

"The consumer is the easiest part of what we have to do," Kuendig told us. "Our struggle is more to increase sales with the trade than the consumer. Walk into any grocery store or supermarket and you'll see 5,000 to 15,000 products on the shelf. Where my company's brand is placed on that shelf is critical to how fast it will move out of the store. If we can get an end aisle display, we know that will mean more volume. The highest leverage point in impacting sales for the packaged goods marketer is in the mind of the retailer."

To Kuendig, the next frontier for marketing is, "How can we get the greatest possible support for our brands from the retailer?"

Can a new kind of database marketing addressed to the retailers play a part? If you want to know the answer, we advise you to keep your eye on what KGF does next.

Marketing executives such as John Kuendig and John Vanderslice are members of a small band of historic explorers in marketing, the Christopher Columbuses and De Sotos and Vasco da Gamas of the new marketing for brand advertisers. "What I am doing is largely uncharted, unlike putting a catalogue together," Kuendig has said. "And nobody can tell me I'm doing it wrong."[2]

On the contrary, it looks like he and his associates are doing it right — and helping to lead a new generation of packaged goods marketers into the new territory of MaxiMarketing.

NINTENDO MAKES HISTORY WITH A VIEWPOINT "THE REVERSE OF MOST PEOPLE"

In 1985, you'd have to be crazy to dream of scoring a big success with home video games. The bottom had dropped out of the once-hot market. Sales had dropped from a peak of $3.2 billion at the height of the craze, just two years earlier, down to a measly $100 million.

But a 100-year-old Japanese toy manufacturer, Nintendo, had shrewdly observed that kids hadn't stopped playing video games. They had simply stopped playing them on home systems, where the games were too simple and the computer images were too crude, and had gone back to dropping endless quarters into the greatly superior machines in video game arcades.

So Nintendo plotted a comeback, with improved graphic quality and far more challenging game complexity. After a successful introduction in Japan, they gave Minoru Arakawa the responsibility for conquering the U.S. market.

The result was one of the fastest and most astounding success stories in U.S. marketing history. In just four years, Nintendo of America went from a standing start to $2 billion in annual retail sales (plus another billion or two of sales by Nintendo licensees). By the beginning of the new decade, over 29 million systems and over 170 million cartridges had been purchased. There was a Nintendo game system in 30% of the households in America. And two million kids (and young adults!) were paying $15 a year for the company's magazine, *Nintendo Power,* barely more than a year after it was launched — the most spectacularly successful magazine launch in history.

The four P's + the Big Double D. How did they do it? Essentially by their masterful application of the four classic P's of marketing — Product, Pricing, Positioning, and Placement — and then by their addition of the Big Double D of the turnaround era, Database and Dialogue.

"I think we look at things the reverse of most people," says Peter Main, executive vp for marketing. (How's that for a statement of the importance of Turnaround Thinking?)

"Real-life consumer demand, not retailer perceptions, drives the company...We are listening more intently than anyone I have ever been employed by to what the market is saying." **(Trend No. 5, Consumer Dialogue)**

When Arakawa had begun trying to break into the U.S. market, he had met with stiff resistance from skeptical dealers. He realized that Nintendo faced a monumental marketing challenge after the collapse of the home video game market in the U.S. So he kept urging Main, a marketing expert who had been neighbor and friend in Vancouver, B.C., to come in and help him. Finally in late 1986 Main, who had been a marketing executive at Colgate-Palmolive and General Foods before becoming general manager of Canada's 150-store White Spot restaurant chain, agreed. Together the two men began to seek the big breakthrough. [3]

By the end of that year, they had sold 1.1 million home systems and a sweepstakes enclosed with the warranty cards was bringing back to their database the names, addresses, and other data from about 7% to 10% of their customers. **(Trend No. 1, Known Prospects and Customers)** The following year they began offering a new incentive to get a reply instead of the sweepstakes. It was a free membership in the Nintendo Fun Club, which included a membership card and free subscription to a bimonthly newsletter. This greatly increased the dialogue with users, but it did not increase the warranty card response rate. Even so, the database grew steadily as sales soared.

Soon the number of phone calls from kids needing help in navigating a difficult game passage grew to 50,000 a week, making it necessary to change the toll-free game-counselor number to a toll call. (To handle the calls, the company has more than 120 "game counselors" working the phones. At last report, the call center was averaging 120,000 calls a week.)

The big breakthrough decision. By 1988, the database had grown to nearly two million names, and the supplying of free newsletters six times a year was becoming a financial burden. The momentous decision was made to drop it in favor of a 110-page paid-subscription magazine costing $15 a year.

In Japan, the publishing company Tokuma Shoten had already created a successful paid newsstand magazine devoted to Nintendo's software. To gain the advantage of their experience, and to avoid having to compete with them in the U.S. market, Nintendo U.S. invited Tokumo Shoten to come over and help them create their new American magazine, *Nintendo Power*.

The company decided to go all out to gain magazine subscribers, and engaged a first-rate direct-marketing agency, HDM Worldwide Direct, to promote subscription sales.

The magazine subscription campaign started off with an expensive bang. All two million names in the database received the premiere July/August 1988 issue free. With it came a letter and reply card offering a $6 annual saving off the cover price, and an 800 number to call for those who preferred to answer by phone.

Successfully breaking the rules. The Burger King slogan, "Sometimes you gotta break the rules," would better fit the Nintendo success story, as they continued to successfully break the usual magazine circulation promotion rules right and left.

The rules say: if you are going to woo subscribers with free copies, you have to give them several issues to give them time to form a habit. Nintendo, gambling on the intense interests of its fans, supplied only one issue free. (The percentage of the database that converted from free newsletter subscription to paid magazine subscription from this first effort is a company secret, but obviously it was phenomenal, perhaps as high as 35% or more.)

The rules say: to sell a new magazine, you've got to sell the sizzle of future contents with long copy. But Nintendo's opening letter was a short, punchy message to kids who were already Nintendo zealots and not necessarily great at reading anyway.

The rules say: a direct-response television commercial must be deliberately paced to give viewers time to absorb the message and respond. But the 60-second and 30-second Nintendo direct-response magazine subscription commercials that were rolled out after *Nintendo Power* was launched had the dazzling speed, intensity, and complexity of a rock video. These commercials spoke the language of — and counted on the split-second comprehension ability of — a new generation of young MTV viewers.

The rules say: you can't expect the first-year revenue from subscribers to a new magazine to cover the editorial, printing, and mailing costs. But the response was so great that the $15 from over a million subscribers in the first year pretty well covered those costs. Nintendo still had to invest $7.5 million in the subscription promotion costs, but Main says it's "worth every penny" because it keeps them in such close touch with their market.

In addition to the direct-response televison commercials, the magazine was being promoted through hardware and software package inserts, store take-ones, and direct mail. At its peak, the television campaign was producing 12,000 to 15,000 calls a day. Not only was it wildly successful, it boosted response from all the other sources as well. And every dollar spent on direct-response TV for the magazine was also a dollar spent on building the Nintendo image of market leader — an outstanding example of the double-duty advertising that we talked about in *MaxiMarketing*. **(Trend No. 2, Response-Driven)**

Within seven months the magazine had a paid circulation of 1.2 million. Less than a year later, it was up to two million. A collective sigh of relief was heaved when the first subscription renewal notices went out and gained a 70% renewal rate, very high by magazine standards.[4]

The secret behind the "secret weapon." "The magazine is our secret weapon," Bill White, Nintendo's director of advertising, told us. "You can't put a value on what relationship marketing has done for Nintendo. The ability to communicate with 1.5 million [now much more, of course] of our most dedicated customers is comparable to what might cost 3, 4, or more times as much through conventional advertising channels."

There are many ways that the magazine supports Nintendo's

spectacular success. One of the most important contributions is the feedback loop created by direct contact with the magazine's millions of subscribers.

Nintendo has received as many as 47,000 letters a month from readers, every one of which was personally answered. But even more important has been the flow of information provided by a card-stock questionnaire bound into each issue of the magazine. In it, Nintendo asked readers what games they purchased during the previous month, what they liked and didn't like about the games they played, and what games they expected to purchase in the coming months. A sweepstakes promotion stimulated response.

What Nintendo learns from the real-time research information — provided by the questionnaire, the game-counselor phone service, the 900-number information line called by 10,000 kids a week, and the Letters to the Editor of the magazine — enables the company to constantly fine-tune the product line. They can respond to consumers' needs, interests, complaints, and enthusiasms with lightning swiftness. They can forecast sales and inventory needs by individual titles months in advance. It is responsiveness to the consumer on a level never before achieved anywhere, as far as we know. **(Trend No. 5, Consumer Dialogue)**

In addition, the deep loyalty fostered by the magazine, the game counselors, and Nintendo's dedication to personal service **(Trend No. 9, E.V.P.)** has well prepared the company to withstand fierce counter-attacks launched by Sega's Genesis and NEC's TurboGrafx-16, even though the latter systems at the moment may be superior technologically.

Important as the magazine is, the turnaround thinking behind it is even more important — the attitude that Peter Main characterized as "the reverse of most people," namely, seeing the market as living, breathing, identified individuals rather than pie-shaped market segments on a chart.

We were struck once-again by the real-world difference between thinking "on the average" and being in direct contact with known individuals when we read a letter to the editor in a recent issue of Nintendo Power magazine. It was from an 84-year-old woman at a retirement home. She was writing about the four hours a day she and her friends spend with their Nintendo Entertainment System. In so many companies, that wonderful lady would never exist among the mass marketing averages, and she would surely never get a personal letter from the company she has come to love.

As an example of the company's extraordinary dedication to putting the customer first, there is the story of the adult user who sent in a game pak with a plaintive request. He had spent three months working up to Level 7 out of a possible eight levels, and then his system had malfunctioned and wiped out all his progress. Could they possibly restore his game pak to where he had left off so he could complete his journey? Nintendo's No. 1 champion game counselor loaded the game pak, rubbed his hands, and spent three hours fulfilling the customer's request!

As the new decade began, the database had grown to five million names, and the company was projecting, for its latest fiscal year 1990, net sales of $4.1 billion.

What next? After you conquer the whole world (well, 80% of them) of boys age 8 to 15, what do you do for an encore?

The company's answer is that there are always plenty of other worlds to conquer. Get more girls interested in playing Nintendo games. More college students. More adults.

And create new kinds of product. Nintendo of America sold five million portable Game Boys and 20 million cartridges for it in the year following its recent introduction. They have licensed Voyager Communications to publish comic books based on Nintendo game characters[5] — and Ralston Purina to introduce a Nintendo Power breakfast cereal, reportedly an instant success. On the back of the cereal box is an introductory subscription offer for the magazine. Subscriptions were also sold as a tie-in with "The Wizard," a movie about winning a Nintendo contest.

Why stop there? Nintendo has built a $2 million traveling show that it plans to move in forty huge truck trailers to 30 top U.S. markets. They anticipated that 1.5 million people would pay an admission fee of about $8 to see a show featuring new games, accessories, live entertainment, and game counselors offering tips and strategies. In a special 200-seat competition area, attendees would vie for the title of "Champion," and then the winners would compete in the Nintendo World Championship on national television.[6] **(Trend No. 7, Involved Participants)**

Another avenue of future development: create new uses for the system. Just think, thanks to the huge popularity of Nintendo, there is now an intelligent box in over 30% of American households. Nintendo and Fidelity Investments have already announced joint plans to hook the box to a modem so that Fidelity can offer investment services to Nintendo-equipped homes. While costly videotex experiments like Viewtron and Telaction were foundering in the face of massive consumer indifference at the "front door," Nintendo has crept in the "back door" of American households with an easy-to-use new interactive computer that the family is already familiar with and likes to use. How this sytem will find itself being used by the year 2000 is impossible to foresee, but it could be as startling as the Nintendo developments thus far.

And despite the quick burn-out of video games in the mid-80's and the fickleness of public taste, it seems very likely that Nintendo is here to stay.

Because of the company's "secret weapon" of direct contact with five million customers, their constant monitoring of what these customers are currently thinking and needing and wanting, and the bold Turnaround Thinking that led them to start with the customer and work backwards to the product and the marketing, it seems far more certain that Nintendo, in one form or another, will remain a household word well into the next century.

STASH TEA — IMPRESSIVE GROWTH VIA NO-COST PRIVATE ADVERTISING

You don't have to be a billion-dollar company to be a successful MaxiMarketer. You can start in the family garage and build a thriving business that can compete with much larger companies.

One of the most outstanding examples of a small company using the principles of MaxiMarketing that we have been able to locate is the Stash Tea Company. It is a young company just outside of Portland Oregon that sells about 30 different kinds of tea, both caffeine teas and herbal teas.

This is the astonishing story of how they have been able to expand their business substantially, soaring in rank to become the fourth largest tea company in America, without spending a penny on awareness advertising or cents-off couponing in Sunday newspapers. Instead it has been accomplished by practicing a kind of guerilla MaxiMarketing, "living off the land" and creeping up on the competition with invisible private advertising.

It would make a neater story if the company's success was the result of the founders designing and carrying out a grand master plan, as was the case of, for example, Federal Express.

The way it actually happened, however, was much more like the way such successes usually occur — a combination of determination, integrity, a good product, the good fortune to be in tune with the times, outstanding improvisation, and an intuitive understanding of how to benefit from an ongoing relationship with the end-users of the product.

The outlines of the company's development reflect almost every aspect of Turnaround Thinking that we have talked about. Identifying and cultivating the best customers. Building a database and using it to drive promotion and distribution. Engaging in a dialogue and building a warm relationship with known customers. Using a multi-channel distribution system in which each channel supports the other.

How Stash Began. Stash* Tea began in 1972 with two young entrepreneurs, David Leger and Steve Lee, blending and bagging herbs and spices in the basement of a Victorian house in Portland and trudging around the Northwest to sell their products. They sold some to health-food stores and restaurants and interested individual consumers, but they soon found that their best market was restaurants.

They also found, in the restaurants they visited at that time — and indeed it is still true in most restaurants today — that a diner who ordered "tea" was simply served an arbitrarily selected brand of caffeine tea. So Stash introduced to the restaurants the idea of "a choice for a change" — a tea list of many different Stash caffeine and herbal teas from which patrons might choose, just as people choose from a restaurant's wine list. It provided a nice touch of elegance and service that both restaurateurs and customers appreciated — and it also boosted Stash Tea sales.

The first big breakthrough. At first Stash Tea was sold to restaurants in bulk. Then the company started packaging the product in individual tea bags. Next came putting the bags in attractive foil packets to seal out air and moisture and keep the tea fresh and aromatic. Then came the big breakthrough idea. A mail-order catalog had been developed for the increasing number of people who had tracked them down and expressed an interest in buying by mail. Why not put an offer of the catalog on the back of the foil packet? So they did just that: "Send for our Stash Tea Catalog of premium teas, gifts, and accessories. P.O. Box 610R, Portland, OR 97297." **(Trend No. 10, Multi-Channel Distribution)**

This message, along with a few lines of charming, appealing copy about the tea, is exposed to thousands of customers when they are in a very relaxed, receptive mood, having just enjoyed a good dinner finished off with a satisfying cup of Stash Tea. And it involves no — repeat, no — advertising cost, since the packet must be manufactured and printed anyway. From this and similar promotions, including asking customers for the names and

---

*Stash Tea got its name from a tradition of the clipper ship days. At that time tea and spices were precious luxury items imported at great cost from the Orient, not the modest commodity they are today. When a ship loaded its prized cargo in Shanghai, the finest tea of the lot was put aside in a box as the captain's "stash" for his own personal use during the long voyage. As soon as the ship docked in America, the captain's stash was tossed over the side to a runner, who raced with it to the tea market. The quality of the tea in the captain's stash then determined the price of the entire shipload.

addresses of friends who might also be interested, Stash Tea built a database of some 100,000 names and addresses. **(Trend No. 1, Known Prospects and Customers)** These people would receive a 24-page four-color catalog four times a year.

A young woman in the company's accounting department, Susan McIntyre, became involved in data processing, and then was made mail-order manager. She became fascinated with the phenomenon of direct-order marketing, and began asking friends at Norm Thompson and other Portland direct-marketing firms to tell her more about it and to recommend books and articles on the subject. Soon she was making important contributions to developing catalog sales and to stimulating the synergistic effect of combining these sales with their other channels of distribution

Each month, about 2,000 additional restaurant patrons would read the tea packet and request a catalog. About 20 per cent of these inquirers would then become mail-order customers, with an average order of $25. And because Stash could sell tea in the catalog at the full retail price, and had no advertising cost involved in getting the customer name, the catalog began producing 35% of the company's total net profit from only 10% of its sales.

Using mail-order sales to break into supermarkets. As we have indicated elsewhere in this book, fighting for shelf-space for new products in supermarkets has become a horrendous challenge in recent years. But Stash has found a way to meet it.

In the wholesale grocery market, Stash sells most of its tea through brokers to distributors and chain stores. To break into those parts of the country where Stash Tea isn't yet sold in restaurants and grocery stores, they have to convince new brokers to handle Stash Tea. These brokers have to convince distributors and grocery chains, and those distributors have to convince individual restaurant owners and grocers. How could this be accomplished without spending far more in advertising and couponing than a small company like Stash could possibly afford?

Well, here's how it works. The Stash sales manager walks into the office of the wholesale grocery buyer and says, "I've got this fantastic product I want you to distribute. Highest quality, great pricing." Well, all sales people say things like that. But then the Stash representative reaches into her briefcase and pulls out a thick sheaf of computer printouts. "And by the way," she says, "here's a list of 3,400 customers in this area who are already buying and enjoying Stash Tea. They're buying through our mail-order division, and your stores will be able to charge lower prices than our customers are paying already." Well, that's a pretty powerful sales argument, and it has been very successful in opening up new markets. **(Trend No. 2, Multi-Channel Distribution)**

When the tea finally reaches the food store shelves in the new market, catalogs mailed into that area inform the mail-order customers where they can now buy the tea locally at retail, for a lower price, thus helping to insure immediate demand for the product in the stores.

Each channel supports the other. You would think that this growing retail distribution would weaken and ultimately destroy the mail-order sales. But just the opposite has happened. Why? Because there is one more step in this ingenious multi-distribution loop.

Like the restaurant diners, many of the supermarket customers who try Stash Tea and like it respond to the free catalog offer they find on the back of the foil packet. This brings in still more names to the database — which then helps persuade still more retailers to stock the brand — which leads in turn to still more retail sales and catalog requests — and on and on! (Figure 11)

Thanks to this system, the number of catalog requests received soon jumped from 2,000 a month to 3,000 a month, and the database grew from 100,000 names to 150,000.

And while these may still seem like small numbers in the vast landscape of national tea sales, remember that these are extra-prime prospects who are extremely likely to become extra-heavy users — people who have not only already tasted and approved of the product, but who liked it so much that they are willing to take the trouble to use their own pencil, paper, envelope, and postage stamp to obtain the catalog of additional flavors and tea products. Also, Stash distribution so far has been concentrated largely in the West Coast and New England states, which means that in those areas its share of market is far larger than the national sales figures indicate.

Catalog does many jobs. The Stash Tea catalog performs double and triple and quadruple duty in building repeat sales and brand loyalty.

It builds Brand Image, far more powerfully and effectively and permanently than any campaign of TV commercials ever could. For these consumers are spending not 15 or 30 seconds at a time learning about Stash Tea, but more like 15 or 30 minutes.

It adds extra dimensions to the advertising effect. Most packaged goods advertising and promotion is painfully limited by the high cost of media and the shackles of mass marketing thinking. To sell a single product, as much as $10 or $20 million a year, or even more, may be spent just on 15-second commercials and poster-like couponing ads in fsi's, neither of which have room or inclination to say very much or show very much. And if the creative people responsible for the advertising were ever allowed to

HOW STASH TEA'S CUSTOMER DATABASE DRIVES SALES

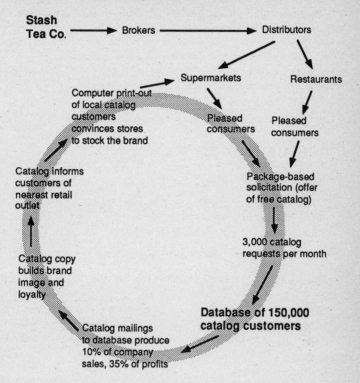

Figure 11

run completely free, unhampered by limitations of space, time, and cost, they might not know what to do with so much freedom. But look at the varied contents of just one issue of the Stash Tea mail-order catalog. See how many different ways it gets customers to "think tea" — drink tea — give tea — and look warmly on Stash:

> • A note on the tea featured on the cover, Licorice Spice. ("For thousands of years, licorice has been prized. It was valued as a cure-all in ancient China, and stored in King Tut's tomb, to comfort him on his journey into the afterlife. The root of this tall, violet-flowered plant is 50 times sweeter than sugar cane...And while most sweets cause thirst, licorice relieves it. It's comforting for a cough and valued by singers to strengthen their throats...Served after dinner, this tea tastes smooth as a fine liqueur. During the

day, it's a sweet treat that's free from calories and caffeine. Kids love it too...Now who could resist a smooth, rich sweet that's entirely guilt free?" (And who could resist such copy?)

• Gift baskets, boxes, glass mugs and tins of tea assortments of all sizes, including The Admiral's Tea Chest, 150 bags in a hardwood chest for $140!

• An historical note on the origin of the name "Stash."

• Tea pots and mugs, and silver tea service items — strainer, jam spoon set, creamer and sugar bowl, teabag rest.

• Breakfast collection of tea, jam, honey, cereal, bread mix.

•33 teas and spices in choice of quantities, packaged in foil, paper, or loose.

• A sidebar on how Stash decaffeinated tea is processed.

• A note on the art of tea blending by Stash Teamaster Steve Smith. ("We're fussy. Take vanilla, for example. After importing the finest 'Bourbon' vanilla from Madagascar, we insist on what's called a 'double fold extract' — twice as many beans per gallon as the pure vanilla you buy in the store.")

• Enthusiastic customer comments.

• List of stores and chains in 25 states that now carry Stash Tea. Offer to send of list of stores in reader's own area.

• Page on herb tea for children, with tea tin, honey sticks, mini-collection.

• Goodies that go well with tea— scone mixes, tea bread mix, short-bread cookies, Outrageous oat granola cereal, Stash jams and honeys.

• Letters of appreciation from environmentally-concerned customers because Stash had changed from styrofoam "peanuts" packing to paper.

• Note on Stash Tea travelling with six Antarctic explorers on 4,000-mile journey.

• Announcement of Stash donation of part of profit from each specially marked package to UNICEF for Oral Rehydration Kits to save starving Third World children, and where to write or call UNICEF if you wish to help too.

• Item about Stash Tea's foster child, Kendagannamma, and address and phone number of Foster Parent's Plan.

• Invitation to send in recipe for tea cookbook being planned.

• Recipe for making mint-flavored hot chocolate.

• An historical note on English Tea Gardens, "the genteel amusement parks of 19th Century England."

• A reminder to "ask for Stash" in restaurants.

• A glass mug of mulling spice, and a note on how to use in wine or cider.

• Bath bags and potpourris for adding fragrance to your bath, closet, and bureau drawers.

* Loose teas and tips of mixing your own custom blend.

• Iced tea pitcher and pitcher-sized tea bags.

• A quick-reference table comparing the flavors and ingredients of all 233 Stash blends.

If the catalog were owned and operated by an independent mail-order merchant, it would simply be another well-planned catalog. But because it is owned and operated by the tea company itself, which also sells its tea in restaurants and stores, it becomes more than just a profit center. It amounts to a new kind of packaged-goods advertising and promotion that bursts beyond the usual limits. **(Trend No. 2, Response-Driven)**

It is a marketing laboratory. The company tests new tea products in its pages, and has found that a new flavor which is a hit in the catalog will also be successful when sold at retail.

It is a dialogue channel. The catalog often prints Letters to the Editor from readers that add greatly to the warm community feeling. This in turn helps turn every catalog customer into an enthusiastic one-person advertising agency, producing free of charge the best kind of advertising of all — word-of-mouth. (This feedback channel also serves as a distant early warning of a problem that needs attention; thus when some of the foil packets started leaking loose tea, catalog customers let the company know right away and the problem was promptly taken care of.)

It is a retail-traffic builder. It drives catalog readers into supermarkets that carry Stash Tea by announcing where the product is available at retail.

It is a public relations communications channel, permitting Stash Tea to get extra value from event marketing tied to the company's dedication to clean water and a better environment.

For example, in the days of the great sailing ships, the precious cargo from the Orient was often tea. So Stash decided to recreate that romantic era. They chartered a 130-foot ketch, the Edna, to sail into Shanghai, load up with ten tons of the actual tea Stash uses in its blends, a whole year's supply, and cross the Pacific with it.

The ketch docked at Expo 86, the World's Fair being held that year at Vancouver, B.C., and then went on to San Francisco, giving public tea tastings and garnering publicity along the way.

Now that's not necessarily big news to a busy newspaper editor. But it *was* big news to the readers of the Stash tea catalog, because the catalog editors were able to tell their readers as much about the event as they pleased.

Similarly, catalog readers were able to follow the adventures of Portland mariner, explorer, and writer Sam McKinney. With a grant from Stash, McKinney spent parts of four years crossing America from Oregon to New York entirely by boat, along inland waterways. His progress was reported in installments in periodic editions of the catalog, and some catalog readers not only followed his story eagerly but called or wrote to find out exactly where he was going to be so they could contact him along the way to say hello. **(Trend No. 7, Involved Participants)**

One innovation by Susan McIntyre won a Gold Echo Award of the Direct Marketing Association. It was a direct-mail test of answering new requests for the catalog with communication that was literally one-to-one.

The control group received just the catalog. The test group received not only the catalog, but a limited-time gift certificate and a letter using exceptional personalization. This personalization included not only name, address, and any specific tea flavor the letter-writer may have mentioned, but also a unique sentence or two of reply written by the customer service manager, such as "Glad to hear you enjoyed the voyage on the Mississippi Queen that you wrote us about, Mrs. Smith." **(Trend No. 5, Consumer Dialogue)**

The conversion rate for the control group was 10.1%. For the test group, it was 32.3% -- and many customers in this group wrote again to thank Stash for having written them such a nice letter! **(Trend No. 6, Building Relationships)**

Does all of this hand-holding and verbosity pay off at the proverbial bottom line? It certainly has for Stash Tea. They have been expanding the business at a compounded growth rate of over 30% a year for the past seven years. They have moved into fourth place in the tea category, and they are still coming on strong.

"But Stash Tea is unique," you may argue, "it's not like the situation our company faces at all." If that is what you are thinking, you are 100% correct. We have never met a marketer yet who didn't say, "My product situation is different."

Furthermore, you could say the same thing about each of the case histories we are examining in detail in this section of the book.

Sorry, you can't just copy Stash Tea. You can't just copy Nintendo.

Your problem is different from theirs. *Every* product's marketing problem is different from all the others.

And the real creative challenge of our time is not simply to write more poetic advertising copy or to create a more amusing show-stopping 15-second commercial. It is to find your own unique, appropriate, demonstrably effective solutions to your own unique problem of getting closer to the customer in the Age of the Individual — new ways to locate, contact, activate, and cultivate your prime prospects and best customers, as Stash Tea is doing so brilliantly. What this book can do, we hope is inspire you to accomplish these aims, point you in the right direction, and give you some idea-starting tips.

AUTOMOTIVE MARKETING FACES NEW CHALLENGES

Wherever cars are sold throughout the world, there is fierce competition among automotive companies As the pressure in the U.S. from imports and other domestics increased, auto makers began casting about for ways to break out of the pack and differentiate themselves from the competition. They began experimenting with expanding their relationships with their own car buyers and instituting elaborate customer satisfaction programs. But just as, for the most part, the automotive world follows look-alike advertising and promotion practices, they began copying one another's loyalty-building and customer satisfaction programs. The real MaxiMarketing innovators were few and far between.

In our chapter on involvement strategies, we told the story of the wonders worked by Ron Fusile when he turned the Buick Open Golf Tournament into the kingpin of an integrated direct-response campaign. Now here are two more stories from the automotive world, one from the U.K. and one from France, which provide more evidence of how pace-setters around the world are beginning to change the way automobiles are marketed.

AUSTIN-ROVER'S CATALYST — WORLD'S FIRST COMPANY-SPONSORED CUSTOMIZED MAGAZINE

In the U.K. as we told you in Chapter Three, Austin-Rover developed a system of database marketing, Superlink, that cut advertising cost of an incremental sale in half.

Now, out of this earlier program, they have evolved a second-generation system that goes far beyond what they did earlier.

It is the Catalyst program, designed by the Systems Market

Link division of Marlow, Bucks, the same agency that was responsible for Superlink.

For nearly a decade, Austin Rover, the largest British-owned automobile manufacturer, had pioneered in building and using a sophisticated database to sell their Rover line of automobiles. Car buyers would receive a cycle of letters familiar to many auto makers and their customers: a welcome letter, an owners' warranty mailing, service reminders, and then — once the car reached a certain age — a sales proposition.

The trouble was, this system did not do enough to assure that the *right* offer was made to the *right* person at the *right* time. This meant that a great deal of costly sales material was being wasted, and a great many sales opportunities were being lost. And the system was still not doing enough to forge a powerful lifetime bond between the owners and the company.

SML came up with a precedent-shattering idea to answer both of these needs. At the heart of their program was *Catalyst*, an elegant glossy magazine that could be displayed proudly on the coffee table along with *Architectural Digest* and *Vogue*.

CAR OWNERS DESIGN THEIR OWN MAGAZINE

A magazine published by an automobile company for its customers is not a new idea. But they decided that this would be no ordinary magazine. It would be the world's first advertiser-sponsored magazine with contents customized by the reader to suit his or her individual interests. Austin Rover could do this by using the new computer-controlled selective binding technology we discussed earlier.

And just how would the previous owners and the prospects let Austin Rover know exactly which areas of interest they wanted covered in their copies of *Catalyst*? Why, by filling out a questionnaire. And guess what other questions would be asked in it? How about: "What is your current car's make and model? Was it purchased new or used? When did you take delivery? When do you expect to replace it? Which Austin Rover model comes closest to fitting the requirements for your next car?" And so on. **(Trend No. 5, Consumer Dialogue)**

The first issue of the magazine was mailed to a compiled database of 800,000 households. It included all Austin Rover owners who had purchased in recent years, as well as a number of additional prospects whose demographic and psychographic characteristics matched the profile of the typical Austin Rover buyer. This first issue explained the concept and provided sample editorial content in six lifestyle areas, along with a section of general appeal. The six special interest areas planned were Sports, Food and Drink, Home and Garden, Entertainment, Female Interests, and Travel.

The magazine was personalized with an addressed letter from the local dealer and also a questionnaire bound right into each copy. It required four passes through the binding machine in order to keep each copy's addressing and personalization correctly matched.

Readers were asked to choose three of the six subject areas for their future copies, and to indicate their choices in the questionnaire— along with the information desired by Austin Rover about their automobile ownership and future buying intentions.

To boost response to the questionnaire, the chance of winning a sweepstakes prize was part of the offer.

The startling response. The questionnaire was filled out and returned by nearly 40% of the car owners who received it, a very high response. With telemarketing follow-up, this was boosted to 54%. **(Trend No. 1, Known Prospects and Customers)**

This meant they now had vital individual data on nearly 400,000 prospective buyers.

Many of the sweepstakes winners were surprised to learn that they had even been entered. They said they had returned the questionnaire simply because they wanted the magazine.

Those who didn't respond received a second issue with a personalized and customized letter and another copy of the questionnaire bound in.

Since then the magazine has continued to be mailed to respondents. Each issue asks readers to update the information about intent to purchase and model most likely to be purchased.

It is estimated that almost half of the cost of producing and distributing the magazine is covered by outside advertising carried in each issue. Of course the readership is a very desirable advertising audience. The special-interest section concept attracts advertising that is natural for that particular audience, for example camera equipment, binoculars, and beverages for those who have chosen Sports as their special-interest category.

The Catalyst Collection. Some 500,000 of the magazine recipients now also receive quarterly The Catalyst Collection, a presentation of various opportunities to participate in lifestyle events offered exclusively to purchasers of Rover cars. **(Trend No. 9, Extra-Value Proposition)** The services sold include such upscale image-reinforcing adventures as wine-tasting weekends, a cuisine club, or a session on a DC10 flight simulator at Gatwick Airport. When the flight simulator was first introduced, more than 40 readers quickly signed up at $1,350 each!

The hardbound book for hot prospects. Three months before the hot prospect is likely to buy a new car, based on intentions expressed in the completed questionnaire and a confirmation phone call, the prospect receives a dealer-imprinted package containing what is called a VIP (Vehicle Information Portfolio).

This is an impressive hard-cover coffee-table book with contents devoted to the specific model in which the prospect has expressed interest.

Just think — while competitors are sending out just another typical new-car brochure showing their complete line, Rover is sending out to prospective buyers, at the most opportune moment, *a whole book* about the model they are most likely to buy.

A survey revealed that over 60% of the people who received the VIP book showed it to a friend or relative, and 70% of them expressed a spontaneous positive reaction.

With the book comes an invitation from the local dealer to take a test drive. (Research showed that only 5% objected to being contacted by their local dealer.) With the invitation there is an incentive to respond that is carefully customized to match the prospect's likelihood of purchase, lifestyle data, and availability of the car model the prospect will probably want.

Telemarketing plays a very important role in the program. Dealers must agree either to the training of an in-house person, who then works with supplied scripts, or to contract the work out to SML's telemarketing agency. Each dealer is expected to qualify and grade local prospects by telephone, and the information they obtain is then fed back to the database. In it the prospects are coded as hot or cold and over time can be switched from one category to the other.

After the sale is made, the new car owner continues to receive *Catalyst* magazine. In addition, the database automatically generates a customer retention program of letters that carry on a caring dialogue between dealer and owner about the warranty, servicing, government safety checks, and so on. **(Trend No. 5, Consumer Dialogue)** Then a few months before it is indicated that the next purchase is due, the customer will be moved back into the hot prospect file.

All car owners who fill out a questionnaire and name a likely future purchase data will stay in the database until they die, leave the country, or buy a competitive car.

The fulfilled mandate and its remarkable result. At the time that *Catalyst* was launched, Austin Rover already had one of the highest customer retention rates of any automobile manufacturer, a whopping 65%.

But after the Catalyst program was introduced, retention

rates for Austin-Rover owners , according to some industry sources, soared to one of the highest rates ever recorded in automotive history.

We were able to learn from Chris Richards, the managing director of SML, that since the introduction of the program, the rate of prospect conversion has increased by 100%.   According to Richards, the magazine continues to be very well received and provides extremely valuable data from the more than 50,000 readers who fill out and return the update questionnaire card in each issue.

These updates report changes in purchase intention, actual purchase behavior, address details, and other information which is then added to the dynamic Rover database.

The results achieved more than fulfilled the mandate the client had given to Systems Market Link: enable us to deliver the *right* message to the *right* person at the *right* time. And to make all this possible, they took a high-tech page out of the future — creating the magazine of tomorrow, a publication offering content custom-tailored to individual interest and a way to establish a dialogue between the the manufacturer and the target market.

Since the magazine was launched, a significant amount of research has been carried out to determine the attitudes of the readers toward the publication. A majority of the respondents said that they would prefer to see more "in depth" articles on one special subject rather than fewer articles on three or four selected subjects.

As a result, Rover modified the format so that readers can now request one 32-page special-interest section from a selection of four subject areas. This is then bound into their customized copy of *Catalyst* in addition to the universal 64-page general-interest section.

As this demonstrates, one of the great advantages of carrying on a continuing dialogue with your market is that your prospects and customers can help you redefine your Extra-Value Proposition as it matures and adjust the fit precisely to the market.

THE VOLKSWAGEN TURNAROUND IN FRANCE

Automobile manufacturers throughout the world have discovered the value of retaining customer loyalty and operating customer satisfaction programs. But very few understand the concept of DPA — Database-Driven Promotion and Advertising. Altogether they spend hundreds of millions of dollars — even billions — on single-dimension awareness advertising when they could be using their television and magazine advertising dollars to establish direct contact with their best prospects and bring them into the showroom in droves.

Volkswagen Audi in France showed how it can be done in an ingenious campaign developed by Alain Philippe at Rapp & Collins France. They ran a DPA insertion in just three news magazines with astonishing results.

The car advertised was the Audi Quattro, the all-wheel drive model which had been introduced several years earlier. It was the first car to use the unique four-wheel drive system which has since been copied by Mercedes-Benz, BMW, and some luxury Japanese cars.

The Quattro had shown very little life in France, and its share of mind in the fiercely competitive auomobile market was very low. Everything tried before had failed to stir up enthusiasm for Volkswagen's truly remarkable engineering breakthrough.

But one short, powerful burst of database-driven advertising changed the picture completely.

The Audi ad was a two-page spread inviting readers to take a test themselves with thirteen questions.

On the left-hand page, the headline asked in big bold letters, "Êtes Vous Quattro?" (Are you the Quattro Kind of Person?)

On the right-hand page, there was a tipped-on sealed 4"x5" envelope containing the 13-question quiz and a reply form. **(Trend No. 2, Response-Driven)**

Total circulation was 1,250,000. At last count the response was close to 100,000, more than *ten times* as many as had been anticipated. This meant that 8% of the readers had taken the trouble to open up the envelope, read through the thirteen questions, fill out the score card, see how they rated, and mail in the reply form with their test score to enter a drawing. The prize was, of course, an Audi Quattro. Note the promotional element added to stimulate response.

Some of the questions in the self-test were whimsical but relevant, such as: "For you, the word car means [check one] (a) a passion, (b) an object you can live without, (c) a necessity, and (d) wheels attached to a chunk of iron." Other questions were more pointed, such as: "When someone mentions four-wheel performance to you, what do you think? [check one] (a) It is a 4x4, (b) it is a Quattro, (c) it is better than two wheels, (d) it is the minimum you want to get."

Previous studies of non-respondents in other product categories make it seem certain that for every reader who actually filled out and returned the Quattro test, there were two or three non-respondents who got involved with it and for several minutes were exposed to the benefits of Audi's four-wheel drive. And the 100,000 respondents received a beautiful 36-page booklet with everything they might want to know about the car, as the next step in a relationship they began when they mailed in their quiz answers. **(Trend No. 6, Building Relationships)**

The follow-up mailing also contained a detailed questionnaire which qualified the prospect further and brought into the showroom just those truly interested prospects most likely to purchase the Audi Quattro.

But wasn't there some way that the power of TV advertising could also be harnessed to serve the ends of this campaign?

Well, there was no way the quiz could be crammed into a 30-second commercial. But France has an interactive home computer system that is almost as common there as the VCR is in many other countries — Minitel, the computerized telephone directory, which also offers 40,000 different advertisements and services viewable on the home screen. So the entire 30-second commercial was devoted to inviting viewers to go to their Minitel, call the Audi number, and take the Audi quiz. **(Trend No. 7, Involved Participants)**

More than 10,000 viewers spent an average of five minutes each taking the test in this way. It provided a tantalizing glimpse of the possibilities for advertisers when the rest of the world finally gets interactive video communication.

As this is being written, we don't yet know the final sales result. But based on the huge number of qualified responses now in the database, the expectation is for a complete sell-out of the inventory.

HOW MICHAEL ANTHONY PUTS ITS JEWELRY RETAILERS INTO DATABASE MARKETING

If you are a manufacturer with retail distribution and a modest advertising budget, how do you get customers into stores all over America asking for your product? By now you may think you've tried everything, to no avail.

Your hang-up may be that you are locked into thinking of *pushing* customers into your retailer's store when maybe the real answer is to *pull* them in. With turnaround thinking, you may be able to help your retailers use the power of database marketing to do one-to-one selling of your products to their own customers and get measurable sales results.

The Michael Anthony Jewelers story provides a striking example of how this can be done.

It is fashionable these days to marvel at how the power of the computer database can bring back the good ol' days of the Mom and Pop store that intimately knew and served each individual customer. Don't kid yourself. Mom and Pop forgot as much as they remembered about what individual customers liked and disliked.

The sad truth is that there are still a great many small Mom and Pop stores, and usually they still don't know who, where, and what their customers are.

These small proprietors tend to be product-oriented rather than marketing-oriented. They cling stubbornly to the old belief that if you carry good merchandise, the world will beat a path to your door. Their only hope for survival is Turnaround Thinking which teaches them to start with the customer, not the product.

The small independent jewelry store is our case in point. In recent years, such stores have been buffeted first by fierce competition from large chain stores and then by discount selling of jewelry on cable television shopping shows. Some have begun to realize the need to embrace the marketing concept before it is too late.

But how? If you have spent a lifetime in traditional passive retailing, how do you suddenly become a sophisticated marketer?

Enter James Porte.

He was an IBM representative who became fascinated with the hidden potential in jewelry retailing. And he was ready to make a big change in his life to something completely different. So he switched careers and soon found himself in the position of marketing director at Michael Anthony Jewelers, a $65 million manufacturer (today a $100 million public company).

To learn the business, Porte spent three years visiting 500 jewelers in 40 states. They told him they didn't need more products — they needed more customers. And when he would ask the jeweler, "Do you have a customer list?" the answer was almost invariably, "Well, sort of!"

Porte eventually persuaded some 350 of these small retailers to let him and his company help them do their own database marketing. He developed a Customer Data Card which every sales clerk is supposed to fill out on each store visitor, if possible. **(Trend No. 1, Known Prospects and Customers)**

There are spaces for name (Ms. Miss Mrs. or Mr.), address, phone, birthday, birth date, anniversary date, birth date of sweetheart. The clerk records whether it is a first visit and how the visitor heard about the store. If it is by personal recommendation, the name of the friend is entered so that a "thank you" can be sent. The customer is identified by sex, age group, type (student, housewife, blue collar, white collar, professional/executive, senior citizen/retired). There is a place to indicate if a purchase was made, and if so, what type of item.

These cards are gathered up by the retailer and forwarded every 15, 30, or 60 days to Michael Anthony, where the information is then fed into the master database.

Of course the jeweler could enter this information in his or her own computer, and the most up-to-date dealers do. But what Porte realized is that many of them are not yet ready or able to do this. So Michael Anthony does it for them at a very modest cost. The service costs $85 for the first 500 customer records and 12¢ for each additional customer.

Each jeweler in the program receives a monthly report summing up the latest activity at his or her store. It shows which customers have birthdays and anniversaries coming up. It provides a monthly summary of each clerk's sales achievement, and tells sales clerks to whom they should send "thank you" notes to recent buyers. The "thank you" cards in this program are no ordinary postcards. The clerk addresses the black envelope with gold ink. The note inside is written in gold ink on shiny black cardboard. It mentions the item purchased and says, "Present this card next time and get 20% off your next purchase." **(Trend No. 7, Consumer Dialogue)**

Michael Anthony also offers the merchants, at cost, gorgeous four-color catalogs, folders, and postcards imprinted with the jeweler's name, address, and specialty. If customers have not visited the store for some time, the computer generates a "we've missed you" mailing and reactivation offer. The offer need not be costly to be warmly received. Even a modest free service such as pearl restringing or jewelry cleaning gets plaudits from the customers and creates productive store traffic.

Many of the small jewelers were stunned and thrilled by the electrifying effect of this traffic-building sales-generating service program. "What are you guys, philanthropists?" they would ask Porte. And the answer was, "No, we simply figure that if we can help you grow, we will get our share."

Store promotion is not necessarily limited to the names on the filled-out cards. Michael Anthony shows the jewelers how, when business is slow, they can attract new customers by mailing to "clones" of their best customers selected from public databases of households in their trading area.

Dealers in the program receive demographic reports showing the make-up of the trading area to guide them in managing their inventory and marketing. One store prided itself on being "the engagement ring specialist" in its area, and 75% of the store inventory was engagement rings. But the demographic report on the store's trading area showed that most nearby residents were over 50 years old, not exactly your hottest prospects for engagement rings. The store was persuaded by the report to change its merchandise policy and positioning to good effect.

Many business and professional people find it hard to take time out of a busy day to go shopping for gifts for clients, employees, family. Porte taught the jewelers to mail out a catalog to such people, followed by a phone call: "Would you like to be part of our corporate discount program? If you see something in our catalog that you would like right now, we can gift-wrap it for you and bring it right over." Local business people are favorably impressed by the professionalism, thoughtfulness, and convenience of such a service.(**Trend No. 9, E.V.P.**)

When Porte first came to Michael Anthony Jewelers, it was a $65 million company. Today it is a $100 million publicly-owned corporation, and it seems certain that the merchant-assistance programs Porte introduced made an important contribution to the company's growth.

James Porte has now left Michael Anthony behind and has moved on to bigger and better things. He founded the Jewelry Marketing Institute to offer jewelry dealers an even broader array of marketing workshops and other educational services, and to keep them abreast of the merchandising programs of a number of other manufacturers in addition to Michael Anthony.

But he is using the same principles, simply on a broader scale. Notice the Turnaround Trends his programs reflect. He teaches the retailer to identify not only the customer, but also the prospect, the visitor who stops in but doesn't buy the first time. He guides them into advertising from which results are distinctly traceable. He shows them how to develop a dialogue and build a relationship with the customers, and to fight price-cutting competition not with more price-cutting but with superior courtesy and service. He shows them how to give up the wastefulness of advertising to "everybody" and benefit instead from the efficiency of focusing their merchandising dollars on their own customers and prime prospects in their trading area.

He not only taught the retailers to wrap their products in service, he practiced what he preached, wrapping every Michael Anthony product in a plan for selling it. He even showed them another channel of distribution: off-site selling, in which the buying decision is made in the customer's place of business and the merchandise is delivered by hand to the place of business.

And most important of all, he has demonstrated how manufacturers and suppliers can grow by helping their retailers grow.

Porte is one of the new breed of turnaround thinkers who is

carrying the tenets of MaxiMarketing to the independent retailer.

What he has done sets an example for retailers in any field who want to turn away from merely offering merchandise and toward becoming a one-to-one marketer.

And manufacturers, too, may realize from his story that helping your retailers *pull* their customers into the stores may be a much better investment than attempting to *push* them in with passive, thinly scattered, unmeasurable awareness advertising.

HOW STEINWAY & SONS TURNED THINGS AROUND IN PIANO SALES

Steinway & Sons has deep roots in the past. They have been making pianos, one at a time, since 1853, and of course are preeminent in the piano field. They make and sell only about 5,000 pianos a year. Nearly 95% of the world's performing concert pianists choose to play only on a Steinway.

With this kind of tradition, and this kind of supply and demand situation, you might expect that the Steinway marketing methods would be a relic of the past too. But you would be wrong.

Sheer necessity has stimulated the company to become a sophisticated database marketer, using the computer to identify and cultivate prospects.

For while Steinway may still be the No. 1 name in pianos, it is also No. 1 in costliness. It takes 23 months for craftsmen to make a Steinway baby grand, and that obviously runs up the price. A Steinway may cost anywhere from $7,000 for a basic upright to as high as $48,000 for a nine-foot concert grand. The prices are often as much as double that of Steinway's competition. And they never do price-cutting or discounting.

At one time this was not a problem. But then the piano industry in the U.S. was hard hit by a flood of foreign imports, which seized 80% of the market. The remaining small number of domestic piano manufacturers began fighting it out for share of market. And it was true that many of their 109 exclusive dealerships, some of which had been run by the same family for 100 years, were still living in the past, with prospect names kept on 3x5 cards stored in the proverbial shoebox.

Steinway's answer has been the development of an artful seven-point program for building traffic and sales for their flagship store, Steinway Hall (across the street from Carnegie Hall, where else?), and for their dealers. It consists of sales training, institutional sales, technical support, advertising support, concert activities, promotion, and merchandising. [7]

Out of the total program, we want to take a closer look here at those aspects of it which are most meaningful and usable for any readers faced with planning their own one-to-one marketing programs to promote a major purchase.

Because of the seriousness of this once-in-a-lifetime purchase, the Steinway salespeople have found that completing a sale often requires perhaps three face-to-face conversations and three or four follow-up letters and phone calls over a period of months. **(Trend No. 6, Building Relationships)**

And since sales, discounts, and other high-pressure methods would be inappropriate to the Steinway image, what has been developed instead is a number of ingenious reasons for getting prospects to pay a visit and ingenious excuses for the salesperson to follow up afterwards.

For instance, Steinway Hall has a small auditorium seating 40 or 50 people, and periodically newspaper ads will invite people to make reservations to come in and enjoy a presentation of "the secrets of Steinway."

And although new pianos are not discounted, another traffic-building event is sale of "slightly used" pianos which have been purchased for a music festival and then sold back to Steinway.

An award-winning campaign of nine newspaper ads presented nine different reasons for paying a visit to Steinway Hall. Salespersons was given ad reprints in advance so they could send each one to their own prospect lists with a handwritten note before the ad appeared in *The New York Times.*

Steinway will sometimes ship a large number of pianos at one time to a dealer. Then the dealer can advertise that they have the largest number of Steinways available in their history.   One dealer sold 50 pianos in three days in this way.

It's a "mortal sin," says Williams Myers of Steinway's direct response agency, Ingalls, Quinn, and Johnson Direct, for a retailer to spend a lot of money to get people into the store and then allow them to get out of the store without capturing their names. Steinway Hall does not commit that sin.[8] **(Trend No. 1, Known Prospects and Customers)**

Each name that is thus captured receives self-mailers and ad reprints from time to time to keep the buying impulse fresh, while it is up to the individual sales person to decide how to pursue the sale.

But where Steinway & Sons has done most to bring its 19th Century dealers into the 21st Century is through its program of dealer-imprinted direct mail. Just as we have seen how Michael Anthony Jewelers was able to give its retail jewelers a boost by enabling them to do sophisticated direct mail to their own customers that they would not be capable of on their own, so Steinway turns its dealers into high-tech direct-mail prospectors.

But direct mail to whom? As Myers has wryly commented, there is no such thing as a mailing list of rich piano players.

So instead, to create a universe of excellent direct-mail prospects, the agency resorted to the powerful list-building technique known as cloning, just as we reported that Michael Anthony Jewelers does for its retailers. The "clone theory," as Myers describes it, is that "my next customer is going to look like my last customer."

To locate clones of Steinway buyers, the agency obtained from warranty cards the names of 3,500 people who had bought pianos at Steinway Hall. They sorted out the cards into 44 geodemographic clusters, and found that four clusters had a very high concentration of Steinway customers. In the top cluster, "the odds are about eight times greater that that person looks like, walks like, talks like, and makes as much money as the last Steinway buyer than if you went through the phone book."

Direct mail to these clusters was extremely successful in producing high-quality store traffic at Steinway Hall.

So next Steinway applied the same technique to its dealerships. Another 3,500 warranty card names, this time from all over the country, were analyzed and the top four clusters determined.

Steinway prints out a count of the number of people in these four clusters for every zip code in the U.S. and shows it to each dealer, along with a sample of dealer-imprinted Steinway direct mail which the dealer can purchase at cost.

The dealers decide which zip codes they want to promote and how many names they can afford. Steinway then handles the entire mailing for the dealer, receives and fulfills the replies at a central location, and forwards the leads to the dealer for personal follow-up.

In this way, Steinway has been mailing out about 300,000 to 350,000 pieces of mail about twice a year for their dealers, "and they love it."

Thanks to this "cloning" strategy and other aspects of Steinway's seven-point program, they were able to register a one-year sales increase of 30% to 40% — sweet music to any company's ears.

ROLAND'S STRATEGY IN ITALY

In Italy, Roland Italia faced a problem similar to that of Steinway and came up with their own MaxiMarketing solution .

Roland is a world leader along with Yamaha in the field of professional electronic keyboards. Top professionals like Michael Jackson and Stevie Wonder play on Roland keyboards.

In Italy, Roland has about 45% of the professional market. The company wanted to expand by increasing its penetration of the amateur music-lover market. But like Steinway, they had a much more expensive product than that of their strongest competition — an "entry-level" Roland keyboard costs about five times as much as a comparable Casio. And like Steinway, they found there was no ready-made mailing list of ideal prospects whom they could approach.

The solution developed by Giulio Spreti of Rapp & Collins Italy was an "Answer and Win" sweepstakes (*Rispondi e Vinci*). Using general-interest magazines (since readers of music magazines were already quite familiar with Roland), the insertions consisted of two pages of Roland's regular awareness advertising and a third page devoted to getting a response. **(Trend No. 2, Response-Driven)** One half of the response page was a highly informative questionnaire, asking for such information as, "Are you an amateur or a professional musician? How long have you been playing? What do you now use?" and so on. **(Trend No. 8,Direct Mass Marketing)** Readers who filled out and returned the questionnaires became eligible to win prizes in a drawing.

The campaign produced about 10,000 responses, which was especially gratifying since the entire magazine expenditure for the promotion was less than $60,000. It is too early to know the final sales outcome of the program, but already Roland has gained three benefits from it:

• valuable research data about the amateur-performer music market

•10,000 prime prospects who can be invited to go to a Roland dealer for trial of a Roland keyboard.

•10,000 potential customers for a new mail-order catalog operation selling items that are hard to find in music shops, such as special effects, manuals, and so on.

DATABASE MARKETING TRANSFORMS PIZZA PIZZA

How do you tell a genuine native of Toronto from an impostor?

Easy. Ask him or her the phone number you need to order from Pizza Pizza. If the answer you get is 967-11-11, you've got a real live Torontonian.

That is the number of Pizza Pizza, and an astounding 80% of

the residents of Toronto can play it back to you.* In fact, if you're under 30 and have lived in Toronto for at least three months, the founder and chairman of Pizza Pizza, Michael Overs, will pay you $100 if you can't recall the number. He hasn't had to pay off yet. (Apparently he has no problem with deceivers. The Canadians are a wonderful people.)

Michael Overs can be confident that you will know that phone number. He has made sure of it. The number is repeated over and over in radio and television jingles. It blazes forth as a huge neon sign at Exhibition Stadium. It's painted on the boards at Maple Leaf Gardens. It's plastered on billboards and the sides of busses. The most recent Pizza Pizza stores don't even have the name displayed out front — just a huge sign spelling out the famous phone number.

And no matter where you are in Toronto, if you call that number, you get a pizza "your way," piping hot in its own insulated bag, delivered to your door within 30 minutes — or your order is free. (The company couldn't obtain exactly the same number for use in Hamilton, Ottowa, Montreal, and Oshawa, but in each case they managed to get and promote locally a similar number ending in "1111.")

On a busy Friday night, up to 100 phone operators wearing headsets accept some 30,000 phoned-in orders and transmit them in seconds to the nearest Pizza Pizza franchise store. Furthermore, they know when and how much you ordered the last time, what toppings you requested, and whether the delivery per-

---

*A marketer in Brazil has also scored great success with the "famous phone number" technique. Amil is Brazil's second largest health plan and the country's fastest-growing company, with a compounded year-in year-out growth rate of 68%. Of course they offer excellent service, and are skilled at segmented marketing, with different plans for each economic group. But perhaps the most singular aspect of their success is the use of TV as a mass marketing medium to reach prospects.

In a country in which the phone numbers have only numerals, no alphabetical letters, they have still managed to burn into the public mind the best-remembered number in Brazil.

Since the name "Amil" sounds the same as the word for "one thousand" in Portugese, they made their direct-response phone number "241-AMIL" (241-1000).

After seven years of featuring the number in billboards, magazine ads, and all of their television commercials, now they even get calls from people who think they are calling a competing health plan.

The visionary president of Amil, Edson de Godoy Bueno, proved the fame of his company's telephone number to one of us in a Rio de Janeiro restaurant. He called over a waiter and said, "Quick, what's the first phone number that comes to your mind?" The waiter grinned and said, "241-AMIL. I know it better than my mother-in-law's number."

son should knock at your front, side, or back door.

Behind this phenomenon is the story of one of the most remarkable database marketing achievements on the North American continent. And like many of the early database marketing success stories, it was not the result of a sweeping strategic master plan but rather of brilliant organic growth and tactical improvisation.

How it all began. In 1967 Overs began his career that culminated in his present role as a pizza king by working as an unpaid pizza apprentice for three months to learn the business. Then he borrowed $3,000, and using his own carpentry skills, prepared a 300-sq. ft. pizza parlor in a 120-year-old building near a new apartment complex dominated by young singles. He made and sold the pizza on the ground floor, prepared the dough and toppings in the basement, and slept upstairs in a rented apartment.

His early experiences in the pizza business taught him two important lessons: (1) couponing, couponing, couponing, and (2) pizza must be hot, hot, hot when delivered. (We never said that couponing doesn't work. It is only when equal counter-couponing by competitors produces a stalemate that it is necessary to explore new horizons.)

Overs and his assistant solved the first problem by working 18 hours a day, delivering coupons in the daytime and running the store at night.

To solve the problem of keeping the pizzas hot during delivery, he consulted a friend in the bedding business and they developed a bedding-lined insulated delivery bag. (Today there are companies in North America that do nothing but produce these delivery bags.)

By 1969, there were four stores. By 1972, there were 10. By 1979, it was up to 20.

The Big Breakthrough. Then came the big idea that played the most important part in turning it into a $100 million Canadian company (the equivalent of a billion-dollar company in the United States).

What do you usually do when you want to order a pizza? You pick up the telephone book and look in the Yellow Pages for the numbers of the nearest pizza places, right?

Overs reasoned that if he could intercept that action by putting the same phone number for all his stores in your head, he would get your business. Okay, so far, so good. But there was still one obstacle. For operators to attempt to take down the orders and then phone them to the nearest franchiser would be a logistical nightmare. And delays and busy signals would be fatal.

Overs turned to the latest computer and telecommunications

technology for the answer. Development of a workable solution required his investing more than $1 million in his own custom-designed phone system based on twin MAI computers, Hamex software, and Northern Telecom's Automatic Call Distributor.

Now, as calls come in, they are automatically and evenly distributed among available answering positions. Each operator wears a headset and sits in front of a computer.

When the customer's phone number is entered (assuming it is not a new customer), the customer's complete history comes up on the screen, including any special ordering or delivery instructions. If the caller is a new customer, a new file is instantly created.

As the customer gives the order, it is entered into the computer by the operator and transmitted instantly to the computer printer of the nearest store, where a hard copy is printed out in seconds.

The benefits of this system are immediately apparent.

First of all, there are the obvious advantages to the customer. There is the convenience of not having to look up a phone number each time or spell out your name and address all over again each time. And the flattery of the operator asking, "Mushrooms and sausage as usual, Mr. Johnson?" **(Trend No. 5, Consumer Dialogue)**

But to Pizza Pizza, it also means a complete, detailed, continuously updated record of each customer's buying history and preferences by name and address. In Toronto alone, the system now has files on 700,000 households representing more than one million customers. **(Trend No. 1, Known Prospects and Customers)**

And because the company has the history of each customer on file, it is able to give different treatment to different customers. **(Trend No. 3, Filling Each Niche)**

If it has been quite a while since you have ordered a pizza, the computer can now generate a phone/mail revival promotion: "We've missed you, Mr. Johnson. Have we displeased you? Please answer a few questions and we'll give you a free pizza."

On the other hand, if you are a terrific customer, you deserve preferential treatment, and thanks to your computer record, you will get it: "Congratulations, Mr. Johnson! To reward you for having ordered one hundred pizzas from us, we are giving you one free!"

Sales soared when the new computerized phone system was installed, and so did the number of outlets.

Then sales jumped again five years later when the "30 minutes or it's free" guarantee was announced. Rob Hindley, the company's marketing director, says that introduction of the guarantee increased sales by 35% within a year.

Note in how many ways the company has turned away from the usual routine way of doing business and toward the new directions outlined in our ten turnaround trends.

The people at Pizza Pizza know who their customers are. **(Trend No. 1, Known Prospects and Customers)** Their advertising is very creative but the creativity is put at the service of response. **(Trend No. 2, Response-Driven)** They can separate their market into heavy and light users, present and past customers, and treat each accordingly. **(Trend No. 3, Filling Each Niche)** They can tell you to a penny how much each customer is worth. **(Trend No. 4, Counting Customers Won)**

They are literally in a daily dialogue with their customers, and by training their operators, can control the dialogue to build customer loyalty and increase sales. **(Trend No. 5, Consumer Dialogue)** By personal recognition of each customer's needs and by initiating follow-up communications, they can build relationships with their customers. **(Trend No. 6, Building Relationships)** And by such means as the insulated bag, the special delivery instructions, and the guaranteed 30-minute delivery, they have succeeded in adding an important service dimension to the product. **(Trend No. 9, E.V.P.)**

If ever there is a Hall of Fame established for turnaround thinkers who have helped to usher in the age of Individualized Marketing, Michael Overs certainly deserves to be honored there.

"THE NEXT DIRECTORY" — THE 21ST CENTURY SUCCESSOR TO THE SEARS CATALOG

In the last chapter, one of the ways we listed of riding the trend toward direct distribution was simply to launch an innovative start-up appealing to the growing demand for the convenience of home shopping.

In the U.K., an astounding start-up has taken a giant leap beyond what the consumer had always expected to find in a mail-order catalog in the U.K. It is as great a leap as Federal Express took past United Parcel Service when it established its air hub system for providing America's first guaranteed overnight delivery service.

"The Next Directory" is the most innovative major new catalog anywhere in the world in the last 100 years or so.

The company guarantees prompt delivery by its own uniformed couriers anywhere in the British Isles within 48 hours for a uniform low delivery charge. Actually, they deliver more than

60% of the orders within 24 hours. If you order on Monday before 4:00 P.M., your shipment leaves the warehouse by 10:00 P.M., is trucked overnight to a depot, and is delivered by courier Tuesday. **(Trend No. 9, E.V.P.)**

But The Next Directory is not just about fast delivery. After all, many U.S. specialty catalogs now offer overnight delivery by air freight for a reasonable charge. It is about a totally different way of shopping at home instead of in a store.

An "art book" catalog. The Directory is beautifully bound in hard covers, similar to an expensive "coffee table" art book. Inside there are swatches of fabric pasted into position alongside the descriptions of many of the men's and women's fashions.

The company discourages ordering by mail, and does everything possible to encourage use of the phone instead. Some 92% of the business is done by phone.

Sizing information, return policy, tissue paper wrapping, deluxe packaging, customer service, availability of merchandise — every last detail has been rethought and reinvented to respond to customer needs and desires.

The cost of producing the first run of 500,000 catalogs came to more than $16 a copy.

All the collective wisdom of the catalog fraternity in the U.K. and the U.S., while admiring the company's daring and creativity, prophesied that excessive costs would quickly sink the venture. Published reports that the first edition of 500,000 resulted in 200,000 sales were greeted with disbelief. There were predictions on every side that there would never be a second volume.

But the second volume did appear in the summer of 1988. This time there were were 650,000 copies distributed. And again the pundits of doom had their say — and reassuring statements from the management of The Directory were discounted.

Then early in 1989, the third volume apeared right on schedule. Could the people at The Directory know something that the rest of the world didn't? We decided to find out, and arranged to meet with CEO David Jones.

The remarkable founder. Jones is an extraordinary person, one who combines the imaginative daring of a visionary with a solid grasp of the realities of the marketplace. He welcomed the opportunity to set the record straight and was more than willing to share the latest numbers with us.

During the first year of operation in the United Kingdom, a market one-fourth the size of the United States, catalog sales totaled $105 million. Although the business plan called for breakeven, the first-year operations did produce a loss due to various start-up problems and a postal strike.

But what was most important about that first year of publication was the change the Directory produced in the mind-set of the British consumer about purchasing from catalogs.

Prior to its appearance, catalog shopping in the U.K. was strictly downscale. The Next Directory proved, just as David Jones and his associate at the time, George Davies, had suspected, that "there were lots of upscale people who were not mail-order buyers who would shop by phone if given the right opportunity."

More than half of the customers of The Next Directory had never purchased from a catalog before.

Jones told us they mailed 730,000 copies of the third volume, with a sales projection, based on six weeks of results, of 430,000 buyers — a remarkably high 60% response. Average order size is $136.

Evidently, the catalog's exceptional presentation keeps customers coming back for more. One out of two who send in an order later order again from the same book. And 18% of those come back for thirds during the same season.

How were the customers generated? Entirely from upscale print media advertising that offers the catalog for $5. The advertising budget was running to $3.5 million annually, the equivalent of a $14 million budget in the U.S.

In the third catalog issued, the cost of printing each copy had been reduced by one-third without any loss of impact, and Jones was predicting a healthy $8.5 million profit from it. And there was every reason to believe that this was only the beginning — an extremely auspicious beginning considering that so many start-ups require several years of struggle before they start showing a profit.

The Next Directory is one more piece of striking evidence that if you can provide people in their homes with a shopping opportunity which offers many of the advantages of shopping in a store and none of the disadvantages (poor stock, poor selection, crowds), an increasing number of will eagerly grab it.

LESSONS IN MARKETING OF THE FUTURE FROM TODDLER UNIVERSITY

The story of Toddler University is a David and Goliath story to warm the heart and stir the blood of every entrepreneur who ever dreamed of going up against a giant and winning.

From a start-up loan of $3,000 to annual sales volume of $30 million in less than four years is quite a parlay. That has been the astounding achievement of Jeff Silverman, the young marketing genius who has shaken up the baby and toddler shoe industry with the business he started at the age of 23, Toddler University.

Along the way, he has demonstrated his understanding and mastery of a number of the principles described in this book, as well as inventing one or two of his own.

If there were a wise Old Man of the Mountain of marketing, and one could climb the mountain and ask him the one all-inclusive secret of success, the answer might be just three little words of timeless wisdom: "Do everything right."

That pretty well describes exactly how Silverman has built his business.

He got the product right, making the shoes appropriately adorable but relieving parental guilt feelings about indulging in sheer adorability by giving the same care to fit, comfort, and age-group needs as are lavished on adult shoes,

He got the image right, with constant clever word plays and visual expressions based on the word "university" in all of the packaging, advertising, and promotion.

He got the advertising copy right, smart and smooth and contemporary, but skipping mushy mood copy and dreamy pictures of saucer-eyed babies and adoring parents, and getting right down to the product features that make Toddler U. shoes superior.

He got the supply situation worked out, after going through some bad times, by making his Taiwan suppliers part owners in his business.

And most important of all, from the point of view of this book, he got the channels of communication with the consumer right, establishing and maintaining direct contact with the parents of toddlers. Almost before he had almost anything else, he made what he considers a critically important investment, and is still a key part of the business today — he established a toll-free 800 number. **(Trend No. 5, Consumer Dialogue)**

He then proceeded to put the number on and in everything – boxes, hang-tags, direct mail, magazine ads. He is passionately convinced that consumers want and need to talk with and be involved with companies they do business with.

Silverman got his first taste of the athletic shoe business when he was a teen-ager, working at a three-store sporting goods chain in Rye Brook, N.Y., and in effect managing one of them by the time he was 16. A competing store in town had the local Nike exclusive, and Silverman had fought to get it for his store. After graduating from college, he wrote a three-page letter of application to Nike in which he recalled the experience. That landed him a job with Nike as product manager for children's shoes.

He quit after eight months, and after a brief detour in another job decided that his destiny lay in starting and building his own shoe company. But all he had was a name for the company, an idea, and a dream.

He made a sketch of his idea and returned to visit the owner of the sporting goods chain where he used to work. That visit yielded $3,000, enough to contract for a logotype design and buy an answering machine. With this he was able to round up $125,000 in working capital from a number of investors, including his mother and a neighbor for whom he had done babysitting as a kid, and was ready to go to Taiwan and find a supplier to make a prototype.

His first office and "warehouse" was his mother's home. Then, he told us, they moved the business into a leaky warehouse renting for $900 a month, and bartered for carpeting by paying for it with a thousand pair of infant shoes.

When he first proposed adding his 800 number at the bottom of his ads, his agency explained to him that just tacking it onto an ad not designed for response wouldn't accomplish very much, and he shouldn't expect much response. In principle they were correct; but the product and the advertising copy were so powerful that the company received 262 calls the first day that the first ad appeared.

The brand he had to beat was Stride Rite, which had a lock on the market for children's shoes with $170 million in sales annually. And Stride Rite sold fit. Even their shoes for infants were sold in a choice of widths.

Silverman designed shoes with a choice of removable footbeds for better fitting of both width and girth. But he also made them fun, with the bright bold colors of children's play blocks. And he designed packaging that was even more fun. A washable shoe comes in a little play washing machine. An athletic shoe comes packed with a little Gatorade squirt bottle. The tissue paper in the boxes is lined like notebook paper. The hangtags assure that the shoes have been passed by the "Dean of Inspection."

The turn to Turnaround Thinking. But Silverman's great product would undoubtedly have died on the vine without great marketing. Especially since he didn't have the vast financial resources that would be required to chip away at Stride Rite's commanding share of mind through awareness advertising in mass media.

So Silverman took the Individualized Marketing route. He started focussing a substantial portion of his limited advertising funds on sharply targeted direct mail and direct-response advertising to mothers of infants and small children. Each mailing was constructed with as much care and persuasive power as it would be if it were designed to pull a direct order. But instead there was a list of the nearest retailers and two 20%-off coupons, one for the addressee and one for a friend.

One early mailing came in a large, bulging 9" x 12" envelope with an actual sample of the removable footbed glued to a sheet inside. Because each footbed had to be glued in by hand, Silverman says it was an "executional nightmare." It was far too expensive by normal direct-mail standards, and undoubtedly many direct-mail experts would have advised against it. But it pulled an astounding *16% response.* **(Trend No. 2, Response-Driven)**

"Reversed co-op advertising." To help pay the freight for these mailings, Silverman used a marketing strategy he calls "reversed co-op advertising." Instead of giving retailers co-op money to advertise his products, he asks them to give him money! Selected retail accounts were asked to kick in $500. In return, they were named to Toddler U.'s "Dean's List" and received a laminated sign announcing their status as an exclusive TU retailer. And their name was included in the dealer listing in the Toddler U. direct mail. [9]

Today Toddler runs ads in magazines like *Parents, Sesame Street, Baby Talk,* and *Parenting* with fairly long, informative copy and always a toll-free number to call for the name of the nearest dealer, resulting in 5,000 to 7,000 calls a month.

This strategy plays an important part in trade advertising directed to the dealers. One such advertisement reads:

IMAGINE. A SHOE COMPANY THAT SENDS YOU
CUSTOMERS INSTEAD OF JUST SALESMEN.

Most shoe companies run ads directing people to their shoes. Toddler U. directs them to an 800 number — which in turn directs them to you.

Every month an amazing five to seven thousand prospects ring the toll-free hot line provided in our ads to get the address of their local TU dealer. Calls that often end up ringing these dealers' cash registers as well. To tap into the industry's most innovative source for kids' shoes — and new customers — simply phone Toddler University at 1-800-237-6751.

Every box of shoes has a little product information tag in the form of a school composition notebook, and all of these always include the company's toll-free number.

In addition, each shoe box contains a registration form asking the customers if they would like to be put on a mailing list for future offers. In this way, Toddler U. has built a database of 150,000 names, including the name and birthdate of the child. **(Trend No. 1, Known Prospects and Customers)** And because they know the child's age, the database will be able to generate timed direct mail suggesting the right athletic shoe at each stage of the child's development, from crawling to toddling to walking, and then for running to nursery school.

The "semi-mail-order-catalog." Most recently, Toddler U. has embarked on a new phase of marketing development — what might be called the "semi-mail-order catalog." And what is that? It is a catalog designed primarily to stimulate sales in the stores . "I think there is a middle ground [between mail-order and retail] today," says Silverman. "People would rather select at home and then go to the store and buy the product. This is the feedback I am getting from parents."*

Does that mean no mail-order sales at all? Not quite. "We will only sell the shoes by mail if there is no store in the area that carries the particular shoe that is being requested," Toddler U. has said. You will recall in Chapter 12 that one of our twelve suggested ways to use direct distribution was to "fill in the holes and gaps in your national retail distribution." **(Trend No. 10, Multi-Channel Distribution)**

But the additional sales that Toddler U. might achieve in this manner are probably trifling in comparison to the potential retail volume. A far more important potential use of the catalog is that Toddler U. would be able to go to the buyers for wholesalers and retailers, as Stash Tea has done, and say, "Look, here are the names and addresses of people in your area who had to buy our product from us because they couldn't find them in your stores. We'd rather that in the future they bought from you rather than from us — wouldn't you?"

---

*Another company reported to be successfully experimenting with a traffic-building catalog is Herman Geist Apparel Co., a manufacturer of women's country clothing. In the fall of 1989, Geist prepared one million copies of its first catalog and mailed them to charge cardholders of its retailers, including Lord & Taylor, Jordan Marsh, Foley's, Macy's, Bon Marche, and Younker's. The catalogs were custom-imprinted with the individual store name, address, phone-ordering information, and branch-store listings, and included style number and price for each item. After printing, the catalogs were shipped to each store's lettershop for addressing and mailing. Younker's of Des Moines was said to have sold 28% of its Geist line within two weeks after having mailed out the catalog. Bon Marche of Seattle reportedly got a 1% response on the 50,000 catalogs it mailed out and sold out 21% of their Geist inventory within three weeks.[10]

The catalog launch called for mailing out 20,000 copies to households with children up to two years old, and another 450,000 copies distributed through retail stores. The catalogs contain value coupons from approximately ten other companies specializing in children's products. When we talked with Silverman, he was also considering binding the entire catalog right into magazines aimed at parents. The LifeTime Value of a customer from birth to age 5 is estimated to be 25 pairs of shoes or roughly $1,000! So a lavish advertising expenditure like binding in a whole catalog would undoubtedly enjoy a satisfying payback over the following months and years.

"I think marketing is everything," says Silverman. "There is a saying that goes something like, 'Marketing people get rich. Inventors' great-grandchildren get rich.'"

It sounds like Silverman is going to do okay. His company's advanced marketing practices add up to an impressive list.

They are capturing the names of prime prospects, either in-house or from compiled lists, and are using this data to conduct a dialogue with the parents that is rich in product information.

They are building a database with dated personal information which will permit him to do as Austin Rover is doing, deliver the right message to the right person at the right time.

They are using the creative techniques of Direct-Order Marketing to create powerful Direct-Communication marketing.

They are in a position to use some mail-order sales as a crowbar to pry open new retail outlets and get others to expand their line of Toddler U. shoes.

They are using Other People's Money to pay part of the cost of direct mail, which is admittedly up to a hundred times more expensive than a single impression from a TV commercial. Thus they are getting the dealers in the "reverse co-op" to share in the cost of the direct mail in return for being listed in it. And getting non-competing advertisers to share in the cost of the catalog in return for being allowed to include their value coupons in it.

They are getting constant feedback from their market by making every magazine ad a direct response ad, and taking 5,000 to 7,000 calls a month in-house.

Today Toddler U. shoes are sold in over 1,000 stores, including JC Penney, Nordstrom's, Dillard's, Gymboree, and Endicott Johnson.

When the company was only a little over one year old and with sales of only $100,000, both Reebok and Avia made offers to buy it ranging from $4.5 to $6 million. How they must now regret they were not successful.

Only a few years later, Toddler U. already had an annual

volume of $30 million and was obviously worth many times what had been offered for it earlier.

HOW MURPHY REALTY HAS REVOLUTIONIZED SELLING OF RESIDENTIAL PROPERTIES

Murphy Realty/Better Homes & Gardens has provided a striking example of the power of E.V.P. in a service business.

While real estate brokers would be classified as being in a service business, more often than not homeowners and home buyers perceive them more as *selling* rather than *serving*. Rather than finding out what you, the consumer, want, they often come across as being more absorbed in what *they* want — namely, your listing if you are selling your home, or your purchase of one of their properties if you are buying a home.

At Murphy Realty, Joseph Murphy and Allan Dalton turned the traditional system around completely, by genuinely putting the interests of the consumer first. The marketing systems they developed so impressed Better Homes and Gardens that it was acquired by them and is now used successfully by some 25,000 salespeople in 1,250 BH&G real estate offices across the country.

These are some of the principles on which their system is based:

• The best time to start building a relationship with a home buyer or seller is *before* the person decides to act, not after. **(Trend No. 6, Building Relationships)**

• It is a disservice to the home owner to claim that the chances of selling are better if the broker has an exclusive listing.

• Home owners need and welcome help in thinking about selling and getting ready for it. **(Trend No. 9, E.V.P.)**

• Since the best chance of selling a property is through multiple listings, the best way to increase that chance is to reward the individual sales person in another brokerage firm who succeeds in selling the property.

• The more home details in a database, the better the chance of matching up a buyer with the right property, i.e., a buyer who wants a home with a swimming pool and a seller who has one. **(Trend No. 3, Filling Each Niche)**

In implementing these principles, they learned to kill two birds with one stone — helping the homeowner and identifying prospective sellers in advance. They do this by offering home owners informative brochures on buying, selling, and fixing up homes, and a chance to borrow a 40-minute videocassette and items from a Better Homes & Gardens library of books and magazines. They even have "library cards" that the brokers can hand out to encourage consumers to visit the local office and make use of the information service. It is part of a Home Merchandising System which teaches home owners how to make their homes more attractive to buyers by generating "curbside appeal" and how to maintain this interest level in every room of the house.

This may seem paradoxical. One of the real estate broker's toughest competitors is FSBO — For Sale By Owner. Yet here is Murphy seeming to help home owners sell their own homes. The answer is obviously that by putting the interest of the customer first, the Murphy system gains their trust and eventually their business.

At one time, Murphy/BH&G was sending direct mail offering helpful booklets to 100,000 condominium and co-op apartment owners a month and getting an average 20% response rate. After three years they were able to build up a database of 75,000 potential buyers and sellers.[11] **(Trend No. 1, Known Prospects and Customers)**

Prospects receiving or requesting information are asked to fill out a questionnaire answering such questions as "What type home are you presently living in? How long do you intend to stay in your present home? What factors make a move unlikely within 5 years? If you do plan to move in the future, what type of home will you be looking for?" Thus they are able to add to the database revealing clues to when and how the prospect might take action in the future.

To reward sales associates in all brokerage firms for selling Murphy listings, they instituted the Cooperative Awards Program. They identify the sales people who have sold Murphy listings from commission statements and send out monthly bonuses and awards to the deserving individuals.

These are only the highlights of the Murphy System, an extremely sophisticated and complex marketing strategy. But the heart of it is: if you are a service company, think more of serving than of selling, and you'll end up doing more selling. And if possible, identify who and where your prospects are *even before they know they are prospects.*

MAXIMARKETING AROUND THE WORLD

As you can see from the cases cited in this chapter, the turn toward putting MaxiMarketing principles to work is not limited to any one country or any one continent.

MaxiMarketing and the Ten Turnarounds in marketing

thinking we have defined in this book are a response to fundamental economic and societal forces affecting all post-industrial markets.

The best and the boldest breakthroughs are taking place all across Europe, in Australia, in Japan, in Hong Kong and Singapore, in North and South America.

Unlike the direct marketing boom of the 70's, which began in the United States and spread to Europe, the new Individualized Marketing affecting all products and services began to happen everywhere more or less at once in the 80's.

New chapters are being written in every country and every business category as this book goes to press. Molson, Canada's mass marketer of beer. The selective distribution division of L'Oréal, headquartered in France, including Lancôme, Biotherm, Vichy, Fluocaryl, and their many other companies. Coca Cola in Sweden. IBM in Spain. Colgate-Palmolive in Denmark. Procter & Gamble in Japan. Sara Lee Corporation in the U.S.

In our final chapter, coming next, we will share with you our views about the present and future impact of The Great Turnaround on advertising form and content, on advertising agencies, on media and research, and suggest how you can get started with your own turnaround thinking and programs.

14

The Future of the Great Turnaround and Your Part in It

3 kinds of resisters...7 roadblocks...A common misconception...The gradual reinvention of advertising, promotion, agencies, and media...The rise in Voluntary Advertising....The turnaround in advertising research...Rethinking accountability ...Serving both long-term and short-term profit needs...The new turnaround landscape...A 5-point star to guide you

In this book we have sought to show you how the coming of the Age of the Individual is beginning to turn around the way people think about marketing and to move it in an entirely new direction.

This great change is actually taking place with breathtaking rapidity, and yet it is easy to be deceived into thinking that it is barely happening at all.

Have you ever stared at the moon and tried to catch it moving? Try as you might, it just seems to sit there motionless. But if you give up, and then look for it in the same place a few hours later — it's gone!

There is only one way that you really detect the motion of the moon. And that is to gaze steadily at the horizon just when a giant full moon starts peeping over the rim. In the same way, you can observe the sun moving upward at daybreak, even though it seems motionless at noon.

If you watch an evening of prime-time television, or turn on your car radio, browse through your latest favorite magazine or newspaper, sort through your day's harvest of mail, the advertising you observe might not seem so different from that of a decade ago. But we have directed your gaze toward the horizon of marketing, where the movement toward a new day is clearly visible in the activities of the many marketers we have cited.

Why aren't these new trends reflected even more in the advertising you read, watch, and hear daily?

In actual numbers, the case histories of the Great Turnaround innovators may add up to the hundreds, far more than we could cover here.

Yet when you consider all of the billions spent on advertising and promotion, the portion of it devoted to the kinds of Individualized Marketing we have looked at would still add up to probably no more than two or three percent of all marketing today.

In view of the compelling need, the exciting opportunity, the present technological capability, and the astonishing results already achieved, why are so many advertisers still hanging back, waiting for others to race on ahead?

We believe it is due to the mindset of many of the decision-makers. In our personal experiences as advertising agency executives for many years and now as marketing consultants, we have observed three kinds of response to the new forces reshaping the marketplace:

1. The Mass Marketing Holdovers. There are those who got their education and experience in a different era. They are most comfortable with what they know has worked in the past. Whether as cautious top managers or foot-dragging middle managers, they are the ones who are most likely to continue resisting the demands of the demassified market and the advantages to be gained from bold Individualized Marketing programs.

2. The Mid-Passage Compromisers. There are those who realize that "the times they are a changin'" but still hesitate to embrace the change unreservedly. What we see them doing is pouring old content into the new forms.

Listen to a frustrated "CEO," attempting to bring about change, who had to deal with such attitudes in the late 80's.

It was Mikhail Gorbachev. In a speech to a Communist Party conference, he spoke with surprising candor of the disappointing progress of his reforms. He told the delegates the biggest obstacle to bringing about change was the heavy-handed application of his programs by managers tied to past practices. He charged the old-style managers with perverting the essence of perestroika, by "filling the new management forms with old content."

In our own world of marketing, we see examples of this happening every day.

We see carefully targeted promotions identifying newly-converted tryers by name and address without any ongoing program planned to retain their loyalty and increase their product usage.

We see toll-free customer assistance lines installed and then nothing done to retain the names and addresses of those who call and then to continue the relationship.

We see relational databases which are enhanced with a wide range of demographic and psychographic information that is then not used for personalization or customization in any of the follow-up material or marketing tactics.

We see direct-response phone numbers added to TV commercials without consideration of how to maximize response or how to make best use of the inquiry that results.

The Mid-Passage Compromisers start to travel down the Individualized Marketing Road, but seem to lack the understanding or willingness to go all the way.

3. The Early Adapters. Then there are the adventurers, the Early Adapters. They sense the Great Turnaround that is taking place, and are willing to take the risks involved in going first in order to stake out their claims in the new territory. But it is not an easy task. Many of the Early Adapters who are in middle management positions have told us that they have to push every step of the way against resistance in their own companies or in their advertising or promotion agencies.

Standing up against The Great Turnaround toward Individualized Marketing is The Great Hesitation — the tendency to think twice and then think twice again before daring to turn away from familiar practices (even though they are not working very well) and plunge into the unfamiliar territory represented by the nine steps of the MaxiMarketing model. There are a great many understandable reasons for this hesitation. Here are just some of the blocks we have observed:

• *Fear of accountability.* Running advertising just because it's the expected thing to do, or because the competition is doing it, can get to be a habit and a very comfortable routine. The idea of being able to measure the results precisely can be frightening, especially to creative people who see a danger of having their creative licenses revoked by the stern magistrate of actual results.

• *The "uncontrollable" and unpredictable direct-response budget.* Believe it or not, in considering a ground-breaking direct-response campaign, a common fear of many product and fulfillment managers is that they will get *too many* responses and the cost of fulfillment will wreck the budget. What a nightmare! Just think, *too many* interested, eager prospective buyers. Better to stick to the old routines in which such problems don't arise.

• *Distaste for "getting your hands dirty."* Compared to the show-business glamour and excitement of a TV shoot, many undoubtedly feel that setting up a database or organizing a customer satisfaction program, preparing an acknowledgement letter, framing a questionnaire, designing a statement or package enclosure, is dull, grubby, low-status work. The implementation of promotional direct mail, cause-related advertising, and such things as dealer sales incentive programs is not considered "mainstream," and its experts are not looked on as being on the same exalted level as the creators of an award-winning television commercial.

• *Fear of the unknown.* Again and again we have heard ,from marketers asked to consider an untraditional way to support brand image and sales, "But we're not in the (magazine business or catalog business or show business, you name it) business — what are we doing talking about putting out a magazine or a mail-order catalog or a video for our customers?"

Often the higher you go on the decision-making chain, the more you find people locked into the scenario they wrote for the company's success many years ago.

• *Vested interest.* There are many people jealously guarding jobs, perks, contracts, and profits based on the familiar old mass-marketing way of doing things.

There was a Letter to the Editor in *Advertising Age* that cast a light on how the factor of vested interest can affect advertising recommendations:

> This writer had lunch in Chicago recently with a media planner from a large ad agency, a young guy far down on the media department totem pole. Discussing his career prospects at the agency, he said the sure way to gain points was to get a client to move heavily into TV as opposed to print. "That's where the money is," he said...One gathers that most agencies could[n't] care less if all the print media bit the dust. They could still fill their coffers with the easiest-to-place multi-million bucks that network and spot TV, combined with their rake-off on commercial production, provide.

> Network TV, with a record $4.2 billion in upfront sales, a 20% leap over last year, is a source of vast agency self-congratulations. This despite the acknowledged network's record shrinking of audience (down to between 60% and 70%) and a per-thousand rate jump of 12% to 18% for the prime time season. [1]

We would not go so far as to characterize agency planning in the words of this irate letter writer. But in some cases there is certainly an agency tilt in favor of television over print. And there is an even stronger tilt toward marketing plans which call for capabilities the agency possesses — and away from recommending to a client a program involving capabilities the client would have to find elsewhere.

• *The demands of Wall Street.* The pressure on publicly owned companies for short-term improvement in sales results is relentless. Often it tips the scales in favor of another campaign of unproductive discounting simply because the result will be another temporary blip in the cash flow, and may rule out investment in developing long-range relationships to build brand and sales.

• *A common misconception about pay-off.* It is generally believed that obtaining, recording, and using data about individual customers necessarily delivers its pay-off only at some vague point in the future when customer relationships ripen. Nothing could be further from the truth about the remarkable short-term Individualized Marketing results you have been reading about in this book. You do not have to abandon the benefits of short-term tactical success in order to gain from a long-term relationship strategy.

When Buick set out to begin developing a relationship with the golfers of America, they proceeded to sell more cars to those prospects in two months with their individualized program than with any other program in the company's history.

The setting up of the Allo Diététique Nestlé phone service had an immediate positive effect on Nestlé's growth in market share.

Mattel's relationship with Barbie Doll owners helps sell doll clothes and more dolls in country after country immediately, as well as month after month.

One of Procter & Gamble's first wholehearted ventures into double-duty advertising and generation of a prospect database — the Cheer-Free launch campaign — resulted in what was said by a competitor to have been the most successful new-detergent introduction in that venerable marketer's history.

The Nintendo magazine played a vital part in the company's first two billion dollars in sales and will continue to play a vital part in the next two billion.

The Kraft General Foods investment in database building began paying off almost at once with such programs for building market share as the Kool Aid and Crystal Lite projects.

A properly constructed database plan should be looked on as neither merely a short-term promotional aid or merely a costly long-term investment with a payoff in the distant future.

Rather it is a kind of dynamic money-making machine in which all the parts in the feedback loop work together to steadily build momentum. (Figure 12) The database inspires marketing programs which reach out to both new prospects and existing customers. The responses from prospects and customers provide

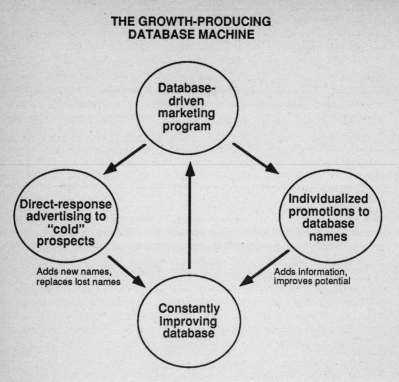

**THE GROWTH-PRODUCING
DATABASE MACHINE**

Figure 12

sales and additional information that enlarges and enriches the database and leads to new and better marketing programs. And so it goes, around and around, in a self-perpetuating progression of income and profit building events. In short, when properly constructed and administered, a machine that helps drive the growth of a business.

Yes, there are some who approach Individualized Marketing as a long-term investment, and there are times when this makes sense. But many more of the best and the boldest, while going against conventional thinking and investing in customer relationships, still manage to reap short-term as well as long-term profits.

Despite all of these roadblocks, we have been impressed with the willingness of some top and middle management to explore new avenues and in time to make a complete turnaround in their thinking. We have seen managers go within the space of a year from "Sorry, it's just not our way of doing things" — to "Okay, let's see what you can do to solve this pesky problem" — to "These results are impressive. Can't you move faster? We've got to expand this one-to-one selling program now that we see what the payoff can be."

So if you are a middle management innovator and encounter resistance in implementing some of the ideas in this book, don't give up too soon on getting approval to go ahead.

Many years ago a man named Robert Updegraff, founder of Pocket Books, wrote a wise little essay entitled *Time Out for Mental Digestion.* In it he pointed out that if you do not understand why you are encountering from others so much resistance to the greatest idea since sliced bread, the answer may be that you have not allowed sufficient time for them to get used to and digest the idea.

We face a period in which the familiar institutions of mass marketing must be rethought and reshaped to deal with the new reality, not only by marketers but by their supporting services as well. And because of the need for "time out for mental digestion" on the part of the armies of people involved, the changeover simply can't all take place overnight. Before everyone gets in line behind the Early Adapters, here are some of the marketing institutions that we believe must change, will change, and are changing:

1. THE COMING REINVENTION OF THE ART OF ADVERTISING

The brilliance of television advertising has been developed about as far as it can go. It has evolved into an extraordinary new human language all its own. For advertisers who have a product with a broad enough appeal and big enough budget, it can be unmatched for effectiveness in creating excitement and desire.

But as we have seen, even for these advertisers it is a frightening game of roulette in which your lucky number fails to come up more often than it succeeds. Even a multi-million dollar campaign on national television sometimes shows little effect on sales. In fact, sometimes sales decline.

And then there are all those other advertisers with more specialized niche products and smaller budgets who either know they can't afford national television or make the mistake of thinking that they can.

Yes, they can and do run awareness advertising in all the other traditional media – in the magazines, in the newspapers, on radio. Yet for these smaller-budget advertisers there is often the uneasy feeling that these other media simply can't compare with the glamour and power of television. And indeed it is a fairly uncommon event when awareness advertising in these other media produces a distinct, traceable, profitable effect on sales. Admittedly some new customers can be influenced and won with this increasingly inefficient shotgun advertising, but often at a prohibitive cost per incremental sale.

So, in recognition of this reality, an increasing number of marketers are taking their first hesitant steps toward increasing their odds of success by turning to a different view of how advertising can be made to work better.

But there is a danger here of what Mr. Gorbachev called trying to "fill new forms with old content." What is called for is not just a modification of the art of advertising to fit a new situation but a whole new way of thinking about advertising communication.

Victor O. Schwab, a mail-order advertising agency pioneer who wrote many wise words about what makes people respond to advertising, taught his creative staff to "start where the reader is" and to lead people by the hand from where they are to where you want them to go.

Today that path from the prospect's need to the purchase and repurchase of the product is often longer than the 30-seconds of mind-blowing images on the small screen or the passage from the headline at the top of the page to the phone number or reply coupon at the bottom. It is a journey from the first contact, established by the prospect's response to the advertising, to the step-by-step building of the confidence of the respondent in the advertised product or service, whether in one long communication or a series of communications.

And it calls at every step of the way for use of the cultivation skills developed over decades of trial-and-error, test-and-observe by direct-order marketers who live or die by their ability to gain the confidence of faraway customers.

Two common errors are made by those who are "filling new forms with old content":

1. *The error of over-reliance on image and awareness advertising creative techniques in advertising where maximized response and continuing contact is the objective.* So much general advertising employs a cleverness and indirection which may or may not be effective in getting the public to laugh and to retain a favorable impression, but are fatally ineffective when it comes to getting people to respond — and, even worse, when it comes to continued communication with people who do respond and want useful information and guidance.

Are we wrong about this? There is a simple way to find out, as we have discussed earlier, and that is the split-run test in which two or more approaches are given absolutely equal exposure.

But this won't help if all of the approaches tested are simply awareness advertising with a response element tacked on. As a benchmark, at least one of the approaches tested must be based on the techniques proven effective in direct-response advertising over the years.

If you are thinking that we are advocating a return to hard-sell mail-order advertising techniques of half a century ago, think again. Instead we are urging the application of the wonderful creative credo of Shirley Polykoff, the great advertising woman who first made Clairol hair coloring acceptable for millions of women with the theme, *"Does She Or Doesn't She? Only Her Hairdresser Knows for Sure."* Shirley's whole advertising philosophy was distilled in just eight words, "Think it out square, say it with flair."

The turnaround from Mass Marketing to Individualized Marketing calls for a new creativity to meet a new set of standards. If the need now is for dialogue and the ability to know and respond to what the consumer is thinking almost before it is thought, then cleverness must give way to clarity and "show biz" to the business of being understood.

2. *The error of focusing all of the talent and money and creativity "up front."* The same kind and amount of attention and loving care that is expended "up front" must also be devoted to the "back end," to everything that happens after the prospect responds to the first advertising message or makes the first purchase. Yet again and again we have answered ads offering a free sample or a booklet or a membership and received a cheap-looking package with either a curt business-like form letter or, more often, no letter at all — a practice that makes a direct-order merchant hoot with derision.

It is as if the advertisers had expended all of the creative talent in the act of reaching out to the consumer, and now that the consumer was interested, there was nothing more to do or say. It's the Casanova Syndrome in marketing. We see advertisers frantically moving on to the next "conquest" while losing interest in yesterday's love.

In both of these common errors, we see signs of the fear that seems to be so ever-present in preparing awareness advertising. It is the fear of telling the prospect too much. And indeed this is a realistic fear if the additional words would be just so much boring puffery. Yet the annals of advertising are filled with legendary examples of ads which held the audience in their grip for an extended period.

Think about your personal relationships. Think of the friend or acquaintance whose conversation sparkles with interesting, enlightening, persuasive information. Could it all really have been condensed into one paragraph...or a 15-second "sound bite"?

The creative challenge posed by Individualized Marketing is to find ways to recreate the same values of a good conversation in your advertising communications, and to find opportunities to do so. The Cheer-Free detergent mailing package containing the free sample sent in response to TV requests showed the same creativity and careful attention to the relationship with the recipient as was lavished on the advertising which prompted the response in the first place. This is a total reversal of the usual back-of-the-hand sales promotion fulfillment practice.

It isn't just a question of getting the right piece of copy in your follow-up communication, although that's a big help.

It's a question of creating a whole mosaic of relationship-building and sales-building elements of information and activation, as companies like Nintendo and House of Seagram have demonstrated so brilliantly and to such good effect in every customer relationship communication by mail or phone.

As another example of this, we pointed.to the page after page of wonderful information about tea in the Stash Tea catalog. If this much information were fired at you broadside, in the form of a booklet about tea, it is unlikely you would ever get around to reading it. But in the easy-browsing format of a mail-order catalog, you are exposed to an astonishing amount of selling information one delightful little bit at a time.

If you would like to hold in your hands and study a veritable textbook of relationship-building, write to Garden Way Mfg. Co, 102nd St. & 9th Ave., Troy, NY 12180, and ask them to send you a copy of the latest *Troy-Bilt Owner News,* their tabloid newspaper of articles and advertising about their lawn and garden equipment. Much of it is written by their customers, a poor way to win advertising awards but a great way to build a warm feeling of community and sell goods.

We're not saying that the Stash Tea way or the Garden Way approach necessarily is right for your own particular marketing challenge.

What we are urging is that you open your eyes to how different these communications are from typical brand advertising and promotional fulfillment material, and then open your mind to daring new possibilities in your own situation.

And we are not only talking about the printed word. A new generation of marketers is communicating with a new generation of consumers with audio discs, videocassettes, computer disks, and "long-form" cable advertising shows. To say nothing of the new art of direct-response commercials which manage to artfully build brand imagery and maximize response at the same time.

A hallmark of good direct-response advertising and follow-up is simply clarity — quite different from what we have come to expect from advertising singled out for praise in the advertising trade press. A great deal of awareness advertising, both in print and on television, can get tangled up in a copywriter's joke so subtle or an art director's special effect so tricky that people just don't get it — and there is no reality check in the form of viewer-responses to tip off the advertiser that a mistake in communication has been made.

Haven't you ever had the experience of turning to a television viewing companion and saying, "That was a really clever commercial. But what were they selling?"

Neither the "upfront" advertising nor the "back-end" contact in the new marketing copy can afford the luxury of this kind of cleverness and obscurity. Yes, it can be droll, it can be witty — but clarity comes first.

The re-invented art of advertising, as advertisers move toward Individualized Marketing, will "take the reader (or viewer) by the hand" and lead him or her to the desired sales result.

It will avoid the mistake of using overly-clever awareness advertising techniques to get a response.

It will employ the same calibre of top-flight creative talent on all the "back-end" communications leading to the sale as it does in the "upfront" message.

It will build the confidence and trust of the consumer with a mosaic of interesting, enlightening, persuasive information.

And it will do this with a clarity which will never leave the prospect or customer in doubt about what meaning was intended.

2. THE COMING REINVENTION OF THE ADVERTISING AGENCY

The turn away from the dominance of mass marketing to the targeting of individuals whom we know by their own special attitudes and characteristics is reshaping how advertising agencies function.

We are seeing agency men and women tackling the challenge of redefining their own organizations and how they do what they do. Here are a few examples of what we have observed beginning to happen in some of them.

Think back to what we told you in Chapter Four about how the Salem Sound Waves campaign was created by the advertising agency, the LKP Integrated Communications Group of Foote Cone

& Belding.   There, as we pointed out, a direct marketing person, a sales promotion person, and a general advertising person literally sit together in the same room at that agency and interact with each other to dream up a multi-disciplined solution to a marketing problem.

The Leo Burnett agency is another innovative stand-out. They brought in a topnotch direct marketing advertising veteran, Jerry Reitman, and gave him free rein to indoctrinate the entire agency in direct-marketing thinking and work hand-in-glove with the brand-advertising account groups.

Outstanding results of this approach have included the Merit and Cheer-Free breakthrough campaigns. Twenty-three out of the agency's 32 blue-ribbon clients now use Individualized Marketing to some degree, including Maytag, Procter & Gamble, Heinz Pet Foods, Philip Morris, and Hallmark.

Burnett has shown that a first-rate mainstream agency can use its mastery of the television medium to put attention-getting humor at the service of both direct-response and brand-building. In their commercial for Meaty Bone dog food from Heinz, they have done an amusing challenge spot in which the dogs in the viewing audience are invited to call 1-800-DOG-BONE. Except that when the canine star of the commercial dials the number, it comes up on the screen, 1-800-DOG-FONE. The human beings in the viewing audience got the number right, and the number of calls requesting the Meaty Bone free sample far exceeded expectations.

Bronner & Slosberg, the agency for Quaker Direct, has the advantage of an unusual combination in its founding partners, bringing together in its top management impressive backgrounds in awareness advertising, direct marketing, and sales promotion. In three years they have reportedly grown from around $80 million in annual billing to over $120 million.

Another new-think agency we referred to earlier was Cramer-Krassert, where the president has deliberately built "a staff with an ability to *think outside a specialty without any danger of losing compensation or status within the agency.*" [Italics ours]

HDW Worldwide Direct, the agency responsible for the extraordinary success of the *Nintendo Power* subscription campaign, has enjoyed meteoric growth as one of the new breed of marketing thinkers under the chairmanship of Murray Bowes.

Direct Resources, Inc., an agency specializing in electronic media, and serving such clients as *Time* Magazine, Merrill Lynch, and American Express, is doing direct-response television which demonstrates that the functions of building brand image and getting responses can be brilliantly combined in a single creatively unified commercial.

This process of evolving a new kind of advertising agency is not limited to the United States but is happening in many parts of the world.

In Europe, the Rapp & Collins European network, with offices in most of the major cities on the continent, began presenting itself in 1988 as more than a direct marketing agency group. They were the first to redefine themselves as an agency network ready to offer expertise at every step in the MaxiMarketing process.

Under the leadership of Jean-Louis Maigret and Stuart Heather, each Rapp & Collins office in Europe has begun to take a wholistic approach to each new marketing challenge, using direct-response advertising, sales promotion, dealer merchandising, frequency marketing, event marketing, and whatever else is needed to enhance brand image and increase sales for their clients. Working in close cooperation with their general agency parent, DDB-Needham, they have pursued a consistent policy of applying basic-MaxiMarketing principles to the needs of such clients as Lancôme, American Airlines, and Gillette throughout Europe.

Of course, the above brief mentions of some of the outstanding practitioners of the new marketing by no means pretends to be a comprehensive survey of all of the agencies worthy of mention. These are just some of the agencies that exemplify how the advertising agency business is gradually evolving in response to the Turnaround Trends we have presented.

The early strides toward finding a new model for the agency of the future are not coming solely from the advertising agency world. Many of the more fascinating examples come from the world of the sales promotion agencies.

Steven Gundersen and Larry Levine, partners in an executive search firm specializing in sales promotion, have pointed out how "Promanad Communications, Inc., a Canadian concern, has evolved from a traditional promotion agency into an integrated marketing communications 'factory.' Promanad produces advertising, public relations, sales and collateral materials, and direct mail, as well as promotional services."

They also pointed to Clarion Marketing and Communications, another agency with promotional roots, that is "merging its creative and strategic process in development of everything from new product consulting to package design, and is doing exceptionally well." [2]

To sell Cadillac's Allanté sports model, Clarion designed a regional test program that identified prospective buyers, sent them a video about the car and an offer for an extended test drive. When the responses came in, Clarion screened them to sift out qualified prospects, then directed them to the right local dealer.

During the test drive, the prospect listens to an audiocassette about the Allanté benefits. In one test market, four out of every 16 prospects who took a test drive ended up buying the car. [3]

THE CLIENT-AGENCY MODEL OF THE FUTURE

In *MaxiMarketing*, we said that the time had come for all advertisers to choose and use the tools of direct marketing. In the years since, we have seen the mightiest of the mighty, including Procter & Gamble, IBM, Bristol-Myers, and Ford Motor Company pick up these tools and begin to put them to good use.

If direct-marketing techniques indeed play such a key role in the new marketing, then does it perhaps logically follow that a brand advertiser or other general advertiser should simply assign its account — or a piece of it — to a specialized direct marketing agency?

Many have done just that in recent years. And often the direct marketing agencies have responded with ingenious relationship marketing programs that many mainstream agencies might not have been capable of producing.

But in the broader landscape of Individualized Marketing as it is evolving, even the specialist direct marketing agency does not necessarily have all of the skills required to implement a multi-faceted program involving targeted sales promotion, public relations, event marketing, field marketing to dealers, and much more.

In some cases this will lead to the client being forced to shop for services among a variety of communications providers when the time comes to execute a multi-discipline MaxiMarketing program — choosing one specialist for direct-response advertising, another for tie-in dealer promotions, another for cause-related marketing, another for publicity.

This can work, as Ron Fusile has demonstrated in the implementation of his Buick Open sweepstakes campaign, but it is not ideal. There is always the risk that it can lead to working with providers who do not really understand the importance of the broad strategy and who may execute their part of the program as just another project assignment.

So we believe you will see a new kind of advertising agency evolving, one that is capable of what we describe as fusion in marketing — first conceiving a new database-driven strategic direction for a client, then firing all of the elements together in the crucible of creative thinking to develop the marketing equivalent of what engineers call a "composite," a substance lighter, stronger, and cheaper than steel. The substance of such an agency's creation will be the much-heralded but little understood "New Advertising" referred to by John O'Toole in his farewell address as Chairman of the American Association of Advertising Agencies.

With fusion of the marketing elements, nothing remains the same as it was. There is a new form of advertising, a new form of sales promotion, and a redefined role for direct marketing.

Advertising works to build image and awareness while at the same time promoting immediate sales and acquiring information for a marketing database.

Sales promotion, while ringing the cash register now, also finds ways to build brand equity and feed information into the relational database.

And Direct-Relationship Marketing, while reaching for long-term benefits, uses the tools of promotion to gain an immediate return on investment.

Often all three of these basic disciplines, plus public relations and event marketing, are fused in a single program in which no one element or its budget can be separated from the whole.

The agency of the future will be a master at creating both the fused upfront advertising and back-end interactions to deliver a marketing force of unprecedented power and efficiency.

This agency of the future will not always evolve out of the mainsteam agencies of the present.

In some cases it will. But in other cases it will be a direct marketing agency which acquires awareness advertising, sales promotion, and public-relations skills and a MaxiMarketing perspective.

Or sometimes it will be a sales promotion agency which sees that the market is moving inexorably from short-term promotions to long-term involvement that creates repeated opportunities for cultivation of the consumer, and which has the foresight to acquire the additional skills needed to meet this new need.

And sometimes this new kind of agency will emerge from a kind of provider you might not even know existed — the specialized companies that create and administer promotional programs, specialty advertising programs, customer-assistance programs, and frequent buyer programs, and who are ready and eager to expand their sphere of operations to include database-building, advertising know-how, and a complete repertoire of the "New Advertising" skills.

But wherever it comes from, the MaxiMarketing agency of the future will not be hesitant to conceive and recommend a brilliant multi-faceted Individualized Marketing program for fear of not fitting into the client's compartmentalized way of thinking.

Clients, on their part, will be looking for a truly wholistic approach, and some agencies will have developed the capability either to perform the entire job in-house — or to supervise the execution of parts of it by trusted agency suppliers, just as an agency today may contract for and supervise on behalf of its client such services as photography, TV production, printing, and media buying.

The advertising shibboleth that will provide the most stubborn resistance to being cast aside is the old habit of thinking about image or awareness advertising as "above the line" and direct mail, sales promotion, and anything else that doesn't earn an agency commission as "below the line."

Christopher Woodward, the marketing director of 3i, the world's largest venture capital company and an important U.K. general advertiser, is one advertiser with absolutely no use for the divisions. He shared his views with us in a recent conversation in this way: "The ridiculous concept of the line separating advertising from all the other marketing activities must be removed. It is all too common for general advertising agencies to deliver prepackaged, off-the-shelf solutions representing the cliché things they are good at doing. They always react with this bundle of creativity when what is needed is strategic and innovative thinking. They just aren't in a marketing mode at all."

Looking to the future, Woodward continued, "What is needed is an outside, totally dispassionate consultant in marketing communications, not a specialist in one area interested mainly in pushing its own specialty."

There are many on the general agency side who would take exception to this view. And certainly there are mainstream agencies offering integrated marketing services in the U.S. and Europe that have removed the "line" of separation. Such agencies are making great strides in developing harmonious working relationships among their various service components and providing successfully "integrated" campaigns.

The ultimate choice as to which agency model fits an advertiser's needs will be determined in part by the client's situation and own capabilities. One thing is certain, however. The number and variety of operational and philosophical models to choose from will far exceed the options available a decade ago.

There will be the providers of a complete menu of services under one agency conglomerate roof. There will continue to be the agencies with special expertise from which the advertiser can order a la carte. And there will be a powerful new force — the agency striving to fuse the advertising and the relationship-building marketing disciplines into an entirely new form of unified agency service.

Dramatic evidence of this was provided by a recent move by DDB-Needham Worldwide, the world's 11th largest agency. In May of 1990 the agency announced a new compensation system that would tie the money it makes to the market performance of its clients' products. Wrote Randall Rothenberg in the account in *The New York Times*: "Keith L. Reinhard, the agency's chairman, has often said agencies must offer integrated communications programs that include direct marketing, sales promotions, and other techniques. Because clients generally pay fees, rather than commissions, for these ancillary services, agencies are less likely to include them in a client's media schedule, Mr. Reinhard said. Shifting to performance-based compensation would remove the incentive to recommend only media that would produce commissions."

Said Reinhard: "We've got to come up with structural reforms and compensation reforms inside our agencies and client organizations which facilitate integrated communications."

A key feature of the new program, Rothenberg reported, is "the requirement that clients give the agency overall authority for coordinating all their communications programs, including direct-response programs, sales promotions, and public relations in addition to advertising. One consultant called that aspect of the plan revolutionary."[3]

Advertisers in the 90's will be making their selection of agencies in an environment of steadily rising media costs and advertising clutter. We can expect rising pressure to make every advertising dollar as accountable as possible.

As a result, there will be more double-duty, triple-duty, and quadruple-duty expenditures. Advertisers will turn around their thinking and increasingly ask: why settle for doing *only* a promotion project or *only* a public relations event or *only* an awareness ad or *only* adding names or information to a database, when so much more can be accomplished for the same amount of money with a truly multi-dimensional effort?

Whatever agency model is chosen, the pressure will be on all concerned, both on the agency side and the client side, to turn their thinking away from the compartmentalized marketing approach that leads to doing advertising by itself, sales promotion by itself, and direct marketing by itself.

On the client side, the turn away from compartmentalized thinking will require a management reappraisal of how marketing and advertising departments are organized.

Instead of the traditional approach of appointing one manager for advertising, another for promotion, and lately a third for direct marketing, it would be more in keeping with the new realities of marketing to break down the dividing line between these three functions. You would put one manager in charge of all of the marketing activities leading up to the acquisition of a new customer, including the awareness advertising, direct-response advertising, and sales promotion. A second manager would then be in charge of all of the marketing activities involved in keeping and cultivating that new customer, including database design and enhancement and all of the communications with — and promotions to — the people in the database.

With this organizational structure, both the front-end manager and the back-end manager would be equally at home with the disciplines of brand-building and sales promotion. A natural consequence would be the development of multi-faceted, wholistic programs that achieve both the short-term and long-term objectives of the advertiser.

Of course the "customer acquisition manager" and the "customer cultivation manager" would work in tandem to maximize sales and profits in this new era of fused marketing activity. And each of them would be in a position to get the best work from their new multi-disciplined marketing agency.

3. THE REINVENTION OF ADVERTISING MEDIA

Pity the poor media planner today. There is such a bewildering assortment of media options that it is almost more than the human brain can contain.

It seems hard to believe that just a few decades ago, media choices were basically limited to magazines, newspapers, direct mail, radio, point of purchase displays, outdoor display advertising, and television.

Today, in addition to these basic media, which are alive and well but changing in character and function, a bewildering variety of new media has emerged— audiocassettes, videocassettes, computer disks, automated voice response to 800 and 900 number calls, card decks, on-line information services for personal computers, take-one racks, supermarket video carts, waiting room and rest room posters, outbound telephone, inbound telephone, interactive video kiosks, school bulletin boards, and on and on. We have also discussed earlier the advertiser-produced magazine and the in-house direct-mail co-op, both of which must be considered as essentially new media inventions.

Almost every week that passes, we read of some novel new media opportunity.

Screenvision puts commercials on movie screens in over 6,000 U.S. movie theatres and at last report was growing at the rate of 20% a year.

Limbi puts ads on the sides of the semi-trailer tractor trucks of the 100,000 members of the Owner Operated Independent Drivers' Association.

American Passage has installed 2,300 Gymboard wall poster displays in some 1500 schools.

The United States Pizza Network, seeking to help the approximately 35,000 independent pizza owners band together to compete with the big fast-food chains, is selling advertising printed on the pizza boxes and also in the free magazine affixed to the top of each box. They hope someday to have a circulation larger than that of *Time*.

We argued in *MaxiMarketing*, and still do, that to indulge in some of these media novelties without some strict form of financial control — such as direct-response replies traceable to each media source, or sales increases measured by scanner data or other methods of accurately measuring media impact at the retail level — often means just finding new ways to throw advertising money away.

The one exception might be novelty media so unusual, so startling, so audacious — like the first Absolut Vodka "music box" magazine ad, or the truck that drove around Manhattan with a brilliantly lit giant Absolut bottle and "ice cubes" in the back— that it causes talk which clearly translates into share point gains.

From our point of view, though, the safest path through the new-media jungle is often a carefully developed *MaxiMarketing* program in which all media chosen are logical contributors to the desired continuum. And that continuum is location, identification, activation, conversion, and cultivation of your prime prospects and best customers.

In this context, an advertising medium which might ordinarily seem inconsequential — a souvenir program — can suddenly become an integral part of an exciting marketing plan. As we have seen, this was the case with the Buick Open golf sweepstakes campaign. A souvenir program containing Buick advertising and intensifying Buick's relationship to the tournament was given to the 275,000 paying spectators, many of them Buick owners and prime prospects.

In the same way, the Minitel (electronic telephone directory and interactive home computer terminal) in France becomes an extension of the VAG Audi television advertising. The message in the television commercial directs viewers to go to their Minitels to get additional information — and thus starts a relationship leading to the dealer showroom and a sale.

A great many of the new media choices are ideally suited vehicles for the contact, involvement, and dialogue strategies of the

90's — new ways to communicate directly and personally with your best customers and prime prospects.

Changes in television advertising. At the time that *Maxi-Marketing* was published, fewer than half of America's television households were passed by cable. But by 1989, 55.6 million of the 90.4 million television households were paying for and receiving cable programming. Cable advertising revenue had risen to an estimated $15.4 billion a year.

Furthermore, under pressure from municipalities to provide better cable service, cable systems were rapidly increasing the number of channels a subscriber could access, up to as many as 40, 50, or even more.

Some systems were also planning at last to introduce pay-per-view, permitting subscribers to pay for just the movies they want to see and presumably making it economic to show first-run movies on television just as soon as they are released to movie theatres. From the advertiser's point of view, this will simply give television households additional opportunities to avoid watching advertising of any kind.

Announcement of plans to market a small low-cost dish antenna for as little as $300 suggested that soon many non-wired homes in urban and suburban areas might be able to tune in as many as 100 channels via satellite.

The result of all this has got to be still greater fragmentation of the television audience, creating both more problems and more opportunities for the advertiser. National television advertising, which has become synonymous with the broadest possible mass marketing and is now becoming less economically efficient, can enjoy a new life as a means to an end rather than an end in itself. It can be a *means* of interesting the best prospects for what is being sold and getting them to identify themselves by responding. And in such cases, the *end* will be to add those respondents to the advertiser's database and to continue the relationship with them through customized cultivation that is measurably profitable.

One promising television opportunity that we wrote about in *MaxiMarketing* makes even more sense today.

It is the so-called long-form television advertising or program-length infomercial that we have discussed in Chapter Ten, supported by advertising in newspapers, TV magazines, or any other appropriate media which flags targeted prospects and urges them to watch the program.

In this book, we have touched on just some of the ways traditional media are finding new life and new media are being invented. It is far from a complete survey — another entire book could be written on this subject alone. But it should provide you with a glimpse of the opportunities for Individualized Marketing in the changing media scene.

It represents a dramatic turnaround, from the time when the emphasis was on delivering big numbers of advertising impressions, to the new focus on putting out just the right message for the right person. And often in a form that allows time for the prospect to really get involved in the message.

By now, we hope we have persuaded you to use direct-response as a yardstick to find out which of all these and many other new media options can do the most for you.

4. A GREAT TURNAROUND IN MARKET RESEARCH

Market research firms are paid over a billion dollars a year by advertisers who need to know what products to make and how to sell them. But the state of the art still suffers from certain significant drawbacks.

One problem is that in-depth research is expensive and often takes a long time to complete. Because of the expense, it may not be economic to update the findings frequently, and consequently the findings are soon out of date.

Another problem is that much advertising research is conducted in an artificial laboratory situation in which consumers speculate on how they might react to a new product, a new positioning, or a new campaign theme.

This has proven to be a special problem in copy research, where there is no completely satisfactory substitute for observing how consumers react to real advertising in a real-world situation.

Individualized Marketing, although it does not provide an answer to all of a company's research needs, does offer exciting opportunities for adding a new dimension to market research. As we have seen in such companies as Nintendo in the U.S., Austin-Rover in the U.K., and Sopad Nestlé in France, it can provide real-time real-world insights into the constantly changing likes, wants, complaints, and needs of a company's customers.

As part of their ongoing communication (surveys, questionnaires, phone calls, customer correspondence, etc.) with many-thousands, even millions, of customers, the best and the boldest MaxiMarketers can often sense with uncanny accuracy where the market is going. It's a turnaround from research that quickly grows stale to a continuous information exchange that is always fresh and meaningful.

Another research opportunity, as we have discussed, lies in

split-run direct-response advertising testing. It can zero in on the right headline, the right picture, the right product, the right offer, the right price, with a precision that other kinds of copy research are not capable of. And this A-B testing is not limited to magazine and newspaper advertising. It can be done in direct mail, take-ones, card programs, the way you handle incoming phone calls — anything involving direct communications with the consumer.

If you have a mail-order catalog for customers not reached by your retail distributors or a company-sponsored magazine, it can become a living, breathing laboratory for product and copy development.

In weighing the possible effectiveness of promotions ideas being considered, offers can be pre-tested against small segments of the database and rolled out only if cost-effective.

And these are only a few of the possibilities. Once you start communicating directly with your prospects and customers, you will constantly discover new ways to learn more about them, how to serve them better, how to activate them to buy your product, and what new products you can develop in answer to expressed needs and wants.

5. RETHINKING ACCOUNTABILITY

During the 80's, direct marketing as a concept spread from the direct-order marketers such as the book and record clubs to the banks, the airlines, the hotels, and other service companies, and finally to many manufacturers and retailers. In due course, what is commonly referred to as direct marketing became the new "in" thing to add to the marketing mix.

The even more fashionable term to use was relationship marketing, and "having a long-term relationship with prospects and customers" was now seen as a good thing to do. Only there was one catch. There was heavy emphasis on long-term relationships, and advocates of direct marketing would get very defensive when asked about the cost in the meanwhile of making all these good things happen.

Direct marketers preaching their gospel of LifeTime Customer Value were out of synch with the hard-nosed world of the product manager in the packaged goods field who waits with bated breath for the latest SAMI figures and worries about meeting this year's sales target. The same problem to a greater or lesser degree confronted direct marketers in all product and service categories which are not based on direct-order marketing. We haven't met a product manager or marketing director yet who isn't fixated on this year's budget and projected sales figures.

Mass marketers distributing their products in thousands of retail outlets are mostly interested in measuring current share of mind and share of market, not in tracking the effect of this year's expenditure on sales in future years.

As the decade progressed, the realization began to sink in that not only direct marketing, but also awareness advertising itself was very often at best a long-term solution. It was needed to support the brand over the long haul, but very few awareness campaigns showed an immediate effect on sales. To get sales right now, management in the 80's increasingly turned to consumer promotions and dealer promotions. Such promotions might cheapen the brand image, but they could, when properly executed, get those vital short-term sales through the door.

So, by the end of the decade, the growth of mass advertising had come to a virtual halt while promotional spending boomed, and some marketers were tinkering with databases and various aspects of customer-relationship building in a minor way, with limited objectives.

THE NEW DIRECTION: SHORT-TERM *AND* LONG-TERM RESULTS

Actually, with turnaround thinking, it is not really a question of being forced to choose between short-term and long-term results. You can have it all. As we have shown throughout this book, the new approach to marketing in which advertising, sales promotion, and direct marketing budgets are fused to implement a single unified strategy, is producing impressive short-term results while also establishing long-term relationships that tie the customer closely to the brand. And at less cost than tackling awareness advertising, sales promotion, and direct marketing separately.

Many of the case histories that we have explored in this book represent a new phenomenon. The new technology of marketing built on the increasingly powerful capabilities of the computer has opened up new vistas which could not be imagined a decade earlier. Being able to send a relevant, motivating advertising and promotional message to precisely those people who are most ready, willing, and able to respond can be counted on to produce astonishing short term results while also setting the stage for a profitable long-term relationship.

But how do you measure the effect of the new marketing when it is part advertising, part promotion, and part database-building?

We were recently involved in developing a customer's club employing targeted sales promotion for a mass marketer selling a $2.50 product through retail distribution. The product is purchased, on the average, only 10 times a year. That adds up to $25 in total annual revenue, yielding a $5 or $6 contribution to profit.

By the yardstick of direct-order marketing, the club was not very successful. Market research told the company that it took about 24 months for directly-accountable sales to earn back the expenditures charged to membership acquisition and the activation mailings to members. But this was not a direct-order marketer and the club was not a direct-order marketing proposition. It was a database-driven program to get the consumer involved with the product and to impact sales in stores.

While the advertising was acquiring club members, it was also making millions of impressions on those in the target market who did not choose to sign up. These impressions, and the word-of-mouth advertising resulting from the various club events and activities, became a potent force for sales in the total market as well as among club members.

When share of market and annual sales growth was used as the measurement for the first year of the program, it showed an overall sales increase that was more than enough to offset the entire cost of acquiring and servicing club members.

The paradox was that what seemed to be a short-term drain on profits when measured in narrowly accountable terms, based on the number of customers enrolled in the program, was actually a net contributor to profit when measured on the basis of total impact on the company's sales that year.

As we rethink marketing in the 90's to become more focused on fusing the advertising, promotion, and direct marketing elements in the marketing mix, we will also have to rethink how we are going to measure short-term and long-term success.

Methods used to measure awareness advertising effectiveness that do not take into account actual sales results are no longer acceptable.

Measurement criteria for sales from promotions that do not take into account negative impact on brand image are no longer acceptable.

And the focus on the long-term payout of Direct-Relationship Marketing without taking into account the immediate impact on sales and brand-image of the direct-response advertising that builds the database is no longer acceptable.

A new scorecard will be needed for the marketing games we will be playing in the 90's. The "synergy effect" of combining all the elements in a MaxiMarketing program has turned out to be far greater than we ever expected. The challenge now is to find out how to measure it fully and fairly.

LOOKING BACK AND LOOKING AHEAD

When the two of us launched our own advertising agency, a generation ago, the advertising communications field was populated by "advertising men," mail-order people, promoters, and publicists.

Today the "ad man" is just as likely to be a woman. The mail-order people have been transformed into direct marketers. And publicists are public relations specialists.

There is the illusion of great change in the advertising communication disciplines. But the reality is that by and large, over the past 25 years, we have seen only evolutionary growth to higher sophistication and greater specialization. The fundamentals have changed very little.

A stumbling block that will trip up communications professionals in the 90's is the failure to realize that evolutionary change is no longer enough to gain the advantage. The propensity to see marketing merely as a series of separate but equal components, linked together in a chain of 'integrated' communications, will keep them from embracing the revolutionary principles of genuine Individualized Marketing discussed in this book.

As the 90's begin, we are seeing a rush to the banner of a New Advertising — which is essentially the same old "above and below the line" advertising disciplines rearranged to give added importance to what was formerly "below the line." It is a New Advertising that fails to reconsider those aspects of the established advertising and promotion doctrines that no longer work very well in the Age of the Individual.

In this new decade, the likelihood of getting a dramatic breakthrough which increases market share is far greater if your New Advertising uses new marketing technologies to contact and get involved with identified prospects and customers than if you merely rely on more creative application of traditional advertising and sales promotion alone. Think for a moment how different the Benadryl success story cited on page 175 is from the conventional 80's wisdom of how to come up with a winning advertising campaign.

For Benadryl, the agency took a relatively minor tactical move and turned it almost overnight into a brilliant Individualized Marketing strategy. By reacting quickly to how the marketplace responded to their pollen-count information service, they were able to establish a productive relationship with over a million prospects and customers. Warner Lambert, on their part, was also quick to shift dollars from conventional marketing programs that were unlikely to produce a breakthrough and turn to this revolutionary new way of building awareness and boosting sales.

Think of the astonishing gain in market share by Miller Lite with their "biggest party ever thrown in Texas" regional marketing extravaganza. They found a way to get directly and deeply involved with two million beer drinkers. They devised an Extra-Value Proposition that set them clearly apart from the competition. And they fused all the skills of awareness advertising, sales promotion, and direct marketing to totally capture the attention and enthusiasm of the Texas beer-drinking crowd.

Think of Nintendo, Stash Tea, Austin Rover, Toddler University, and other companies large and small that we have observed. Note how they responded to the opportunities made possible by the Ten Turnarounds in marketing we have described and the big rewards they have enjoyed.

What these turnaround-thinking companies have shown is that what you *do* with your marketing communication, whether it is "integrated" or not, is what makes the difference between standing still and moving ahead.

In the real New Advertising of the 90's, Individualized Marketing will increasingly be seen as the right way to go. And, we believe, the MaxiMarketing model shows the way to get there.

This concludes our view of where turnaround thinking is taking the world of marketing in the 90's.

Now it's time to do your own turnaround thinking.

Where do you begin?

For openers, how about focusing on the most relevant Idea-Starter questions at the end of each of the ten trend chapters? Decide which of the questions are relevant to your own situation, then informally explore with appropriate associates how your answers might lead to new tactical and strategic moves.

We would be surprised if you did not come up with some really promising ideas that you want to develop further. We've seen it happen again and again in meetings and workshops we have conducted on four continents.

Another way to begin putting into practice the lessons learned from the turnaround trends we have highlighted is to take a MaxiMarketing audit of your company's advertising and promotion practices. These are some of the questions you might ask:

• Are you identifying and contacting your best prospects and customers?

• Are you using your advertising budget to begin the process of getting involved with potential heavy users of your product or service?

• Are you clear, before you begin planning your advertising and promotion, about whom you want in your database and what you are going to *with* them and *for* them?

• Are you taking the prospect by the hand and leading him or her to the sale in a carefully linked series of marketing steps?

• Are you conducting an ongoing dialogue with your prospects and customers that gives you a real-time research advantage in the marketplace?

• Are you capturing in your database information about every sale and every customer name and address that you can?

• Are you taking advantage of all the distribution channels you might possibly be using?

• Are you taking steps now to set up your database so that you will be a winner in the battle of the databases that is likely to come to your field in the 90's?

• Are you fusing your advertising, promotion, and direct marketing budgets into a single unified strategic marketing program that maximizes the impact of every dollar you spend?

• Are you identifying and eliminating the waste in your present advertising and promotion programs, even if it means giving up some of the company's long-held beliefs about where and how to spend advertising and promotional dollars?

• Are you cultivating your relationship with the 20% of your customers who give you 80% of your business?

• Are you boldly exploring the new media options available to facilitate interaction with your best prospects?

• Are you ready to invest in exceeding customer expectations without a guarantee of an immediate payback in the same quarter?

• Are you courting each individual prospect and customer as if the future of the company depends on it?

• Are you identifying the segments and niches within your database that are ideal for targeted promotions and new product development?

Making such an audit is not a simple task. With each issue raised, there may be the challenge of examining established practices and long-held beliefs. In some cases, you may decide little if anything needs fixing. But where you do see a new opportunity, we hope you will go for it and enjoy the satisfaction of breaking new ground. There will never be a better time than right now — with all the examples we have provided fresh in your mind — to get started.

DO MORE for those special people in your database — your best prospects and customers

LEARN MORE about the behavioral, psychographic, and attitudinal characteristics of individual prospects and customers.

CONNECT MORE of the steps involved in identifying, contacting, activating, converting, and cultivating new customers.

SELL MORE to people you have contacted by identifying and satisfying their own special needs and wants.

MEASURE MORE of the sales results of each advertising dollar spent , taking into account the full short-term and long-term effect.

Figure 13

By the time this book falls into your hands, there will have been even more extraordinary developments in many fields than we have told you about. And you may worry that you have already been left behind and it's too late to catch up.

The answer is that it is never too late.

Certainly there is an advantage to being first in your field — there always is.

But if it is too late for you and your company to be first, there is also a lot to be said for being second. You have a chance to study and learn from your competitor who went first, to learn from their mistakes and improve on their model.

And if it is too late for you to be either first or second, it is still not too late to get started with your own innovative Individualized Marketing program that builds on your company's unique strengths and opportunities. Innovation is never out of style. There is always a better way to do things waiting to be discovered by those who dare to reach beyond what has already been tried.

For inspiration, we will leave you with our five-point guiding star (Figure 13).

Whatever you do, you are part of marketing history. And if you act boldly, you can help write it.

By casting off the shackles of outmoded mass marketing

thinking and entering the Age of the Individual, you can invent your own new ways to get closer to your customers and serve them better in a mutually rewarding relationship.

In the 80's, Nike proclaimed, "Just do it!" and it became the rallying cry of a generation of fitness lovers. In the 90's, it is also a good slogan for marketers.

Certainly it makes sense to exercise proper business caution in moving into this new territory. But it is also important not to let undue caution keep you from acting at all. At some point, once you're ready, *just do it.* And do it even better than the marketers you can learn from in this book.

Be better at keeping a dialogue going with the consumer — at exceeding your prospect's and customer's expectations — at applying every step of the MaxiMarketing concept.

This is the challenge and the satisfaction of being part of The Great Marketing Turnaround.

NOTES

INTRODUCTION

1. "Adam Smith's Money World" WNET, February 6, 1990.
2. "Campbell Cutting 364 From Staff," *The New York Times*, May 2, 1990, p. D1.
3. "Round Research Pegs in Square Marketing Holes," *Adweek's Marketing Week*, May 16, 1988, p. 12.
4. "Reaching Individual Consumers," *The New York Times*, October 3, 1989

CHAPTER ONE

1. "Stalking the New Consumer," *Business Week*, August 28, 1989, p. 54.
2. *Adweek's Marketing Week, Marketing to the Year 2000*, September 11, 1989.
3. "The Time Is Now to Prepare for the Census," *Adweek's Marketing Week*, November 13, 1989, p. 60.
4. "Marketers Mine for Gold in the Old, "*Fortune*, March, 1986.
5. "Why All Those People Feel They Never Have Any Time," *The New York Times*, January 2, 1988.
6. "Time — the Currency of the 90's," *Advertising Age*, November 13, 1989, p. S-2.
7. "How Kimberly-Clark Wraps Its Bottom Line in Disaposable Diapers," *The Wall Street Journal*, Thursday, July 23, 1987, p. 1.
8. "Shifts in Marketing Strategy Jolting Advertising Industry," *The New York Times*, October 3, 1989.
9. "With American Honoring Walesa, Little Poland Is Filled with Pride," *The New York Times*, November 17, 1989, p. B1.
10. "Food Marketer: Slow the 'Frenetic' Pace of New Product Introdutcions," *Marketing News*, March 28, 1988, p. 17.
11. "Panic Creeps in Amid More Sluggish Sales, *Advertising Age*, September 11, 1989, p. S-4.
12. "At Budget Hotels, Growing Pains," *The New York Times*, November 17, 1989, p. D1.
13. "Retailing Falls on Hard Times," *The New York Times*, October 15, 1989.
14. "Beauty Firms Question Their Dependency," *Adweek's Marketing Week*, January 22, 1990, p. 3.
15. "Have :15s Hit their Peak?" *Advertising Age*, November 13, 1989, p. 16.
16. "3 Networks See Declines Continuing," *The New York Times*, February 8, 1989.
17. "The Big Boys' Blues," *Time*, October 17, 1988.
18. *Adweek's Marketing Week*, December 21, 1987, p. 50.
19. "Zapping of TV Ads Appears Pervasive," *The Wall Street Journal*, April 25, 1988.

20. "Free Choice: Too Much, All the Time," *The New York Times*, February 14, 1990, p. C1.

21. "Shifts in Marketing Strategy Jolting Advertising Industry," *The New York Times*, October 3, 1989.

22. "RJR CEO: What's in Megamergers for Me?" *Adweek*, November 3, 1986.

23. "Are There Fewer Viewers?" *The New York Times*, April 30, 1989.

24. "Sales Promotion: It's Come Down to Push Marketing," *Marketing News*, February 29, 1988, p. 8.

25. "Consumers Who Stick with Brands Decline," *The Wall Street Journal*, August 26, 1986.

26. "Preserving Value of Brands," *The New York Times*, October 27, 1988.

27. "No Frills, No Sales," *The New York Times*, October 5, 1986, p. F-2.

28. "A Timber Company Takes on the Diaper Kingpins," *Adweek's Marketing Week*, February 12, 1990, p. 28.

29. "An Iconoclast Takes a Look at the Future," *The New York Times*, August 1, 1989.

30. "A Critic Gets Forceful Responses," *The New York Times*, August 22, 1989.

31. Horiwitz column of August 4, 1987, quoted in Sid Bernstein column, "The Test for Ad Ideas," *Advertising Age*, November 16, 1987.

32. "A Cold War Over Coffee,"*The New York Times*, October 29, 1989.

33. "What Have Snoopy and Gang Done for Met Life Lately," *Adweek's Marketing Week*, November 13, 1989, p. 2-3.

34. "The Failure of Marketing Programs," *Marketing & Media Decisions*, May, 1986, p. 160.

35. "Automakers Fight Ad Gridlock," *Advertising Age*, October 30, 1989.

37. "Coupon Distribution Grew by 9% in '89," *Adweek's Marketing Week*, March 5, 1990.

38. "Trying to Slip the Cuffs on Coupon Fraud, "*Adweek's Marketing Week*, June 26, 1989, p. 57.

39. "Catalina Cuts Couponing Clutter," *Advertising Age*, May 9, 1988, p. S-30.

40. "Facts: The Final Frontier of Promotion," *Promote*, November 14, 1988, p. 28.

41. "Short-term Focus Hurts Reputation of Brands: Survey," *Advertising Age*, December 14, 1987, p. A-8.

CHAPTER TWO

1. John Naisbitt and Patricia Burdene, *Megatrends 2000*, New York: William Morrow and Company, 1990, p. 307.

2. "Marketing Gets a New Emphasis," *The New York Times*, March 16, 1990, p. D5.

3. *Ibid.*

4. "A Turning Point," editorial, *Advertising Age*, May 16, 1990.

5. "Many Historic Walls Are Falling," *Adweek*, April 9, 1990, P. P28.

CHAPTER THREE

1. Michael J. Weiss, *The Clustering of America*, Harper & Row, New York, 1988, p. xii.

2. "Donnelley Sems to Be Asking All the Right Questions," *Advertising Age*, May 16, 1988, p. S-5.

3. "The Al Franken Decade," *Adweek's Marketing Week*, November 13, 1989, p. H.M. 6.

4. "American's No-Nonsense Marketers," *Adweek's Marketing Week*, June 5, 1989, p. 18.

5. *Ibid.*

6. "Sticking to Databasics Keeps Rover Sales Rolling," *Adweek's Promote*, November 16, 1987, P. 19.

7. "Stealing the Right Shoppers," *Forbes*, July 10, 1989, p. 104.

8. "Quaker Bets Direct Promotion Is the Right Thing to Do," *Adweek's Marketing Week*, January 8, 1990, p. 4.

9. "The story Behind Quaker Direct," *Direct*, February 20, 1990.

10. "Data Bases Uncover Brands' Biggest Fans, *Advertising Age*, February 19, 1990, p. 3.

11. "The Story Behind Quaker Direct," *op. cit.*

12. "No Hang Ups Here," *Direct Marketing*, August, 1989, p. 16.

13. "Direct Marketing Analegics Give Competition a Headache," *Direct*, December 20, 1989, p. 5.

14. "Electronic Coupons," *Target Marketing*, July, 1987, p. 12.

15. "Card the Customer," *Target Marketing*, November, 1989, p. 56.

16. "Frequent Reader Clubs: A New Book Battleground," *Adweek's Marketing Week*, March 12, 1990, p. 28.

17. Editorial, *Direct Marketing*, May 1986, p. 160.

CHAPTER FOUR

1, Stephen Fox, *The Mirror Makers*, William Morrow and Company, New York, 1984, p. 48.

2. "A Lesson 'Direct' from Bill Bernbach," *Advertising Age*, November 13, 1989, p. 48.

3. "Highbrow or Low," *Advertising Age*, October 30, 1989.

4. "The Strategy for Benson & Hedges," *The New York Times*, February 13, 1990.

5. "Integration, Who's Making It Work," *Adweek*, February 5, 1990, p. P14,

6. *Ibid.*

7. "A Cigarette Campaign Focusing on Blacks Is Under Attack," *The New York Times*, January 12, 1990, p. D1.

8. "Salem Uses Music to Make Waves," *Adweek's Marketing Week*, February 6, 1990, p. P16.

9. "General Advertising Creative Guru Becomes a Direct Marketing Mutant," *Direct*, January 10, 1990.

10. David Ogilvy, *Confessions of an Advertising Man*, Atheneum, New York, 1963, p. 90-91.

CHAPTER FIVE

1. "Computer Communities," *Newsweek*, December 15, 1986, p. 66.

2. "High-Tech Shocks in Ad Research," *Fortune*, July 7, 1986, p. 58.

3. "Jergens to Capitalize on Bath Additives Market with New DM Campaign," *Direct*, April 10, 1990, p. 17.

4. "Farm Journal Thrives in Fertile Asphalt Soil," *The New York Times*, December 13, 1989.

4. "Toward an Age of Customized Magazines," *Adweek*, February 13, 1989, p. 36.

5. "Isuzu to Run Personalized Ads," *The Wall Street Journal*, December 8, 1989.

6. "New Equifax Clustering System," *DM News*, February 19, 1990, p. 1.

7. "Porsche 300,000: the New Elite," *Advertising Age*, February, 1990.

8. "Sears Stores Look to Database Marketing in the 90's," *Direct*, January 10, 1990, p. 10.

9. "Flying High," *Marketing Communications*, October, 1984, p. 49.

10. "Fitting Airplanes to Passengers," *The New York Times*, November 18, 1989, p. 35.

11. "Marriott Pulls a 4% Response," *DM News*, August 15, 1986, p. 70.

12. "Casinos Leave Nothing to Chance," *Adweek's Marketing Week*, January 9, 1989)

13. "Segmentation Pays Dividends for Barnes & Noble," *Direct*, November 20, 1989, p. 43.

CHAPTER SIX

1. "Spray It Again, Sam," *Adweek's Marketing Week*, September 18, 1989, p. 44.

2. "Why Were Lee Ads So Darned Efficient?"*Adweek*, March 2, 1987, p. F.C.24.

3. "Burger King Ads Don't 'Do It' For Sales," *Advertising Age*, May 16, 1988.

4. "When an Ad Takes Off but Product Stalls," *The New York Times*, April 27, 1990.

5. "The New Era of Ad Measurement," *Adweek's Marketing Week*, January 23, 1989, page 22.

6. Tom Peters, *Thriving on Chaos*, Alfred A. Knopf, New York, 1987, p. 98.

7. "Did Golden Arches Tie-in Tarnish Olds Image?" *Adweek's Marketing Week*, May 22, 1989, p. 20.

CHAPTER SEVEN

1. "Wanted: Stores That Care," *Adweek's Marketing Week*, April 18, 1988, p. 10.

2. "Gerber's High-Energy Baby Marketers," *Adweek's Marketing Week*, May 22, 1989, p. 20.

3. "Exclusive Beginnings Put Perfumes in Demand," *The Wall Street Journal*, November 30, 1988.

4. "Riding High at Low Tide" *Target Marketing*, August, 1989, p.16.

5. "Is Consumer Stress Reducing DM Sales?" *DM News*, December 15, 1988, p. 26.

6. "The Idea Store," *Direct*, September 20, 1989, p. 45.

CHAPTER EIGHT

1. Stephen Fox, *The Mirror Makers*, William Morrow and Company, 1984, p. 74.

2. Rosser Reeves, *Reality in Advertising*, Alfred A. Knopf, New York, 1960, p. 39.

3. David W. Stewart and David H. Furse, "Analysis of the Impact of Executional Factors on Advertising Performance," *Journal of Advertising Research*, December,1984/January, 1985, pp. 23-26.

4. Thomas Whiteside,*The New Yorker*, September 27, 1969; quoted in Fox, *op. cit*, p. 187.

5. "BK Franchisees Pan Ad Theme," *Advertising Age*, January 29, 1990, p. 3.

6. "Burger King Courts Health Fans, Kids," *Advertising Age*, December 4, 1989.

7. "Sharon Fogg," *Adweek's Marketing Week*, March 5, 1990, p. P 13.

8. "Woolworths Gives Kids Their Own Club," *Adweek's Marketing Week*, July 10, 1989, p. 14.

9. "Marketing Perks to Members Only," *Adweek's Marketing Week*, Promote section, May 2, 1988, p. 16.

10. "Mattel Launches First Dm Campaign To Boost Sales And Build Database," *Direct*, March 10, 1990, p. 20.

11. "Swiss Magazine Reaches New Heights as Catalog," *Advertising Age*, October 27, 1986, p. S-33.

12. "'Morris Report' Data Base Delivers Direct Dividends," *Advertising Age*, May 16, 1988, p. S-1.

13. "Is Consumer Stress Reducing DM Sales?" *DM News*, December 15, 1988, p. 26.

14. "Kohler Turns On Consumer Plumbing Awareness," *Advertising Age*, October 27, 1986, p. S-30.

15. "Distiller Finds Little Comfort as Cataloger," *Advertising Age*, October 27, 1986, p. S-31.

CHAPTER NINE

1. *Adweek's Marketing to the Year 2000*, September 11, 1989, p. 231.

2. "German Beer Scores with Two-Way Rub," *Adweek's Marketing Week*, June 12, 1989, p. P25.

3. "Miller Bash Invites Lone Star Loyalty," *Adweek's Marketing Week*, August 7, 1989, p. P16.

4. "For the Microbrews, the Big Moment Is the Micro-Event," *Adweek's Marketing Week*, October 9, 1989, p. 17.

5. "Divine Extravagance? Elizabeth Taylor Didn't Like the Sound of It," *Adweek's Marketing Week*, January 30, 1989, p. 52.

6."Dutch Treated to U.S.," *Promote*, July 4, 1988, p. 19.

7. "Power Wheels Christmas," *Adweek's Marketing Week*, Sept. 18, 1989, p. 47.

8. "Now Playing in Your H.S. Gym," *Adweek's Marketing Week*, September 18, 1989, p. 46.

9. "Fragrance Sniffs Out Daring Adventures," *Advertising Age*, November 6, 1989, p. 47.

10. "Buick's New Horsepower," *Direct Marketing*, December, 1989, p. 14.

CHAPTER TEN

1. "Direct Marketing Analgesics Gives Competition a Headache," *Direct*, December 20, 1989, p. 5.

2. "A Positive Reaction," *Direct Marketing*, February, 1990, p. 73.

3. "Realty DR Television program helps generate home-buying leads," *DM News*, April 15, 1989, p 2.

4. "Backup Boondoggle," *Video*, January, 1990, p. 14.

5. "Alaska Sets Budget, Dusts Off 1984 Ads," *Advertising Age*, October 23, 1989, p. 86.

6. Video Brochure Cuts Through Clutter, *Direct*, March 10, 1990, p. 16.

7. "Turning PCs into Salesmen," *Newsweek*, March 12, 1990, p. 69.

8. "Carmakers Steer Disks to PC Users," *Adweek's Marketing Week*, January 25, 1988, p. 59.

9. "Software Selections from Santa," *DM News*, December 1, 1989, p. 31.

10. "Lincoln-Mercury Video Mailing to 200,000," *DM News*, October 1, 1989.

11. "Why Supermarket Pamphlets Demand Attention," *Adweek's Marketing Week*, January 30, 1989, p. 17.

12. Claude Hopkins, *My Life in Advertising*, Crain Books, Chicago, 1966, p. 83-84.

13. Everett M. Rogers, *Diffusion of Innovations*, Free Press, New York, 1962, p. 162.

14. "Ad or Show or Both," *Target Marketing*, March, 1989, p. 50.

CHAPTER ELEVEN

1. "Service — Marketers Aren't There Yet,"*Advertising Age*, December 11, 1989, p. 47.

2. George Fields, *Gucci on the Ginza*, Kodansha International, 1988. p. 109.

3." If the Customer Has an Itch, Scratch It," *The New York Times*, May 14, 1989, p. F3.

4. "Building Good Will Through Guarantees,"*The New York Times*, November 23, 1989, p. C1.

5. Oldsmobile news release, February 9, 1990.

6. "Coping with Home Electronics," *The New York Times*, January 13, 1990, p. 52.

7. *Ibid.*

8. "Selling Turntables in the Age of the Compact Disc," *Adweek's Marketing Week*, June 26, 1989, p. 24.

9. "The Real Truths About Promotions," *Advertising Age*, October 16, 1989, p. 42.

10. "Mutual Funds Turn to the Hard Sell," *The New York Times*, January 7, 1990, Sec. 3, p. 1.

11. "Building Good Will Through Guarantees,"*The New York Times*, November 23, 1989, p. C1.

12. "How a Small Chicago Bank Went Wild and Raised Interest," *Adweek's Marketing Week*, June 5, 1989, p. 41.

13. "Going to School at a PACE Warehouse," *Adweek's Marketing Week*, October 2, 1989, p. 34.

CHAPTER 12

1. Menus' Hot Item: Home Delivery, *The New York Times*, September 5, 1988, p. D1.

2. "Carnation Delivers Pet Food,"*Advertising Age*, February 20, 1989, p.31.

3. "Cake Company Turns to Mail," *Adweek's Markeking Week*, November 9, 1987, p 8.

4. "Medicine by Mail Becomes a Booming For-Profit Business," *Adweek's Marketing Week*, January 1, 1990, p. 22.

5. "Jeno to Deliver Grocery Service," *Advertising Age*, July 17, 1989, p.6.

6. *Ibid.*

7. "Giorgio's Star Rises Beyond Beverly Hills," *Advertising Age*, February 27, 1984, p., M-29.

8. "Philip Morris Plans to Offer Cigarettes by MO in January," *DM News*, December 15, 1989, p. 1.

9. "Starbucks Coffee Co. Catalog a Response to Customer Demand," *DM News*, May 1, 1989, p. 11.

10. " Cooking Good at Williams-Sonoma," *Catalog Business*, May 15, 1988, p. 41.

11. "Retail Store, Mail-Order Catalog: Synergistic Growth," *Direct Marketing*, April, 1983, p. 44.

12. "Selling Off the Package Is Prescription For Success, claims Dr. Cookie," *Direct*, January 10, 1990, p. 35.

CHAPTER 13

1. "Kool-Aid Uses DM to Build Share," *DM News*, November 1, 1988, p. 45.

2. "Wacky Warehouse Builds Kool-aid's Market Share," *Direct*, January 10, 1990, p. 4.

3. "Marketer of the Year," *Adweek's Marketing Week*, November 27, 1989, p. M.R.C. 37.

4. "The Power of Nintendo," *Direct Marketing*, September, 1989. p. 21.

5. "Comic Based on Nintendo Characters Is Due," *Adweek's Marketing Week*, January 22, 1990, p. 6.

6. "Nintendo Wired For $95m Push," *Advertising Age*, January 15, 1990.

7. "Steinway Finds Key to Domestic Market," *Adweek's Marketing Week*, July 18, 1988, p. 50.

8. "Steinway Hits High Note," *Direct Marketing*, January, 1989, p. 30.

9. "Making the Grade at Toddler University," *FNM*, May, 1988, p. 21.

10. "Women's Apparel Manufacturer Bows New Traffic Catalog To Aid Retailers," *DM News*, January 22, 1990, p. 10.

11. "Meredith Real Estate Operation Pulling an Average Response Rate of 20% with Mailings," *DM News*, January 15, 1987, p. 6.

CHAPTER 14

1, "Why Agencies Prefer Television," *Advertising Age*, January 22, 1990.

2. "Many Historic Walls Are Falling," *Adweek's Marketing Week*, April 9, 1990, p. P28.

3. "Ad Agency Abolishing Fixed Fee," *The New York Times*, May 7, 1990, p. D1.

Index

A NOTE FROM THE AUTHORS

Would you like to be kept informed on future developments in The Great Turnaround and learn more about how to apply the basic principles of MaxiMarketing? If so, indicate your special interest below, detach this page, and mail or fax it to:

MaxiMarketing, Inc.
Grand Central Station
P.O. Box No. 6652
New York, NY 10163-6023
Fax No. 212-779-1856

I am interested in (check one or more):

☐ Receiving information about the trend toward Individualized Marketing worldwide and how I can use the ideas in my own marketing planning.

☐ Seminars, workshops, lectures, and in-house training.

☐ Receiving information about the MaxiMarketing Intensive Consultation offered by the MaxiMarketing Institute.

☐ Receiving information about the MaxiMarketing Idea Generating Intensive offered by the MaxiMarketing Institute.

Name...Title..

Company ....

Address..

City...State............Zip.........................

Fax No. .... Phone No. ....

MAXIMARKETING, INC. was founded by the authors and Richard Cross to track and report on continuing developments in The Great Marketing Turnaround and to provide information and assistance in the application of MaxiMarketing principles. We welcome your inquiries.